Forty years ago, Stuart Goldstein was a   ⌐
Writing class at Trenton State College. His talk that day, filled with compel-
ling stories about his career in politics and as a communications strategist in
the financial services industry, inspired me to pursue a similar career path.

Today, Goldstein applies his gift of storytelling to bring us the story of Moe
Fields, a gripping narrative about a father's extraordinary work ethic and
indomitable spirit in the face of adversity.

We all have our Moe Fields. I lost my dad more than 20 years ago, and now
am the proud father of two young men. This treasure of a book reminds us all
about the importance of keeping family memories and traditions alive through
generations. It is a poignant and thought-provoking memoir that captures the
enduring power of role models in our lives.

Andy Polansky,
Executive Chairman, Weber Shandwick

Stuart Goldstein tells the story of a father's love for his sons in a captivating
way. I was drawn in from the very first paragraph.   You begin to realize that
his story is our story.

Ralph Savino, my dad, had a similar background to Moe, although he grew
up on the streets of the Bronx – different boro, same trials and challenges to
overcome. My dad, a man of integrity and grit, with a warm loving heart, also
put his energy into providing for his family. He held a construction job and
opened two small businesses in order to do so.

I went to high school with Stu Goldstein. We had no idea about his family's
car accident or the major health crises the family faced. He tells this part of
the story with a degree of understanding and a wrenching honesty that comes
only with age.

My dad is my hero, as Moe is to Stuart, for all the life lessons both men have
taught us. This book is a gift to all the memories you cherish

Stuart has written a life-affirming story with anticipation that makes it hard to
put down—and hard not to talk about.

Joanne Savino Cicchelli,
Paramus High School '68

MOE FIELDS

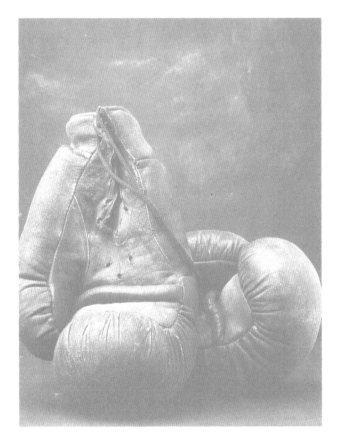

by **Stuart Z. Goldstein**

Publisher: Pen Paper Press
New York, New York
Copyright August 2020

ISBN # 978-1-7366322-0-8
ISBN # 978-1-7366322-1-5

C: 10,9,8,7,6,5,4,3,2

Legal Disclaimer:

Moe Fields is a true story. However, in fairness, what's true in life (or non-fiction narrative) is often a matter of perspective. The author does not claim sole ownership of truth. Each of us in my family may have experienced these life events differently. Some may see nuance where others see black and white. This story cannot represent the ultimate truth in the life of Moe and his family. For that reason, the names of characters have been changed to respect the privacy of family members who may feel or recollect things through a different lens. Also, the names of other characters used in the book are not intended to represent actual people or historical circumstances. These names are simply literary conveniences to help tell the story. Love has a way of shading the things we see and believe. The one constant, however, is that we share the value of family.

DEDICATION:

For my dad, who taught us to respect and value hard work; to persevere when you're knocked down; to fight for things that matter; and to know he believed in us.

For my mom, who taught us the importance of first impressions; the determination to face life's difficulties with quiet grace and resolve; and who raised the bar of expectations for the lives we would lead.

For my brothers, who honor the promise we made to our parents that no matter differences encountered on our journey we "stick together" and to "look out for each other".

For my family, who despite the trauma, triumphs and tragedies, found inspiration to teach the next generation the stories that bind us and the importance of unconditional love.

ACKNOWLEDGEMENTS:

Inspiration: Eritt, Jessica, Adam, Brooke and Samantha Maren

Editorial: Daryl Betenia, Sydney Shaw, Rosalie Jenkins, Robert Cole, Mark Spinner

Graphic Design Book Cover: Pam Brooks

Early Readers/Supporters: Joanne Savino Cicchelli, Daryl Betenia, Sydney Shaw, Mark Spinner, Jeff Barrie, Rosalie Jenkins, Charles Kaufman, Patrick Donovan, Francesca Cardinale, Shawn Kathryn Laurenti, Michael Falk, William Chrietzberg, Stephanie Harmon, George Taweel, John Vrettos, Sue Keenom, Prajakta Shah

Publishing/Printing Advisors: Jeff Barrie, Charles Nurnberg, Rachel Kerr

Navy History: Sid Maiten, Barry Maiten

CHAPTER 1

The Boxer 1934

———

He could not feel the pain—his pride got in the way. Blood showered down across his chest as he landed against the ropes. For the first time, his nose had been broken. He did the only thing he knew how to do: He fought back. His name was Moe Fields.

The blood continued to flow down Moe's face and chest. He spit to his right, clearing the blood in his throat. He was unaware of the crowd as the blood sprayed down on people in the first row. A woman stood cheering Moe on, proudly wearing his blood on her pale-yellow dress. The outside of the ring was a blur. At that point, Moe's pain was numbed by a determination no one had seen before.

He clearly knew he was out-classed by a real professional. It can't be the money. After all, this was bootleg boxing at the back of a neighborhood bar in the 1930s. The boxer got paid $20 per match and a percent of the betting, but the purses for the fights weren't very large. No one here ever really made it to the professional ring. Most were just working stiffs who fought to make a few dollars during the Depression.

There's something mysterious about boxers. You see a guy like Moe get his nose broken and you wonder why they go on. He's out there sucking blood down his throat, in a frantic effort so he can breathe.

With Moe, it seemed as if he couldn't feel the pain. Maybe it was the adrenaline. Maybe there's a switch in a fighter's head that turns off when they get in trouble. Suddenly, there's nothing left between you and the outcome of the fight, except the inner voice that just won't quit. In the ring, you're alone, as alone as you'll ever be in life. Some say it's a false bravado that keeps you going. Others call it pride. Moe was hurt badly, but he just didn't know how to step back. He would not give in. And he would not be defeated.

Murray Goldman, the Jewish kid from Williamsburg, used the alias Moe Fields so his family wouldn't know he had become a boxer. He was 6-foot-2 and had unusually large hands and lightning speed. At 19, he had only been fighting a year and a half. The Daily News described him as one of the more promising boxers in the 1932 Golden Gloves amateur tournament. But that was then. He no longer cared about a boxing career. His goal was to make money and help his family. Moe Fields wasn't a character he played. Getting in the ring was a metaphor for the way he chose to lead his life.

Moe weighed in at just under 200 pounds, which was light for a heavyweight fighter. Most of his earlier opponents were bar room brawlers from the neighborhood. All of them were older than Moe by at least 10 years, but he had not expected tonight he would be fighting for his life against an ex-professional.

As a boxer, Moe was dangerous because he could switch seamlessly to fighting southpaw. His opponents often entered the ring thinking they were fighting one boxing style and then Moe would mix it up in the middle rounds, switching to a right jab and a vicious left uppercut. But perhaps his greatest talent was that this tough street kid knew how to take a punch.

The crowd cheered as Moe furiously threw punches at his opponent, Ritchie "The Mugger" O'Brien. It was a sizable crowd for a Saturday night at Rosie's. As the sound of the fight could be heard in the bar, customers flowed to the back of the building, to a small boxing ring that staged local fights. A small group of men circled the ring, taking bets. As the tide of the fight seemed to change, people continued to bet more money with reckless abandon. Smoke and the smell of booze filled the air. The heat from the lights hanging over the ring was intense. No one believed the fight would last this long.

Ritchie O'Brien was one of the few bootleg boxers who had ever been a "professional." Ritchie never made it to the big-time fights. During his career, he served pretty much as a punching bag for faster, up-and-coming contenders like Zeke Jones or Mike "the hammer" Morin. But at 6 foot and one inches, 250 pounds, Richie was not to be taken lightly.

His fighting stance was awkward. He remained hunched forward. His elbow always pulled in to cover his midsection. This, of course, left his head open to a left jab, but Ritchie always took this punishment in stride. The fact that he could take a lot of punches made up for his limited skills.

During his career, Ritchie's brawling style would surprise even his more talented opponents. He got the title "The Mugger" in the fight of his career against Charlie "Chuck" Thompson. Thompson had been coming up the heavy weight ranks rather quickly-maybe too quickly, according to some fight observers. He was two fights away from a shot at the title when his handlers signed a fight with Ritchie O'Brien. No one ever figured Ritchie would give Thompson such a beating.

Thompson was slightly smaller at 6 foot, but he was a very stylish boxer. He bobbed and danced around the ring, constantly throwing jabs. Jab, jab, left, right...jab, jab...but Ritchie kept coming. Attack, attack, attack-that's all O'Brien knew. Thompson never counted on the head butts or elbows Ritchie used. When Thompson went down in the ninth round, no one was certain if it was a clean punch or just the cumulative effect of the head butts. At 30 years old, Ritchie won his largest purse for a fight and the well-earned nickname.

Ten years later, Richie was still mugging it out in the back of a bar. Slower and rounder, the years had worn Richie down. The hair on his head had thinned and the facial scars from his earlier battles were more pronounced.

But Ritchie still knew that one good solid punch could take an opponent out. Except tonight, the young Moe Fields would not go down.

Moe threw six or seven combinations that backed Ritchie up for the first time in their match. His hands landed like jackhammers. Then he switched to southpaw and peppered Ritchie's face with jabs for the second half of the round. He was now bleeding from his mouth and a cut over his right eye. What Moe lacked in size against Ritchie, he made up for with incredible speed.

Ritchie backed away toward the opposite rope, with Moe in pursuit. His breathing had become labored. He was not in the best shape and his prime was long gone.

Moe switched his fighting style once again and Ritchie looked confused. Moe moved quickly to his left, landing combinations, and then, a right upper cut. Moe's eyes were fixed on Ritchie. He would not stop or let up for one second. His breathing labored from the blood, still flowing down this throat. He spit to clear his airway. This time it landed in the ring.

Suddenly, from out of nowhere, a right-cross sent Ritchie against the ropes. Ritchie bounced forward and butted Moe in the head. Ritchie "The Mugger" O'Brien, realized he was now being mugged. Desperate and in trouble, Ritchie was pulling out all stops.

Moe, dazed for a second and bleeding from cut above his eye, brought his gloved hands to his head. Ritchie hit the midsection. Taking two steps backward, Moe shook his head and recovered. As Ritchie came in for the kill, Moe hit him square in the face. He followed with a powerful left upper cut to the chin. Before Ritchie's head could recover, Moe hit him three more times in the midsection. Ritchie gasped for air and wobbled. Moe landed one more right cross. The fight was over, before Ritchie landed on the canvas.

There was a moment of deafening silence. Moe, bleeding freely from his eye and broken nose, looked at O'Brien's body slumped down before him. He looked to his corner. Everything seemed to be moving in slow motion and then he heard it. The crowd had erupted into a roar. Moe could suddenly hear again. The referee grabbed Moe's arm and signaled for him to return to his corner. People were going crazy. Fans around Moe's corner were standing and cheering. The ring floor had blood everywhere, from O'Brien and Moe. The fans had never seen a more-hard fought match.

Some would say it was disgusting and barbaric to see these two men beating each other like that in the ring, but isn't this what life is really all about, at its most basic level? Isn't the challenge we all face in life the decision about who's willing to persevere? Does anyone really want to give in or give up? No one wants to admit when pain reaches past the threshold of what we can tolerate. Are the boxers blind to the damage their bodies experience? Are they just too stubborn to step back and say enough is enough? At the end of a fight, one man wins and another walks away bloody in defeat. But every fighter knows they gave their best. They took the punishment and they didn't quit. At this final moment, there is a nobility and respect only fighters share. The people who watch and cheer can only wonder about what they've seen. We ask ourselves in this moment of truth whether we, too, would have the heart to get back up and fight.

As men circled the ring at Rosie's paying off bets, no one complained, not even those who lost. This was a fight the folks in Brooklyn would be talking about for some time—and everyone would remember the name—Moe Fields.

CHAPTER 2

Brooklyn 1930

The tenement building was a six-story walk up in the Williamsburg section of Brooklyn. Isaac and Tonia Goldman lived on the fourth floor, with four children in a crowded apartment. Berta was the oldest. She was almost two years older than her brother, Morris, who preferred to be called Murray. After Murray was Asher, who was two years younger. Sammy (Samuel) was the youngest by seven years to Berta.

Isaac Goldman, a cobbler by trade, worked long days fixing shoes in a shop owned by David Migorsky. Isaac was a big man, and could be stubborn as hell. He didn't talk much. If the children got out of line, he didn't hesitate to communicate with his hands.

He and Tonia were also sticklers about going with the children every Saturday morning to Synagogue. This was a Jewish family in the traditional way, with Friday night candles and prayers recited before dinner. All the children could read Hebrew from the Siddur and the Torah. They understood and spoke some Yiddish, learning from their parents who spoke Yiddish at home. Ironic, in this family of values, Jewish values, Isaac Goldman became such a compulsive gambler.

By 1931 the children ranged from 10 to 17 years of age. Isaac would come home for dinner early. There wasn't much shoe repair work. After the dishes were cleared, Isaac would often announce he was going out for some errands or an appointment. Murray knew better. His father was going out at night to gamble.

The card games were usually somewhere nearby in the neighborhood. Whenever Isaac did well, the children would find a small gift or toy by their bed the next morning. No one in the Goldman home asked why they got gifts or where Isaac spent his evenings. Children were expected to be seen but not heard from.

Occasionally, Murray would follow Isaac. Murray had turned 15 only one month earlier. He loved his father but resented his time away from the family. Isaac was not a bad father, just an absent one.

Over time, the gambling became an obsession. The strain between Tonia and Isaac grew. During the Depression, most families were struggling to survive. Isaac may have rationalized his compulsion by convincing himself he was doing something to help bring home more money, but he lost more often than he won.

Through a window in the basement of a nearby tenement building, young Murray saw with his own eyes Isaac's humiliation. His father more often lost card games and the family's rent money. The thought of not having a place to live did not bother Murray. However, he was sad to see his proud father shrugging his shoulders as money was gathered up from the table. Isaac's meager cobbler's salary disappeared.

One winter evening that year, as Isaac was returning from his regular game, three young men in their twenties attacked him near an alleyway. Isaac had won that night. His pockets were filled with cash. His mind drifted off as he thought about what gift of clothing or toy to buy the children.

Before he realized it, the three men surrounded Isaac. Outnumbered, he knew he was in danger. Isaac immediately called out for help, but no one could hear him in the alley way. Isaac seized the initiative. He struck the first man in the jaw. The man went down. Soon the other two men wrestled Isaac's arms behind his back. A very strong man, he was not easily overpowered.

The third man scrambled back to his feet. Now he had a lesson to teach this old man. He hit Isaac in the face, knocking off his thick glasses. Three, four, five more blows followed to the midsection. Isaac slumped forward. The young man then landed another two blows to the face. Blood flowed from Isaac's split lip. Dazed and uncertain of his fate, Isaac was now helpless. The men held him up as they rummaged through his pockets for money. But the young man that Isaac hit was not finished. He wanted revenge. Again, he began to beat him.

Suddenly, without warning from the shadow of the alley came a figure. He moved so swiftly, he went undetected. A quick kick to the groin silenced Isaac's beating and sent his assailant to the pavement. Before his friends could react, one was hit from the side in the lower back. Without slowing down, like a battering ram, the shadowy figure hit the last man repeatedly until he, too, went down. Isaac, off balance, fell back toward the remaining mugger. From the shadows stepped Murray Goldman. He reached over Isaac's slumped body, hitting the mugger square in the face. Blood flowed from the man's nose. He pushed Isaac's body into Murray's arms and ran.

Several minutes went by before Isaac realized what had happened. Murray bent down and wiped the blood, with his hands, from his father's face. He found the broken glasses off to the side of the alleyway. The wire rims were bent out of shape, but the glass was still intact. Murray helped put the glasses on Isaac, though they remained crooked on his face. At first, as he checked on Isaac, he was relieved he seemed still dazed but generally ok. Then he grew angry. Murray began yelling at his father for the first time in his life. He hated gambling and said so. Isaac, still bleary from the beating, sat there quietly and took the verbal assault from his brave son. When Murray finished, Isaac looked into his eyes. He then reached up and slapped his son across the face. Murray stood stunned. "Don't ever talk to me that way," a defiant Isaac responded. "I am your father."

Isaac struggled to his feet, with Murray's help. The two of them walked home in silence. It was very late. Tonia was waiting by the door. She could see Isaac's bruised face. Murray said nothing. He went to his room. For the next hour, he could hear Isaac and Tonia fighting. "I can't do this anymore," Tonia told him. "You have not kept your promise. I can't. I just can't." The next day, Isaac moved out.

Murray knew life would never be the same. His parents had argued many times about Isaac's gambling. Tonia worried constantly about money. Would they have enough to pay the rent that month? During the Depression, a family's first month's rent was free. Murray was fond of saying to friends, "We moved often." It was common for the older children to work odd jobs to help contribute to the family. Would it be enough to get them by?

Isaac rented a room in someone's apartment not too far from home. Families would force their children to share a bedroom so they could rent rooms to neighbors or strangers to cover their monthly rent. However, a cobbler's pay could only stretch so far. With Isaac gone, it would be difficult keeping the rest of the family under one roof.

Two months later, Murray was shipped off to Tonia's brother, Uncle Victor. Tonia reasoned he was old enough to be out on his own more. Uncle Victor had no children. He lived in another section of Brooklyn with his wife. She thought Murray would not be too far away. He would have a better life, with more food to eat. But Victor was a mean-spirited person who immediately saw Murray as a burden. Since no one in the Goldman home talked about why Isaac left Tonia, Victor concluded this son sent to live with him must be at fault.

Murray stayed at his Uncle's home for only three weeks. Uncle Victor openly and often expressed resentment toward his nephew. For the first time in his life, Murray felt alone. He left quietly one morning before Victor was awake. He walked home and waited outside to say goodbye to his brothers and sister. Sammy clung to his older brother. He did not understand why

Murray could not come home. "Tell Mama not to worry," Murray instructed his siblings. "I'm going away, but I'll be back."

His brother Asher asked Murray where he was headed. "Don't worry, I will be ok," he responded. After hugging his sister and brothers, Murray bent down and held Sammy in his arms. "Samuel," Murray said, "remember what I always tell you. Be strong. Never, ever...give up." The two stared at each other. As tears came to Sammy's eyes, Murray pulled him close and held him tightly. Then Murray took off down the street toward the train station.

He ran alongside an open freight car as it headed toward Philadelphia. Murray had hopped freight trains many times, just for the excitement and to get away from New York for the day. The air was cold and crisp. Murray sat on a box, rubbing his hands together. He could only wonder what adventures lay ahead of him. There would be no anguished thoughts about the family he left behind. The prior trips on the train had prepared him well for his new-found freedom.

CHAPTER 3
The Circus

During his last visit to Philadelphia, Murray remembered a poster at the train station advertising jobs for a traveling circus. For Murray, it was like a dream come true. He wanted to see what life was like beyond Brooklyn and Philly.

The circus manager, Georgio Lecardi, was surprised to see the new young recruit knocking on his door. "How old are you?" he asked. Murray was very tall and looked older than his age.

"I'm 18," he replied.

"Do you have any special skills? Ever juggled? Worked the trapeze? Been on a horse?" Murray shook his head, several times. "Good," said Georgio. "You're hired. What's your name?"

Looking up surprised, "Mor...Morris Goldman, but I prefer to be called Murray."

"Well Murray, you are now a rigger. Your job is setting up the tents and any other odd things we need you to do. The pay is lousy, the food is lousy, the work is hard, but nothing...nothing you ever do will be as much fun as being here."

Lecardi, a short, round, balding man in his 50s, then took Murray back to meet the rigging crew.

The next several months were grueling for Murray. His hands were often wrapped with rags to protect against rope burns and blisters. But he carried his own against many of the men twice his age. With a sledge hammer in one hand and wooden stakes in the other, he and the rigging crew set the foundation for circus tents. Then, a line of men would grab hold of the ropes and pull the heavy canvas into position.

Sweat poured heavily from Murray's brow as he worked in the hot afternoon sun. The circus moved south to Delaware, Maryland and then Virginia. Tents went up on Thursday and they were taken down on Sunday. Monday through Wednesday were traveling days. When he wasn't working on the tents, Murray watered the animals and swept out the train cars carrying the horses. For many, this was considered the least pleasant job. Murray shrugged and grinned as circus performers passed by the train car.

His afternoons always included free time to watch the circus performers practice and, sometimes, join in the fun. He particularly enjoyed watching the lion trainers and exercising with the acrobats. Murray had no acrobatic skill. But he was fine climbing the stairs to an eight-foot platform and then jumping down to catapult one of the famous Kartuski brothers to another brother's nearby shoulders. Whoosh!! Murray would send another Kartuski flying.

It was on one of these fun-filled afternoons in June that Murray first saw Mariana Escobar. She wore black riding pants and a purple blouse. Her dark curly hair ran down past her shoulders. She was the most beautiful woman Murray had ever seen. He watched her as she walked across the circus yard. "Wow," Murray said quietly to one of the Kartuski brothers. Joseph Kartuski smiled. He told Murray the girl was 26 years old. She was too old for him, Murray thought. He was past 16 and his hormones were raging.

Mariana's home was in South America, where she learned to ride horses with her brother Enrique. Every day Mariana and Enrique would practice with four white stallions in the center ring. She would begin by riding around the ring. Soon she was standing on one horse, then two, and, eventually, she'd stand straddling four horses as they galloped around the ring. Enrique would stand in the center, holding a whip and using a long stick to keep the horses together.

Mariana had seen the tall, young muscular Murray Goldman practicing with the acrobats many times. He brushed his long, dark hair back across the forehead with his hand. Mariana's brown eyes were fixed on his every movement. He was over 6 feet tall. Perhaps he was too young, she told herself. But Murray carried himself with enormous confidence.

One day, as the Kartuski brothers were warming up, she called to Murray for help getting on her horse. Close up, Murray was overtaken by her beauty. She was only 5 foot 4 inches tall and just 110 pounds. He could not get over how good she smelled. Was it lavender, he asked himself? As he lifted Mariana up on to the horse, her breasts gently brushed his face. He paused for a minute, holding Mariana in the air. He did not hear the Kartuski brothers calling.

Several more encounters like this would follow. Soon Murray's free time was spent watching Mariana, helping Mariana—falling in love with Mariana. He dismissed the idea that she might be interested in this young, homeless boy from Brooklyn. If she found out his real age, he'd suffer an embarrassment greater than he could handle. He pulled away from watching or spending time with Mariana for several weeks. But his mind—and his dreams of her—would not yield.

The Saturday night performance in Virginia had gone extremely well. While tired, Mariana was in a festive mood. She saw Murray after the show and insisted he come back to her compartment on the train. A bottle of wine saved for special occasions was opened. She quickly drank a glass and then poured another. Murray waived off Mariana's offer to drink with her. He didn't want wine.

Mariana then surprised him by speaking openly of her interest in him. He hesitated until she had finished her third glass. He gently grabbed her arm and pulled Mariana close. He could still smell her perfume. Slowly, he began to kiss her neck. She leaned her head back as he moved from one side to the other. Mariana had not been with a man in a very long time. She responded with a hunger bottled up over a long period of time.

Gently, she kissed Murray and began to explore his mouth with her tongue. Soon, the pace quickened. Murray had never been with a woman before. He wasn't certain what to do. But he wanted Mariana more than anything he had ever wanted in his life. He decided to close his eyes and to just follow his instincts.

His hot breath moved past their lips and tongues. He lifted her up in the air to kiss her breasts exposed by the V-neck riding costume. Her hands pulled his head closer, as Marianna wrapped her legs around Murray's waist. They moved a few feet before falling on the bed. Soon they were naked and Murray was lost in a world he had never known before. Suddenly, she pushed him away. He looked at her as she pulled back. Was this it, he feared? Was she coming to her senses? Then, just as quickly, she began kissing him again. She had made her decision.

They kissed again as he slowly rolled Mariana over. What he lacked in finesse, Mariana found he made up for with boundless energy. The night would not end for many hours. He was filled with her smell, drenched with her sweat and spent of his love.

Murray woke to find himself still in Mariana's arms. He closed his eyes again. He never wanted to leave her. Mariana moved slowly, stretching. "I have to go," he told her. "They will be looking for me. I'm late for morning chores."

"Ok, but I'm not done with you," she replied. "You must promise me, you will not talk about us to anyone. Promise me."

Murray pulled her close and kissed her neck. If only he could freeze this moment in time. "I promise you." Looking at the clock on the wall, Murray knew he was late for morning chores. He stole one more kiss and got dressed.

Mariana could not recall a more satisfying evening. She stared out the window for a long time. After breakfast, she walked back to the animals. She did not wish to disturb Murray, just to gaze at him from a distance. He was young, she thought to herself. But it wasn't just the physical lovemaking that impressed her. She had never been with someone who was so "in the moment," so focused on her needs or her satisfaction. For her, Murray was every bit of a man, and maybe more, than she had ever known.

The workdays gave way to long nights of passionate lovemaking. Mariana and Murray seemed inseparable. She was flattered by the affection he showered on her. He wasn't certain how long the time with Mariana would last, but he was not going to over analyze the situation. He was happy. He had a new purpose in life. He was grateful to find love.

In the fall, the circus headed north again toward Chicago. Murray had made many friends and was well liked. Next to Mariana, his favorite pal was Louis Kimmel. Louie, as he was called, was a dwarf. Among the circus performers, he was known as Louie the Lionhearted. The nickname was given to him because everyone knew it took courage for Louie, being so small, to go out there every night and face the crowd. His job was dressing up and performing with the clowns.

Louie was more than three times Murray's age. But he found in Murray a thoughtful friend and they shared a common heritage. Louie was also Jewish.

Leaving Brooklyn involved more than saying goodbye to his family. Murray quit high school before completing the eleventh grade. He also gave up the weekly trips to Synagogue with his family. Murray was not religious, but he felt at home in a synagogue. He knew the Sabbath prayers by heart. He also strongly identified with Jewish history and culture.

Louie loved making people laugh, but few people cared to have a dwarf as a friend. Even in the circus family, no one really spent time with Louie. It was different with Murray. He didn't see Louie in terms of size. Louie was educated.

"Look, you will have lots of time during your stay with the circus," Louie told his young friend. "I can give you books to read. And I can teach you things from the books I've read on history, geography and even some literature."

Murray turned out to be a quick study and anxious to learn.

The circus reached Chicago in September. Big cities usually involved an extended stay, which gave the performers more time off. Louie seized the opportunity and suggested he and Murray attend Rosh Hashanah services at a nearby Synagogue. The two of them walked a mile into town to celebrate the Jewish New Year. Along the way, they talked about their families.

Louie's mother had died many years ago. His father had not loved him. The other kids in the family were normal in size and he was a dwarf. "God did not intend for us to judge people by their physical makeup or color of their skin," Louie said quietly to Murray. After that, the conversation ended as they walked along. Eventually, Murray reached over to pull his friend closer. He put his arm on Louie's shoulder to console him. Ironically, it also gave Murray the warm feeling of the family he missed, as well.

That morning, the Beth El Synagogue was sea of prayer shawls and Kippahs. Above the murmurs of the congregation, the Cantor's voice sang out. Murray and Louie knew they had come to the right place. This Cantor could sing. Seated way in the back, Murray could see the wave-like motion of prayer, as people stood for the opening of the Ark. Behind the dark burgundy curtain were six beautiful Torahs. It was just like Brooklyn.

At the end of services, people turned to each other, and to Louie and Murray, wishing them a "Shanah Tova" or good holiday and new year. For two wandering Jews, the warmth of strangers gave them a feeling of belonging. Isaac had taught Murray that a Synagogue was always a focal point of community. It was a connection you would find in different towns across the country.

CHAPTER 4

In the Shadows

The Chicago crowd on Friday night filled the big top to capacity. Circus performers enjoyed big cities. More people could afford the admission fee, and they genuinely seemed to have more fun. On this night, a near fall off the high wire brought loud gasps. A death-defying pyramid almost ended in tragedy, as two men dangled by their hands from the wire. Murray joined the other riggers, who rushed out with a net. Soon shrieks of fear turned to cheers as the performers regained their balance. With tragedy averted, they continued their act.

At the end of the evening, Mariana and Murray walked back to her compartment on the train. She had waited for him to finish a few chores, before the circus closed down for the night. Mariana seemed anxious and upset. She began expressing concern to him about the future— their future. "I can't do this anymore," she told him. "I care about you, but I don't see where this is going. Soon, you'll return to New York. I don't want to be alone."

Murray could sense a breakup coming with Mariana. "I'm not going back to Brooklyn," he pleaded his case. "I want you. Only you. Why can't we just give ourselves more time. "They had been inseparable for three months. He knew instinctively the odds were against them.

In the distance several train cars away, Murray suddenly heard a scream. He put his hand to her lips to quiet Mariana. Again, he heard screams. He ran from her and moved closer to see the source of the noise. His concern turned to horror as he circled the next train car. The circus lights broke through the darkness. He could see Louie helpless on the ground. His face was filled with blood.

Two strangers stood in the shadows. They were drinking and laughing. They had been taking turns beating him. Louie's eyes saw Murray. Louie was crying. At that moment, something snapped inside. Murray blindsided the first man with a fist to the jaw. The man was going down when Murray grabbed his left sleeve with his right hand. Pulling him back straight, he punched the man square in the face with a left. He was aiming for the nose, but hit a few inches lower. Blood and teeth dropped from his mouth.

"What have you done?" Murray asked. He could not imagine the horror Louie suffered, as he was sprawled on the ground. "You've made a mistake," he told the man, with blood filling the front of his T-shirt. He knocked the man senseless twice more. But his anger was not satisfied. He spun the man, twisting his right arm behind his back. The bone cracking sound and screaming came instantly.

However, he was so focused, he did not hear the second man approaching. A large board cracked him in the head. Murray went down on one knee. Dazed and bloody, he struggled to get control of his senses. He would not give in to the pain. Once again, the second man came at him. He raised the board high. Murray drove his fist deep in the man's solar plexus. Gasping, he went down on one knee.

As the noise of the fight grew louder, a crowd of other circus performers joined them. The Kartuski brothers grabbed the men and waited for the police to arrive. Murray lay back on the ground for several minutes. He could not get the pounding in his head to go away. He soon felt a small hand rubbing his forehead. He opened his eyes. It was Louie.

"Are you ok?" Louie asked. Murray looked up at his friend, still bleeding himself. He smiled. "Yes, I'm fine."

Murray sat up and closed his eyes for a moment and then looked up again. "Why? Why did they do it, Louie?"

"I don't really know," Louie replied. "There are people out there in the world who just hate. I guess they hate anything or anybody that is different."

After a long silence, Murray reached over to grab Louie's arm. "Well, now I know how you got your name," Murray responded still groggy. "I don't understand," Louie said.

"A person must have the heart of a lion to take this kind of abuse and still want to make people laugh." They both hurt, but managed to smile. Louie bent down, picked up Murray's head and gave him a hug. "Thanks Mighty Moe for coming to my rescue." Murray wasn't certain how Louie came up with "Mighty Moe," but he liked it.

CHAPTER 5

Going to the Fights

Two weeks passed. Murray was working at the back of the train sweeping horse dung from the cars. The smell was not as strong in the cooler Chicago air. Nevertheless, few had the stomach to handle this chore. Murray seemed oblivious. He had not seen Mariana in a week. They had not finished their conversation. Each of them avoided the other, as if by not talking, no one would get hurt.

Louie walked back to where Murray was working. Bandages still covered wounds he received from the beating. He covered his face with a handkerchief to try and stench the smell. "Doesn't it bother you?" asked Louie.

"What?" Murray responded.

"Doesn't the smell bother you?"

"No," said Murray matter-of-factly. "I've got two brothers at home who smell worse than this." Both Louie and Murray broke up laughing.

Louie could not wait to tell Murray his surprise. Big cities like Chicago offered many opportunities. With the help of circus manager Georgio Lecardi, Louie had managed to get two passes to the professional boxing matches that Friday night. Several known fighters were expected, the most notable being the heavyweight, Mike "the Hammer" Morin.

Louie wanted to thank Murray for saving him from an even more savage beating than he received. He figured a boy from Brooklyn would enjoy seeing the fights. Mr. Lecardi gave the two men the night off. He, too, was proud of young Murray Goldman. His actions upheld the traditions of circus family. Not everyone in the circus got along, but differences didn't matter when it came to taking care of their own.

Murray was thrilled. He had never seen a professional boxing match. He had listened often to fights broadcast on the radio. Mike Morin was a familiar name. He could recall the famous Murton versus Morin fight. Phil Murton from Philadelphia was your classic boxer, moving around the ring, peppering Morin with a steady left jab. But he was no match for the brawling tactics of Mike Morin. He worked Murton's arms as well as the mid- section with punches, to the point where keeping his guard up was difficult.

Then Morin hammered Murton till he dropped in the ninth round. Murray could still hear the announcer yelling the count over a scream- ing crowd. The thought of seeing Morin in person was so exciting. Murray stopped worrying about Mariana. He knew what he knew. He was still a kid. Mariana wanted a family. Murray could only think about Friday night and going to the fights with his pal Louie.

The boxing hall was already crowded when Murray and Louie arrived. Fans were rowdy, anxious for the fights to begin. Three matches were sched- uled before the heavyweights. Murray and Louie made their way down the aisle looking for their seats. As the ring got closer, the two of them looked at each other and shrugged. Louie pretended to be surprised. He knew a week ago that Georgio Lecardi had gotten them ringside seats. A deal was struck with the boxing promoter in exchange for a block of circus tickets. Murray couldn't believe it. He was sitting in the third row at ringside, waiting to see Mike "The Hammer" Morin fight Jimmy Sullivan.

The welterweight fight went fast, a fourth-round knockout. Then the middleweights went at each other furiously. It wasn't clear who had the advan- tage. Both fighters had landed on the ropes and both had kissed the canvas, but a cut prematurely ended it in the tenth round. It wasn't an ordinary cut. The eyebrow was raining blood down the fighter's face, into his eye and down his arm. Louie was amused by his young friend's concentration on the fighters. His shoulders and arms moved almost as if he were in the ring himself.

The light heavyweight bout ended suddenly in round two, a complete mismatch. The fans booed as Bobbie Castle used Ken Jones as a punching bag. Murray lost count of the punches as Jones back pedaled across the ring. His legs wobbled, but he wouldn't go down. Then, in a burst of lefts and rights, Bobbie Castle knocked Jones through the ropes and out of the ring. The crowd loved the finish.

Murray stood up smiling. He applauded Castle with the crowd. Louie laughed. "You really like this, don't you?" asked Louie.

"I don't know," Murray responded with a shrug as he sat down. "There is something very simple about it, Louie...only two guys out there in the ring. And it's not just speed or strength."

Murray's eyes moved from Louie towards the ring. "Out there, it's heart." He turned back to Louie. His expression was reflective, as if there were questions unanswered. His hand reached for Louie's shoulder,

"I don't know where else you are ever tested like right there," Murray said pointing to the ring.

The heavyweights came out to a restless but upbeat crowd. This was the match they had waited for all evening. Jimmy Sullivan, like Mike Morin, was a brawler. Both were rated as potential contenders for the heavyweight title. Sullivan was slightly taller, with a longer reach. Morin was compact, a huge chest. His short muscular arms hit opponents like two sledge-hammers, which is how he came by his nickname. Each fighter had a reputation for the occasional use of an elbow or head butt. Neither had ever been knocked out.

From the first bell, the fighters collided at the center of the ring. Five rounds later they were still at each other nonstop. The advantage during the round changed quickly, from Sullivan to Morin and back the other way. A missed jab or right cross was an opportunity to regain control. Murray was fixed on the action. He could hear Louie above the crowd telling him the fight was like two Roman gladiators.

Murray didn't know what a Roman gladiator was. "Courage," Murray said to Louie. "What you see in Mike Morin is sheer courage." Morin bobbed and weaved. He punished Sullivan's midsection. He also took the best punches Sullivan could dish out, but he never backed up. Morin may have moved sideways to ward off Sullivan's attack, but backing up from an opponent was just not his style. Murray couldn't put his feelings into words, but he admired Morin in a way he had never looked up to anyone.

In the seventh round, Morin rocked Sullivan with two rights to the head. It was the first major turn in the fight. Murray was on his feet. Sullivan moved to his right. At that point, Morin physically grabbed Sullivan and threw him back against the ropes. Morin would not let him escape. He unleashed a savage attack.

The crowd jumped to their feet, wild with excitement. Sullivan's face was puffy and swollen. Dazed and desperate, he lunged forward off the ropes butting Morin in the face. Grimacing with pain, Morin moved to the right. Blood flowed from a cut above his eye and from his nose. The blood blurred his vision. Before he could recover, Sullivan came around with a powerful left cross. Morin went down on his knees, leaning against the ropes near the corner.

Sullivan moved away as the referee came in for the count. Murray knew it was somewhere in these hazy few seconds, when going home would have been easier than standing up again. "Here is where a fighter must find heart," Murray told Louie. "Quitting is not an option. Failure is not an option." Murray knew instinctively that words could not describe what Morin felt. But it is there in a fighter's eyes. At times like this, fighters really find out what they are made of. Murray stood at his seat, hoping beyond hope Morin would respond.

By the count of eight, Morin was up and on his feet. He waived off the referee, then he motioned to Sullivan. His arms defiantly gesturing, "Come on, let's go." Sullivan, convinced this was false bravado, moved in to finish him off. Sullivan did not see the left upper cut. His head flew backward. Morin came around with a right that rocked his opponent. Another right and then a left. After the third right, Sullivan landed on his back. He was out cold.

Morin paused for a moment leaning against the ropes. The crowd was on their feet screaming. As the referee waived his hands to signal the end of the fight, a smile came to Morin's face. The blood dripping down his face and the pain in his head didn't matter. All that mattered is he had gone the distance. He had won.

Murray stood by the ring for the longest time watching Morin. This was a special night for him. He felt something he had never really felt before. He had found a hero in Mike Morin. Perhaps he had also found a purpose.

As they left the boxing hall, Murray thanked Louie. They stopped for some food before heading back to the circus. Louie joked about Kenny Jones being knocked out of the ring. They both marveled at Mike "The Hammer" Morin's stunning comeback. "Guts," Murray said, "it's determination and guts."

CHAPTER 6

Time to go Home

Murray tried unsuccessfully for several days to talk with Mariana. She said she was too busy while practicing, and afterward, she would disappear. Murray was persistent. He could feel her pulling away for some time now. Murray couldn't be what she wanted and he couldn't let go of her. Finally, on Thursday night, following his chores, he went to Mariana's train car. It was late.

The light was on. He could see her shadow moving behind the curtains. "Mariana, are you in there? We need to talk. I want to see you."

When the door opened, Murray realized Mariana had moved on. She held a glass of wine. He knew that look in her eyes. Her lips were full. The kind of fullness that only comes from rubbing them against someone else. He knew those lips all too well.

Stanley Dombrofsky, the strongman from the trapeze act, came out from the shadows and stood behind her. "Oh, I'm sorry for coming over so late," Murray told her. "I didn't know you had company." Shocked and hurt, he turned to walk away. Mariana stepped from the car to watch him. She knew how hurt he would be. But Mariana knew loving him was not enough. Love is never enough. She feared Murray might grow tired of her, and then what? She could not wait and wonder if they had a future.

Murray walked a long time by himself. He felt betrayed. She was his first love. How could she turn him away? No one had ever gotten so close to him. A sense of distance and loneliness shadowed him. Like the circus clowns, no one saw beneath the smiling face. Only Mariana's eyes could see the feelings he held deep within. He longed for her arms to hold him again.

As he walked further and further along, his thoughts turned to family back in Brooklyn. It had been a year since he left. The sounds of the tenement buildings and neighborhood streets still echoed in his head. He missed his father, Isaac, strange as that seemed. During his time with the circus, he occasionally wrote to his mom, brothers and sisters. But when he missed home the most, it was always Isaac's face. He hated what gambling had done to his family. Yet he loved his father.

Louie was asleep when Murray came knocking on his door. It was not like Murray to be out roaming around in the middle of the night. He knew something was wrong. Calmly, Louie listened to the story about Mariana. Louie could feel his young friend's pain. Murray would not give in to the hurt bottled up inside. He decided it was time to go home.

The train back to New York would leave on Saturday at 10 a.m. Louie went with Murray to the station. They drank coffee and talked until the conductor yelled out for everyone to board the train. Louie was sad to see him go. They both promised to write. "I'll never forget you," Murray said as he leaned down and hugged Louie Kimmel goodbye. Louie tried to clear his throat, but the words would not come. His small hand wiped his eyes. He patted Murray on the arm. Then he waved for him to get on the train. "Whatever you do with your life," Louie said, "stay true to who you are. Stand up for what you believe. Fight if you must, but let your good nature and love win in the end."

Murray would never forget this little man. He made people laugh and he taught everyone he met much about humility and courage.

CHAPTER 7

Brooklyn

Brooklyn felt like a pair of old winter gloves, familiar and warm. Murray knew these streets so well. He walked the neighborhood for most of the morning. A bag hung over his shoulder. He passed the diner near Broadway Avenue in Williamsburg. The smell of fresh coffee washed over him. A fire truck siren wailed in the distance. He took in the sounds and smells of the city. He was home.

Lemberg's bakery was bustling with customers when Murray arrived. Mrs. Lemberg, as usual, was pushing the apple strudel. "Vel dahling," she said in a heavy Yiddish accent, "you don't vant to pass up the strudel today. Nobody makes strudel like my Joseph Lemberg."

"You there, tell these lovely ladies vat a great strudel we make." Murray smiled at being singled out by Sophie Lemberg. He indeed was an expert on the strudel and most other baked goods made by Mr. Lemberg. "Ladies," Murray began, "I have traveled all the way from Chicago. The one thing that I heard people talk about over and over again on the train is if I ever get to Brooklyn, I should run to Lemberg's for a piece of apple strudel." With that, Murray dropped his bag. "I hope you have enough left," Murray said. "Vait just a moment young man," responded Sophie, "I have to finish with these customers first."

The two women quickly ordered large pieces of strudel and then left the bakery. Murray and Mrs. Lemberg began to laugh. "Come over here Murray Goldman and let me look at you." After a big hug and kiss, Sophie Lemberg stepped back. "I cannot believe this is the same boy," she commented. "You've filled out. You've gotten so big...and strong. She grabbed his muscular arms and pinched. "Where is Alvin?" Murray asked. "He'll be back soon. He is delivering a cake to the Mrs. Bloomawitz."

Alvin Lemberg had been Murray's friend since elementary school. They were different in many ways. Murray had always been more of a street kid. His intelligence came from an intuitive understanding of people. Alvin read books, lots of books. Alvin did exceptionally well in school. Murray was less of a student, except for math. Murray could calculate numbers in his head, even complex math exercises. Alvin and Murray were like brothers, but more open and maybe closer than some brothers often get. There was no competition here. The two of them nurtured each other and built a strong bond of respect.

Alvin returned from delivering the wedding cake for Avram Bloomawitz's daughter. He burst into a smile at the sight of Murray eating apple strudel and drinking coffee with Mrs. Lemberg. The two shook hands, then hugged. "It's good to have you back," Alvin said. Murray did not speak, but he realized how much he missed his friend.

Murray and Alvin sat for hours in the back room of the bakery catching up on their adventures. He told Alvin about Louie and Mariana. He went into some detail about working in the circus and the cities they had visited. He also talked about seeing the Morin-Sullivan fight in Chicago. Alvin could tell by Murray's long and enthusiastic description of the fight that something else was going on. He was animated in telling Alvin the blow-by-blow details of the fight. It was not like Murray. He was usually not such a talker. "So, what you're telling me is that you came back to Brooklyn to be a fighter?" Alvin asked.

Murray sat stunned. "Alvin, how did you know that already? I haven't shared that thought with anyone," he responded. Yes, he told his friend. He wanted to try. Alvin was not surprised.

There was something inside Murray, which even he could not explain. He didn't know if it had always been there? But the night he saw Mike Morin pick himself up and knock Jimmy Sullivan out cold, he knew he had to find out.

Alvin laughed. He would not try to persuade his friend to give up the idea. At moments like this, it was important for a friend to just be a friend. Besides he knew how determined, even stubborn and single-minded Murray could be. The thought of him in a boxing ring brought a chuckle and smile to Alvin's face. Murray saw he had his friend's blessing and he began to laugh as well. They could tell, once again, they were about to embark on another great adventure together.

Murray knew he could not stay at home. The family, without Isaac, was just getting by. There was little in the way of extras; extra food, extra clothing. He was 17. He was on his own now.

Alvin left to talk to his father. Mr. Lemberg agreed to let Murray live in the bakery's backroom. He was already an extended member of the Lemberg family, having eaten at their home upstairs many times. Murray was very appreciative. He insisted on working for Mr. Lemberg, to help in the bakery.

That evening Murray went home to see his family. His brothers and sister greeted him at the door. They were excited and happy. Each of them rushed to tell their older brother some tidbit of news. Asher had become a weightlifter. Berta had gotten a part-time job at Moskowitz's candy store. And Sammy was wearing a new pair of thick eyeglasses. He had grown at least three or four inches.

After a brief round of hugs, Murray left his siblings for the kitchen.

Tonia Goldman sat at the table sipping hot tea from a glass mug. As the door swung open, Tonia looked up to see Murray. She did not get up. Her hands quickly covered her eyes and she began to cry. He went over. He kneeled down beside her. "Mama, it's ok. I'm home now." Tonia pulled her glasses off and grabbed Murray, pulling him close to her. With the back of her hand, she tried to dry her eyes. But she could not hold back the flood of tears. He sat there in his mother's arms as she wept. He could not imagine she felt such pain. Slowly, he stood up holding and hugging her. Murray towered over his mother. He tried to reassure her, as he stepped back and dried her eyes. Tonia grabbed her son's hand. She kissed it and squeezed it with both her hands. Her prayers had been answered.

Tonia rushed around the kitchen preparing food, as Murray sat at the kitchen table talking with his brothers and sister. The stories would go on for hours. Berta asked about his girlfriend. He had mentioned her so often in his letters home. "So, what happened to Mariana?"

"Well," he replied, "She didn't mind coming back with me to Brooklyn, but she insisted on bringing the horses. I told her they wouldn't fit in the house." They all laughed.

"Sammy," Murray motioned, "come here. I have something for you." As Sammy walked over, he reached inside his coat. "I saved this just for you Sammy." He pulled out a picture of Mike "the Hammer" Morin and Jimmy Sullivan. Sammy's mouth opened and his eyes grew wide as he looked at the two famous fighters. "This is it?" Sammy asked. His older brother nodded. Sammy leaped at his older brother with a hug. He could not describe in words how much he had missed him.

By eight o'clock, Murray looked at Tonia and asked about his father. She paused for a moment, as she washed the dishes. He could see the sadness in his mother's face as she turned around.

"You should go see him. He misses you. He may not say it out loud, but I know the man. He misses you very much." Murray put his coat on to leave. He explained to Tonia his arrangements with the Lembergs. The Goldman clan gathered at the door. Sammy was clinging to his brother's arm. "Don't worry Sammy," Murray told him, "I'm not going away again. I will see you every day. I promise."

As he headed out the front door of the tenement, he stopped for a moment. Across the street he could see someone playing handball under the streetlight. It was a girl. She was very fast. He watched for a few minutes. His attention then turned to his father, Isaac, as he walked down the street.

The door to his apartment opened. Isaac peered through his thick glasses, stunned by the sudden appearance of his son. "Moshe, is that you?" Isaac often called Murray by the Jewish name he was given at birth. It was always used to convey his affection and love.

Isaac could not believe how much taller Murray had grown. He stepped through the doorway. Isaac reached up with a hand on the back of his son's neck, pulling him into his arms. Without warning for the first time in Murray's memory, Isaac began to cry. He wept openly. Whether the tears were joy at his return or guilt over breaking up the family, it did not matter to his son. Murray loved Isaac. He knew somehow that much of his determination and pride came from his father. The ties that bind them could not be broken and the love could not be diminished.

Isaac asked Murray many questions about his time away from home. He wanted to know everything. Afterward, he asked him about his plans. Murray wanted more than anything to share his dream with his father, but he could not. Isaac would not approve his decision to be a boxer. Instead, he told his father he was staying and working with the Lembergs at the bakery. He would find a better job later. Isaac asked his son to visit, now that he was home. Murray agreed to do so.

By 10 p.m., Murray was once again on the street. He breathed a deep sigh of relief. As he walked, the sounds of the city were everywhere. Cars roared by. Drivers leaned on their horns loudly as traffic came to a stop. Somewhere, music blared from a radio. It felt good to be home in Brooklyn again.

CHAPTER 8

Getting in the Ring

As they headed to the boxing gym on Tuesday, Alvin was telling Murray about the great lineage of Jewish boxers who dominated the sport throughout the 1920s. Alvin was an avid reader. While he did not have any skill at sports, he read the newspapers every day. He began telling Murray one of his favorite stories about Benny Leonard, a Jewish kid from the Lower East side of Manhattan who became the lightweight boxing champion of the world.

Like Murray Goldman, Benny Leonard learned to fight in the streets of New York. On a pound-for-pound basis, he was considered by many to be one of the greatest fighters ever. He held the title for eight years, longer than any fighter in that era.

In 1922, Benny Leonard moved up a weight class to try and take the welterweight title from the champion, Jack Britton. There were still many in Brooklyn who believed Leonard should have won that fight. It was so ironic, because Leonard had beaten Britton twice before, in 1917 and 1918.

According to Joseph Lemberg, Alvin's dad, Leonard was disqualified for knocking Britton on his ass in the 13th round with a clean right cross, and then, as Britton was laying helpless on the ropes, Leonard did what any kid in Brooklyn would do—he reached down and continued to beat him.

Leonard was not about to let his opponent regain his senses. The judges disqualified Leonard. The commotion in the ring was out of control. People screamed that he was robbed when they announced Leonard's disqualification.

"Fix." "Fix." "A rising tide of voices could be heard across the crowd," Alvin told Murray. "Soon the supporters of each boxer were yelling at each other in the audience. Then the fists flew. The boxing hall turned into the largest public brawl ever seen in New York. The chaos continued for almost an hour, before the police restored calm. By the time that happened, more than two-dozen people were sent to the hospital and a greater number dragged out by the cops.

Leonard didn't care," Alvin explained. "He had made his statement about who owned the ring. His manager got him out of the building, before the police took their turn beating the crowd with night sticks."

"That's it," Murray responded.

"Well, my dad told me, Leonard continued to defend his lightweight title for several more years. He had fame, he had money and he had glory. Then, suddenly, and without warning, he came home one night after the fight with Jake Musgrove. It was an early round knockout. Bennie's mother had been sitting in the kitchen, listening to the fight on the radio. "Benjamin, it's time. I want you stop fighting."

"As my dad put it," Alvin said, "a Jewish boy never disobeys or refuses his mother's instructions. Leonard retired the next day. He won 89 of his 96 fights, with 70 knockouts."

Murray smiled. Alvin told such wonderful stories. The 20's and 30's were considered the golden era of Jewish boxers, with folks like Barney Ross, Maxie Rosenbloom and Leonard. Jews had won 26 world championship titles. The sport was only exceeded by baseball in popularity.

"Hey," Alvin pointed out, "Jews were no different from any other ethnic group, trying to get ahead in America. Eventually, there would be other routes to success and Jews would find them. But during this period, when people were struggling to survive and no one could afford an education, boxing was an expression of Jewish pride."

By the time Alvin and Murray reached Clancy's gym, it was filled with sweat-covered young men. Everywhere there was movement, some pounded punching bags, other boxers were pounding one another. After some discussion with the gym manager, Frank Celentano, Murray was invited to tryout. Celentano was a fighter in his heyday. He was smart enough to get out before getting seriously hurt.

Murray walked over to the ring and took off his shirt. He did not own a pair of boxing shorts. Alvin helped lace up the gloves. Murray climbed into the ring in street shoes, wearing his pants and a sleeveless T-shirt. His arms were long and his hands were big as a shoe box. Celentano called over Jackie Bennett. Jackie was wet with perspiration from hitting the big bag. He was clearly older than Murray, but he was about the same height and maybe 20 pounds heavier.

After a brief introduction, the two fighters squared off. Murray took a couple of quick jabs to the face. Jackie Bennett circled to the left. Then Bennett hit Murray with two stinging body shots. Murray did not flinch. Jackie went for a left and then a right combination. Murray caught his right hand, with his left. He countered with a right to Jackie's jaw. The lights went out and Jackie landed on the canvas.

Murray stared down at his unconscious opponent. The gym manager stepped into the ring, pushing him aside. He held Jackie's head and put smelling salts under his nose. Slowly, Jackie came around. Over his shoulder the manager, Celentano yelled, angrily, to Murray, "tryouts are over kid."

Murray looked at Alvin as he climbed down from the ring. Alvin shrugged. Nothing more was said. Murray felt like his dream seemed lost in a matter of minutes. Murray put his shirt back on and grabbed his coat. He had reached the gym door, when a voice called out,

"Hey kid, where are you going?"

Murray looked back to see Celentano motioning with his hand. "The locker room is over there. Willy will show you where to change. And next time, bring a pair of shorts." Alvin and Murray looked at each other and began to laugh. Murray knew the gym would soon become a second home.

Nine months later, Murray was an accomplished amateur. He showed great discipline and worked very hard to prove himself. He was light for his weight class, but Murray's hand speed for a heavy weight was very fast. No one doubted his punching power. Celentano, the gym manager, saw great promise in Murray. He coached him through more than a dozen amateur fights. Most had ended in knockouts. The 1932 amateur Golden Gloves tournament was several months away. Celentano was hopeful Murray would be ready.

By the 1930s, amateur boxing was growing in popularity. But boxing was not regulated well and amateur events were worse than professional fights. Many fights were complete mismatches between boxers. The crowds were convinced these fights were fixed.

However, the public attitude changed with the start of the Golden Gloves amateur tournament sponsored by the New York Daily News. The newspaper saw an opportunity to redefine amateur boxing, with fights that would be strictly policed. Fighters had to get physical exams and they had to agree to tough rules enforced by Golden Glove officials.

The Daily News funded these tournaments at considerable expense. They also benefitted from the ready access the newspaper had to the fighters and the news stories they'd write about local kids who were making their way in the ring. Thousands of would-be fighters applied to be in the tournaments. By 1932, a new screening process was put in place to narrow the field of competitors. Murray's early amateur success under his manager, Celentano, guaranteed him a spot in the inter-city sectionals of the Golden Gloves.

Murray's routine started every day at 4:30 a.m. He hated running, but he would do what he had to do to succeed. He ran through the dark Brooklyn streets until sunrise. The city was calm and quiet. The pounding of his heart and heavy breathing were the only sounds he could hear.

By 6:00 a.m., he would round the street back to Lemberg's bakery. Mr. Lemberg and Alvin were already working in the bakery. Murray immediately began to help, carrying in large sacks of flour and stacks of heavy metal trays used in the oven. At 7 a.m. they took a break for breakfast. Sophie Lemberg would bring coffee and food down to the bakery. For Murray, it was always the same, three raw eggs in a glass, a bagel and black coffee. Alvin winced at the sight of his friend drinking eggs like it was juice.

By noontime, Murray would be headed for the gym. He jumped rope, hit the speed bag and then the heavy bag. Then he sparred for thirty minutes with other more experienced fighters. He was liked and respected by the other fighters. He didn't talk much. At 4 p.m., Murray returned to the bakery, helping Mr. Lemberg clean-up for the following day. He was very hardworking, Mr. Lemberg often told Sophie. After an early dinner, Alvin and Murray went out, though his training schedule required him to be home early. Sometimes Murray stopped to see his family or visit his father. At other times, he and Alvin walked the streets looking for girls or grabbed coffee at a diner and talked.

Murray told Alvin about the Golden Gloves tournament that was coming up soon. But Alvin was not prepared for his next question. "Alvin, would you be in my corner during the fights?"

"Uh, I don't think you want someone like me in your corner. I'd be useless. One of those girls over in the corner of the diner would know more about what to do then me."

Alvin rambled on for several minutes, but he could see it didn't matter to Murray. His friend could be stubborn as hell. He muttered something about "knowing Alvin had his back."

"OK, ok. Yes," he told his friend, "I'll be there, but I'm going to insist on one condition."

Murray couldn't imagine what Alvin wanted. "What? What do I have to do?"

"Win!" Alvin responded, "You have to promise me you'll win."

CHAPTER 9

First Glance

The streetlights had already come on as Murray reached home to visit his family. He could see two figures playing handball under the lights across the street. The game moved quickly and it appeared the girl had the advantage.

Sammy was sitting on the steps watching from the distance. "It's Asher and that new girl," Sammy said. "She beats him every time. And you know Asher, he hates losing."

Murray could hear Asher arguing with the girl over losing a point. Asher's large body builder frame towered over the girl, but she never backed down. She was poking him in his chest and telling him he was wrong. She wasn't about to be bullied. After several minutes of argument, the girl agreed to play the point over. She knew exactly what she was doing. She hit the next ball low to the wall and Asher ran, tripped and fell almost flat on his face. She moved so fast. It had only taken a minute for her to win the point again. Murray watched with a smile on his face, as his brother picked himself off the pavement. "She's quite an athlete," he told his brother Sammy.

"What's her name?" he asked. "Sugar. Franny Sugar," Sammy responded.

Murray looked again as his brother got up and chased hand balls back and forth across the court. Shaking his head, he grabbed Sammy by the arm and went upstairs to see his mom.

CHAPTER 10

Test of Courage

The Golden Glove city tournament ran for several weeks. Boxers had to register to fight using their real name, but could use a nickname for the promoters. The registration forms listed him as Morris Goldman (aka "Moe Fields".) Murray understood his father would not approve of his decision to be a boxer. He knew Isaac would probably come down to try and stop him. He did not want a confrontation with his father, so he decided on using an alias. His boxing had to remain a closely guarded secret. Aside from Alvin, he initially told no one.

By the first week of the tournament, the Daily News ran a feature story on the fifth straight win for a new fighter out of Brooklyn. The headline read, "Moe Fields Wins by a Knockout." Murray never explained to anyone how he chose that name. After five impressive knockouts, most people assumed his real name was Moe Fields.

Murray was very low-key, after each victory. He agreed to do newspaper interviews, as long as they didn't take his photo. He was careful his family and his father did not find out he was boxing. If the newspapers ran a photo, it was usually of Moe Field's back with his hands stretched out looking down at an opponent on the canvas. After a fight, he and Alvin would quietly slip away from the boxing arena. He avoided the crowds of well-wishers and the women who would hang around to meet the fighters. Eventually, they would find their way back to Lemberg's bakery to eat.

Alvin talked with him about the upcoming boxing tournament quarterfinals, which were scheduled for the following Thursday night. Murray was set to fight a black fighter, Reggie Peterson. His nickname was "Ripping Reggie." He was a very strong fighter. His chest was massive. Both Murray and Reggie had an equally long reach, but Reggie was also known for a dangerous left jab. Reggie would frustrate his opponents by jabbing and then moving around the ring. The movement made him a difficult target. After several rounds, the jabs would redden his opponent's face. Sometimes, he would actually open cuts above or below the eyes. His fans would get excited. "Rip 'em up, rip 'em Ritchie," they yelled.

The subject of fighting quickly faded. Murray and Alvin sat and talked about their families and what they hoped to do with their lives. Alvin's parents wanted him to go to college, but he thought he'd be happy just taking over the family bakery. Murray didn't think he could go back to finish high school. Too much had changed in his life. He just wanted to find a good job and maybe someday start his own business. Alvin envied his friends' discipline and drive. "Nothing could stop this guy," Alvin thought to himself. "Nothing and no one." Alvin smiled as he listened to his friend.

On fight night, Murray arranged with Alvin to sneak his younger brother in so he could see the match. Sammy was sworn to secrecy. Frank Celentano, Murray's manager, cautioned him about the jab. He kept telling him to try and cut off the ring, so Reggie couldn't dance away. Celentano knew his fighter wasn't listening. He kept glancing at the audience. "He's coming Moe, he's coming," Celentano assured him. Sammy waived to his big brother, as he reached ringside.

Celentano, once again, asserted his authority. With a light slap to the face, he gave Murray his final instructions. He knew Murray was up against a first-class fighter. He could only hope he would follow the game plan and Peterson would tire in the later rounds.

As the bell sounded, Reggie Peterson came out quickly. "Moe, Moe, Moe," voices from the crowd yelled in support of the undefeated Moe Fields. Peterson danced and jabbed, hitting Moe with several blows to the head. The blood vessels in Celentano's neck were bulging, as he screamed red-faced across the ring, "Move, Moe. Move. Don't let him control the fight."

Soon Moe returned the punishment with two hard shots to Reggie's mid-section. Reggie winced, as he tried to protect his ribs. The tone of the fight had been set.

Reggie continued to pepper Moe's head and face. Celentano watched from the corner. He was not certain which would give way first, Moe's head or Reggie's ribs. Moe was a powerful inside puncher. The fans could see Reggie gasp with each blow. The battle waged on. This was not the same Murray Goldman who helped out at Lemberg's bakery. This was Moe Fields, an unyielding, tenacious fighter. He kept coming at you, calmly, with grit and guts. His eyes were fixed on his opponent. He moved toward you. He did not know how to step backward. He just kept coming. He did not believe he could be stopped. And then it happened. In a split second, Moe's world went into slow motion. He did not see the punch.

The sounds of the arena were blocked out. The ring spun, as his body jerked backward. Moe landed on his butt, his arms reaching back between the ropes. The slugfest was almost over. The undefeated kid from Brooklyn had been knocked on his ass by a stronger competitor from Harlem.

Moe could hear the slow and slurred speech of the referee counting out the number four. He knew there wasn't much time. He pulled on the ropes to help himself up. "I'm ok, I'm ok," he could hear himself saying over and over. His breathing was labored. Sweat poured off of him. He knew he had to convince himself and the referee that he could continue. But there was no sound. At that moment, Moe wasn't certain if they would let him go on. His legs were wobbly. Then he heard it. It had always been there, when he needed it. A voice inside him said, "What the hell are you doing? Get up. Get the fuck off the floor. It's not time to go home. You can't give up. You can never give up. There's no retreat, and there's no surrender."

Moe's head started to clear by the count of seven. He looked to his corner. He could see Celentano and Alvin yelling. Below the ring, he saw Sammy's thick glasses fixed on him. Moe instinctively knew Reggie would move in quickly, as soon as the referee let go of his gloves. In situations like this, fighters would usually try and move away from their opponents. Getting out of the corner and clearing one's head was a priority, but Moe would not budge. He held to his position in the corner. There was no backing up or running away.

Reggie came at him. Moe ducked Reggie's right that was intended to end the fight. He hit Reggie with a hard right to the ribs and he doubled over. Moe followed with a left upper cut, then a right cross. The crowd was on its feet. Moe could hear again. This time the cheering was for him. Reggie fought back valiantly. No more pretense. The boxing match had fast become a slugfest. The advantage turned several times in the next few rounds.

Moe then landed a crushing right, in the eighth round. It was Reggie's turn to hug the canvas. This fight was no longer about skill. Each had bested the other, but neither was giving in to the punishment. He stood in awe as Reggie pulled himself up from the ring floor. This was now a test of wills, of wanting to win. There is something unique in the human spirit, when the brain no longer listens to the pain. The will to win, the will to live another day, rises up in us to conquer our fear. We have in each of us the ability to will ourselves to win. We just need to search for it. To accept nothing less of ourselves than giving everything we have and more.

Both Reggie and Moe were exhausted. The ninth round seemed as if it would go on forever.

In the tenth and final round, Moe slipped under a missed jab by Reggie and hit him in the mid-section. Again, he jerked to protect his ribs. Moe missed with a left, but then caught Reggie on the jaw. He went down. Reggie was up by the count of eight. His legs were still shaky. He moved to his left, while shaking out the cobwebs in his head. Moe tried to come inside, but Reggie held him off with jabs. Both fighters showed caution as the match was coming to an end. The bell rang. It was over. Each had gone the distance. Each had won the test of wills.

As they waited for the decision, Moe and Reggie paced nervously near their corners. The wait seemed longer than in previous fights. The referee then summoned the fighters to the center of the ring. "Ladies and gentlemen," the voice rang out over the loud speaker. "We have a split decision." The announcer waited for the noise to quiet down. "Our first judge scored the match 105 to 103 for Reggie Peterson. "Our second judge scored the fight 106 to 102 for Moe Fields. The fans grew quiet, as the announcer paused. "And the third judge's score was 105 to 103 for Moe Fields. The winner, by a split decision is Moe Fields."

The crowd was on its feet applauding both fighters. Each of the fighters were surrounded by a small crowd. The gloves were pulled off in the corner. Celentano started to congratulate his fighter. Moe patted his manager on the back, turned and walked toward Reggie's corner. "No one could ever understand what it was like," Moe thought, "except the two guys slugging it out there in the ring."

Moe pulled and pushed himself through the crowd around Reggie. As he made his way through, the crowd backed away. At the center, Reggie looked eye-to-eye with Moe. Reaching out with his right to shake hands, Moe put his left on Reggie's shoulder. "Toughest fight I've ever had," Moe said. "You're one damn good fighter. It could have gone either way."

"You're not so bad yourself," Reggie responded, "that is for a white boy." Moe smiled, then Reggie reached over and gave Moe a hug. These were two kindred spirits. Moe headed back to his corner. He realized that night he won the fight—and made a new friend.

CHAPTER 11

Bootleg Boxing

───────

The semi-finals match was scheduled for the following Monday night, which gave all the fighters time to rest up. Murray looked forward to the break. It had been a grueling week. His head still hurt from Reggie's jab.

The Friday night after the fight Murray and his brothers went with Isaac to synagogue. Isaac stared long and hard at Murray's face, "Moshe, have you been fighting?" Murray looked at Sammy, who stood on the other side of Isaac. "No. Well, actually, I tangled with two guys yesterday, while making deliveries for Mr. Lemberg. They got one cake, but not the money I was carrying. It happened near our neighborhood. Sammy saw me. He started yelling. They saw him and ran off." Isaac stared ahead for a moment through his thick glasses. Suspicious, he then turned to Sammy. "Is this a bubameiser?" Isaac asked. Sammy knew this was a Jewish word for fairy tale. He looked up through his own thick glasses and blinked twice, "No papa, no bubameiser. Moshe is telling the truth."

The ark, where the Torahs are kept, was opened and the Goldmans turned their attention to God. The voices of the congregation sang out the sacred prayer, "Shima Yisrael Adonai Eloheinu Adonai Echad, Hear o'Israel the lord my God, the lord is one." Their voices were strong and free. In this place of worship, every Jew felt part of something larger than himself. Murray stood in prayer next to his father. He thought, as he looked around, at how important this place had been to him all his life. His eyes turned toward the Rabbi, as the congregation began to pray. Murray did something he rarely did. He began to sing.

Saturday had gone by rather quietly. Murray spent most of the afternoon with his family. Toward evening, his brother Asher coaxed him into going to the gym. Asher was anxious to show off his weight lifting. They took Sammy along to watch. The gym smelled from sweat. Asher saw two friends working out in the corner. Before long, they were all trying to outdo each other. Murray was still sore from the fight on Thursday. He decided to do some light exercise with his brother. Murray did not have the roundness of muscles or v-shaped chest of his younger brother, but he could easily lift more weight. Two hours later they left the gym. Murray felt good.

On Monday morning, Murray received word to meet Frank Celentano down at the boxing arena. Murray entered the hall where six men from the Golden Gloves Governing Committee were waiting. Someone had reported seeing Murray at the weight gym. The Committee wanted to know if it was true. Murray paused for a moment. He was wanted to answer honestly. He didn't really understand what the big deal was.

"Yes, I was at the gym, but I was mostly stretching and loosening up after the fight. I was sore as hell."

As he tried to explain the situation, a member of the Committee cut him off. "Thank you, Mr. Goldman. We appreciate you're coming down here and for your honesty."

Before an hour had gone by, the Committee voted to disqualify Murray from the semi-final fight for what they described as "over training." A Committee member tried to explain to Celentano that the vote was not unanimous, but the majority wanted to send a message.

The Golden Gloves organization had strict rules forbidding fighters from weight training once the tournament had begun. The rules were viewed by many as unreasonable and even excessive, but with the backing of the Daily News, they were not about to have the fights compromised. The Rules Committee of the Golden Gloves were committed to keeping the integrity of their tournament, even if it meant losing a talented fighter like Moe Fields.

Celentano protested for over an hour. After the meeting, he went to each committee member one-on-one, pleading his case. The decision was based on a technical rule. Surely, Murray had not violated the spirit of the rules with one workout. The decision of the committee was irreversible. Reggie Peterson would now compete in the semi-finals, replacing Moe Fields.

Murray waited outside the hearing room as Celentano pleaded his case. He could hear loud voices and arguing. He still didn't understand what the fuss was about.

The news of his disqualification hit like him like a brick. Murray was in shock. He had worked so hard during these last few months. He was so close to winning it all. The shouting and arguing between Celentano and committee members continued in the hallway. But it was over, and Murray knew it. He left.

The bus ride back to Brooklyn was long. Murray stared out the window. He made his way back to Lemberg's bakery and told Alvin what happened. After a few minutes alone with his parents, Alvin returned and took his friend for a walk. It was already early afternoon and most of the work around the bakery had been finished. Alvin knew better than anyone the sacrifices Murray had made and the hard work he gave to winning the boxing tournament. But he was certain his friend would spring back from this disappointment. He just needed time to clear his head. It was this particular quality Alvin so admired about his friend. You couldn't keep Murray down for long.

They took the train out to Coney Island and walked the boardwalk for an hour. Murray was quiet and distracted. In his dreams of being a boxer, he had not thought much about his struggling family. These were not the easiest of times. Alvin finally got his attention, reminding him about the time in grade school when they first became friends. Alvin was always very smart. Other kids resented that he knew the answers. "Hey, Jew boy," the bullies would taunt him. Murray wasn't bothered by the smart kid, but he did resent hearing Alvin being called a "kike" or worse. Twice he defended Alvin against the bigger boys. At first Alvin liked him, because Murray protected him. Then one day in school he found another surprise. In math, his friend had few equals. He could calculate numbers in his head, faster that Alvin figured them out on paper.

Alvin knew there must be something for him beyond boxing. He didn't know what is was, but he tried to reassure his friend their future would be bright. Murray did not respond. He stared out at the ocean. He hoped Alvin was right. The Depression had not been easy on families. Many had ended up like his, split up or separated by the lack of money. Murray was coming of age. He had to get control of his life. The disqualification in the Golden Gloves tournament was like a cold shower. He began to think more about how he might help his family.

They arrived back in Brooklyn late that night. By now, Murray had shaken off his bad news. Alvin tried to joke with him, as they walked near Williamsburg. Rosie's bar was two blocks down the street. A large sign with a green shamrock hung above the open doorway. As they walked past, they could hear the loud cheering coming from inside. "What's going on?" Alvin asked someone exiting the bar. "It's bootleg boxing," the man said. "What?" Alvin asked again. "Look, there's a fight going on in the back," he responded.

Alvin shook his head. Rosie's bar had a reputation for brawling. As he turned back toward Murray, his friend had disappeared. He looked up and down the street, but he didn't see him. Suddenly, he caught a glimpse, as he pushed past the doorway crowd. The building was long. Once past the bar and tables, Murray walked through a narrow dimly lit hallway. Smoke was thick in the air. The crowd jumped to their feet, as Murray reached the entrance to the back room. The noise was deafening. Hot, bright lights were shining down on Brian "Bulldog" Mullooly standing in a boxing ring. Below him, laid out on the canvas, was Joey Polito. Brian had a menacing smile on his face, with one front tooth missing.

The ring announcer and fight promoter called out above the noise, "Bulldog Mullooly wins by a knockout." Men were moving around the crowd exchanging money. The gambling payoffs continued, as the announcer called for a new challenger to fight Mullooly. Twice more, the announcer asked for a challenger. "I have $20 for the first man who can knock the Bulldog down," he yelled out.

Alvin pushed through and joined his friend in the back of the bar. He could hear the announcer repeating his challenge to the audience, for a fighter to get in the ring with Bulldog Mullooly. Alvin could feel it. Instinctively, he grabbed for his arm, but it was too late. Murray had raised his hand in the air. Alvin quickly tried to stop him. "Please Murray, this is not the time or the place. There's got to be another way.

"Look Alvin," he said, " I was scheduled to fight this week anyway. Except this time, maybe I'll earn some money."

The announcer spotting Murray's arm, yelled to the crowd, "Ladies and gentlemen, we have a new challenger." He was half out of his shirt and heading for the ring. Alvin, in close pursuit, cautioned him this was not the Golden Gloves. These guys fought dirty, with elbows and head butts. Bulldog stood in the ring growling and waving to mock his opponent. Murray was not intimidated. He climbed into the ring. The gloves were quickly laced up, while the betting started. Murray immediately realized the gloves were not thick like the ones used in the Golden Gloves. He knew thinner gloves would result in more damage to the fighters.

The announcer soon walked over. "Hey kid, what's your name?" Murray looked up, hesitated and then replied, "Moe Fields."

"Where are you from?"

"Brooklyn."

"Ladies and gentlemen," the announcer yelled to the fans. "Tonight, Bulldog Mullooly faces a newcomer at Rosie's. He is a tough homegrown kid from the streets of Brooklyn. In the far corner...his name is Mooooo Fields." Cheers spread from the eager crowd. This was primal. No one cared who was being sacrificed. These were working men, many of them angry and unemployed. After an hour or so of drinking, they just wanted to see the bloodiest fight possible. "And in this corner," the announcer continued, "with 17 wins and only 1 loss here at Rosie's is Brian "Bull...dog Mu...lloo...ly."

Mullooly ran to the center of the ring. Then he ran to the ropes and growled at the crowd, as if he were a wild animal. He did not appear to have a neck. His body was overweight. He had to be in his mid-30s. His hair was thin and scraggly. The announcer kept his distance. He could smell this fighter and it wasn't pleasant. Sweat was dripping from his face and body. The toothless grin and growls encouraged his screaming fans, "Bulldog! Bulldog!! Bulldog!!!"

As betting on the fight was completed, the ring announcer called the boxers from their corners. Suddenly, without warning, the young fighter lunged at Mullooly, grabbing him around the head. Using all the strength in his legs, he drove Mullooly backwards into the ropes. Mullooly tried to reach up from the headlock. His arms were flying helplessly in the air. He could not pry himself loose. Moe bounced him off the ropes, whipped his body around and let go. The crowd was screaming. Mullooly spun around, and completely disoriented landed near the side of the ring. The announcer and referee jumped between the two fighters. But Moe had already turned and walked to his corner.

Alvin stood in his corner and was equally shocked by the attack. As he walked back to the corner, Alvin looked at him, "What the hell was that all about? I know I said that these guys fight dirty, but I didn't expect this."

Moe smiled and calmly looked up at Alvin after spitting in a bucket. "I just wanted to wipe that smile off his face and give him something to think about."

Order was soon restored. Once again, Bulldog Mullooly and Moe Fields were called to the center of the ring. Mullooly was not smiling this time. He looked agitated. He had been taken off guard by this young fighter. As the instructions were given, Moe looked into Mullooly's eyes. Then without warning, he smiled. It was a corny, almost a mocking smile. As Moe turned toward his corner, the smile still painted on his face, Alvin could see Mullooly being restrained by the announcer and referee.

"Have you gone crazy?" Alvin asked. "First, you want to wipe the smile from his face, then you go back out there with this shitty grin. This guy might just kill you."

"You don't like that smile?" he responded. Alvin looked up to the sky for answers but knew it was hopeless.

The bell rang for round one. Bulldog Mullooly was already three quarters of the way across the ring. Moe waited, three steps out from his corner. Mullooly threw a looping right hand. Moe ducked under and chopped the mid-section. Two more hits to the ribs followed. Mullooly spun around with his left. Again, it was high. Moe pounded at his stomach with shots. Mullooly backed to the ropes. He bounced backward like a slingshot. It was his turn to use his weight to push and wrestle Moe to the other side of the ring.

The crowd alternately cheered each fighter. Anticipating that Mullooly would hold and punch him on the ropes, Moe bounced and ducked under his right cross. As Mullooly turned to face his opponent, Moe landed a left upper cut. A right overhand punch followed. Bulldog's legs wobbled. Moe was not finished. He back-pedaled to the center of the ring. Mullooly pursued. Moe unleashed a barrage of quick punches, working from the mid-section to Mullooly's head. Fans could not get over the speed he demonstrated in hitting his opponent. Bulldog tried to cover up, but the young fighter's hands kept landing at will. Mullooly heard the crack before the pain registered in his brain. His jaw was broken. The sounds of the audience quickly faded and the lights above the ring spiraled into darkness. His body hit the ropes and thumped to the canvas.

Moe had not moved from his punching stance. The crowd was on their feet, "Moe Fields! Moe Fields!!" The referee stepped in to clear him away from the fallen fighter. When he reached the corner, Alvin praised his friend's victory. He smiled, "I wonder how Reggie Peterson did tonight."

He declined the ring announcer's request to stay and take on other challengers. He had gotten it out of his system. Enough fighting for one evening. The hurt and anger he felt about the Golden Gloves passed. He collected his $20 plus $10 from the betting pool. Soon he was back out in the street with Alvin. People coming out of the bar would stop to compliment him on the fight. "Great fight Moe." "Hey, Moe. Are you a wrestler or a fighter?" Alvin and Murray looked at each other and broke up laughing. Alvin realized that his friend had caught Mulooly off-guard with his ring behavior. Nothing worse than a fighter losing his temper....and losing control. It was late now. The boys decided to head home.

CHAPTER 12

Helping the Family

———

Two days later, Alvin read the Daily News headline, "Peterson wins Golden Gloves tournament with a KO in the ninth round." Alvin knew he could not keep the news from Murray. He feared his friend's reaction. As they sat in the bakery eating buttered rolls and drinking coffee, Alvin nudged the paper across the table. Murray looked up. Alvin pointed to the story. He smiled. "He's one helluv a fighter. I'm glad he won." With that said, matter of factly, he got up and went back to work. Alvin sat there surprised by his calm reaction. It could have been him in that headline. Murray didn't give it a second thought. "What's done is done," he'd tell Alvin.

Fighting at Rosie's, however, became a routine, at least twice a month. He did not want to take on all challengers. He understood there were many locals who only fought out of a need to make an extra $20. "There's no point and no satisfaction in stopping these Brooklyn guys from feeding their families," he'd tell Alvin. "I'd rather go late and fight the guy who was dominating that night. That's the best paying fight." He decided to fight the guys no one else would fight and no one else could beat. Rosie's would pay double or even triple to have him keep the action going. Alvin bet on his friend, though Murray frowned on gambling. Fridays at Rosie's was not about gambling to him. He was simply a fighter, earning his wages, and he enjoyed it. His last stop of the night was usually to drop off half his winnings with his mom.

When he wasn't boxing, Murray looked for other jobs. Tuesday and Thursday nights he delivered plumbing supplies. The truck pulled up to the curb. Murray stepped out. His brothers Asher and Sammy, and Alex Zacropolous, a friend from the boxing gym where Murray trained, usually came along to help carry the load. The cargo was always the same—a large supply of pipes and radiators. The radiators were the toughest, each weighing over 100 pounds. The destination was the fourth or fifth floor. "Do we have to do this again?" complained Asher. "This is the second delivery tonight."

"Asher, you and Alex take this one," Murray said. "I'll take the other."

Asher stood shaking his head. Sweat still poured off of him from the last delivery. Murray walked to the back of the truck. He placed two thick pads on his right shoulder. He pulled the steel radiator legs on his shoulder. "Sammy," he called out, "you go ahead and see if the stairway is clear." Off they went.

Asher stayed behind a few minutes grumbling to Alex. The two of them eventually grabbed the radiator and joined the climb. He and Sammy were on their way down, when they met the struggling pair at the third-floor landing. He did not speak. He smiled at the sight of Asher struggling, tapped Sammy on the shoulder and headed down to the truck.

It was almost ten o'clock by the time he returned the truck with Alex. Normally, he would head back to the bakery and go to sleep. In his pocket was $30. He was tired, but he had another excuse to stop home and give money to help with the rent.

As Murray reached home, he found a young girl sitting on the steps leading into the building. Her hair was long, curly and brown. She was tossing a handball in the air.

"Excuse me, little girl you'll have to move aside so I can go upstairs."

"Yeah, well you and what army is going to make me?" she responded. "Isn't that your brother I beat all the time," she said, throwing the ball at Murray. "I bet I can beat you, too."

He caught the ball and handed it back to her. A grin on his face, he put one foot on the steps and leaned toward the girl. "What's your name?"

"Francine Sugar, but I like people to call me Franny."

"Well Franny, I've seen you run my brother all over that handball court. I agree, you probably would beat me. But if you let me by, I promise to let you prove it another day."

Franny was intimidated by this grown man, which was not easy to do. He had broad shoulders, thick black hair and the darkest brown eyes. Quietly, she moved over on the steps to let him pass by.

Murray was still thinking about her, as he reached the fourth floor. His daydreaming was soon interrupted by the yelling he heard down the hall. The noise was coming from the apartment where the Goldman family lived. He recognized the voices immediately. Asher was being loud and disrespect-ful. Tonia was close to tears. Murray could not figure out what the argument was about.

"Asher, the whole neighborhood can hear you," Murray told him. "You better shut up and apologize to mom. I don't care what the issue is, you treat your mother with respect."

"It is none of your goddamn business," Asher yelled at him. "Don't start with me," he cautioned, pulling his shirt sleeves up over bulging biceps.

Murray paused for a split second looking into his brother's defiant eyes. He said nothing. In a split second and without warning, his right hand caught Asher with a glancing blow to the chin. Asher hit the wall and slowly slid down to the floor. He was out cold.

Murray then turned to Tonia.

"I'm sorry mama. You know papa would have done the same thing," he said. "That boy has to learn respect."

Murray handed her $20 and then left.

CHAPTER 13
A Night at the Savoy

———

By the time Murray reached 20 years of age, he was a sophisticated street kid, boxer and budding entrepreneur. On a Saturday night, he walked the streets of Brooklyn in a charcoal grey pinstripe zoot suit, floppy hat and spats. Joined by Alvin or Artie Schwartz, another childhood friend, the destination was a dance club in Harlem. People who lived in the neighborhood took him for being much older, 27 or 29, including a local loan shark who tried repeatedly to recruit him as an enforcer. He needed someone like Murray, who had quick hands, for collecting gambling debts. Murray wanted no part of gambling or anything else that was illegal.

He never lost a bout at Rosie's, though his nose was broken twice, by Richie "The Mugger" O'Brien and later, by Tony Calabrese. In Brooklyn, Moe Fields became a well-recognized name. People would pack Rosie's on the nights Moe came to fight. Even Isaac had heard talk of the fighter, while working in his cobbler shop. He passed by Rosie's bar one Friday night after going to Synagogue. But he did not like fighting. Murray never knew how close he came to being discovered by his father. And ironically, Isaac never found out that this local boxing hero was his own Moshe Goldman.

When Murray wasn't fighting, he was always finding new ways to make money. He worked at Lemberg's bakery early in the day, fixed cars at the local garage and delivered radiators at night. On days when there were no deliveries or cars to work on, he would wash dishes, work down at the docks or find other odd jobs. He brought his mother as much money each week as Isaac did. His efforts helped the family survive.

At the same time, Murray started to accumulate money for himself. Soon he could buy whatever he wanted. He liked buying clothes and shoes. He also bought his first car, an old broken-down model T-Ford he would fix when he had time. He worked hard, and money gave him the freedom he wanted.

One Saturday night in late spring, Murray and Artie Schwartz headed up to the Savoy ballroom in Harlem. As he and Artie entered the ballroom, they could easily be mistaken for a couple of gangsters. Dressed to the nine's, they would swagger into the mixed ballroom crowd. Murray was already six foot two. Artie was six foot. The padded suits on their broad shoulders made them seem even larger in size.

Quietly they strode over to the bar. Music was blaring from the orchestra. This was dance music. People snapped their fingers, waved their hands and skedaddled their bodies to the hard drum beat and frenetic rhythms. Next to boxing, this was Murray's favorite place. Stoically he watched and listened from the side of the room. After the band took a break, he'd make his move. He handed Artie his jacket and walked through the crowd. Artie lost sight of his friend as the music started up. Soon, however, the crowd seemed to be forming a circle around three dancing couples. Artie moved toward the action, breaking into a smile at the sight of Murray cutting up the dance floor. The girl he danced with was petite. He twirled her, threw her up in the air and pulled her through his legs. Each of the three couples tried to out-do each other. They had the club in a frenzy, laughing and screaming their support. Murray loved the Savoy, where blacks and whites mixed. It was a place where people could just be themselves, letting down their guard and avoiding pretensions. The young crowd came for the dancing and the music. And for an evening, they could travel far away from their daily struggles.

He used his handkerchief to wipe the sweat from his forehead as he came off the dance floor. He wasn't certain where his rhythm came from, but dancing was as natural to him as breathing. He took his jacket back from Artie. They returned to the bar for drinks. Next to Alvin, Artie was his second closest friend. He was the opposite of the bookish Alvin. Like Murray, Artie was a street kid. He also had style. He was an immaculate dresser and a shameless womanizer. Artie really knew how to schmooze people.

Standing near the bar crowd, Murray suddenly felt a nudge at his back. He had not expected trouble, but knew this was no accidental push. "Hey white boy, what are you doing in my neighborhood?" He turned, bringing his hands up. His eyes moved quickly across a small group of young black men and women. At the center of the group nudging him was Reggie Peterson. Murray started to laugh. He stuck out his hand. Reggie grabbed it, pulling Murray toward him. The two fighters hugged.

Reggie turned to his small entourage, "Hey everybody, I want you to meet a friend of mine. This is Moe Fields. He's the toughest fighter I ever faced in the ring." Murray's grin was ear to ear. It was not like the overly confident Reggie Peterson to heap such praise on an opponent. He could feel the admiration of Reggie's friends as they reached out to shake his hand, one by one.

Ruby Smith chose to be the last in the group. After shaking seven or eight hands, Murray was anxious to finish. He wasn't paying attention, as he continued talking with Reggie. Finally, he felt a soft, warm hand. He turned his head from Reggie to shake Ruby's hand. As she raised her head, Murray stopped talking. Her bright hazel green eyes greeted him with a smile. Her skin was light brown. Her lips were red and full. Her smile was wide. For a moment, the room devoid of sound blurred. It was like being in the ring, when the fighter shuts out the crowd. The moment passed quickly, as two more people pushed by Ruby to greet him.

Afterward, he was whisked away by Reggie to the bar. They stood drinking together; straight vodka with a twist of lemon. Murray looked back to find Ruby, but she had gone. Reggie explained to him that after the Golden Gloves, he decided to turn pro. He had already fought and won two fights. He knew it would be years before he could get the big-time payoffs of boxing, but this was his only route to get there.

As Reggie talked about his plans, he looked around to see if they were alone. Reggie wanted to tell Murray something he held inside for a long time.

"Moe, I felt real bad about your being disqualified at the Golden Gloves. It should have been you out there in the finals."

"Reggie, thanks, but I don't believe in looking back. The only round that counts is the one you're in. I hear you really pounded the crap out of that guy."

"Well I gave him one for you in the ninth round."

The two young boxers laughed and talked for an hour.

Suddenly, he caught a glimpse of Ruby walking past. She was headed toward a table twenty feet from the bar. She wore a gold dress with straps, and it was low cut across her chest. Her long legs and slender body moved gracefully. Murray excused himself. "Reggie, bear with me. There's something I have to do," said Murray.

He reached Ruby just as she was getting ready to sit down. "Would you like to dance?"

She turned around. She looked up into Murray's face. It was a strong chiseled face. His eyes were large and dark brown. His hair was slicked back off of his forehead. To her, he was one of the most beautiful men she had ever seen.

"I was waiting for you to ask."

The music was slow. Murray held her close. The smell of her perfume was intoxicating. She leaned her head back and looked into his eyes.

"You know," he began in a low voice, "I think I have always loved you."

Ruby smiled. "But we just met tonight," she replied, her eyes widening and a big smile stretching across her face.

"Yes, but it doesn't take long. This is just my first opportunity to tell you."

"Are you always so direct?" she asked coyly.

"Yes," he replied, staring back at her.

She rested her head on his shoulder. Ruby was completely taken by this handsome young fighter. He exuded the same confidence and determination as Reggie. She was turned on more than she was comfortable admitting. Ruby was never at a loss when it came to knowing what she wanted. She wanted Murray.

The two of them danced and talked the night away. "I see you've met Ruby," Reggie's voice interrupted as he was getting ready to leave. "Be good to her Moe, that's my cousin." Murray smiled, "I'll see you again soon."

It was getting late. Soon, he walked Ruby out of the club with Artie close behind. He hailed a cab, handed the driver money and instructed him to take the lady home. As he opened the car door, he gently pulled Ruby into his arms and kissed her. Stepping back, she gasped for breath. Then without warning she leaped up in his arms, kissing him back as her arms squeezed tightly around his neck. Ruby had her own ideas about men and love. She, too, could be direct. Before stepping into the cab, she asked Murray if he would meet her at the Savoy the following week.

He and Artie talked about their evening all the way back to Brooklyn. Artie was impressed meeting Reggie Peterson. He did not mention Ruby or his concerns about an interracial relationship. Artie knew his friend didn't care. Growing up in a Jewish community, his parents would not accept anyone who wasn't Jewish. For Murray, it was not about religion. He didn't except boundaries of any kind, whether in life or when it came to love.

CHAPTER 14

Ruby, Ruby, Ruby

———

The next week seemed to breeze by. Murray had difficulty concentrating on work. His mood was upbeat. He could not wait for Saturday. He wanted to see Ruby in the worst way.

On Friday night, he fought Pedro Gonzalez at Rosie's. Pedro was a good, tough street fighter. In the fourth round, Murray was cut above the left eye. He had never been cut before in a fight. By the fifth round, blood was dripping into his eye. His vision blurred. Suddenly, he felt the pressure to try and finish the fight. Gonzalez tried to jab at the eye. Murray caught him with a lucky punch. Two more solid rights to the head and Gonzalez went down. A dozen stitches were needed to close the cut. He dropped off half of his weekly earnings to Tonia. When asked, he told his mom cut his head working on a car.

The next night, Artie and Alex Zacropolous joined Murray for the ride up to the Savoy. Artie had tipped Alex off about the girl. They did not expect to see much of their friend that evening. The Savoy was crowded when they arrived. Music was blasting away. The dance floor was filled. Murray waded through the crowd near the door.

Ruby stood alone by the bar. Her dress was a bold royal blue. Her hair was straight with a slight curl as it reached her shoulders. The dress was cut out in the back. You could see her bare shoulders as she leaned against the bar. She turned her head from the dance floor toward the door. She had been waiting for him. Murray stood a head taller than the crowd. His suit was dark with pinstripes. To Ruby, he seemed like a movie star. Her smile greeted him across the room. He studied each part of her closely, as he approached. He had waited so anxiously for this moment. Her green eyes looked up at him.

"Hi, Moe," she said pulling him close to her. He had not anticipated this. She reached up and kissed him. It was more than a friendly kiss.

Ruby then stepped back. She reached up toward the bandage over Murray's right eye.

"Does it hurt?"

"No, not really. Just some stitches."

"Should I assume the other guy looks worse?"

"Yeah, I think you could say that," he replied with a smile. The music was slow and romantic.

"Let's dance," he said, waving toward the dance floor.

Murray stared into Ruby's green eyes. The dancing provided a good excuse to hold her in his arms. When the music stopped, he turned to walk lead her back to the bar. Then he paused and turned around to face Ruby.

"Can we get out of here. I know a place where we can go."

Ruby nodded in agreement.

The cab ride was expensive, but he didn't care. He only thought about being with Ruby. The third-floor apartment in Manhattan was small. Artie Schwartz had borrowed it from another friend. Murray turned on a light in the kitchen. He then returned to Ruby standing in the living room. Ruby reached up and kissed him. Murray returned her kiss. His tongue explored her mouth slowly, then with passion and desire. He brushed the dress off her shoulders, as he kissed the side of her neck. Her back arched backward. He reached down and kissed under her neck. As he stood straight again, she pulled his belt toward her. They kissed again. Her mouth could swallow him. His tongue reached deep inside.

Suddenly, Ruby stopped. She pushed him away. He stepped back. She wanted him to see her, to see her as few would ever get to see her. Murray stood quietly. He didn't know what to expect. She looked into his eyes, as she pulled her dress down to her waist. Slowly, she reached behind and unhooked the bra. Her breasts were modest but full. He removed his tie and shirt. His shoulders were round, his chest hairy. He pulled the sleeveless tee shirt up over his head. Ruby watched his strong muscular form. Her dress dropped to the floor. Soon they both stood naked.

Murray stepped toward Ruby. His hands slowly rubbed the skin on her arms. He gently moved his hands toward her chest, touching her as her breathing became more labored. He pulled her close and they kissed wildly. Murray lifted Ruby up. She wanted him so badly. He entered her with one long, slow thrust. He held her up with one hand on her lower back. She threw her head backward. Her arms held him around his neck. He pulled her close, kissing her neck and her breasts. The light through the windows illuminated their naked bodies. Murray was dripping with sweat. His arms ached. Ruby let out short breathy screams. They kissed, each gasping for air. They stood a moment quietly hugging, before he set her down.

He walked her to the bedroom, where they laid quietly and kissed. They were soaked. Ruby put her head on his chest, with her leg across his body as she caught her breath. She couldn't recall ever feeling like this. He laid back against the headboard.

They slept like this for hours, in each other's arms. Ruby woke at 4 a.m. She could hear the sounds of sirens in the street below. She could not stay the night. She walked to the window. Murray opened his eyes to see her naked form. She had the most beautiful body, he thought. "I have to go," she said as he sat up in bed. He walked over to the window and kissed her one more time before they started to dress.

"I want you to hold on to these," Ruby said, as she handed him her black panties. "I want you to think of me. I want you to take this out when I'm not around. I want you to smell me. Most important, I want you to come back to me."

He smiled as he looked down at the underwear. He put them in his left pocket. He wouldn't ever forget this night or this amazing woman.

After putting Ruby in a cab, Murray walked the streets of Manhattan. He stopped at a coffee shop in mid-town. Three raw eggs in a glass were ordered, with a cup of coffee. The waitress watched as Murray slowly drank the eggs. She shook her head and walked away. He couldn't stop thinking about the night. As he went to pay the bill, he realized Ruby's underwear was in his pocket. He walked back to the counter and left a tip. When he walked outside, he pulled the black underwear from his pocket. He had to smell her one more time. The smile on his face was warm and loving.

Murray then headed back home to the bakery. Mr. Lemberg was baking bread when he arrived. Murray could not sleep. He did not want to let go of Ruby's image. He changed his clothes and then insisted on helping Mr. Lemberg.

CHAPTER 15

Learning a Trade

Two days later Murray started a new job at Weinberg's plumbing supply company. Nathan Weinberg was a smart businessman. He had apprenticed as a plumber many years ago, and then started his own business. He understood and valued the importance of learning a trade. He imparted lessons learned to his two sons, Steven and Benjamin, who worked with him in the business. Murray and Bennie Weinberg became good friends. Bennie admired the taller and street-smart Goldman. After a month, Steven also took a liking to Murray. He could see the guy was quiet, hardworking and ambitious. Nathan offered Murray the chance to learn a trade. He would soon be turning 21. He knew bootleg boxing provided extra cash, but hardly represented a way to make a living long term. He didn't want to end up like Bulldog Mullooly. Plumbing was not a glamorous job, but he didn't care. He liked work with his hands and Mr. Weinberg was a good teacher.

After three months, he stopped looking for other part-time jobs. He was working almost every day for Mr. Weinberg. Mr. Lemberg encouraged him to skip his chores at the bakery. "Murray, you have a chance with Weinberg to learn the plumbing trade—and, more importantly, how to run a business," Mr. Lemberg told him.

"But I'll always be indebted to you and Mrs. Lemberg for taking me in and treating me like family," he responded.

Mr. Lemberg put the bag of flour down on the counter in the kitchen. "Come here." He grabbed Murray's arm and gave him a huge hug. Murray towered over Lemberg. "Someday, I know you will make us all proud with what you accomplish. We believe in you son. Don't ever doubt we will always be there for you."

For the first time, Murray began to think about the future. He took to heart Mr. Lemberg's advice, listening carefully to the daily lectures Mr. Weinberg gave his sons. How true it is, he thought that, often, it's easier to teach a stranger life lessons than your own children.

Mr. Weinberg could get dramatic when trying to get his sons' attention. "See these hands," he'd say, "these hands help clean out other people's toilets. But you know, their stuffed-up toilets help put bread on my table during this lousy Depression." Murray stared at Mr. Weinberg's hands. "Nathan," Murray said, "I hope you wash those hands before you eat." Mr. Weinberg stopped for a moment and then he and the boys began to laugh. Murray always looked for the humor in situations and the plumbing business was a good source.

CHAPTER 16

Love has no Color

For six months, Ruby and Murray were a steady item, both on the dance floor at the Savoy or spending sweaty nights at a friend's apartment locked in each other's arms. "There is something so natural about us being together," Murray would tell her. "It's like I always know what you're thinking and the passion between us could last forever."

"Yes, there's something magical when we're alone," she told him. "But are we living in the real world?"

Ruby lived at home with her parents in a neighborhood in Queens New York. They were not happy when she told them about Murray, but they knew better than to try and control their headstrong daughter. Sam Smith, Ruby's dad, held a job working on the New York subway system. Jobs were scarce, but he took the assignments no white person was willing to tackle, like fixing tracks underground. He'd tell friends, "The rats in the subway are bigger than cats."

Sam was a burly man. He didn't fear the rats, but just in case, he hooked a baseball bat on his belt to protect himself. Mary, Ruby's mom, cleaned homes for wealthier white folks.

Ruby was quick to tell her parents about Murray being a boxer and his friendship with Reggie Peterson. Her cousin was admired by her family—and in the community—for his discipline and his success. If Reggie vouched for him, she figured her parents might accept the relationship for now, even if they still hoped it was a passing phase.

New York City was not the like the rest of the country, where racism and segregation was visible and threatening. In Manhattan, Murray and Ruby could walk the streets together. They didn't hold hands or show outward signs of affection in public. People stared at them but left them alone for the most part. As time went by, they began to take for granted how unaccepting the world might be for an interracial couple.

As June rolled around Murray decided to take Ruby on a weekend trip to Rhinebeck, in upstate New York. He boxed extra matches at Rosie's bar, for three weeks in a row, to raise the cash. With one bruised rib and a borrowed truck, the two of them set out on a grand adventure. Ruby wore the most beautiful yellow sundress. They drove in the country for three hours. Ruby loved to sing. She had a terrific voice. He was thankful, since the truck didn't have a radio.

By two o'clock they had reached a lake, about 30 minutes from Rhinebeck. Murray pulled off down a dirt road leading to the water. The area was isolated. Soon they were stripping off their clothes.. Still in his boxer shorts, he spread out a large blanket on the grass. He looked up to see Ruby naked from behind entering the water. "Aaaah!" she let out a brief scream, "This lake is cold."

She turned to look at Murray. Her breasts gently touched the water. She watched as he lowered his shorts and walked toward her. Before the water reached his knees, he dove in. He surfaced again next to her. He brushed his hair back and pulled her close. He then leaned down and kissed her. They both swam out twenty yards to deeper water. There they rolled in each other's arms through the water. Ruby laughed at Murray's exploring hands.

After twenty minutes they pulled themselves onto the blanket. Both of them rolled on their stomachs and laid quietly in the sun. The air was warm. Murray was too hot to sleep. He rolled on his side and stared at Ruby, for the longest time. Her skin was like silk. His hand reached over and he let his fingers walk across the smooth skin on her back. Soon, he moved closer and started kissing her lower back. His hands reached up to her waist and she slowly turned over. Her back arched, as he started to kiss the inside of her thighs. His tongue reached inside of her. Ruby was breathing harder. Her hands ran through Murray's hair. She lifted her knees and pulled his head deeper between her legs. She rotated her hips and her breathing became heavier. "Uhh.....uhh!" came the groans as she climaxed. He loved the taste of her. Her wetness covered his lips and filled his nostrils.

Ruby pulled him up to her lips. She could taste herself on his lips. Her arms reached for him to come on top. He was quickly lost inside of her. He kissed her as he very slowly thrust his hips in and out. Then she pushed him to the side. She rolled him on this back and climbed on top. Slowly, she twisted and moved. Murray looked up and grabbed her breasts. Her head leaned back toward the sun. She bounced in short movements, followed by a slow circular motion. Her head came down to kiss him. He didn't want it to end--and for a moment --it seemed endless.

She laid on Murray's chest motionless for a long time. He pulled a blanket over them and they soon fell asleep. An hour later, a cool breeze woke them. The sun was setting. The two lovers got dressed to resume their journey. They ate dinner in Rhinebeck and stayed overnight at a local motel outside of town, off the highway. Murray went into the hotel by himself to book the room. He was not looking to draw attention to Ruby or himself.

The next day, they visited some of the greenhouses near Rhinebeck, which specialized in growing violet flowers. The area was well known and often referred to as the Violet Capital of the country. Murray couldn't resist. He bought a small string of violet flowers. Ruby placed them in her hair with a bobby pin. She looked radiant.

By early afternoon, he and Ruby started to drive back to New York City. They stopped on the way to get some lunch at local diner. He took a table near the back. The waitress came over. She stared at Ruby, holding hands with Murray. The two of them seemed oblivious to the surroundings. They joked and laughed over lunch. An hour later they were quietly drinking coffee, when trouble walked through the door. The two truck drivers sat down at the counter. They were loud and abusive to one another. They ordered coffee and burgers. Then one of them spotted Ruby, looking past the shoulder of his friend. "Hey, Charlie," he said nudging the man next to him. "I do believe I spotted a nigra."

The first man's voice sounded southern, but his friend definitely had a New York accent. "What do you suppose that white boy is doing with that black bitch?" he asked Charlie.

The diner was small. The voices of the men could easily be heard from Murray's table. He raised his hand in a calming gesture to Ruby. He was ignoring the men. He could not have known this would only antagonize them more.

"Ralphie, I believe that nigra lover is just plain ignoring you."

Ralphie was on his feet. He headed toward the table. Murray looked straight into Ruby's eyes, as the man towered over them. "Look, no one here wants trouble. Why don't you just leave us alone."

"I just came over to get a closer look at your nigger bitch. She's cute. So, you like white men, do you?" His arm reached out toward Ruby. Before his hand reached halfway across the table, Murray's elbow hit him hard and fast in the groin. Ralphie doubled over, gasping for air. As quickly as his head came down, Murray grabbed the back of his hair and drove his face into the table. He rolled to the floor limp and unconscious. The table and Ralphie's face were full of blood.

Murray grabbed Ruby and started for the door. The owner of the diner came out from the kitchen. An older man, the owner was yelling at the truck driver. Charlie back handed the man in the face. He reached over the counter, where a large kitchen knife was sitting on a cutting board. "Where I come from," he growled, "we carve up nigger lovers." Murray heard the words and turned around. The knife stuck him in his forearm. He could feel a burning sensation. The blood gushed out, as the man pulled the knife out. The truck driver was not finished. He went to slash Murray. This time Ruby jumped in the way to protect him. The knife ran across her back. She screamed in pain and then fainted into Murray's arms. The blood gushed down her bare back.

Now it had gone too far. Murray gently laid her on the floor. He would not be pushed back. He didn't care about the knife. "You just made a big mistake," he said walking toward the man. This time he could see the knife coming at him. As the man lunged forward, Murray circled to his right. The blood gushed from his arm down to his right fist. He hit the man so hard that the guy flew back against the counter. The knife fell to the floor. He grabbed the man by the shirt and pummeled his face. By the fifth punch, Murray pulled himself back. There was blood everywhere, some of it his and some from the truck driver. He had knocked out several teeth, which were littered on the floor. The man's body dropped to the floor like a piece of wood. His jaw was broken.

Murray stepped back. He turned to see the owner standing over Ruby, trying to stop the bleeding with a towel. Murray's lip was also cut. He ran to Ruby. "It's not deep," the owner assured him, "but she is going to have a nasty scar." Murray reached for a rag to tie around his arm. "You better call the police," he told the owner.

"No. No. You don't want that around here," the owner cautioned. "You're not in the City. I'm not certain the police here will be any nicer than these truck drivers. I'll help you get some bandages on her, but you better leave quickly. I'll call the cops as soon as you're gone."

As much as it bothered him, he knew the old man was right. "I'm sorry you had trouble," Murray told him.

"Look son, it's none of my business, but you can't fight the world. People just won't accept this," gesturing to Ruby. "They don't understand."

Murray could not shake the man's words, as he drove her back to New York City. She slept in the truck most of the ride back. Her yellow dress ruined, her back bandaged.

Several hours after taking Ruby to a City hospital, Murray brought her home. She required quite a few stitches to close the wound. Murray's arm was also stitched and bandaged. His head and arm ached. Ruby's parents were very upset at the sight of their injured daughter. Murray tried to explain, but emotions ran high and Ruby was too weak and tired to defend him. Ruby's mother hurried her to bed, and her father insisted Murray leave.

His head throbbed as he drove back to Brooklyn. He thought about the first time he saw Ruby. He hated racial intolerance. He could not understand why people judged each other on the basis of their skin or religion. As a boxer, it didn't matter to Murray what was outside. It was only a question of whether you had heart, whether you got up when you were knocked down, whether you could lift yourself off the canvas and still win. Murray saw only a woman. He didn't see a black woman. He tried to ignore the accepted wisdom that it was better the races did not mix. He would stay with her, if given the opportunity. He feared, however, that the events could not be undone. Love can't always overcome fear and ignorance.

The next day, Murray sat with Alvin sat and talked for two hours. Alvin was horrified at the danger his friend faced, which he recounted in detail. He could not hide his reservations. In Alvin's eyes, it was bad enough that she wasn't Jewish. Alvin was not prejudiced, but saw the world in very practical terms. Jews should marry Jews, gentiles marry gentiles and Negroes marry Negroes.

Alvin was thankful neither Murray nor the girl were hurt more seriously. He listened to his friend and he expressed sympathy, even if he did not agree. He didn't think their future together was realistic in a world divided by race. But he also knew when Murray set his mind to something, he was determined to make it happen. It's the only way he knew.

A month went by before Murray made his way up to the Savoy. He had tried to call Ruby several times, but her parents answered the phone and they would make an excuse. She was either out with friends or asleep. He wondered if her parents would ever forgive him. He wanted to see her again. How he wished to hold her in his arms.

He and Artie Schwartz sat at the bar listening to the music. He waited. An hour or two went by. Artie got up a few times to dance. But Murray just sat there staring out at the dance floor. He was day-dreaming when a man sat down next to him at the bar.

A familiar voice quietly said to him, "Moe, she's not coming." he turned to see Reggie Peterson. Murray's eyes were sad. He did not speak.

"Look man, Ruby told me the whole story. I appreciate what you did. And I think I know how you both feel. But it's no good, Moe. Ruby's folks are crazed over this. I tried to reason with them. I told them I'd trust you with my own daughter—and you saw the world differently than most folks. To them, however, white people are only trouble. There's just no way to put this thing back together. You both have got to let go and get on with your lives."

He could still hear the old man from the diner telling him over and over, "Son, you can't fight the world." Now, he was hearing the same words from a close friend. He sat quietly, as Reggie talked to him. Murray never said a word. He figured Ruby asked Reggie to talk him. She could not face him.

She felt as much pain and conflict as Murray did. She hoped Reggie could somehow make this all less difficult for both of them. It was not. Love does not work that way. Reggie apologized to Murray. As he stood to leave, Reggie reached to shake his hand and gave him a hug. "You're the best Moe. Yes, the best, as a fighter—and as a man. There's no one I respect more. Take care of yourself." Reggie patted him on the shoulder and then left.

Murray sat alone for fifteen minutes. The band was taking a break. There was no music. He just stared out at the crowd. He could still see her there, gracefully sweeping across the ballroom floor. Soon the band started up again. Artie returned and Murray stood up. "Look, I got to go." It was early, but Artie realized his friend needed him. The two of them started for the door. Murray paused to look back, just one more time. A big smile came to him. "No regrets," he told himself. "No regrets." He turned, shook his head and started out the door. He loved that girl. He never went to the Savoy ballroom again.

CHAPTER 17

Betty by the Door

More than a year passed since he saw Reggie Peterson. He had opened his heart to two women. Each time, his heart was broken. He would not do so again. Women were always available to him. Until now, he had resisted. He had not fancied himself a womanizer. He knew what it felt like to be alone in the world. He often felt alone. He wanted to be connected to someone. He wanted to be loved by someone. But he realized it wasn't going to happen for him. He decided to just let go. He was determined to just enjoy the attention that he received from his bootleg boxing success.

After the fights, women always hung out in the hallway near the dressing room or waited in the alley by the street. They wanted to be with a fighter. Some women were happy to be with any fighter. Some wanted only to be with Moe Fields.

One night, a buxom blonde named Betty couldn't wait for Moe to return to the dressing room. As soon as his handlers left, Betty snuck through the crowd lining the hallway and entered the door. Moe looked up, naked from the waist up and wrapped in a towel. He had just come out of the shower. Betty pulled her blouse open. Her breasts were completely exposed.

"I didn't come for no small talk," she told Moe. "I want you. I want you now." As he stepped backward toward a massage table in the center of the room, Betty was already on her knees and grabbing at Moe's towel. He started to laugh, but the humor was quickly gone as this short, round woman scooped him into her mouth. He couldn't believe it. He could feel the vibration, as Betty started to hum.

This was not the first woman to be aggressive with Moe. He had regular visits from women of all ages, sizes and ethnic backgrounds. The single common trait these women shared was their determination. There were no demands, no expectations. Most importantly, it was not about love. It was just for the sex. They saw boxers slugging themselves in the ring. They saw blood and it turned them on.

Moe sat back as Betty bobbed up and down. He could see her left hand was reaching down between her legs. He quickly decided he must have her. Betty seemed a little dazed. Moe turned her around and pushed her over the table. He lifted her skirt up. She was not wearing underwear, which surprised Moe, but only for a split second. Betty let out a small scream. Once again, Murray was dripping in sweat as he leaned over Betty. She held onto the table with both hands.

"More, more," she kept telling Moe. "Oh, please don't stop."

Without warning, the table Betty leaned on started to slide across the room. In slow motion, the two bodies would move an inch at a time, to keep up with the table. Betty pushed back hard on Moe. Finally, the table hit the opposite wall and Moe had his way with her. His strong legs pressed upward. His arms held her waist. She was moaning, this time louder than before. He could wait no more. She screamed in delight. He then fell on top of her, gasping to catch his breath. Betty giggled, as their bodies separated. She dressed and left 15 minutes later. She had what she wanted. She stood right outside by the door and took a drag on a cigarette. A big smile came to her. She exhaled and then left the bar.

Moe sat quietly in his dressing room. The fight had gone six rounds, which was a bit longer than usual. He had no idea he would be going extra rounds in his dressing room. He smiled at the thought of Betty. He wondered if he'd get this lucky next week.

Murray began to realize how much he liked women. Each time, he was learning something he thought might be valuable in his life. But he wasn't certain if he'd have the stamina to keep up with the physical demands after each fight night. He accepted being happier with women who didn't want to be with him forever. He was afraid of getting too close to someone again. He'd rather be with women who simply wanted to be with a fighter.

CHAPTER 18
Taking up the Challenge

___

The bootleg boxing career and Murray's love life continued with great adventures. He worked at Weinberg's plumbing. In the evenings, on Tuesday and Thursday, he would visit his family. His mother, Tonia, would make a big meal. She appreciated Murray's financial help. She was very proud of him. The children all worked and contributed something. But the money Murray gave her each week kept the family going. Isaac could not always be counted on to provide enough to buy food and clothes. The Goldman family did not live in comfort, but with her son's support, they didn't suffer.

Murray horse played with Sammy before dinner. It was Sammy's favorite time of the day. His brother was so strong. He loved being roughed up. Asher and Berta each worked part-time jobs. At dinner, Murray would catch up on what each of them was doing at work.

Occasionally, the discussion was interrupted by the sounds of a saxophone or trumpet. "That's our neighbor's kids upstairs," said Tonia. "They're all musicians. It's like having a band in our backyard."

On this particular night, Berta was telling Murray about a boy who lived upstairs. His attention was drawn away by the sounds of a saxophone playing. He was not a musician, but he loved that sound.

"Murray," Berta insisted, "you're not listening. I want you to go with me on a date. Ziggy Sugar asked me out. I can't go alone. He has a sister. She's a nice girl. We can go to the movies. If you don't want to hang around with us afterward, take her home."

"I'll think about it."

He had never seen Berta act like this. She had never expressed interest in boys. Mostly, she hung out with a small group of girlfriends.

He started to notice his older sister was growing up. She had become "zaftig," a Jewish expression for having a round body and fairly large breasts. Her hair was neatly tied in a bun, and she started wearing lipstick.

Berta feared the worst. She couldn't go out with Ziggy without a chaperone. It wouldn't be proper. She had no idea how long it would take for her brother to commit. She didn't know what more to say or do. She couldn't bear it if her brother said no.

After dinner, Murray excused himself to head back to Lemberg's bakery. He had promised to help Alvin and Mr. Lemberg do some extra work re-arranging the supply room. He fended off Berta's nagging with a promise to give her an answer before the following weekend. Tonia stood on the sidelines, shaking her head in amusement. She kissed her son goodbye and left for the kitchen.

As Murray exited the apartment, he could hear footsteps coming down the stairs. He immediately recognized the girl he met on the front steps a few years back. She had challenged him to a game of handball. He watched her beat Asher under the lights across the street. He couldn't get over how much older she now seemed. Her brown hair was curly, full and it stretched down her back. In her hands, she held a saxophone.

"Hi, was that you I heard playing upstairs?"

"Yeah, so what?"

"I don't know much about music, but you play very well."

"You're right, you don't know much about music."

Franny was very much a tomboy, athletic and competitive. Growing up in Brooklyn, she started off most friendships with a bit of sarcasm and untrusting behavior. She was both refined and a street kid. You had to be tough to survive.

Murray shook his head at her response. He was not put off by the gruffness. He admired she wasn't intimidated by his brother Asher or by him. He smiled at her, as he turned and headed down the stairs to leave. Then he heard her call out, "And I can still beat your pants off at hand ball."

He paused at the next staircase, chuckling to himself. Slowly he turned and looked at her. She was pure tomboy, but he couldn't get over how pretty she had become.

"Ok," he replied, "I think it is time you showed me."

Franny Sugar stood at the stairs stunned. She had not fully calculated the consequence of Murray accepting her challenge. This guy was not like his younger brother, Asher. He had an air of confidence and worldliness that unnerved her.

"When," she asked, hesitantly?

"Right now," he replied matter-of-factly.

"Right now?"

"Yes, right now! I'll wait for you across the street."

Murray started down the stairs. Franny headed back to her apartment. This time she realized she may have bitten off more than she could chew. She put away the saxophone. Her handball outfit consisted of a T-shirt, high cut shorts and rubber sole shoes. She tied her long curly hair back in a ponytail.

She could see Murray under the streetlights, as she reached the front steps of the building. He had taken off his long sleeve shirt. His broad shoulders were accentuated, by a sleeveless T-shirt. His arms were long and muscular.

"Do you want to warm up?" she asked, offering him the ball.

"No," he responded calmly, "let's just play."

Franny shrugged her shoulders. She bounced the ball a few times and let one rip against the wall. Murray reached for it in vain. Franny hit two more. He missed.

"Are you sure you've played this game?" she asked.

Murray eyes opened wide. Shaking his head as he smiled. He was impressed. She had speed, and seemed very confident. He couldn't help notice how much she had changed since their last encounter. She had the legs of an athlete, firm and quick. She also had breasts.

"What are you staring at?" she stopped and asked.

He shook his head.

"Are you ready?"

"Yeah."

Franny hit the next one off to his right. Her strategy was intent on making him run. This time, he moved in swiftly and with his huge hand slammed it back. Franny, caught off guard and out of position could not get to the ball. She looked up at him surprised. They volleyed the next two balls several times. Franny couldn't get over how fast Murray picked up the game. No push over, she thought. And the more they played, the tougher he got as an opponent.

Franny had all to do to keep up with his speed and stay ahead in points. She had not anticipated how hard Murray could hit the ball. And those long arms of his could reach almost everything she dished out.

Franny was ahead by one point. They had played for over forty-five minutes. Both of them were sweating freely. It was her turn to serve. This volley was particularly fast and furious. Neither one of them would accept defeat. Murray came in on a ball Franny had lobbed off the wall. The play was so aggressive, he crashed into the wall as he slammed the ball. Instinctively, she knew she could not reach the ball in time.

Suddenly, she dove in the air. Her arm fully extended out, reached the ball low to the ground. She clipped it with her fingers before landing. The ball reached the wall and then dropped to the ground.

Murray ran over to her. She was lying face down on the cement. Franny did not move. Slowly, he rolled her over. Her knees and elbow were bleeding. She appeared to have tears in her eyes. She clearly was in pain.

"Are you ok? C'mon, I'm going to take you inside."

He lifted her up in his arms.

"I got it," she whispered, with quiet satisfaction.

"What?"

"I got it. I got the point. I told you I would win."

He started to laugh. Here she was hurt and bleeding, but winning was the only thing on her mind. Who was this remarkable girl, he asked himself? She's lived here right under my nose, in the same building as my own family.

CHAPTER 19
Double Date

Two weeks passed before Murray agreed to go out with Berta and Ziggy. He arrived early at Tonia's apartment to have dinner with the family. Berta quickly finished eating and excused herself. She was so nervous. A half an hour later she emerged in a pink floral dress. He couldn't get over how nice she looked. Berta had always been a rather tall and large girl. Her nose was a bit wider than most. Her eyes were spaced far apart. And her lips were large, but they were accentuated even more by the deep purple-red lipstick. At times, Berta could be selfish and demanding. But Murray knew what really drove her was a need to be accepted and loved.

Berta, like many girls, knew she was not born beautiful. Berta was a Goldman. The Goldman boys were all big boned. She wished only for someone to look inside her heart. How strange that in spite of her size, how many men treated her as if she was invisible.

Ziggy Sugar, on the other hand, was a short and slightly built young man. His face was round and his dark naturally curly brown hair was everywhere. Ziggy had one special quality: his sense of humor. He didn't really tell jokes. He just had a humorous way of looking at life and poked fun at things.

Ziggy thought Berta was special, though he hadn't found the courage to tell her. Ziggy was shy in expressing his feelings. He had been sickly growing up and often felt out of place with kids in the neighborhood. He was not athletic. He had no special skills and he was only an average student. But Ziggy's sense of humor often endeared him to people. He was thrilled Berta found him funny. Theirs was a slow courtship. They would have short conversations in the hallway or while passing on the stairs of their building. This had gone on for six months. Both Ziggy and Berta tried to avoid the fact they liked each other. Perhaps they feared that what they hoped for would escape them.

Ziggy finally asked about a date in a moment of laughter. He figured he could turn the situation into a joke if she said no. The fact that Berta immediately said yes, stunned them both. A silence came down around them like a curtain as they stood motionless in the hallway.

Will I ever know another moment like this in my life, Berta wondered to herself? They stared at each other without speaking for what seemed like hours. Then a dog came out of nowhere leaping up the stairs running between them.

"Brownie," a voice yelled from behind. "Brownie, come back here."

Old Mr. Abelson slowly climbed the stairs. Laughter broke the silence for Ziggy and Berta.

"So, will you go?" Ziggy asked, not knowing how to retreat.

"Yes," she replied.

Tonia left the kitchen when she hear the knock on the door. Asher and Sammy followed her, as she invited Ziggy and Franny Sugar into their home. Murray left his cup of coffee by the sink to join the others. He walked through the kitchen door and saw Franny standing there.

"You?" he asked from across the room.

He could not believe it was Franny, the tomboy handball player he had met just a few weeks earlier. He almost didn't recognize her. She was wearing a dress. Her hair was no longer pulled back, but draped across her shoulders. She was as tall as Ziggy, at least five feet three inches. In a dress, her athletic form filled the contours. Finally, she responded, "Yeah, it's me. And I bet you're still nursing that beating I gave you on the handball court."

Franny would not back off. Being tough and holding her ground came natural to a kid growing up during this period. She and Ziggy were among six children in the Sugar family. The father, Saul, a tailor, was a quiet man who came and went each day. He did not get involved much in the affairs of the family. He read the Jewish Daily Forward newspaper every day. It was one of the few Yiddish language publications in America. The family scraped by during the Depression because of one special blessing: Leonard Sugar.

Lennie, as he was called, was a musical prodigy. By his teenage years, Lennie had already mastered six or seven instruments. As the oldest child, he became the surrogate father. Saul worked long hours as a tailor and was rarely home. Lennie forced his younger siblings to do their schoolwork each day and held them accountable when report cards were sent home. He also insisted his sisters and brothers learn to play music. "If you can play an instrument," Lennie would repeatedly tell them, "you'll always make a living."

Lennie was smart and determined to make something of his life. At times, he could be extremely tough on his siblings. He would chastise them for not practicing their instruments and criticize them when they did practice. Meeting his exacting standards became a goal for the children and a source of competition, especially among the girls.

After Lennie, came Rachel, a trumpet player who adopted the nickname Boots. Franny was next in line. She played saxophone and clarinet. Lennie knew Franny was gifted, because she could read music. While Boots had an ear and could pick up a tune by listening to it, Franny had the discipline of a well-trained musician. Lennie could give Franny any sheet of music and after a single glance, she could play as if she knew the song all along.

Next came Maier, another trumpet player, and then Ziggy. Ziggy was the only Sugar who never mastered an instrument. He dabbled on the clarinet, though he never showed any real talent. He essentially was tone deaf. Last, there was Myrna or "Micky" as she liked to be called. Micky played the flute.

A seventh child died from pneumonia at three years old. Lennie took this loss very hard. He talked often of the special red-haired boy.

By 17, Lennie was good enough to play with a musical orchestra in the Catskills. He was a serious and frugal boy. He dreamed one day of being a big band leader, though in his heart he knew the idea would face many obstacles. He contributed much of his earnings to the family, and used the rest to rent instruments he would use to teach his siblings. When they were old enough, they too, would be encouraged to join bands and earn money for the family.

Franny was his favorite. He admired her determination to practice her instrument. He was also proud of her athletic prowess, which none of the other Sugar children possessed. Lennie was an avid tennis player and a good athlete in his own right, but even he could not keep up with his kid sister on a handball court. In every aspect of her life, no one ever would take her for granted.

Lennie would frequently tell the story about when Boots and Franny were returning from a school band practice as young teens. They had to walk through some rough neighborhoods. A group of older boys were hanging out on a street corner. They started harassing the girls. First, with words. Then, on seeing the musical instruments, they quickly circled the girls and demanded they turn over the instruments. Boots was struck with fear, "let's give them these stupid instruments." Franny would not budge, "I'm not giving this case to anybody. If they want it, they'll have to take it."

The Depression was far from being over. Franny understood that if she lost her saxophone, the family might never afford to buy her another one.

Suddenly, Boots shoved her trumpet case into Franny's hand and took off through the circle. "I'm getting out of here," Boots yelled. The boys could care less about Boots. They wanted the instruments and she had them.

Franny thought quickly. She grabbed each music case by the handle and held on tight.

"You want my instruments, well here they are." With that, she began to spin counterclockwise with all her strength.

She quickly hit one boy square in the face with the trumpet case. Next, the saxophone case caught another boy in the ribs. Franny twirled faster and faster, pushing against the circle of boys until she hit one and he went down.

At that moment, there was a break in the crowd and she ran as fast as she could. Seeing their friend land on the ground, the boys hesitated. It was only a second of hesitation, but that's all she needed. Franny Sugar was just too fast. She was gone. They chased her for several blocks before giving up.

By the time she reached home, Boots had already told Lennie the whole story. But she left out the part about leaving her sister to fend for herself. Boots had prepared Lennie by telling him that their instruments were stolen by a gang of boys. The sibling rivalry between the two ran deep. She and

Boots would never really be friends. Franny's victory on the street was doubly sweet, when she walked in with both music cases still tightly gripped in her hands. Boots was dumbstruck. Lennie beamed with pride.

Murray's face broke into a big smile, as he listened to Franny talk about beating him at handball. He liked that she spoke up for herself. These were qualities he thought were important.

"Look little girl," he said walking across the room. He couldn't imagine Franny was more than 16 years of age. "I'm no little girl," Franny responded, "I'm almost 19...and a lady. And I expect you to treat me that way."

Murray froze in his place, glancing toward Berta and Ziggy who stood pensively at the door. He began to laugh. He knew he had his hands full.

"C'mon, let's go," he said as he opened the door.

There was something about Franny that he liked. They were both fiercely independent and held their inner most fears to themselves. They were competitors and they were determined to be survivors.

Following the movies, the brothers and sisters stopped for food at a local diner. As they walked up the boulevard, Berta and Ziggy were silhouetted by the streetlights up ahead. Their giggling and laughter broke the evening silence. Murray was not much of a talker. It wasn't that he lacked words, he just tended not to like small talk. But he wanted to know more about Franny and was not afraid to ask.

For all her gruffness, Franny could seem very sensitive and shy. Franny had never really gone out on a date with a man. Having a normal conversation was more challenging than the short digs about handball. She thought Murray was much older. She had seen him in the neighborhood, walking with his friends in his dark suit and hat. Beneath the tomboy front, Franny was indeed all woman. However, no one had prepared her for being one.

Soon the silence gave way to conversation, and Murray and Franny talked much of the way home. "So, your brother Sammy told me you're a fighter. Why?"

"Well, I think it was always in me, to be one. I mean, don't get me wrong. I'm not really a violent guy. I saw this boxing match in Chicago. This guy Mike Morin was so strong and determined. He was all alone in the ring, with nothing between him and the outcome. I wondered what it took to be that guy?"

"And are you that guy?"

"Yes—and no. After I got disqualified during the Golden Gloves tournament, I almost didn't care anymore. I trained and dreamed of being a professional fighter, like Morin. But then I just wanted to earn enough money to support myself and help my family. I'm a bootleg fighter now to get by. I still have to figure out the future.

"What kind of future do you see for yourself, if it's not fighting?"

"I'm not certain yet. I know I can't keep boxing forever. I think I've proved I can take a punch and give one when I have to. I have nothing to prove on that front. I've been working at Weinberg's plumbing. The pay is good. I'm learning a trade. I'm starting to wonder if maybe I can start my own business. What about you Franny?

"My dream was to play a sax solo at Carnegie Hall. It lasted until my appendix burst the week before the concert date. Now, I'd settle for a regular gig playing in a woman's band in the Catskill mountains. My brother Lennie rides the band circuit from hotel to hotel. The money is good."

Ziggy and Berta were waiting by the entrance to their building. Each had big smiles on their faces. Before Murray and Franny reached them, Murray paused for a second, "I'd like to see you again."

Franny stood quietly for a moment. She didn't know how to respond. She didn't know what she was feeling. He was certainly attractive, but she had never really dated guys before.

She considered herself naïve about men. She hadn't even kissed a boy. This Murray Goldman seemed like a grown man. Then with a mix of sarcasm and humor in her voice replied,

"You want a rematch at handball or something?"

"Yeah, something," Murray replied.

With that, the couples climbed the stairs and said goodnight. Franny and Ziggy continued up the stairs past the Goldman flat.

Berta and Ziggy soon became a regular item. Murray and Franny would periodically join them. These were happy times. They'd go to the movies, take the subway to Coney Island or drive to upstate New York for a picnic. Murray never pushed Franny to express affection. He could see she felt awkwardness between her tomboy image and the woman she'd become.

By summer, she would get her wish. Lennie had arranged for Boots and Franny to work in an all-women's dance band traveling to all the hotels in the Catskills. Lennie hoped that by keeping the girls together, they'd look out for one another.

CHAPTER 20

A Summer with Kathryn

Murray did not take the news well. The thought of not seeing Franny all summer bothered him. He had actually grown to like this young girl. He was guarded about letting someone get close to him. His past experiences with love did not go well. He wondered if summer would change things. If that's what Franny wanted, so be it. Murray knew he couldn't change her mind. He accepted that life was unpredictable. Maybe she's not the one, he told himself. He was not going to sit around and wait for her.

With Franny gone, Murray decided he would hit the nightspots and dance halls, where he could continue to attract beautiful women. Blonds, brunettes, red heads, Murray knew and loved them all. Artie and Alvin would often join their friend on these adventures, knowing that at the end of the evening they'd likely be going home without him.

Some of the women were older, in their thirties. Some of them worked and some didn't have to work. He grew fond of Katherine Winsford, a rich Shiksa who had an apartment overlooking Central Park. Katherine's husband, Robert Montgomery Winsford III, traveled often and could care less about his wife's antics. She would explain to Murray that theirs was a marriage of convenience. At first, he wasn't certain what she meant by that explanation. Eventually, Katherine would confess that her husband preferred the arms of another man. However, for the sake of public appearance, he insisted on marrying a woman he could never love.

Katherine, like Murray, did not come from wealth. Robert Winsford had become both her salvation and her curse. When they were together, Murray could not control Katherine's hunger for affection. She could not keep her hands or mouth away from him. Surprisingly, he was never put off or offended by her aggressive behavior.

Katherine regularly invited Murray back to her apartment. If he seemed distracted, she'd do something outrageous to command his attention. She'd sit at the kitchen table in a nightgown. One night, she suddenly began pouring maple syrup down her breasts. She'd sit there slowly rubbing with both her hands to spread the syrup across her chest. If he didn't respond, she'd pour more syrup on her legs and rub her hands upward on her thighs. Her head would be pulled back. When she'd began to moan, he started to chuckle. Katherine was a seductress. She was irresistible—and a tad crazy.

Murray welcomed the wild nights with Katherine. There was no pretense about love, living together or marrying. Katherine just wanted to know a man's hands touching her. She wanted to feel him inside of her. She made a deal with the devil, she regretted. At 35, she was at her peak in life, but she was starved for passion.

Katherine grabbed him at the strangest times and in the oddest places. Sometimes before he even stepped through the doorway to her flat. As they slow danced at the nightclub, her hands would sometimes slip down across his butt or sitting down, she'd reach down inside his thigh. She was out of control, and Murray loved it.

Eventually, he would finally get to meet Robert Winsford. Katherine had plotted all day to drag Murray back to her place following an early evening at a night club. They had both been drinking, though Katherine was more inclined to drink heavily. Giggling and laughing they entered her apartment. He resisted her initial attack in the foyer. A long hallway in the apartment led past the kitchen to the living room and the bedrooms beyond. They kissed very passionately for a moment. Then with one hand reaching down inside his boxer shorts, she grabbed Murray. As they reached the first bedroom, he and Katherine could see two bodies in the light streaming through the curtains. It was clear from the noise that they were having sex.

Murray stood motionless. He was in shock. He stopped walking, even as Katherine gently tugged him. He realized the two bodies embracing in the bed were men.

"Katherine, is that you?" asked the voice. Robert was very nonchalant as he paused, his hand on the other man's shoulders. "I'm sorry for not calling ahead, but I just got into town. This is George. We met on the plane. Look, why don't you and your friend take the back bedroom and we can talk over coffee in the morning."

Murray never thought anything could shock him. He didn't know what to say. Katherine had told him about Robert. He believed her. He just thought how odd it was that the two of them could reach such an accommodation.

Katherine saw the startled look in Murray eyes. A sadness overtook her. This was not the life she envisioned. She grabbed his hand and led him down the hallway. She hoped, with some privacy and time, the two of them would soon forget Robert was in the other room. Katherine was even more determined that evening to love him like there was no tomorrow.

Hours passed before Murray and Katherine collapsed on the bed. Katherine curled up in his arms. They slept until 5:30 am, when he glanced at the clock. He was not anxious to be there for the morning conversation with Robert and George. He pulled on his clothes and bent down to kiss Katherine goodbye. She was groggy. She worried he might not see her again. He smiled, as he kissed her again.

"Are you kidding me?" he asked. "We have the whole summer. The only question in my mind is how often we can physically handle a session like last night." Katherine smiled. It was a smile filled with satisfaction. She then laid back down on the bed and fell fast asleep.

CHAPTER 21
Jerry Katz

The summer of 1936 seemed to fly by quickly. Franny and Boots were living their dream playing in an all-women's dance band almost every night. Boots joined two other trumpet players for an upbeat solo number. The trio would stand mid-way in the song, swinging left and right as they blew their brains out. The dance floor was packed with people shaking and moving to the music. After a break, the band would reassemble. The orchestra leader tapped her baton on the music stand. A young woman stood in the first row with her saxophone. She played by herself for two minutes. The tone of the solo saxophone was rich and haunting. The song was Summertime, from the 1935 show Porgy and Bess. The audience sat almost motionless. At the lip of the saxophone was Franny Sugar.

Slowly, as the band joined in, people crowded on the dance floor. Franny was lost in her solo. On this occasion, she did not read the music. Franny played from memory....and from the heart. Above the orchestra, the audience heard Franny's sax sweetly caress each note.

From a distance, Jerry Katz watched and listened. The spotlight showered down on Franny Sugar. He was in awe of this talented young woman, with long curly brown hair. Jerry was a college student at Columbia University. He worked summers as a waiter to earn extra money for school. His father was a respected surgeon in New York City. Jerry intended to follow in his footsteps.

He was used to getting what he wanted. He decided at that moment, he wanted to meet and date Franny. He approached her with small talk, after the band finished playing that night. He offered to take her for something to eat. He told her how much he admired her discipline and skill as a musician. He admitted he had no natural talent of his own for music. Franny did not read anything into Jerry's friendly conversation. She had met and talked with many people who worked at the hotel. She thought about Murray occasionally, but Brooklyn seemed far away.

When Franny was not practicing or playing her saxophone and clarinet, she'd be down at the handball court. It was here that Jerry would try to impress her. Franny had already played and beat several waiters. As the two defeated opponents walked away, Jerry approached from another direction. She stood there wiping the sweat from her face with a towel. The shorts were cut high on her legs. Jerry looked at her with desire in his eyes.

Jerry was built athletically. He was at least five foot ten inches with curly blond hair and deep blue eyes. He was an avid tennis player, more likely to be found playing doubles then hanging out at the handball court. However, he finally made his move, where he thought it counted.

Franny quickly took up his challenge, not expecting much more competition than she had just easily disposed of. As the points climbed closer to the magic number of twenty-one, the volleys became heated. Jerry knew he could control the outcome, but he played the game tightly. He was not out to humiliate her. He wanted to impress her with his determination.

Physical competition had always been an important measure for Franny. But she did not anticipate he would take the last two points of the game. She stood center court still looking at where the ball failed to reach the wall. Jerry spun her around quickly. Pulling her close, he leaned down and kissed her. Franny had never been kissed before. Her eyes bulged with shock and surprise. Jerry knew there would be a price to pay for this indulgent act. The response came quickly. But Franny did not slap Jerry with authority. The act was more a token protest over not being asked permission. She could not deny a certain truth. She liked kissing Jerry.

After a week of feigned indignation, Franny and Jerry started seeing each other for what remained of the summer. Four weeks went by fast, but this first infatuation would remain special to her.

When they weren't working, they competed in sports, hung out at the swimming pool and took long walks around the lake near the hotel. They spent long afternoons making out on the grass at the lake. He wanted her to stay overnight in his room. He had his sights set on having sex with her, but she was not that kind of girl.

She set the boundary lines and Jerry accepted them. He was the first guy she had ever kissed or let touch her breasts. She was curious to know what love was like. At the same time, she wanted it to be with someone she could love forever.

As summer drew to a close, he talked about coming to see Franny in Brooklyn. She was already 19 years old. She imagined the possibility of settling down one day, perhaps with a doctor named Jerry Katz. She knew he respected her talent. She felt certain he would allow her to pursue her music career.

She returned from the summer in the Catskills a changed person. She was no longer a tomboy trying to become a young woman. The gruffness was gone. Franny had known love. She glowed with confidence as she headed back to Brooklyn.

CHAPTER 22
Murray and Franny

───────

Three weeks passed before Murray and Franny crossed paths. The changes in her were noticeable to her family and friends. She insisted on wearing dresses, even if it meant sharing clothes with Boots. She tied her hair back less frequently, preferring to have it naturally fall across her back and shoulders.

Murray was speechless when he ran into her in the hallway. He was climbing the stairs, all decked out in a dark gray double-breasted suit. It was Saturday night and he was headed to a nightclub. He stopped by to drop off his regular contribution of money for the family. As he reached the stairwell, he could smell the air of perfume. He sensed the figure of a woman pass by behind him and start down the stairs. He paused as he watched her move, "Franny," he called out "is that you?"

He waited a moment. When she turned around, her eyes smiled. For a few minutes they made small talk and then she excused herself. She then headed off down the stairs. It was unlike him to be so surprised. After a minute, he followed her down the stairs. He caught a glimpse of the curly blond hair that escorted Franny down the street. Murray didn't quite know what to think, but a feeling he never felt before slowly started to swell inside his head. He didn't think about Katherine or any of the half dozen women he had been with that summer. The image of Franny going out on a date played over in his mind. Murray Goldman was jealous.

Franny's evening with Jerry was like a dream. He picked her up at the tenement building in Williamsburg, Brooklyn. They'd hop the subway to Manhattan. He had gotten tickets for a concert at Carnegie Hall. He could not know how special this was for her. She delighted in telling him about the music scholarship that she was offered at 15, and the invitation to play a solo at Carnegie Hall. Oh, how she had wanted to play in that concert. She practiced for three months. Her teacher said she played flawlessly. Then, two weeks before the concert, Franny was stricken with appendicitis. Her parents, who were immigrants, didn't understand the danger. At first, they thought she had a stomach ache. She almost died.

Franny would never forget the disappointment she felt. It took months, after surgery, before she had the strength to play her saxophone. Jerry could tell how proud she was to be at Carnegie. And even though the dream was cut short, she could still imagine herself up on the stage.

Franny and Jerry talked all the way home. Much of their discussion was small talk. But Jerry kept bringing up the time commitment he would have to give to his studies. Columbia University was very far from Brooklyn. He wanted so badly to succeed at a decent medical school. He was torn between his desire to spend more time with Franny and the inner drive to be a doctor, no matter what the cost or sacrifice. He wasn't certain if he could tell her. He didn't know if she'd wait for him.

It was late as they reached Franny's tenement building. Before they started up the stairs at the entranceway, a figure stepped toward them from out of the shadows.

"I'm sorry fella, but this is as far as you go."

It was Murray Goldman. He stood there with shirtsleeves rolled up over his muscular forearms. His suspenders gave added shape to his large chest. He could easily be taken for a longshoreman. Gently, he pulled Franny away from Jerry. "Murray, what are you doing?" she asked. "You have no right coming out here like this."

Murray did not respond. He could not explain himself. He looked at Jerry and said in a slow deliberate voice, "I think it's time for you to go home."

Jerry took two steps back. For only a moment he paused to think about the situation. He didn't know who Murray was or why he thought Franny needed protection. He realized, however, he was standing in front an oak tree without an axe. "Franny, I'll talk to you," he said over Murray's shoulder. Then he left.

Franny was furious. How dare Murray behave this way. She had not seen him the whole summer. Did he really assume she would only be thinking of him? She looked down at him from the top of the entranceway stairs. "Who do you think you are Murray Goldman?" she asked. He just stood silent, his suit jacket now draped over one arm. He expected more. He waited for her to let him have it. Franny said nothing more. She grabbed the door handle to enter the building.

"Look, I'm sorry," Murray called out to her.

Franny stopped and stared at him. She was clearly upset. Murray had always seemed such a grown man to her. His behavior was childish. For the first time, however, she was seeing him not through the eyes of the neighborhood tomboy, but through the eyes of a woman.

She glared once more at him, as she shook her head. Without saying anything, she turned to go inside. Murray walked down the street in the direction of Lemberg's bakery. He had made his statement to her or did he? He had never fought with anyone over a woman. Murray felt confused. Why did it matter so much to him?

Two weeks later the same scenario occurred, on the way home from a date. Murray had not seen or talked to Franny. He wasn't certain how to put his feelings into words. Part of him envied Jerry. This blond-haired guy had something he wanted. Once more, he stepped from the shadows by the front steps to intercept them. This time she was calm. She sarcastically introduced Murray as her body guard. This time, Jerry stepped forward toward Murray. As he sheepishly looked down at the ground, Jerry sucker punched him.

He knew this was desperate act, but Jerry was not walking away this time. Murray pulled his head back. Blood appeared at the corner of his lip. Again, Jerry came at Murray swinging. He landed a punch high on Murray's right cheek. He did not retaliate. He could have easily knocked Jerry out. Instead, he ducked twice..three times. After several more swings, Jerry eventually tired. He backed away trying to catch his breath. Murray was standing straight up. Aside from the blood on his mouth and a red spot on his cheek, he had barely broken a sweat. "All right, all right, you win."

Jerry apologized to Franny and then left. Murray sat down on the stairs to the building. Franny stared at him for the longest time. Now it was her turn to feel confused.

"Why didn't you hit him?" she asked. "I don't understand, you could have clobbered him."

"He's your friend isn't he?" Murray responded. "I guess I care about you too much to hurt him."

That was as far as Murray could go in trying to explain himself. He got up from the stairs. He looked at Franny and wiped the blood with the back of his hand. Then he walked off into the night.

Now it was Franny's turn to ask herself soul searching questions. She sat on the stairs and watched the cars pass by on the street. "Was Jerry just a summer romance," she asked herself? After coming home from the Catskills, he was increasingly focused on his studies and career. She sat for almost an hour trying to figure it out. But instead of thinking about Jerry, why was she so worried about Murray? It wasn't like him to act this way. "This guy could have any girl he wanted. Why was he hanging out waiting for me?" she asked herself. He was not college-educated like Jerry. He would never be a doctor like Jerry. But she felt something for Murray she had not really thought about all summer. They were cut from the same cloth. She knew what a hard life he led. It was not unlike the struggles she and her family had faced. But in spite of all the despair and uncertainty, Murray didn't seem to fear anything. She was drawn to him, because she knew Murray would survive against any odds.

In time, her life decisions were made for her. Jerry Katz eventually faded into memory. He stopped calling and he stopped coming around. He made his decision about his priorities. He might think about Franny, but he accepted that he couldn't succeed at medical school and maintain a relationship. He never knew what to make of Murray Goldman. He was grateful to escape, after slugging the guy. Maybe it was the competition for Franny's affection that scared him away. He just decided to let it go.

He would always be Franny's first love. The first guy to make her realize she had become a woman. But he couldn't be her soulmate. He was too privileged. He had options beyond what Franny knew in her life. Their summer romance could not last. Back in the real world, she knew she'd always be second to Dr. Katz's career. Franny was not willing to settle for being second for anyone.

The weeks and months ahead changed everything. A serious courtship began to grow between Murray and Franny. Whether they admitted it to each other or to themselves, their competitiveness and drive as individuals became the foundation of their love.

Murray was not going to college. However, in a room, you could feel his presence. The concentration in his eyes could be felt on the back of your neck. His smile came naturally and could put you at ease. And beneath this calm exterior, you just knew not to take this guy for granted. She never doubted his ambition. At 21, he was making more money than anyone in their neighborhood.

The fateful night came one year later. He had arranged to take Franny out to dinner. She stood downstairs waiting for him in front of her building wearing a new dress and shoes. He was late. She looked as far as she could down the street, but Murray was nowhere in sight. Soon she turned to go inside when she heard the honking from a car that pulled up across the street. It was Murray waving her toward the car. He had worked for months to restore this model T Ford. Franny's face glowed with excitement.

As they pulled away, the car backfired. They laughed and laughed. The evening together was wonderful. Franny asked what seemed like a million questions about the car. She knew he had invested a good deal of money fixing it up. After dinner, as they walked outside, Murray turned to take Franny in his arms. Very slowly he leaned down to kiss her. Franny paused for a minute. She then put her arms around his neck. She pulled him closer and kissed him back.

They reached the car in a particularly giddy mood. Their feelings about each other were stronger than ever. They talked non-stop as he drove down Flatbush Avenue. Suddenly, a car came out of a side street at a high rate of speed. He swerved and tried to avoid the car, but the driver clipped the front end of his model T. Before they knew it, their car was spinning like a top. Franny was thrown from the car. Luckily, she landed against a wooden fence along the roadway. Once the car stopped, Murray jumped out to find her. She was laying upside down against the fence. Her new shoes were missing.

Murray surveyed the situation quickly and realized that the fence had softened her landing. She did not appear to be seriously injured. He turned, as he heard a police car coming on the scene. Then he looked back at her once again. It was a defining moment in Murray's life. He looked at this young woman lying there. Her dress had been thrown up over her head. Her under-wear clearly visible. With a wry smile of relief on his face, he said to himself as he pointed at her, "Yes, that's for me."

Franny woke up the next day in the hospital, bruised and sore. As her eyes opened, she could see Murray towering over her bed.

"Hi little girl," he said affectionately. "How do you feel?"

Murray gave her time to come to her senses and then explained what happened. She sat up in bed and looked around the room. Her eyes gave her away, as she glanced at the floor near her bed.

"Are you looking for these?" Murray asked, as he brought her new shoes from behind his back? "I had them fixed this morning, while you were asleep."

Slowly, she smiled. Her new shoes had survived intact. He handed her the shoes.

"Look," Murray started, "I know this may not seem to be the best time, but I realized I could have lost you last night," Murray said. "I guess it got me thinking. I love you Franny Sugar. I hope you know that. I've been on my own for so long. I didn't think I'd ever want to settle down or be with just one woman. But I do. I want to be with someone who shares my dreams . I want someone to wake up to every day, someone who will inspire and challenge me. I've never really felt that before meeting you. So, I'm asking you, will you marry me?"

Franny began to cry. She could not put into words how long she had wanted Murray to express these feelings. She knew how much disappoint-ment he experienced in his life, especially when they talked about love. She, too, had feared waiting to find one man who would value her. It was clear to her that he was not going to disappoint her.

"Yes, I'll marry you."

Franny motioned for Murray to lean down so she could kiss him. His arms reached under her shoulders and raised her off the bed.

She cried out in pain. Her body still hurt like hell. He gently laid her back down on the bed, but she would not let go of her arms around his neck. Murray bent further down.

"I love you Murray Goldman."

"I love you too, Franny. I will share with you and I'll take care of you," He told her.

"I'll take care of you forever."

CHAPTER 23

Hope and Love

Francine Sugar and Murray Goldman were married at City Hall in the fall of 1938. It was a small ceremony with just a few family members and friends. Alvin Lemberg was his best man. It took almost two years before Ziggy and Berta married in 1940.

Everyone in both families were certain Berta and Ziggy would tie the knot first. They met first. They dated longer. And when Berta wanted something, she was stubborn and unyielding until she got her way. Yet they were happy for their siblings. The families were now linked forever. Berta felt liberated. The path had been cleared for Ziggy.

Franny and Murray were so very much in love. The honeymooners left for a weekend in the Catskill mountains. Like two kids they chased each other through the woods at a Catskill resort. They reached the lake and Mrs. Goldman with wild abandon ran into the cold water. She waited for her husband to approach. With all her strength, she pulled her arms forward and the burst of water showered down on Murray. Her laughter could be heard echoing through the woods. He took the cold water in stride and kept coming. He dove in fully clothed. For a minute she didn't see him. Then without warning, he appeared from beneath the surface. He lifted Franny up in the air, his hands around her waist. She screamed and laughed, all at the same time. Murray poised for a minute with her in his arms. Her hands brushed back his hair away from his face. Her feet dangled off the ground. He lowered her slowly, gently kissing her as her hands pulled his face toward her. They were no longer two kids who lived in the same tenement house in Brooklyn. She had already turned 21 and Murray was 23. He had been with many women, but with Franny it was different. He had found more than just a wife. He had found a life partner, who shared his dreams.

After several minutes of passionate kissing, he lifted her and scooped her up in his arms. "C'mon buster, you can do better than that," she chided him. Just as quickly as he scooped her up, Murray spun and effortlessly tossed Franny in the air. She reached back, not knowing where she would land. A huge splash surrounded her. He could see her go under several feet away. With a sheepish smile on his face, he walked over and extended a hand to help her up. Now, brushing her own wet hair away from her face, she grabbed for his hand. As he leaned forward to pull her up, she put her arm around his neck and pulled him toward her. "I love you," she said, as he, off balance fell forward into the water. Soon they were both on their feet wringing the water from their faces and laughing.

The weeks and months ahead seemed effortless. From tenderness to playing pranks on each other, their love was filled with good humor and a certain competitiveness. They could be tough with each other, but never mean spirited. Once, Murray rigged the toilet so it backed up on her at the most inopportune time. She could be heard through the door, "Oh, my god, oh, my god." She thought it was her fault, until she saw her husband gloating as she opened the door. "You didn't really break the toilet, did you dear?"

Franny's payback came a week later. He sat down for dinner and began eating his mushroom barley soup. But as he stirred the soup, low and behold he found a large cockroach sitting smack in the middle of the bowl. She had really gotten him this time. It took a lot to get Murray's goat. From his plumbing experience and working in deserted buildings, he had seen and smelt it all.

But the sight of a bug in his soup disgusted him. He started to gag, but he wouldn't admit it. Franny waited patiently inside the kitchen, her ear pressed against the door to hear her husband's panicked reaction. The silence was broken by the slurping sounds of someone eating soup. Had she gone too far? She certainly didn't intend for him to actually eat a cockroach. She gasped and then ran through the door. She found him sitting there, the soup spoon perched near his lips and slurping away at the empty spoon.

Her initial expression of frustration gave way to a big smile. Murray reached for her and pulled her onto his lap. "You got me," Murray confessed, as he squeezed her tight. They both giggled and hugged.

Murray loved to surprise Franny. Sometimes he'd bring flowers or take her on a spontaneous outing to Coney Island. He was very much a product of Brooklyn. Maybe he was a bit more refined and worldlier than most. His image as a boxer fit him well. He didn't verbalize his feelings often. He didn't leave her notes before going to work or write poetry. However, she could always count on him to do sweet things when she least expected it.

For her, the world now seemed a less uncertain place. This was an uncharacteristic feeling for most people coming of age during the 1930s. Just as things started getting better, it seemed they got worse again.

Franny had no idea how they would make a living, but instinctively she knew her husband would be successful. The lean years in New York were still visible everywhere. The street corners were filled with vendors and homeowners trying to sell goods to make a few dollars. People didn't think much about careers, just survival. Many just worked hourly or day-jobs as laborers, trying to make a few bucks. But a calmness filled Franny. She felt her life now had a purpose and a clear direction. She was unmistakably lost in the hope of love.

CHAPTER 24

Rocco Rosetti: Lasting Three Rounds

Murray Goldman, still awfully young, had become a married man. It was highly unusual to the times, but he kept a regular job working at Weinberg plumbing. He worked hard. No task too hard or skill too challenging to learn. Even so, he also sought to earn extra money. Murray tried to leave Moe Fields behind. Franny did not approve. The fighting should be his past. She did not want him to get hurt.

As a young man, Murray found his heart inside a boxing ring. He learned not to fear anything or anybody. He once tried to explain the feeling to Franny. His manager, Frank Celentano, taught him that fighting came down to a "triumph of the spirit." He followed the punishment his friend Reggie Peterson experienced as a professional. At times, he was jealous. Murray wanted more in his life. What he took from his fighting years was attitude. Every challenge during this period in his life reminded him how often he could absorb pain and still persevere. In those moments of victory, he reassured himself. He was alive. He knew how to win.

Like his father, on occasion, Murray would go out at night. Except it wasn't a card game that drew his attention. He missed the crowd at Rosie's bar. On Friday night, he could hear the noise in the back. It was late. The ring announcer was egging on the crowd for someone to fight the undefeated Rocco Rosetti. No one moved. Rocco had been on the bootleg fight scene for several years. He knocked out 38 opponents and nearly killed two fighters. Moe Fields had crossed paths with Rocco during their time at Rosie's, but avoided the confrontation. Rocco's skills were fine-tuned during his years fighting as a professional. At 42, he was long past any hope of a shot at the title. His managers never had the influence to get Rocco the fights that would serve as a stepping-stone in his career. And then sports writers claimed Rocco had the guts of a fighter, but lacked the control. His opponents out boxed him and out-scored him in the ring. "He was simply too emotional," wrote a boxing commentator. "Crazy," is the way another reporter put it. Something happened when Rocco Rosetti entered the ring. If he got hurt, he'd completely lose his composure and his game plan.

But Rocco was well suited for Rosie's bootleg boxing scene. The crowd wanted blood. In his final boxing years, Rocco had gained quite a following in the local neighborhood. It wasn't uncommon for Rocco to lose his temper and get a fighter in the corner, where he beat them into unconsciousness. His 260 pound, six-foot four-inch frame would tower over his opponents. At

Rosie's the referees were not capable of pulling Rocco off someone, once he got angry. Rocco got angry frequently.

Murray moved through the crowd at Rosie's toward the ring. He had not been a regular for some time now. Murray envisioned a life beyond boxing. He wasn't afraid to work. He wanted to own and run a business. He had dreams. He had ambition. He could see the Weinberg family did quite well in the plumbing business. If only he and Franny could get past the war. Everyone knew a war was coming. The news on the radio was filled with stories about Hitler and Germany. It was just a matter of time. Murray was focused on saving as much money as he could, to prepare for a war—if a war came.

The ring announcer still begged the crowd for someone to fight Rocco. He had already knocked out two contenders. These fights had ended quickly. The crowd wanted more. No one was anxious to face Rocco. They valued their life. The announcer finally did something rarely done at Rosie's. Ringside was flush with the energy from the crowd and cash to bet. "Ok," said the announcer, "who's willing to come up here and take on Rocco Rosetti?

For the challenger who steps in the ring, I have this crisp $20 bill. And for the man that lasts three rounds with Rocco, I have two crisp $20 bills."

The crowd went wild, cheering for someone to accept the challenge. It would be perfectly acceptable if someone else got their brains beat. People held out cash waiting to place their bets. The cheers soon died down. No one was coming forward. The ring fell silent. "Ladies and gentlemen," said the announcer, "You leave me no choice. I will pay any man or woman $75 if they can stay in the ring with Rocco Rosetti for three rounds."

This was an extraordinary sum of money for a bootleg fight. While gambling revenue could easily cover the expense, fighters rarely shared in the gambling profits at Rosie's. Once again, after several minutes, the roar died down and folks started laughing at the lack of takers. "I am shocked," the announcer yelled, "is there no one here who can go three rounds with this fighter?"

"Why don't you fight him," a drunk patron yelled near the ring."

The ring announcer ignored the comments. "Hey, it's way too early for everyone to go home," he called out. "Surely, there must be someone out there? Step forward. Please step forward."

The announcer's frustration was growing more evident. His tone sounded almost sarcastic. Soon a very heavy-set man walked down to the ring and waved the announcer to come over and talk. After several minutes, the announcer returned to the center of the ring. "Ladies and gentlemen, I have just chatted with my good friend Ian Knight, the owner of Rosie's. We have a great tradition at Rosie's of giving customers what they want. He has agreed to pay the unprecedented sum of $100 to anyone who lasts three rounds with Rocco."

The crown went wild, screaming and cheering. As the crowd calmed down, a voice called out, "I'll do it." Chaos took over ringside. Patrons strained to see where the voice came from.

"Who said that," the ring announcer yelled out. Anxious to get the fight going, he motioned with his hands, "Everyone, please quiet down. Did someone say they'd fight Rocco? Please show yourself."

Soon a tall figure started to make his way down the aisle. The crowd was on their feet, cheering the contender. The ring announcer strained to see the fighter. As Murray reached ringside, the announcer walked over and asked his name. They talked for a minute and then the ring announcer grabbed the microphone.

"Ladies and gentlemen, it looks like we have a fighter in the house. Someone you may know. He is no stranger to Rosie's. He is homegrown. He's a former Golden Gloves competitor. At Rosie's, he has been undefeated in 25 fights. At 220 pounds and standing six foot two, from the streets of Brooklyn, I give you Moe Fields."

The crowd jumped to their feet clapping and cheering. It was unclear whether they remembered Moe Fields or they were just happy to have someone get in the ring with Rocco Rosetti.

Moe climbed into the ring, with his boxing gear in hand. While the crowd continued to cheer and place bets with the bookies at ringside, the announcer walked over to Moe Fields.

"What took you so long? You've been standing in that crowd for 15-20 minutes."

"The money," replied Moe. "I wasn't getting in the ring with this guy unless there was more money."

Moe smiled, as the announcer shook his head and walked away.

Moe stripped down to his sleeveless T-shirt. There was no time to change his clothes in the locker room. He had not actually planned to fight this night.

Suddenly, Moe turned serious as he looked across the ring at Rocco's bulging arms and trunk-like legs. His plan was to jab and move around the ring. He felt he had enough experience to last three rounds and collect his whopping $100.

The bell rang. The fight was on. Rocco moved across half the ring, before Moe could leave his corner. Moe jabbed with his left and moved to clear the circle. Rocco's head snapped back. The opportunity was there and Moe took it. He landed a hard-right cross to Rocco's face. Pandemonium broke out, as Rocco went down on one knee. The smoke in the arena was thick. People were drinking and whooping it up. Rocco was stunned, as the referee started the count. Moe was equally stunned. He had hardly broken a sweat. He returned to his corner.

Life is never as easy as it seems to be. Rocco was up by the count of eight. He blinked his eyes to shake the cobwebs. Blood filled his face with rage. He started spitting to his left and right. The ref had his hands full trying to hold Rocco back. He broke free and came at Moe. His arms were swinging wildly. Moe had been deceived by the early knock down. Rocco was more than a match for him. Moe tried to move in a circle and get his jab working. Rocco cut him off and pummeled him. Moe moved back against the ropes, hoping he could escape. Rocco would not let him go. He grabbed Moe in a head-lock and kept punching his face. It took forever until the referee could separate them. By the end of round one, Moe was bleeding from a cut above his right eye. His lip was split. His head felt like he had been hit by a truck.

The bell for round one rang out. The fighters retreated to their corners. Moe wished he had brought Alvin along. He missed his friend being in the corner. Moe feared no one, but he was smart enough to know he was about to take a beating.

By the middle of round two, Rocco had broken Moe's nose. Blood spurted out and filled his T-shirt with crimson. Moe had difficulty breathing. Rocco had driven him into the corner. He must have hit Moe with 10 unanswered blows to the face and body. Moe grabbed Rocco's arms and held on. Moe's legs were clearly wobbly. The bell sounded. Moe was saved from certain defeat.

At ringside, a boxing old-timer climbed up to help Moe in his corner. He must have worked the ring in his day, because he knew what to do. He wiped the blood from Moe's face, clearing his eyes. He held an ice bag on Moe's nose.

"Son, you're taking quite a beating out there."

Moe looked at him. His head was aching, but Moe managed to smile. "Yeah, I know," he responded. "Do you have any advice?" Moe asked.

"Well, you're from Brooklyn, aren't you? I think you better go out there and show him what you're made of."

"That's it," Moe asked. "That's your advice?"

"Yes, that's it. Get out there and kick the shit out him. And you better not waste any more time doing it."

The bell for round three rang. Moe knew he would not last a third round by moving around the ring; too much time and too little ring. He couldn't shake the old man's advice. He stood flat-footed near his corner. He knew Rocco was coming in for the kill. He ducked Rocco's right and hit him square in the solar plexus. He could hear Rocco gasp for air. He had found Rocco's sweet spot. He stood up and hit him with a left to the jaw.

Moe drove him back against the ropes with a series of punches to the mid-section. He worked the ribs, hitting Rocco with everything he had. Moe could swear he saw steam coming from his face. He had angered the bull. He had a choice to either try and run, until the round ended, or square off with the meanest fighter he had ever met.

The fighters were oblivious to the crowd. People were jumping up and down at their seats. As the noise level grew, for Moe it felt like the room was shrinking. The crowd pressed forward toward the ring, as fans clamored to get close to the action. The referee remained a silent observer. The ref wasn't certain what was coming, but he did not want to be in the middle of these fighters.

Rocco suddenly lunged at Moe, hitting him square in the face. He went down. Slowly he used the ropes to regain his footing. He crouched down low and came up with a powerful right upper cut, which caught Rocco by surprise. Rocco fell back a few feet. Moe pursued and hit him again with a right cross. Rocco tried to steady himself. Moe caught him again with a left upper cut. He drove his fist into Rocco's right ribs with everything he had left.

His legs wobbled. Moe's instinct took over. His hands worked faster, like he was on the speed bag. He switched his fighting stance to try and confuse his opponent. As a southpaw, Moe had an equally strong jab with both hands. His right cross was then followed by a left to the body. The adrenalin had taken over. Moe was angry for the first time in the ring. He let go of trying to protect himself. He wanted Rocco gone.

A right upper cut caught Rocco, just as the bell rang ending round three. He was hurt, but Rocco would not go down for the count. The crowd was out of control. It would be 30 minutes before the noise subsided. Few remembered ever seeing a fight like this before at Rosie's. A chorus of "Moe, Moe, Moe," erupted.

Moe returned to his corner. Every inch of his body hurt. The old man climbed up to his corner once again and handed him a towel. Moe wiped the blood off his face and chest. "You did well, son," said the old man, as he patted him on the shoulder. This guy was a complete stranger, but at the end of the fight his words meant the world to Moe.

The ring announcer called the end of the fight. Moe's head was pounding from the beating he took. For the first time, he had regrets. His body told him he had miscalculated. What was he thinking? He was married now. How could he face Franny? It was time to leave Moe Fields behind, but was that possible? He would always be Moe Fields. Nothing really changes you at the core. No one could break his spirit or his pride. Win or lose, whether he was a fighter or a plumber, Murray Goldman and Moe Fields shared the same space.

He had lasted three rounds with Rocco Rosetti. He collected his $100 from the announcer. But his biggest challenge was still ahead of him. How would he get home?

CHAPTER 25

The Freight Train wasn't going Anywhere

———

Artie Shaw arrived at Rosie's as quickly as he could. Moe was still sitting in the dressing room. He held an ice bag on his nose. Blood was everywhere. It was obvious he had taken a vicious beating. It was the first time he had come by himself. Usually, Alvin or Artie would be in his corner. It wasn't their experience that counted. He just felt certain his friends would look after him. This time, it didn't look like Moe was going home.

"What the hell happened," Artie asked. Moe looked up. "I think a freight train hit me," he responded.

"But if it makes you feel any better, I don't think the freight train is going anywhere tonight."

Artie shook his head, partly in disapproval and partly out of concern. He helped wipe off blood from Moe's chest and arms. He could see the gash under his right eye. He almost didn't recognize whether he still had a nose. He tried to help his friend get his clothes on. He winced twice. Artie suspected he had some broken ribs. "Ok, my friend, I think it's time we paid the hospital a visit."

Moe protested. He didn't believe he needed a hospital, but he was too tired and hurt to argue. Artie flagged a cab and off they went. The emergency room nurse took him to the exam room, as soon as they arrived. At first, she thought he was in a car accident. His face looked pretty banged up. He had two or three lacerations above his left eye and below his right. She didn't see his nose until Murray took the ice and towel off his face. She summoned a doctor.

It would be a long night. Artie sat patiently. Murray had three broken ribs. He could hear him yell, as the doctor grabbed and twisted his nose back into place. The doctor cautioned him his nose might soon be beyond repair, if he broke it again.

Murray was only half listening. He was thinking about Franny. He did not tell her he was boxing again. She wanted him to stop. Was it really about the money he wondered? He had always done what he wanted to do in life. It was just that simple. But now it was different. He could not lie to his wife. At the same time, he didn't think she would understand. He realized, however, he had found someone he trusted and loved. He would have to come clean with her.

It was 4 am by the time he left the hospital. He had asked Artie to call Franny and let her know he was all right. The walk home was difficult. His ribs hurt. His nose was swollen and bandaged. Artie tried to make small talk, but Murray was pre-occupied.

Franny was standing at the door waiting, when Murray arrived. She couldn't go back to sleep, after Artie called from the hospital. She was not happy he was boxing again. He had told her he quit. It was one of the issues they discussed before getting married. She knew it wouldn't be easy for her proud husband to just walk away.

He looked exhausted as he came through the door. Franny thanked Artie for taking care of him. She closed the door. Her arm held on to him. "Look, I'm sorry I didn't tell you."

"Shush....Let's just get you to bed right now. We can talk in the morning. I'll get you aspirin and more ice for your nose. I'm just thankful you're ok. I trust the other guy looks worse."

Murray smiled, but didn't respond. He was too weary. He let Franny guide him down the hall to their bedroom. She helped him out of his clothes. "I love you, Franny," said Murray, as his head hit the pillow. He was out cold. she shook her head.

Murray woke the next day. It was mid-afternoon. He was sore from head to toe. The headaches would last weeks. The aspirins didn't help. At first, he thought it might be related to the broken nose. The ice helped bring down the swelling in his face, but the headaches remained. He slept for days. He wasn't eating much. He didn't want Franny to worry. He blamed the broken ribs for his laziness. At times, he laid in bed and felt the room spinning. Artie had stopped by to see him. He wanted Murray to go back to the doctors. He refused. In two weeks, he was up walking around again. The dizziness was gone and his appetite was returning. However, the ringing in his ears remained and his head throbbed for two more weeks.

Murray knew he had to find another way to earn extra money. His job at Weinberg plumbing taught him a skill and paid a modest wage. But his dreams required more.

CHAPTER 26

The Heckler

———

The shaking and vibration of heavy bulldozers could be felt coming up the street. A crowd started to gather. They came to see them finally tearing down the Heckler building. The six-story building was almost 100 years old.

It had been condemned. Workers at the site feared going near the building. They thought it might just collapse at any moment.

The gruff voice of Nick Garragi filled the air. "What the hell are you guys waiting for?" Nick was the manager of the demolition crew and an expert with explosives. He was a big burly man with jet-black hair and a black handlebar mustache. He barked at the men standing idle by the work site, as he came across the street from a local coffee shop.

The men stepped back as Nick made his way toward the building. Ed Kelleher finally stepped forward, "It's Goldman." he said pointing to the soon to be pile of rubble. "Him again?" Nick asked. "This was the third demolition site he's showed up at in a month. Kelleher, go in there and tell him he's got 15 minutes before I bury him in the rubble. We have to finish this job."

"Look Nick, you may be my boss, but there's no way in hell I'm going into that building. And I don't think you'll find anyone here who feels different than me."

They all thought Murray Goldman was crazy going into these old abandoned and condemned buildings just to salvage copper pipes and fittings. Not even the fearless boss of the demolition crew would venture in there, especially after they set the dynamite charges.

Nick had told Murray he'd have until 10 a.m. to get what he wanted out of the building. It was late fall and the temperatures were brisk. Murray had been inside over two hours. Nick couldn't spare any more time. He walked to the entrance and yelled with all his might, "Goldman, it's time to go. You got five minutes and then we're going to blow you to kingdom come."

Nick took two steps back, as a rattle of dust and small debris fell from above. For all he knew, Goldman could already be buried below somewhere. He retreated from the entrance and stood back by his men, huddled around a fire in a metal garbage can, smoking cigarettes and drinking coffee.

"This guy has to be the craziest son-of-a-bitch alive. He must have the biggest set of balls I've ever seen," Nick joked with Kelleher and the men. Soon, one of the men pointed toward the building. Murray must have been carrying thirty pieces of pipe on his shoulder, as he stepped through the entranceway. His overalls and face were covered with soot and dust.

"How the hell did he carry all that stuff out of there?" Kelleher asked himself out loud. They all stood there shaking their heads.

"It's all yours." Murray called out to Nick and the men. "Thank you. I'm done here." He walked another thirty or forty yards to a truck parked out on the street. It had been a good morning for salvaging plumbing supplies. He would make a good sum of money selling these pipes. He'd also have just enough time to drop off the load before heading to his regular job at Weinberg's plumbing business. As he drove away, he could hear men shouting in the background. About a quarter mile away, he could feel the road shake from the explosion and looked back to see the cloud of dust. The Heckler building was no more.

CHAPTER 27
The Brookly Navy Yard

The outbreak of World War II changed everything. Murray Goldman started working at the Brooklyn Navy yard in 1941. The Navy needed men with experience to help prepare ships for possible war. He joined a workforce of 18,000 men and women. After Pearl Harbor, however, the effort at the Navy yard grew more urgent. The government employed more than 42,000 mechanics, technicians and plumbers. The Navy yard was a city unto itself.

By 1942, the war machine was in high gear. The country was now completely mobilized. People tried their best to continue their lives as normally as possible, but nothing would ever be normal again.

Everyone knew someone, a brother, a relative or friend who had gone overseas or was on their way. Murray had wanted to enlist, but at 27, he was no youngster. Franny begged him not to go. They had been married several years. She wanted so desperately to start a family. Luckily, the Navy wasn't anxious to lose his talents in the Yard. Aside from his experience in plumbing, he quickly developed a reputation for someone who could fix things—almost anything.

Murray took his job seriously. He felt he was an important part of the war effort. He would stay on the job as many hours as they needed him. He loved his wife and he loved his country.

Murray's best friend Artie Shaw and his youngest brother Sammy also worked at the Navy yard. Sammy tried to enlist, but was rejected because of his poor eyesight. Even as a young man, Sammy wore thick glasses and would be useless if he couldn't see well enough to function in military combat. Artie Shaw was an only child, with an ailing mother. His father had died when he was a teenager. He knew he couldn't go off to war and leave his mom, at least not at the outbreak of the war. But everyone knew their turn would come.

The news of bombs dropping on London or the fighting in the Europe was everywhere. The time would come when new recruits would be needed. Murray knew the war would not end without him.

Franny Goldman took a job at a local factory. With more men leaving for the war every day, it was up to the women to keep the factories running. Franny would tell her husband, "Look, what women did during the war would remain one of the great untold stories in America. Men went off to war. We stepped up and stepped in. The men fought to guarantee our freedom. The women made it possible for the nation to survive." Knowing his wife as he did, Murray never challenged her description of the sacrifices women made.

CHAPTER 28

Surprise and Loss

On Tuesday night, dinner was on the table when Murray came home. Franny had insisted in the morning he be home on time. Murray knew something must be up. She had been acting strangely the past several days.

"Hi, honey," he called out as he came through the door. He walked through their small living room to the kitchen. Franny had pots on the stove and was pulling a chicken out of the oven. "So, what's new honey?" he asked.

"I see you decided to show up after all," Franny said, with a mild sarcastic tone in her voice.

"Am I late?" he asked. Artie wanted me to join the guys down at McKinnon's bar and, I must admit, I was tempted. Then, I thought about this young, beautiful woman who would be waiting here at home for me." As his voice trailed off, he suddenly grabbed Franny by the arm and spun her around, lifted her off her feet and held her in his arms.

"Stop, stop that," she protested with laughter in her voice. Murray lowered her slowly and then reached down and kissed her. He gazed at her. After a minute or two, he whispered, "Maybe we should eat later." She surprised him. She would not say no. She reached to turn the stove off, as Murray held onto her outstretched hand.

They soon disappeared down the short dark hallway to the bedroom. The light through the partially open blinds silhouetted Murray's body. He pulled his t-shirt off and leaned down to kiss Franny. He was not in a hurry. He knew moments like this were special.

After what seemed like an hour, their sweaty bodies fell apart. They lay on the bed quietly for ten minutes. Franny soon broke the silence, "Murray, I need to tell you something." He turned toward her and moved closer. He rested on his elbow, as she stared up at the ceiling pensively. "What is it Franny?" he asked.

"I'm pregnant."

"You're what?" Murray asked. He sat up straight in the bed.

"Pregnant! We're going to have a baby."

He paused, looking down at her. He could sense she was waiting for his reaction. Why did he sense that Franny was afraid? Yes, the country was at war. Yes, he was likely to get shipped overseas. But Murray felt certain this would only be a short interruption in their life together. She continued looking up pensively toward the ceiling. She didn't know if Murray really wanted a child, even if she did.

"Franny," he responded. "I couldn't think of anyone I'd want to be the mother of my children more than you. You've made me a very happy guy!"

The words brought tears to her eyes. She reached up and hugged Murray. She held tight for what seemed like the longest time. She wanted to be in his arms. It was the one place where everything always seemed less uncertain.

Almost three months passed by. Murray and Franny walked on clouds. They could barely contain their excitement. Workdays went quickly. Nights were even more passionate than before. There was something about being pregnant that made Franny feel womanly, even sexy. At first, Murray was nervous. He'd ask her if making love could hurt the baby. As tough as he seemed, he always had a gentle side.

Franny was so happy. She felt freer about herself than she ever did in her life. It was as if nothing else in the world mattered. Rushing home to each other, the reality of the approaching war in Europe faded away. They'd sit up until late into the evening talking about moving somewhere. Maybe New Jersey or California.

Murray wasn't certain if he wanted to be a plumber. It came to him easily and he was good at it. But he also thought about opening a store or restaurant. He didn't mind working long hours. He wanted in the worst way to own a business. This would allow his wife to be at home with the children. He imagined several children running around the house, though he kept this idea to himself. After all, both he and Franny came from families with lots of siblings. He hoped they'd be boys.

She, on the other hand, wasn't convinced she wanted to stay home. She still had dreams of being a musician. She wanted to return to work and play in a band someday. She did hope their first child would be a boy. She knew how much it meant to Murray, to have a son. She also knew she wanted a daughter. She would teach her how to play handball and stand up for herself.

Franny wanted a daughter who would be strong and independent. She knew from her own life how tough things might be a times. Franny longed to teach her children the survival skills she learned.

As much as they tried to ignore the news, the war was everywhere. At the movies they would see the latest reports of battles in Europe. On Sundays, war reporting would interrupt radio programs. Each of them knew Murray would soon face having to go to war.

It was nearly four months into the pregnancy, when Franny woke up in the middle of the night. At first, the pain was dull. It must be gas, she thought. She turned and tossed for an hour, hoping it might subside. Soon, the pain grew stronger and sharp, like a knife cutting into her stomach.

The rain was pouring outside. It sounded intense. She tried her best to lay perfectly still. She tried to convince herself the pain would go away. Her body was slowly starting to throb. She reach out for Murray, who was in a deep sleep. He walked around to her side of the bed and turned the light on. The sheets were filled with blood, Franny's blood. She pulled at her hair and began to cry, "Oh, god, please don't let this be happening to me."

He dressed quickly. By this time, Franny was too weak to stand on her own. Murray wrapped a blanket around her and carried her down to the street. He held her close, covering her face from the driving rain. As he reached his car, he placed Franny in the back seat. His head was now soaked, as he walked around the car to the driver's side. The car would not start. He made a half dozen attempts. No response. He quickly abandoned the car, in search of a taxi. But it was the middle of the night. He carried his wife for eight blocks before he could flag down a cab. His arms hurt. His head pounded. He remained silent on the way to the hospital, except to try and reassure her, "everything will be ok."

By 4 a.m., the doctor came out to find Murray sitting in a dimly lit hallway. His head was buried in his hands.

"Mr. Goldman," the doctor called out.

He stood up, motioning the doctor in his direction.

"Hi, I'm doctor Reagan. Your wife has lost a lot of blood. It will be touch and go for a while, until we see if we can keep her vital signs stable."

"Wait, I don't understand. Is it the baby?"

"Mr. Goldman, your wife had a miscarriage." The doctor paused for a minute. He could see the information had not registered with him.

"I'm sorry, but she lost the baby. She must have hemorrhaged in her sleep. What we don't know right now is if your wife will survive. She's lost a good deal of blood. We're giving her transfusions, but we won't know how her body will respond."

Murray jumped to his feet. He towered over Doctor Reagan. "Are you saying I might lose my wife?"

We're doing everything we can for her. We are hopeful she'll pull through this. The next 24 hours will be critical."

The news hit Murray hard. His body slumped back against the wall. The baby was lost. Franny might be lost as well. How could this be happening, he asked himself. Why? Why her? Why now?

"Doctor, can I see her"?

"Well, maybe we should wait until morning. She's extremely weak."

Murray had taken two steps closer to the doctor. Doctor Reagan looked up at Murray. He could tell Murray Goldman was not about to take no for an answer.

"Doctor, I don't think you understand. I want to see my wife."

"Well, I guess it would be ok for you to go in, but only for a short stay. We are giving her blood and fluids. She knows what happened. She needs to stay calm now. It's very important she sleep. Her body must have time to rest and repair itself."

Franny's head was turned away, as he entered the room. He pulled a chair next to the bed. He gently reached out to touch her hand. She was asleep. He did not feel the tears streaming down his face. Murray could not remember when or if he ever cried before. He sat there for an hour, long after the nurses had asked him to go.

Murray left the hospital just before 6 am. He walked the streets until the rain stopped. His clothes were soaked. He thought only of Franny and how she would take the news. He refused to accept the idea of losing Franny. He didn't believe in fate. He would will her to live. He would focus only on being strong for her, so she could deal with the loss of this child.

By 11 a.m., he returned to the hospital. He went home and took a hot shower. He removed all the bedding and any trace of the horrible event that had taken place the night before. He wanted Franny to come home and for them to resume their lives together.

She seemed to be sleeping when Murray entered the room. As he approached the bed, her head turned toward him. He could see the tears running down her face.

"Hey, what's going on here?" he asked.

He reached down and wiped her cheek with his hand. He caressed her face.

"Look at me," he said softly. "Look at me."

Franny's eyes moved to avoid direct contact with Murray. The tears came. She could no longer hold it back. She sobbed uncontrollably. Again, she turned away from him.

"Franny, I'm not going anywhere. I want you to look at me," he called out. Gently, he touched her arm and she turned her head toward him. Her eyes were bloodshot from crying. Suddenly, for the first time, she could see tears streamed down Murray's face. His voice cracked as her eyes met his.

"I love you Franny," he leaned down close to her and whispered. "This doesn't change anything. I wanted this baby, too. I promise you, we'll have another chance. I promise you! It's important that you rest and get stronger. We have each other. Nothing can hold us back."

Franny's hand reached up to touch Murray's face. She trusted him and it gave her peace.

His arms slowly lifted her up from the bed. He embraced her, quietly for several minutes.

Her body trembled with emotion. The tears flowed. He then set her back down.

There is in life an unspoken code between a man and a woman. We may not have certainty. We may not always have longevity. But in the eyes of the person we love, we see ourselves. We see our hopes; our dreams and we understand with great clarity what it means to give ourselves over to something that's shared with another human being. Whether in tragedy or celebration, these moments elevate us. We come to understand that true love is unconditional.

"You need to rest now. The doctor said you lost a lot of blood."

Murray's hand brushed the hair from her forehead. "Please close your eyes and try to sleep. I'll stay here with you. I won't leave."

Franny finally fell asleep. He sat nearby. His eyes fixed on her face. She finally seemed to be at peace. He wondered what was next? How might losing the baby change her? How might it change them? He was thankful he did not lose her. The rest of life would always be within their grasp.

It was early evening. Murray's eyes opened. He had fallen asleep in the chair. His body felt stiff. As he lifted his head, he could see Franny laying on her side. She was staring at him.

"How long have you been awake?"

"About an hour," she replied.

"You ok"?

"I'm better."

He stood and pulled the chair closer to the bed. He reached out for her. He kissed her hand. Then he held her hand against his face. His eyes looked deeply into hers.

"Franny, we have to move beyond this. As long as we're together, we'll be ok."

Her eyes told him she knew he was right. She knew her husband would never quit on life and neither would she.

CHAPTER 29

War Beckons

Fall came early. As he reached the street, the crisp air shook the sleep from his eyes. It had been six months since the miscarriage. Franny and

Murray had resumed their routines. They continued to enjoy their lives as a young couple. But the news of the war dominated.

Murray grew increasingly worried as more and more of his friends were drafted. He didn't fear the war. He just didn't want to be a foot soldier. He knew the time was closing in for him to make a decision.

Two weeks passed. He took Franny away from the city. He rented a small bungalow upstate. On Saturday, as they walked in a nearby park, he broke the news to Franny that both he and Artie had received draft registration notices. "The problem, as I see it," he told his wife, "if we wait, the Army will grab us. Artie and I want to serve, but we'd prefer being on one of those big ships at the Brooklyn Navy yard. By enlisting, I'm hoping we'd get assigned to a Navy facility on the east coast. This would allow us the chance to come home on leave, before they send us overseas." Murray was calm and spoke matter-of-factly. He certainly didn't want Franny to think he was excited about going to war.

Franny listened patiently. She knew this day would come. Why should her life be untouched, when so many people were making sacrifices? Now her turn had come. There would be no turning back or talking Murray out of his decision. She reasoned in her mind that Murray might be safer on a ship. However, she was no fool. She realized once Murray enlisted, he'd have little control on where he was sent or whether she would see him again.

As they sat in the park, Franny responded, "I can't help but think of the child we lost. I so wanted for us to have a family. If you go overseas, who knows how long the war will go on? How long will I have to wait?" The reality started to sink in. And as it did, she became even more emotional. "Tell me. I'm pretty tough. But will I ever have children?" Her eyes welled up with tears. She had unburdened herself of the fear in her heart. The only thing left were these tears of resignation.

"Franny, I am coming back. It may take time, but nothing on this earth will keep me from coming back."

Murray could see how upset she was by the news, but he didn't have a choice.

"Look, you need to trust me. I want to start a family. I want you to be the mother of my children. And hopefully, they'll all be boys. Well, one girl, if you want it," Murray said with a smile.

Franny could not hold back. She laughed nervously, as tears streamed down her face. She knew Murray meant what he said. He had this way of talking. She never doubted he would keep his word. As much as she wanted to cling to him, she had to hold on to his promise. She had to be strong, if only to assure herself that their dream survived.

Murray and Artie Shaw joined the Navy in July 1943. He had never been to sea. However, he was confident his plumbing experience working on ships in the yard would be useful to the Navy.

After filling out all the paperwork, they returned home to say their goodbye to family and friends. It would be several days before they had to report to the Navy facility in Lido Beach, Long Island, New York. Murray visited his parents and siblings. Mr. Weinberg wished him luck and promised him his job would be waiting when he returned. Next, was Lemberg's bakery, for coffee, cake and good wishes from his surrogate family. Last, was seeing his father Isaac, who said little but wouldn't let go as he hugged his son and said goodbye.

On Saturday, Franny and Murray walked the streets of Brooklyn for hours together. They held hands. Each of them was lost in their own thoughts about the unknown future ahead. Franny wondered about all the wives, who like her, had to see their husbands or boyfriends off to war. She was already 26 years old. How long would the war go on? She understood from the news on the radio what was at stake. She did not have a right to ask for something, when so many others were sacrificing for their country. She found her patriotism that warm day in July.

Murray couldn't imagine what the war was like. He had seen the newsreels at the movie theater. For him, there was adventure in the air. He recalled leaving home at 15 and traveling with the circus. He had been to six or seven states. Soon he'd be traveling overseas to foreign countries. But he was no longer a kid. He would soon be turning 28. Leaving Franny would put their life together on hold.

He took her arm as they stopped on a street corner. The traffic with honking cars raced by. He could smell pizza being cooked nearby. Smoke rose from manhole covers. He turned toward her and held her tightly. He didn't speak right away. He just held her. Franny was caught up in the moment. She wanted the world to stop, so she would never have to leave Murray's arms.

As he let go, he stepped back to speak. "No. Don't say another word," she said. "I know what you're thinking. I am not worried. I love you Murray Goldman. There's nothing more you need to know."

He remembered the handball court and how he watched Franny, without her ever knowing. He had married a woman without peers. She didn't want him to think about her. She just wanted for him to come back alive.

On the morning of July 16, 1943 Murray kissed Franny goodbye. He met Artie Shaw at the train station. They both looked out the window, as it left Brooklyn. Soon their lives would be inextricably linked to over 600 strangers on a ship headed for war.

CHAPTER 30
U.S.S. Catoctin

The USS Catoctin was originally built as a merchant ship. It was launched in January 1943 as the SS Mary Whitridge. The Navy acquired the ship the prior August and brought the vessel from Long Beach, California to the Philadelphia Navy yard. The Catoctin was then converted to serve as a high command ship, with the latest radar and communications technology available. Its mission was to support the Atlantic Eighth Fleet and play a key role in planning and serving as a headquarters ship for the three branches of service in the Mediterranean.

Once the basic installation of new equipment was completed, the Catoctin would make its way down the coast from Philadelphia to Virginia. Here the ship would be in port for a month, where it would take on supplies and bring aboard a full complement of sailors. Most of the men, who joined the Catoctin, had never been on a ship. The Captain ordered drills each day to get the men seaworthy.

In port, a crane would lift large nets onto the ship, loaded with food, fruits, vegetables and other hard goods. Murray Goldman and a large contingent of men were ordered to help retrieve the supplies and organize their distribution on the ship. Jack Selby, a tall and broad-shouldered sailor, worked alongside of Murray. Jack was from Mobile, Alabama.

The men had worked until late afternoon unloading the nets. As the third wave of supplies reached the Catoctin, a small crate of oranges broke open and spilled onto the deck. Several sailors, including Murray and Jack, scrambled to scoop up the fruit. These oranges were precious treats. Some had not seen fruit since before their seven-week boot camp training.

Murray still had lightning reflexes and quickly scooped up 3 oranges, as others around him pushed and shoved. As he stood up, Jack Selby cursed at Murray's good fortune and then hit him square in the jaw. He didn't know if he had accidently bumped into Jack, as the men rushed for the fruit. He tried to apologize, but Jack was angry. He came up empty handed. Murray tried to hand Jack an orange. Jack swung and hit him again.

At this point, Murray dropped his oranges. He was not someone who got angry quickly, but Jack was pressing his luck. He held back, until he saw Jack moving in to hit him again. "Bam. Bam." Murray began hammering Jack with lefts and rights to the body and face. Jack hit the deck twice. By the time he connected with a right cross, the lights went out for Jack Selby. The sailors gathering up oranges stopped to watch the fight. They were still cheering when a whistle blew and the ship's Ensign stepped through the crowd. The sailors quickly refocused their energy on stuffing oranges in their side pockets and slowly walking away.

The Ensign arrived just as Jack was being helped to his feet. "Who started this?" the Ensign asked. Neither sailor responded. Frustrated, the Ensign told them they would be written up and likely to lose pay for fighting. "Get back to work. And you better find a better way to communicate," the Ensign said as he walked away.

Jack Selby would never forget the beating he received from Murray. He had no idea he picked a fight with a trained boxer. Unlikely, as it turned out, the two men became friends after that first encounter. They worked together, trained together and when the fighting started, the two of them would man the 40-millimeter canons near the rear of the ship.

The Catoctin sailed from Norfolk, Virginia, to join the Eighth Fleet on March 5, 1944 and reached Algiers on March 19.

In 1942, the Navy's Eighth Fleet, under the command of Admiral H. Kent Hewitt, had led the successful amphibious assault and invasion of North Africa. The assault, under the code name, Operation Torch, was a joint effort between the British and the Americans. It was not, however, without some controversy. The Allies were deeply divided over war strategy. The U.S. had been lobbying for Operation Sledgehammer, which would have involved an all-out assault on Europe, crossing the English Channel. Churchill, however, felt more time was needed. He wanted to see Germany weaken before the assault on Europe. He argued for a second front from Russia to draw German resources away from Southern Europe. President Roosevelt eventually agreed to go along with Churchill and Operation Torch commenced in November 1942.

Admiral Hewitt and the Eight Fleet followed up with a major campaign to take Sicily in July 1943. Operation Husky, as it was called, required an amphibious and airborne assault that lasted six weeks. The taking of Sicily, by the end of August, opened up the Mediterranean sea-lanes for Allied ships and paved the way for the Army's invasion of Italy.

Murray Goldman and Artie Shaw had taken a rather circuitous route before reaching their Navy assignments. From Lido Beach, Long Island, they were sent to Dearborn Michigan for 7 weeks of training. Murray's knowledge working in the Brooklyn Navy shipyard and his years of plumbing experience were immediately recognized. The newly re-commissioned Catoctin was a logical assignment. Artie, on the other hand, was sent to serve on a battle ship. They would not see each other again until after the war.

As part of the Catoctin's Repair Division, Murray quickly established a reputation for being able to improvise and resolve issues with the ship's operating systems. He could look at the engineer's drawings and quickly guide the repair crews.

It was obvious to the Commander, the ship was overloaded and top heavy with sophisticated communications equipment. Because of this equipment, the ship would have limited firepower to defend itself. The Commander knew he would not have enough time in Virginia to fix the ship's shortcomings. There was a war going on and the Catoctin had to be in Algiers. He directed the Repair Division to keep at the task of addressing problems that could slow the ship down or interrupt its ability to function.

While Murray had not given it much thought, he became aware once he arrived on the Catoctin that he was one of the older men on the ship. Aside from the officers, Murray was surrounded by sailors almost a decade younger. He guessed some must have lied about their age and enlisted at 17. He admired their determination to fight in the war.

The Repair Division consisted of 50 men who specialized in tackling the vessels infrastructure, including the boilers, fire systems, plumbing, electrical work, heating and refrigeration. They also had to be resourceful to address special construction needs the ship might have, while at sea.

Sidney "Sid" Mayer was a refrigeration specialist. His father had been in the business. He knew more about fixing this equipment than any sailor twice his age. Murray figured he was one of those young sailors who must have lied on his enlistment form. He wanted to join the Navy so bad. He was afraid if he waited, the war might be over. Like so many others, he joined the Catoctin in Virginia a month before it sailed for Algiers.

There were 633 men on the USS Catoctin, but Mayer realized there were very few Jewish sailors. His shipmates came from all over America. For Sid Mayer, many had strange southern accents. Mayer came from Lower Manhattan in New York City. He thought living in New York was like a melting pot, but he had never met anyone from Alabama or Mississippi before. Mayer didn't mind. He rather liked that everyone was different.

However, after three weeks aboard the ship, Mayer came across only one other Jewish sailor. His name was Schwartz, Jacob Schwartz, from Bayonne, New Jersey. The USS Catoctin was like a small city. A sailor rarely saw his friends unless they worked together or shared similar duties on the ship. Mayer came from a religious family. He realized without other Jewish sailors, they wouldn't have the ten men needed for a prayer minyan each week. The unknown of what sailors might face, once they arrived in Europe, only heightened their interest in prayer.

A week later, Mayer was standing below when he heard the announcement come over the public address system, "Goldman to the quarterdeck. Goldman to the quarterdeck." He didn't make much of the announcement, except he knew from his basic training that sailors rarely ventured up to the quarterdeck.

While in port, the quarterdeck or main deck was the most important place on the ship. It was the central control point for all major ship activities. Once the Catoctin was underway, control of the ship would transfer to the bridge. But a sailor called to quarterdeck was normally there for an important reason. With its deck markings and specially painted lines, this was not an area where sailor could just hang out.

Mayer didn't pay too much attention, but it did peak his curiosity. Who is this Goldman guy?

Murray Goldman had been asked by the ship's Captain to hand pick a small team within the Repair Division, to tackle problems on the ship that cut across specialized groups or needed urgent repair.

He picked an eclectic group that included Dick Riordan from Detroit, Tony Marano from Queens, New York, Steve O'Malley from San Diego, California, William "Buster" Johnson from Georgia—and Jack Selby from Mobile, Alabama. Across the board, this group was much younger than Murray Goldman, but they shared a common thread having all worked in construction, plumbing and electrical jobs starting as teenagers. Buster was a former weightlifter. He was strong as an ox. Tony Marano was the smartest and most well-read member of the group. Marano had a special talent for anything electrical. But all of them looked up to Murray Goldman, who wasn't afraid to roll up his sleeves and get his hands dirty.

It would take the entire two weeks at sea for the Repair Division to correct mistakes and shortcomings they found from the work completed in Philadelphia and Virginia. When the repairs were finished, nothing they did was pretty or perfect. But this was a critical time during the war—and perfect didn't matter.

By the time the Catoctin reached Algiers, she was fully seaworthy. Commander Olsen was very pleased with the hard work done during the voyage, especially considering how frequently his young sailors were hanging their bodies off the side of the ship and heaving up their breakfast. As much as the crew was getting the Catoctin ready for its mission, the two weeks at sea was preparing his crew for life on the ocean.

The ship was so top heavy with equipment that it bobbled like a cork in the water. It was not uncommon for new and young sailors to be seasick on their first trip. But even seasoned Navy men on the Catoctin were experiencing sea sickness.

Murray Goldman was no exception. He was a leader in all things, including his frequent timeouts to gather his senses and vomit into a bucket below deck. Among his Repair Division team, their frequent turns heaving into the bucket became a source of humor for the group. The only sailor not bothered by the back n' forth motion of the ship was Riordon, from Detroit. None of the guys could figure out why. But Riordon was a good sport. Most times, he would just smile and shake his head, as his friends ran for that bucket.

CHAPTER 31

Lessons in Algiers

The Catoctin would stay in Algiers for several months, while waiting for orders from the high command. During this layover, the Commander ordered the ship to be loaded down with heavy iron and concrete. The crew spent almost a week bringing onboard heavy blocks of cement to load in the bowels of the ship. Iron bars from a deserted railroad depot were lined up along mid-ship to act as stabilizers. While he didn't want to slow the ship's speed, the Commander needed to prevent the top-heavy Catoctin from causing half the men to be seasick.

Meetings were being held on the Catoctin, with frequent visits by senior military officers from the Navy, Army and Marines. Fighting in Italy was well underway. The Germans and Italians were in retreat, after the success of Allied forces in Sicily. Regular planning sessions were scheduled to coordinate the next phase of the U.S. led attack.

While in Algiers, Commander Olson would grant shore leave to sailors, but the standing order of the day was sailors had to travel in groups of three or four. Usually, sailors followed orders. Officers tried to explain that there were dangers in Algiers. Most sailors heeded this advice. Some, were too giddy with excitement. This was the farthest they'd ever been from home.

North Africa seemed very exotic. Sailors visited outdoor markets selling goods they never saw before. At night, the bars became havens for foreign soldiers. There were belly dancers and amazing food. The music was a blend of modern and middle-eastern. The women of Algiers were beautiful, especially to a group of sailors and soldiers so far from home. The troops in Algiers didn't speak Arabic which made it hard to converse with the locals, but companionship didn't require conversation.

The Commander's orders were better understood, following one weekend when a group of sailors separated and two did not return to the ship. They had left the ship in a group of six, but after a night of drinking two sailors split on their own. One left with a woman he thought would bring him bliss. A second sailor just wondered off, promising to rejoin his buddies later in the evening.

The view that North Africa was no longer at war ignored the realities. Yes, the Germans were gone, but Arabs in Algiers killed hated foreign soldiers and sailors. It didn't matter if they were American, British or German. In North Africa, they were all seen as occupiers. Their uniforms were trophies within the Arab-Algerian community.

Azzam's bar was a well-known watering hole for soldiers on leave in Algiers. Young sailors and soldiers felt safe going there, because it was so popular and crowded with Americans and the British. But in Algiers, nothing was as it seemed.

On one Saturday night, a group of sailors had arrived hours earlier from the Catoctin. The drinking was in high gear. Near the bar, the sailors watched as three Algerian women danced. They had dark skin and long curly hair. Breasts bulged from their tight dresses. Their faces were covered, as per custom. One of the women picked a blond sailor out of the crowd. She danced up to him and pulled his head into her chest. The crowd went wild with applause. Later, the sailor was seen with the woman. They sat at the end of the bar for almost an hour. She laughed and drank with him. He was having a good time, loading up with alcohol while his lady friend was ordering just to increase the bill.

She spoke only some broken English. But she let her hands communicate what she really wanted, gently rubbing the sailor's leg. She grabbed him deep in his crotch. He couldn't resist. He whispered something to her. Soon, they were leaving the bar, his arm around her shoulder. Two sailors tried to slow him down, urging him to stay with the crew. He acknowledged his mates with a wink and said "Don't worry I'll be back soon." They walked a block down the street. The woman pointed to a second-floor window. As they climbed the stairs, the sailor was smiling. He had only been with a woman once. He was 19 years old.

The door opened to the small apartment. The woman walked in and turned on a small dim light. She moved to the wall on the other side of the room. The sailor came through the door and walked two steps toward her. From the shadows behind the door, a man's wrist came forward. In one stroke, he slit the sailor's throat. The knife was long and curved. The movement was so quick. There was little warning. The sailor looked at the woman and blinked twice. He had not lost consciousness. His mind was still trying to process what had happened. His eyes blinked once more, staring at the woman, and then his life ended.

The Algerian man quickly stripped the sailor, emptying his pockets on the floor. Blood filled the dirty old carpet where the sailor's body fell. The woman did not move. She had played this role of seductress before. She began to lose count on how many sailors and soldiers had crossed her doorway. Americans, British, she did not care where they came from. This was

Algeria. But she was curious. She had yearned to sleep with just one of them, to know why they had wanted her so much. However, this would not be her fate or theirs.

She collected her bounty for the sailor's uniform and headed out to a different bar. She was happy to be rewarded for two uniforms each night. The sailor's body would be rolled up in the old carpet and carted away. No one would ever see him again.

Across town, a second American sailor strolled around the city, as if he was sightseeing. The night sky was dark. Stars filled the landscape. In the distance, a full moon helped light his way. However, Algiers was a city without laws or anyone to enforce them. His fate was sealed, when three men stepped from a dark alleyway. He was stabbed multiple times.

One of his attackers held his mouth to muffle the screams. The pain was excruciating. His eyes bulged with terror. The sailor wondered if anyone had seen him. The knife made sharp sounds, as it plunged deep into his back. First, it hit his kidney. Then the attacker worked up his back toward his lungs. Three…four…five thrusts found their mark. The sailors white uniform filled with red crimson. His head tilted upward. He thought only of his family back home in Ohio. There would be no one to save him. He would not be returning to the Catoctin.

By morning the two men had not reported back to the ship. Inquiries were made among the other sailors that left together. The Commander put the ship into lock-down. No one could leave the Catoctin, until an investigation was completed. The word spread through the ship quickly. The Catoctin wasn't the first or last Navy vessel to lose men in Algiers, but after this incident no one disobeyed the Commander's orders.

CHAPTER 32

The King's Visit

The Catoctin sailed from Algiers to Oran and finally to Naples, Italy by early July 1944. In Algiers, the ship served as the flagship for Admiral Hewitt, Commander of the Eighth Fleet. The crew wasn't aware, but for several months the Catoctin had been the headquarters for the planning of the invasion of southern France.

The Repair Division had been hard at work fixing boilers that would break down on the trip to Naples. The Catoctin was only making 16 knots. The ship had installed two small 20 and 40-millimeter guns, which were hardly adequate to protect it from an enemy attack. The Navy did its best to keep the ship safe. It was often accompanied by a destroyer. But if in danger, the Repair Division had to ensure the ship had enough speed to try and escape.

"Goldman to the quarterdeck. Goldman to the quarterdeck."

Sid Mayer stood below deck, when the announcement rang out. He swore the public address system (PA) called out that name every day, or so it seemed. He had still not met this guy Goldman after three months on ship, but Mayer figured he must be an incredibly important guy.

When he reached the quarterdeck, the Captain gave Goldman another job for his team. The planning for the invasion would require senior leaders of the Army, Navy and Air Force to stay aboard the Catoctin for meetings and planning sessions. Murray's team was asked to work with the Refrigeration Unit to make the ship as comfortable as possible for these senior officers. It was summer time in the Mediterranean. Sid Mayer from the Refrigeration Unit suggested the men route air ducts through the refrigerators on the ship. Murray's team would fabricate and install pipes working with Sid, so they could deliver cool air to the bridge of the ship and the rooms of command-ing officers.

Late in July, it finally became clear to the crew just how important a role their ship was about to play in the war. The Commander had announced over the PA to prepare July 24, the following day, for a visit by senior military leaders. The word spread quickly that King George VI of England would be visiting Admiral Hewitt on the Catoctin. Both U.S. and British high command officers would accompany the King. This would be one of several American and British ships visited by the King to bolster morale.

The entire crew of the Catoctin was standing ready, when the King boarded the ship. There was a war going on. Nevertheless, the men were in dress uniforms. The only thing missing for the Brits were marching bands. On the quarterdeck, a group of officers assembled without music. The King and the Admiral walked the line greeting and thanking the officers, which included representatives of each country and branch of service.

The King then surprised the Catoctin's Commander, asking if he could walk down to the next level of the ship and greet the enlisted men. This was unprecedented. King George was a rather quiet spoken and shy person. The Commander and other senior officers followed the King. He walked along half the starboard side of the ship shaking hands and waving to sailors he could not reach. He thanked each man for their service.

For many, these sailors had never been away from their homes in the U.S. Alabama and Mississippi were a good distance from London England. The idea of meeting the King of England seemed strange. "Where is England," one sailor asked. The men, however, were blown away at how down to earth English royalty seemed to be. It was certainly a memorable day for the ship's crew. News reports filled the airways back in England about the King's visit with U.S. and UK forces. These visits also bolstered spirits back home and rallied support for the war.

While in Naples, the Catoctin granted limited leaves to sailors. This would likely be their last time ashore, until the ship's next mission was completed. With only weeks left, the sailors tried to enjoy a few summer days in Italy. Unlike Algiers, the Italians greeted the Americans with open arms. They had tired of Mussolini and were happy to be liberated.

The sailors were welcomed everywhere, in restaurants and bars and even into the homes of local families. Sid Mayer met Murray Goldman during a shore leave in Naples. Mayer was walking off the ship with Jacob Schwartz, when they heard Goldman's name being called out as he headed off the ship. Mayer was an average size guy. He made it down the gang-plank and there was Goldman. Mayer tapped him on the shoulder. He didn't know what to expect.

"Are you that guy, Goldman, I keep hearing over the PA system?"

Murray Goldman smiled. "Yes, I'm that guy."

At this point, Mayer was joined by Schwartz, and to Mayer's surprise, Murray was standing with Jeff Katz and Leo Mitchell. It had taken almost six months, but Mayer had finally found other Jewish sailors. "Do you think we have enough for a minyan," Mayer asked? Murray and the men gathered around and laughed.

The sailors walked around Naples together for several hours. At cafes, they'd stop and swap stories about family back home. More sailors would gather, wherever there was food or a bar. Murray had written to Franny often since leaving New York.

As evening came, the loneliness of war and being far from home got to some of the men. Women in Naples were excited to meet Americans. On these evenings, there was more love spoken between men and women, than Italian or English. From bars and cafes, young couples—and young strangers would couple up and disappear. Promises of staying in touch after the war would follow passionate hours of escape. In war, everyone lived in the moment. The war was far from over. There is something about uncertainty that brings people together like magnets. Perhaps, in a brief passionate encounter they found hope.

CHAPTER 33

Invasion of Southern France

On August 13, 1944, the Catoctin left Naples. The men were aware a new operation would soon be underway, but very little information was communicated. Word spread quickly that the Secretary of the Navy, James Forrestal, and the commanders of the 7th Army, the 12th Air Force and French Naval Forces were all on board the Catoctin.

By the next day, the ship arrived off the coast of southern France, at early dawn. The crew was put on high alert, as the long-planned assault, code name Operation Dragoon, got underway. The ocean off the coast was filled with Allied war ships. The invasion of southern France was underway.

The Allies had to seize the port cities of Marseilles and Toulon. Access to these ports would ensure the Allies could resupply their growing force of soldiers in France, Italy and the rest of Europe. Some crew members argued the southern attack was even more important than the Normandy invasion, which had occurred three months earlier. The southern landing was critical, because of supply routes it created.

Originally, the Allies had planned to attack southern France simultaneously with the invasion at Normandy in June of 1944. However, the Allies were delayed. Their forces on the mainland had met heavy resistance from the Germans as they moved north in Italy. Troops and resources had to be diverted to ensure success in Italy. The invasion of southern France would be pushed back to August.

The U.S. and Allied commanders did heed the lessons learned from the Normandy invasion, where German embankments on the hills caused high casualties. This time, the Allies strategically picked a less hilly terrain for the assault, off the coast of Toulon.

On August 15th, the invasion began with a parachute drop by the 1st Airborne Task Force behind enemy lines. These foot soldiers would take the high ground. A major amphibious assault followed, backed by heavy naval gunfire and naval air attacks.

The Catoctin played a key role in planning the Allied assault. The ship remained with the Eighth Fleet, which stood miles offshore. However, the crew could still see some of the action in the distance. Puffs of smoke were visible, where Allied paratroopers tossed smoke grenades marking the enemy's large gun embankment. Then, suddenly, the crew could hear loud explosions behind their ship. The deafening sounds came from the powerful guns on two U.S. destroyers near the Catoctin. The crew watched as the destroyer found its mark and the German gun embankments disappeared.

Within the first two days, it became clear the Germans did not have the troop strength to resist the invasion. The Allies achieved success, moving quickly inland and liberating France in four weeks. While U.S. forces moved north, the French First Army liberated Marseille and Toulon. The ships of the Eighth fleet dispersed after the initial attack proved successful.

The Catoctin had done its job on August 15, guiding the Allied invasion, but it was not out of danger. Each night, a crew of sailors would circle the ship in small boats. Their mission was to use smog machines to cloak the ship with a large smoke screen, so its position was hidden from German air attacks. The crew was hugely effective, until the third night after the invasion. It was near 3 a.m., when the Catoctin's Commander sounded the alarm for battle stations. German planes could be heard in the sky. Suddenly, a panic swept across the ship. The moon was full and gusting winds had cleared the smoke screen protecting the ship's visibility.

On the brightly lit ocean, the Catoctin was a sitting duck. Sailors scrambled on deck, as they heard the German planes descending. The Catoctin radioed for help, but help would not come in time. The Commander ordered the gunners to begin firing, in a last-ditch effort to try and scare off the German pilots. But the Catoctin was a radar and communications ship, with limited weaponry. The German personnel bombs fell and shrapnel exploded, cutting through the ship. Two sailors, who left their positions to see the planes overhead, were killed instantly. A fire broke out below. Crewmembers were racing up the stairs from the lower decks to try and escape.

Murray Goldman and his team had already bedded down for the night. As the general alarm sounded, they moved quickly to man their stations on the ship. Crew members awakened by the alarm ran, some tripping as they tried to get their pants on. Others ran without shirts or shoes. Below deck no one knew what was happening, but they all knew their lives were in jeopardy.

The German pilots circled and made two passes at the Catoctin. The screams of men injured as the bombs landed could be heard through the ship. As men ran up the stairs, one grabbed Murray and warned him not to go below. A fire was raging in the lower decks, near the ship's boilers. Murray pushed the man aside and headed down toward the fire.

Murray Goldman understood the danger to the ship. He was determined to help stop it. He walked quickly down the steps, as sailors ran past him in growing numbers to reach the top of the ship. Dick Riordan and Steve O'Malley followed close behind.

A fire below ship was beyond anyone's comprehension. There was little room to move around below ship. Murray motioned for Riordan and O'Malley to get whatever fire equipment they could find. Murray knew they had to reach the boiler room, if they were going to avoid a major catastrophe. With hoses and buckets the men organized other members of the crew to work together, so they could get enough water down to the area by the boiler room.

The heat from the fire was intense. Murray knew he had little time to shut the boilers down and avoid an explosion deep within the ship. Lives were at stake. An explosion below would likely sink the Catoctin. The only option was to get through the fire and reach the main valves controlling the boiler.

The hair on his arms was gone and he was burned in several places, as he raced through the narrow corridor of fire. He had not thought about how he would get out, once the boiler was shut down. He reached the wheel of the main valve. He grabbed wet towels to throw on the wheel and turned it with all his strength. At first, the wheel would not budge. Murray backed off. He could feel the heat from the fire in the wheel. Several more attempts would prove unsuccessful. Sweat was pouring off of him. He wiped his brow with the back of his hand. He grabbed a long piece of pipe to use as a lever, placing it through the wheel. With his foot firmly placed against the wall, Murray pulled the pipe with everything he had left to give. He heard a creaking sound and the main valve slowly started to turn. Again, he pulled. Finally, he was able to shut the boiler down.

But as he turned back toward the corridor, the fire was everywhere. He had saved the ship, but how would he save himself? Murray began coughing from the smoke. As he tried to move forward, he could feel the intensity of fire surround him. He backed up to decide his next move. He had only minutes before there would be no way out. He had a choice to make. He started running down the corridor, through the smoke and fire.

About half the distance, he began to feel water cooling off his body. At first, he couldn't tell where the water was coming from. He looked up to see if pipes were leaking, but he kept running as fast as he could. Soon he could feel the water coming more intensely. He realized hoses were spraying the corridor. His team and others had made it down to where Murray was located. He was grateful. Murray smiled and thanked the sailors manning the hoses. He started heading back toward the surface.

Suddenly, another explosion from the German pilots rocked the ship. Murray and his men were thrown from the stairs. They were just one level down from the main deck. Injured men were everywhere.

Above ship, there was chaos. Small fires had broken out on deck. Men were being carried from below, many with serious injuries. It would be several hours before calm returned to ship. Murray soon reemerged on deck. He was carrying a young sailor in his arms. Murray's face and arms were now black from soot. His t-shirt was covered in blood. Murray was coughing from the smoke, as he struggled to reach the main deck. Other sailors ran to help Murray, but they could see it was too late. The young sailor had died in Murray's arms. The sailors on deck tried to pry Murray's arms loose. Murray refused to let him go. He knew the boy was gone, but Murray could not bear it. By the end of that night, six men on Catoctin had died and 31 were wounded from the attack.

Murray and his team were successful in stopping the fire near the boilers. Their effort had averted a calamity for the ship, but there was no celebration. They had simply done their job, as they saw it. Men had died that night. They were thankful to survive the attack.

The mood on Catoctin turned solemn and gray in the weeks ahead. The Allies has pushed the Germans north in France. The Eighth Fleet was spread across the Balearic and Tyvrhenian Seas. The Catoctin was not a war ship. The sailors thought the ship was an unlikely target for attack. How could this happen to us? How could so many good men die? Through young eyes, the cause of war seems just. The cost of war is never fully contemplated.

It would take time for the men and the ship to heal. Sailors couldn't stop talking about the wounded. Everyone knew someone who was injured in the attack. The worst of the injuries were transferred to an Army medical facility ashore in Toulon. The Commander of the Catoctin yearned to give his sailors shore leave.

In an effort to lift their spirits, the Commander held a ceremony to single out and recognize two dozen men for their quick action and bravery under enemy fire. Murray would receive a commendation and a promotion. Both Riordan and O'Malley would also receive commendations.

Murray would now receive the title of Ship Fitter, with three stripes, which was just below the title of Master Chief. He would say nothing to his own team or his friends aboard ship. Murray could not help thinking about the young sailor who died in his arms. He did not know the sailor before that night. In time, he realized he might not remember his name. But as he held him in his arms, Murray had felt the young boy's last breath. He was just gone so quickly, Murray thought over and over again. This was one life he could never forget.

After the ceremony on the quarterdeck, Murray left his friends and headed below ship. He walked below until he found an isolated area near the galley. His eyes welled up with tears. He could hold his grief no longer. His thoughts raced through his mind. He wondered if Franny was ok? He wondered if he'd ever see her again. Was his family ok? He could not erase the picture in his mind of that young sailor. Who would tell this sailor's family? How would life ever be normal again?

Murray, who had always been stoic in the face of tragedy, cried quietly. Then, as he heard men coming toward the galley, he hid his face in a handkerchief and blew his nose. It was not his nature to show emotion. But now, Murray began to appreciate how tentative and unpredictable life could be. This feeling would nag him.

CHAPTER 34

Toulon

The attack on the Catoctin was the last by German pilots. As the Allies pushed north, the German threat eased. Some pockets of German resistance remained, but the taking of Marseilles and Toulon gave the Allies the needed supply route to kill or capture the remaining German forces in France.

After repairs were made to the ship, the Catoctin reached Toulon in early September. The French army had liberated this port city several weeks prior. With the Germans gone, Catoctin docked and gave its sailors their first shore leave.

Just as in Naples, the sailors found a warm welcome. There was plenty of kissing and hugging between French citizens and U.S. sailors. Murray left the ship with his team from the Repair division. They headed for the biggest bar, best food and the loudest music.

Murray ate and drank with his team. They joked with him about being such an old guy, until the music started. Murray, like all the men, just wanted to let go. He went over to a French girl and asked her to dance. Buster Johnson was bent over laughing, as Murray tossed and twirled the girl over his shoulders and between his legs. Tony Marano was no slouch on the dance floor. He grabbed a girl and joined Murray. The group partied for hours.

Murray left his young team at the bar. He was headed back to the ship, when he ran into Leo Mitchell and Jeff Katz. Much to Sid Mayer's delight, he found his minion of ten Jewish men on the Catoctin. He also found that Murray could lead Jewish services for the men, while they were aboard ship. The men would gather on a Saturday, if conditions permitted, and pray together.

Murray had gotten to know this group very well. When Leo and Jeff saw Murray, they pulled him aside in the street to talk. Leo and Jeff had found a Jewish family in Toulon that had been hiding from the Nazis. The thought of finding Jewish survivors was not lost on Murray. It was late, but he asked Leo to take him to this family.

Michel Dumas and his wife, Claire, had been hiding with their two children in the attic of a building near the outskirts of Toulon. Their non-Jewish neighbors had saved them, when the Nazis came through the town searching for Jews. Since that time, the neighbors would bring them what little food they could find. The family never left the attic, for almost two years. On occasion, they would sneak down to their neighbor and wash themselves. Their children, Luc and Avril, were old enough to understand the daily danger they faced, if discovered.

It was more than three weeks, since the liberation of Toulon had freed the Dumas family. Slowly, they were eating again and gaining strength. All of them looked gaunt. Their neighbors celebrated their freedom with them. They helped Michel and Claire reclaim their apartment lower down in the building, though there was little left of their possessions. Luc and Avril were happy to sleep without fear once again. At night, the family would gather around what was left of their damaged dining room table and thank God for saving them.

Murray spoke very little French. When he arrived at the Dumas apartment, he was relieved to find that Jeff Katz was pretty fluent. Murray could see the family had been through a difficult time. There were stories in the Jewish community, whether you were in New York or among soldiers fighting at the front, about the Nazi treatment of Jews. Murray was shocked hearing the first-hand accounts by Dumas family. He asked Michel if there was enough food and clothing. He promised to bring supplies and money to help the family.

Back on the Catoctin, Murray Goldman was determined to keep his promise. He was able to collect some money from his Repair team and from the Jewish sailors on the ship. He then called in a favor from a friend in the ship's galley. With two duffle bags of food and clothing from the ship's supply room, Murray was ready to return.

The Jewish high holidays would begin in a week, with the Jewish New Year of Rosh Hashanah. Murray was excited. This holiday represented a time of renewal. He had been troubled by the death of sailors on the Catoctin. He didn't talk about it, but he could not let it go. Finding the Dumas family and understanding their struggle to survive gave Murray purpose—and it gave him hope. He asked Leo, Jeff Katz, Sid Mayer and four other sailors to help him sneak food and clothing off the ship.

They arrived at Michel's apartment with bags of surprises for the Dumas family. As Claire Dumas was emptying the food, she stood in the dining area and began to cry uncontrollably. In her hand was the biggest bar of butter she had ever seen. It had been three years since Claire had seen butter. Michel went to comfort her, but soon joined her with tears of joy. He wiped his tears with his sleeve. He motioned to the sailors to come to the dining table and eat with them. The sailors were nearly settled, when Michel stood up to say a Hebrew blessing over the wine and bread. The Dumas family had little except the clothing they wore, but they were alive.

He asked Jeff to thank Murray and all of the Americans for their generosity. With that, Michel raised his glass, "nous sommes reconnaissants d'être en vie et pour célébrer cette fête avec vous." Jeff leaned over to his fellow sailors and interpreted, 'we are grateful to be alive and to celebrate with you."

After dinner, Murray called Luc and Avril over to the table. He gave Avril his white Navy hat. She was a shy 10-year old and the hat was very large, but she smiled and thanked him. Sid came over. Her turned the hat inside out and placed it back on Avril. The men joined in laughter as the hat nearly covered her face.

Murray had guessed that Luc Dumas must be near 12 or 13 years old. As Luc came over, Murray held out a dark blue bag. Luc immediately recognized it was a Tallit bag. But it wasn't any Tallit bag, it had been with Murray since his Bar Mitzvah. Jeff Katz explained to Luc the significance of this gift. Michel immediately shook his head. He explained this was a gift neither he nor Luc could accept. Murray slowly raised his hand to cut off the conversation. He asked Jeff to explain in French how important it was for Luc to keep his Tallit. "I do not have children," he said to Michel. "But I hope someday to have a son like your Luc. I want him to know about something more than war."

The sailors weren't certain how many Jews in Europe would survive. Clearly, everyone knew about German atrocities. Luc might never wear his Tallit or have a Bar Mitzvah. Still, Murray felt Luc would remember this visit by a group of Americans. For him, it was more than just restoring Luc's faith as a Jew, he wanted him to restore his faith in people.

Luc took the Tallit bag from Murray, after his father, Michel, told him it was ok. Luc turned to walk away and then stopped. He looked back at Murray and in French said, "Thank you. Thank you for helping my family. We are here to see another day. I will not forget this night." Murray didn't understand everything Luc said, but the boy ran to him and hugged him. That was enough.

The dinner with the Dumas family ran late into the evening. Soon the sailors would be rushing back to the ship. Murray promised Michel he would continue to send money to his family. Murray kept this promise for several years, even after coming home from the war.

A week after leaving Toulon, Sid Mayer could hear the PA system call out, "Goldman to the quarterdeck. Goldman to the quarterdeck."

Mayer couldn't figure out why Goldman was needed so quickly after leaving port. The ship still needed work from the damage it suffered, but none of that seemed to require Goldman. The thought crossed his mind about the dinner they all attended in Toulon with the Dumas family. Murray Goldman certainly bent, if not broke the rules, when he took food and clothing from a U.S. ship, during a time of war.

Mayer saw Jeff Katz and asked if he knew why they called for Goldman. Katz shrugged, though he, too, wondered about the dinner. Katz hoped he and the others would not soon be joining their friend on the quarterdeck.

Hours would go by, well into the afternoon, before anyone saw Murray Goldman. His Repair Division team was also growing concerned that no one saw or heard from him. Anthony Marano and Steve O'Malley finally caught a glimpse of Murray, as he walked back to his bunk on the ship. They called out to him, but he did not turn around or stop to talk.

Later that evening, Marano found out Murray had been court-martialed for taking clothing and food from the Catoctin, without permission. An officer, Ensign Robert Conmy, told Marano that the Commander was lenient with Goldman, because of the bravery he demonstrated when Catoctin was attacked. The Commander also considered how valuable Goldman had been in helping resolve major repairs on the ship.

Conmy told Marano that Goldman was demoted to Seaman first class, a significant drop in rank but he didn't get a cut in pay. The Ensign didn't want to penalize Murray's family at home in the U.S. Goldman was confined to his quarters for a week. Conmy explained the Commander was pissed Goldman wouldn't tell him who helped him take the food and clothing off ship.

Marano was pleased to hear his friend Murray didn't get more severe punishment. He spread the news among their team and Dick Riordon made certain that Jeff Katz told his friends.

Jeff, Leo and the other Jewish sailors were also relieved to hear Murray had not given them up at the court-martial. They all felt he had done the right thing in helping the Dumas family in Toulon. If he had to give their names during the court-martial, they, too, would have accepted the consequences.

As he laid in his bunk down below ship, Murray was not remorseful. He knew he was breaking the law when he took the food and clothing. But his conscience could not bear what he saw in Toulon. He'd do it again. The title meant nothing to him. He had to be true to himself. He made his decision without regret. A man had to find his own voice in the darkness of war.

He wished he could have done more. His eyes stared off in the distance. He wondered how many more people there might be like the Dumas family. Then he closed his eyes and went to sleep.

His confinement went quickly. While he was allowed his regular meals, his team and his friends would sneak Murray cookies or fruit. He didn't really need the extra food, but he realized it was their way of affirming their respect for him and their support for the decisions he made. These lessons about being your own person were not lost on them.

CHAPTER 35

Sailors on Leave

The Catoctin returned to Naples at the end of September 1944 and remained there until January 1945. As they entered the bay of Naples, the crew could see several sunken German war cruisers from the invasion of Italy. The Catoctin moved slowly through the debris field, before reaching port.

The news on the war was increasingly positive. The Allied forces in Europe were making great strides in pushing the Germans back. Paris and Florence had been liberated. The Soviet army was closing in on Warsaw and they had crossed the border into Romania. The end of the war in Europe was in sight. However, the news of Japanese Kamikaze pilots crashing into

American ships was not lost on the Catoctin crew. The word from the Pacific was that the fighting was fierce with many casualties, but the Americans were pushing ahead.

Naples was a welcome sight for the sailors. While the ship still needed repairs from the attack in August, the Commander knew they'd be in port for three months. The ship leave policy would be liberal. The men would get to celebrate the Christmas holidays in southern Italy.

Weeks passed in Naples. The Repair Division had demanding work schedules to complete. But if you weren't scheduled, you could go ashore and spend days touring this port city. The men would always travel in small groups of two and three, a lesson not forgotten from Algiers.

At night, sailors would congregate at local bars and trattorias. Romano's was a large and favorite restaurant and bar, with music and a small dance floor. Sailors could meet young Italian women at Romano's. On a Friday and Saturday, a crowd filled the place.

Murray Goldman walked the city of Naples. He learned some Italian greetings, so he could make his way through the town. He enjoyed going to the open markets on Wednesdays and Fridays. The signs of war were every-where, but the Italian people were warm and welcoming. They were already trying to put the war behind them. To their delight, American sailors were ready and willing to spend money.

He first saw Cosima di Benetto at the Farmer's Market. He had been strolling around town. He came upon an open plaza. Spread across tables, farmers were selling anything they could grow to make money. For a sailor, the sight of fruit was a special treat. Murray walked along the rows of tables, which also included vegetables, nuts and bread.

He stopped to buy apples at one stand. He waited in line. Cosima had just paid for melons and turned to leave. The bag ripped. A melon and several lemons spilled onto the ground. Cosima bent to pick up the fruit. A large hand reached down next to her, "can I help"? Murray went to help scoop up the fruit. Cosima seemed totally embarrassed. Her eyes kept looking everywhere but at Murray. Finally, they both stood up.

Cosima was about five foot six inches tall, with thick black hair and dark eyes. She was not skinny. Her Capri pants fit tightly against her hips. Her breasts pushed out at the button of the V-shape where her blouse opened. Murray's first thought was she was quite voluptuous.

Still embarrassed, Cosima thanked Murray for his help. He was taken aback that she could speak English, though her accent was strong. Cosima finally stopped looking down or away. Her first glance was at the tall, large frame of a man that stood in front of her. Eventually, she looked straight into his eyes. She couldn't get over his strong features. He could have been

Roman, except for the nose that had clearly been broken. Or, he could just as easily have been from Sicily, with his olive skin tone.

Her faced blushed as she thanked Murray for coming to her rescue. They walked together through the row of tables. They both spoke hesitantly, trying to determine if they could understand each other. Soon Cosima became more at ease. Murray was not like other sailors she had met. He was not pushy. He did not say things that appeared to be false compliments or attempts to flatter her. He asked her about life in Naples. He seemed genuinely interested in learning what it was like before the Germans left.

Cosima was surprised, in conversation, he freely mentioned he was married. He talked about his wife back home and how much he missed New York. Cosima was also married. Her husband was a soldier in the Italian army and fighting in the north. She had not heard from him in many months. As they walked, they talked about the difficulties of war. Cosima was happy the Germans were gone.

Murray and Cosima left the plaza and walked down a narrow street. The sun was bright. The shade from the buildings provided some relief. At the end of the street, he asked Cosima if she'd like to stop at the café on the corner. She hesitated, but then agreed. Their conversation was slow. Neither of them was in a rush. They talked about their spouses and families. Each of them was aware they were sharing information with a total stranger. But war is a lonely place. Maybe the only place where a stranger can be your best friend.

After an hour, he told Cosima he would leave her so she could finish her errands and go home. At first, she was taken aback, as if maybe he was bored or didn't like the conversation. Soon, it came to her. He was simply being a gentleman. She expected, based on her previous experience with Americans that he would ask her out. Being married did not stop the Americans. But she realized he was not like the others and she regretted jumping to that conclusion.

Murray thanked Cosima for talking with him. He joked that being away from home for almost 18 months, with a bunch of sailors much younger than himself was not always the best company. He told her he enjoyed meeting her and hoped their paths would cross again.

She had not had someone to talk to in a long time. Her husband, Franco, had been gone for two years. Cosima's family lived near Tuscany in the north. Most of the time, she kept to herself in Naples. As Cosima watched him leave, she wondered if they would see each other again. The fact that they were both married gave Cosima comfort. The thought of making a new friend with an American sailor intrigued her.

A few weeks passed by before he ran into Cosima again. He was sitting at a café trying to read an old newspaper. Cosima could tell it was Murray from across the plaza. She had been taking her morning stroll through the neighborhood. She wasn't certain why, but instead of turning on the next street Cosima kept walking toward him.

Murray had not looked up, until Cosima said hello. He jumped up, somewhat surprised to see her again. He invited her to join him and waved to the waiter. In his worst Italian, he asked,

"Can we order two cappuccinos?"

"Well, this is a nice surprise," he said.

Cosima was wearing a light-yellow dress. The sun loved Italian women on a warm day. The sunlight cut through the dress and showed every contour of her body. Murray wasn't looking, and yet he couldn't help but notice. He smiled to himself.

"I walk this way every day," she told him, turning and pointing to the plaza.

They sat for almost an hour talking. Neither one of them were anxious to end the conversation or leave. Cosima described about how beautiful it was in Tuscany, especially near Siena. She so missed her family. She worried about the fighting continuing in the north. She had lots of questions to ask him about America. What was New York City like? Were there any Italians living in New York? Murray laughed. He realized that if you didn't live in America, you would never understand Italians could be found in every city.

Murray was looking around to see if the waiters wanted them to leave. In New York, the manager of a restaurant would come to your table and tell you people were waiting for the table by now. Cosima explained that a café in Italy would never ask customers to leave. You could sit there all day after drinking one cappuccino and no one would say anything.

Soon, Cosima got an idea and she motioned to him. They left the café and walked for twenty minutes, talking as she led him through side streets. He didn't have a clue where they were headed, but the day was warm and Murray felt very relaxed. He had not been this laid back in a long time. It was almost hard to forget there was a war going on.

They paused at a street, as she tried to remember the right place to turn. She quickly got her bearings and pointed for them to go down a narrow and shaded walkway. He could feel a cool breeze coming toward them. As they reached the end of the street, they came upon a clearing. The sun was bright and before them stood the horseshoe shaped bay of Naples.

Cosima stood back waiting to see Murray's reaction. He shook his head and smiled at the beauty of the sun shimmering across the aqua green colored water. Closer to the right side of the bay, he could see where war ships were docked. On the left, the bay was filled with small fishing vessels. Across the bay, in the distance, she pointed out the city of Sorrento, which sat along the coast.

He sat with her on a bench overlooking the bay. She pointed across the water and talked about Sorrento and Positano. "Out in that direction was the Amalfi coast, one of the most beautiful areas of Italy," Cosima explained. "It's difficult driving there. The roads along the coast had been damaged from Allied bombings."

"Would you take me there?" he asked. "I may not get this chance again."

Cosima was surprised by his sudden and forward request, but she realized he was just reacting to her long description of the coast. All he wanted was a friend to spend time with. He wanted to experience Italy with someone who could help him appreciate the landscape and the history.

Another three weeks would go by. Murray and Cosima would meet more regularly, whenever he could get shore leave. Their friendship grew. The conversations became more familiar. She took him to different parts of Naples and along the coast toward Pozzuoli and Bacoli. She borrowed an old car from a neighbor for the ride to Bacoli.

These sightseeing trips would be filled with laughter and stories about their families. As their friendship grew, their ability to communicate improved as well. She was surprised to learn about the nightclubs Murray described in New York and his days as a boxer. At times, their time together turned serious, as they each confided their fears about the war. Cosima had lost a cousin in the war. He was only 20 years old.

Murray never overstepped the boundary lines he had set down in his own mind. Cosima was beautiful. He valued the friendship. He missed Franny terribly. Since the attack on his ship, he worried if he'd make it back to Brooklyn. The Allies were making good progress, but it was only a matter of time before the Catoctin set sail. What if the rumors were true about them heading for the Pacific?

She felt totally at ease with Murray, as if she knew him for years. In Italy, it was not respectable for a married woman to be seen with another man. She didn't care. He was someone she could spend time with and escape the loneliness of war. She prayed her Franco would return to her. Her first waking moments of the day were spent looking out her apartment window and hoping Franco would be coming up the stairs, near the garden below.

By December, the holiday mood was taking over on the Catoctin and in the city of Naples. Everyone wanted to be somewhere else, but the sailors would make the best of the season. The cafes and bars were filled with revelers.

Cosima had arranged to go with Murray by bus to Sorrento. He worked double shifts for a week, so he could get an overnight pass off the ship. They could reach Sorrento in two hours, but she insisted they stay overnight to enjoy the city during the holiday season. "The lights in Sorrento at night were so beautiful."

He arranged to meet her early on a Saturday morning, before the nine o'clock bus arrived. He sat and waited, but she did not show up. It was not like her to be late. Murray waited until ten thirty. Something must be wrong, he told himself.

He left the bus station and walked to Cosima's apartment. He had only been there once before, when he walked her home after dinner one night. He remembered it overlooked a plaza, near the café with the orange sign on top.

He made his way to her home in about twenty minutes. The widows in the apartment were open. She must be there. He climbed the stairs to the third level and knocked on the door. No one answered. He knocked again, but still no one answered. He went to turn the doorknob, but it opened before he could reach it.

Cosima stood there in a nightgown. Her hair was frizzy and her eyes were red. As Murray entered the apartment, she leaned against the door and slowly slid to the floor crying. "Cosima, what's wrong? What happened," he asked. She struggled to speak, but the words would not cross her lips. Soon, she fought to catch her breath, as she cried uncontrollably.

Murray reached down to lift Cosima up off the floor. She fought his arms. Her head lurched from side to side. She began to wail, as she threw her body against the wall. Her night gown clung to her sweat soaked body. She crawled along the floor.

Once again, he tried to pick her up. She could not be consoled. He sat down on the floor next to her. He waited for her to calm herself. Eventually, she let him put his arm on her shoulders.

"It's ok, Cosima. It's ok," Murray said over and over again. She lay quietly for a minute. "He's gone. He's gone…," her voice trailed off. Cosima lifted her left arm and held out the crumbled piece of paper that communicated her husband's death. "My Franco was killed two days ago."

She cried quietly in his arms. He didn't move for fifteen minutes. Soon there was silence. Murray picked Cosima up and carried her into bed. Her body trembled. She must have been awake half the night. He calmly put her down, but she would not let go of his arms. "I'm here, Cosima. I won't leave you," he told her. "Please don't let go of me," she begged.

He sat down on the bed beside Cosima. She buried her head in his chest, with his arms wrapped around her shoulder. Murray eventually dozed off. They would sleep for two hours.

Cosima woke, still in his arms. Franco had been away for such a long time, she almost forgot what it was like to be in a man's arms. Franco was gone now. He was not coming back, as she had hoped. She would never know the firmness of his embrace, the touch of his hand on her breast, his soft kisses down her stomach. Her memories of Franco were already hazy. How could she survive? She was alone.

As she gazed out the window, Murray woke and tried to comfort her. "Cosima, I'm so sorry. I don't have words. I know how difficult this is." Cosima sat up. Her bloodshot eyes looked at Murray. She reached to kiss him. Murray instinctively pulled back. He was dumbstruck. She turned toward him. He paused for a moment. He looked into her eyes. Tears began to well up again. He leaned toward her and kissed her forehead. "Please Murray, please. If you're my friend and you really care about me," said Cosima, "please make love to me." She cried again uncontrollably. "Why can't I die? I am dead without Franco. I am lost to the world" He could taste the salt of her tears, as he pulled her close in his arms.

Murray wanted to find some way to calm her. They had talked so often about their fears. War is war. He knew more than anyone what she had lost. Suddenly, Cosima reached up to kiss Murray again. He turned his head to avoid looking in her eyes. This was not right he thought, but he could not ignore her pain.

He kissed her slowly at first and then increasingly more passionately. Maybe he felt this way toward her all along. He would never have crossed this boundary with her, but at this moment he wanted her as much as she wanted him. Was its Franco's death? Was it the uncertainty of war? Could either of them imagine life beyond this moment?

They could not stop kissing. Cosima's passion had lost control. Clothes fell to the floor. In bed, her hands would grab Murray's hair. She would pull and push, as his hips became more forceful. There would be long pauses, as they each fell back into the bed to rest. Neither one of them wanted this moment to end. They took turns reaching out, to hold each other, to make love, until there just wasn't any energy left between them.

After sleeping the day away, they woke in each other's arms. Their bodies separated. This wasn't the beginning of a relationship. It was the end. Life doesn't give us everything we want. No one owns love. We rarely get to experience that passion and reckless abandonment for more than short intervals in our lives. Perhaps, what matters most is the lasting nature of those moments. They stay with us. They fill the voids when we need them. They give us the inspiration to continue, even after we lose love.

Franco would not be coming home. He had not lost sight of his own commitment back home. But for a brief moment, Cosima and Murray both found hope in each other's arms.

By late afternoon, he had showered and left Cosima's apartment. She watched out the window, as he walked across the Plaza. Her thoughts turned back to her husband. She had waited so long for Franco to come home. Her life, as she knew it, was over. She sat at the kitchen table dabbing the tears from her eyes. She could not bear to eat. The picture of Cosima and Franco's wedding stood on the counter. He was her first and only love. Her heart ached.

Soon she tired. She took the picture into the bedroom and held it to her heart until she fell asleep.

Murray walked for hours after leaving Cosima. He could not imagine her pain. He wondered what Franny might have done, if he had been killed during the German attack on his ship. When death comes for you, he imagined, you try convincing yourself the person you love is strong enough to eventually move on. But what if that's not true, he wondered? How do you let go of someone? How would Cosima survive the loss of her husband?

It was getting late so he headed back to the ship. He had not taken the overnight liberty as planned. He felt a new determination to get home. He wished the war would end and life could be normal again. He laid in his bunk, staring off into space, until his eyes closed.

Christmas week the Catoctin announced a rotation schedule, which allowed all sailors one day to celebrate the holiday in Naples. For the Italians, it was the first holiday season without German occupation. The mood in the city was very festive.

Murray had not seen Cosima for ten days. He worried about her, but he wasn't certain if she might have regrets. They had become such good friends. He didn't want to lose that special relationship. What now?

The walk to her apartment seemed so much longer than before. She opened the door part way. Her long dark hair fell on her shoulders. She wore a crisp white blouse. Her eyes were dry, and she wasn't wearing any makeup. She was just so naturally beautiful.

"I'm sorry I haven't come sooner. I didn't know whether I did the right thing, when I was here last. I didn't know if you might need time alone."

Cosima listened. She reached out with her fingers and touched Murray's lips to silence him. Coming from behind the door, she reached up and whispered in his ear.

"I love you Murray. I love you for being with me. I love you for helping me get through this." she kissed him on the cheek.

"Do you want to talk," he asked, as he motioned for them to take a walk.

Cosima got her coat. They walked toward the Bay of Naples. The conversation was like two old friends that had not seen each other in years. She talked about Franco in great detail. She spoke of first love and the remorse of not having his child. She was coming to terms with her grief. Murray felt good when she explained that she could not have survived Franco's death without him. She thanked him for his warmth and loving nature. Only once during their conversation he wondered if she wanted him to stay with her in Naples. But if love can grow from friendship, then perhaps friendships can be reclaimed.

Cosima finally did get to take Murray to Sorrento, the week after Christmas. The town square was decorated with beautiful lights. They walked the streets, stopping occasionally to look inside the shops. Cosima said Sorrento was known for its woodworking artisans, who made the most beautiful inlaid wood designs. In the shops, they found tables, desks and small jewelry boxes with very intricate designs.

Murray walked around the shop, as Cosima talked to the owner. He was an elderly man. Cosima chatted as he worked on a small music box. He told her his small shop had been in his family for more than 80 years. A picture of his father hung on the wall near his workbench. As they left the shop, Murray searched for his sailor hat in his back pocket. He took a backpack off his shoulder and looked inside. He apologized, but he must have left the hat on a table at the shop they visited. He asked Cosima to wait for him at the street corner, while he went back. Nearly ten minutes later, Murray came strolling toward Cosima. His white Navy hat was tilted down across his right eye.

Cosima suggested they go for dinner at her favorite trattoria. Murray ordered calamari and pasta, his favorite. They drank wine and talked the night away. Afterward, they walked back to the house where Cosima had rented a room.

It was the first-time they had been alone together, since they made love at Cosima's apartment. Cosima came to bed in a thin nightgown. Her breasts pushed through the material. Murray wore his sleeveless t-shirt and boxer shorts. At first, they laid in bed staring at each other. They both wanted each other so badly, but then what? How could they ignore the fact that the war would keep them apart? Would Cosima want to wait yet again for another soldier to return to her? And what about Murray's wife? After getting to know Murray the past three months, did Cosima really believe he could leave his wife? Murray was everything she could ever want and yet he was everything she couldn't have. Life is like that, at times.

Cosima turned over and faced the wall. Murray crawled under the covers to get closer to Cosima. He put his long arm around her body and held her close. They would not make love again and he knew this was for the best. He could not get Cosima's lips and body out of his mind, but his heart was in Brooklyn. Cosima pulled Murray's hand to her heart and quickly fell asleep.

Sorrento was a wonderful two days. On the bus headed back to Naples, Murray stared out at the sunken war ships laying sideways in the bay. He was deep in his thoughts about the war.

Cosima was staring at the people on the bus, a mix of locals and some sailors. She was happy to have taken Murray on this trip. However, she realized the time was coming for him to leave. She felt resigned.

CHAPTER 36

Catoctin Sets Sail-Given New Mission

On January 5th, 1945, the Commander of the Catoctin communicated orders to ready the ship to leave Naples. The destination was unknown, but the ship would depart in 10 days.

The Repair Division was kept busy addressing minor and major issues on the ship, before leaving port. Shore leave was more limited now. Murray wasn't certain if he'd get to see Cosima. He spent several days taking on extra assignments, hoping to gain favor with his XO. He wasn't alone.

Tony Marano, from Murray's Repair team, had met and married a young girl from Naples. The entire team was shocked, when Tony finally told them the news. Dick Riordan kept asking him if he was going to hide the girl on the ship, all the way back to America. Tony just waved him off.

He explained to Murray he met Cara Esposito during a shore leave in Naples. Tony had been touring and stopped to visit this beautiful church, which somehow had avoided being hit during the bombing raids. He noticed Cara praying at the church. She was thin and only about five foot two inches, but she had the most angelic face. He asked to walk her home from the church. They hit it off immediately, though she kidded Tony about speaking Italian with such a heavy accent.

Tony met her family and asked her father's permission to see Cara. Mr. Esposito was nearing sixty years old and much older than his wife. He was leery of soldiers, whether Italian or American. He didn't trust their intentions. Moreover, he knew the war was far from being over. He was impressed, however, by Tony's respect for old world customs and values. The more he got to know Tony, he could see his Italian upbringing in America was very much like his own.

Cara and Tony were a natural pairing. He had spent every shore leave over the past three months with her. He promised himself he wasn't going to be one of those sailors, who loves and leaves the girl behind. The couple married Christmas week. Her father was concerned about Cara waiting for Tony and the war to end, but Tony had won him over by the commitment and love he showered on his daughter.

Tony asked Murray for his help. He was desperate to get one more shore leave before the Catoctin left Naples.

A week before the ship left port, Murray approached his XO. The officer told him only 65 men would be granted shore leave that weekend. Murray said he wanted to say goodbye to someone he had met. But if his team could get only one pass, he wanted it to go to Tony Marano. The XO was impressed by Murray's gesture. He shook his head with a smile, when Murray told him Marano had gotten married. The XO had seen too many of these war time marriages, whenever and wherever a ship landed at a port. He often wondered if the women would ever see these men again. "Tell Marano I offered my congratulations," said the XO, "and he will be granted shore leave to say goodbye."

Murray was disappointed that he would not see Cosima again. He had made the decision to give up his chance at shore leave, so Tony could say goodbye. Murray might not admit it, but in many ways he was a romantic. He was happy for Tony. He also hoped the girl would wait for him, after the war.

When he heard the news, Tony ran and hugged Murray. He couldn't stop thanking Murray. You would think Tony had won the lottery. Aside from his comment to the XO, no one on the ship knew about Cosima. Murray told no one.

The next day, Tony Marano left the ship early in the morning to see his wife. The men on shore leave lined up to sign out, before departing the ship. Murray had gone about his business down below. It was early afternoon when he heard the PA announcement, "Goldman to the quarterdeck. Goldman to the quarterdeck."

Murray knew he hadn't gotten into trouble, so he assumed there must be a special work assignment that needed his expertise. When he reached the quarterdeck, his XO was waiting with a piece of paper and a smile. "Goldman, I called in some favors to get this for you. Please make good use of it and go quickly. You must be back here by midnight."

At first, Murray seemed confused. He took the piece of paper and quickly recognized it was a shore leave pass. A hundred questions raced through his mind, but there wasn't enough time. "Thank you, sir. Thank you." He must have thanked his XO several times and then ran back to get a clean uniform on.

Murray ran through the streets of Naples until he was completely out of breath. He reached the plaza where Cosima lived. From the street below, he called her name. Cosima was completely surprised to see Murray from her window. Quickly, she disappeared. Murray waited until she came down. Under her coat, he could tell she was wearing the same yellow dress she had on when they met.

"We don't have much time," Murray explained. "Our ship is leaving in a few days and this was the last chance for sailors to get shore leave."

"I guess we knew this was coming," Cosima replied.

Murray shook his head acknowledging what they both understood and yet they both feared.

"Can we go someplace and talk?" Murray asked.

Cosima and Murray drifted from a cafe to dinner at a local restaurant. They both felt there was so much to say and not enough time. They might never see each other again.

"These past few months have meant so much to me," Murray told her. "I believe the attack on our ship and having someone die in my arms really hit me. I began to wonder if any of us would survive the war? And if we didn't die, could we ever let go of what we witnessed? You may not know this, but you gave me hope. You helped me remember who I am."

Cosima began to cry, as Murray spoke. She knew it was not easy for him to verbally express his feelings, but she had been in his arms. She understood more than anyone, how important they had been to each other.

"It was easy being your friend and even easier to love you," Cosima responded, wiping tears from her eyes. "You may not realize it, but you saved me too. There are many ways to die. The worst is when we die inside, deep inside, but our bodies and our eyes continue to function. I don't know what I'll do when the war is over. I do know that I will have you in my heart, always."

Murray reached for his shoulder bag. He pulled out a gift wrapped in plain brown paper and handed it to Cosima. "What's this?" Cosima asked.

"Something I bought for you when we visited Sorrento," Murray replied.

Cosima unfolded the paper and found a beautiful jewelry box. It had a light natural wood finish and on the top was the inlaid design of a rose. The rose was a soft mauve color.

"Remember when I forgot my hat at the shop?" Murray asked.

Cosima smiled.

"Well, I wanted to get something for you that I hope will remind you of me."

The night was getting late and Murray knew it was time to head back to the ship. He walked Cosima back to her apartment.

"Murray, I think your wife is a very lucky woman," said Cosima.

"I hope you will remember me."

With that, Cosima pulled down on Murray's jacket and kissed him.

Her lips pressed against Murray. She wanted more, but that was not to be.

"I love you. Please take care of yourself," Cosima told him. "You can always write or come visit," though Cosima knew this was unlikely.

She followed Murray down to the plaza and watched as he walked away into the darkness. Her mind drifted off. At least, unlike Franco, the only other man she had loved had not died. For years after the war Murray would remain for Cosima as a reminder of the possibilities in life. He had given her renewed purpose and resolve.

CHAPTER 37
Heading to Yalta

***

The Catoctin left Naples on January 15, 1945. Much to the surprise of the crew, the ship headed east as they reached the Mediterranean Sea. After the Allies took back much of France, it was assumed the Catoctin would head west and north to support the final push in Europe.

Several days later, the Commander and his officers began briefing the men on their new mission. The Catoctin was bound for Sevastopol, a deep port on the Black Sea. It was off the coast of Crimea. The ship would serve as the headquarters for the planning of a war time conference at Yalta, between President Roosevelt, British Prime Minister Winston Churchill and the Russian General Secretary Joseph Stalin.

Stalin had refused to travel further west than Yalta for a meeting with Allied leaders. The conference would be held at the Livadia Palace, which had previously served as a summer home for Nicholas II, the last Russian tsar. Stalin's decision forced President Roosevelt on an arduous two-week journey, traveling eight days aboard the war cruiser, the USS Quincy, boarding an airplane for the 1,200-mile flight to Crimea and then driving 80 miles to Yalta, which took more than four hours over war torn roads.

The coastline around Yalta was not deep enough to accommodate military ships. Both the British and the Americans would send their command ships to a port at Sevastopol and be greeted by Russian troops. War ships like the USS Quincy and the destroyer, USS Murphy would remain at sea. The town of Yalta was a two to three-hour drive from Sevastopol, along the coast.

The Catoctin would reach its destination by January 26 and the crew needed to make the ship ready to receive a sizable advance party of military and non-military personnel. Aside from housing the planners for the upcoming conference, the ship would serve as an offshore hospital and provide food and transportation for various generals and dignitaries.

Sid Mayer was picked, along with two dozen men, to serve as military drivers and escorts. The escorts received early briefings on the details of who would be attending the conference, with drivers assigned to specific personnel. Many of the attendees were in route to Sevastopol already.

After the briefings, the crew was all business. The men went about their tasks quietly and quickly. However, you could feel the undercurrent of nervous energy on the ship. The sailors could sense from what they were told that something historic was about to happen. There had only been one other meeting of the supreme leaders of the Allied forces. Even if Churchill or Stalin never stepped on their ship, Catoctin would be playing a role in deciding the future of the war.

The journey to Sevastopol would take ten days. The preparations were well underway. Daily briefing meetings were held with the Commander to review the different logistical responsibilities on the ship and the command protocol crew members would follow.

Five days out of port, the Commander shared the news with his direct reports that following the conference at Yalta, President Roosevelt would be staying on the Catoctin for one night before returning home. The officers sat stunned. Who could have ever imagined the President of the United States would visit their ship, and do so in the middle of the war.

The Commander explained the President was traveling with his daughter, Anna, so additional planning had to be completed. Two hours after briefing the officers, the PA system rang out a familiar announcement, "Goldman to the quarterdeck. Goldman to the quarterdeck."

Murray Goldman, like everyone else on Catoctin, was working tirelessly to prepare the ship for the mission in Sevastopol.

He was below ship when the announcement came. Buster Johnson, on his team, walked down to Murray and tapped him on the shoulder. "Murray, the XO is calling you," Buster told him.

"Maybe they need a plumber to help at the war conference."

Murray smiled. He was used to the give and take among his team members. He tried to set the tone with his own dry and off beat sense of humor.

Murray reached the quarterdeck only to find that instead of his immediate XO, the Commander of the ship was waiting to talk with him. "Goldman, I just briefed the officers. The crew does not know it yet, but I've been informed by central command that President Roosevelt plans to visit the Catoctin and stay overnight after his meetings in Yalta.

Now, you may or may not know it, but the President is not well. At this point, he's pretty much bound to a wheelchair. This is not to be shared with anyone. I need you to figure out how to build a bathroom on ship for the President and to get cool air pumped into his room. Can you do that for your Commander-in-Chief?"

Murray stood silent. He listened intently. There was nothing funny about this request from the ship's Commander.

"Sir, I will do my very best to make the President comfortable," Murray replied.

The sailors on Catoctin were not versed in the large-scale politics of the upcoming Yalta conference. They understood, however, the war might soon be coming to an end in Europe. They instinctively didn't trust the Russians. The meetings at Yalta would decide how to restore control in Europe, once Germany surrendered.

Murray didn't concern himself with the scuttlebutt or speculation about the Yalta meetings. He had been given a mission. In his mind, he had very little time and he would be single minded in his purpose. He was determined to do his best for the President's visit.

To complete his assignment in the short time he was given would be demanding. It would require construction and plumbing, some of which wasn't normally possible on a ship. Since the President was in a wheelchair, Murray needed to give the President and his aides as much accessibility as possible.

Murray was aware that a second crew from Catoctin had been asked to build a 400-foot-long wooden ramp, which would allow the President to be brought aboard the ship. It was suggested that a simpler approach would be to hoist the President onto the ship using a small crane, but the President said no. He could not abide that image. Even as his health declined, Roosevelt wanted to project a wartime image of a vibrant leader, determined to protect what he saw as the greatest nation on earth.

He pulled his team together and he briefed them on the Commander's request. He knew the news of a visit by Roosevelt would leak out, but he asked his team not to be the source of those leaks. Murray used a small area below ship to begin making the parts and cutting pipe. He received permission to cut through a metal wall, so the space for Roosevelt was enlarged. His mission was to create the first handicapped bathroom ever built on a Navy vessel.

The Catoctin reached Sevastopol on January 25, but the Commander waited until morning before allowing anyone to board or disembark from the ship. A Captain in the Russian army, with a contingent of soldiers, could be seen waiting at the port. The Russian army controlled all of Crimea. The Americans were now in their territory and they expected them to follow their direction.

The Captain boarded Catoctin and was greeted by the XO. Immediately, it was clear that neither one of them spoke the same language. The XO motioned for one of his subordinates. "Get him down here as quickly as you can," said the XO.

Soon the PA system was as loud as it's ever been, "Goldman to the quarterdeck. Goldman to the quarterdeck."

Murray was working in the stateroom they were building for Roosevelt. His men were drilling holes when the PA system first rang out. The sounds of construction below ship were deafening. A second PA announcement was sounded. Sid Mayer knew where Murray was working. He ran down the corridor and entered the room.

Sid alerted Murray to the announcement and followed him up to the quarterdeck, where an impatient Captain of the Russian soldiers was pacing back and forth. Mayer knew Murray could speak several languages, at least enough to get through basic greetings and simple instructions. With a boat-load of young sailors from Alabama, Arkansas, Mississippi, Oklahoma, Nebraska, the older guy from New York was likely the XO's best option.

After speaking to the XO, Murray looked at Sid. He walked over to the Russian and smiled. The Russian did not smile back. He was a large barrel-chested man, maybe six-foot inches tall and 240 pounds. He had a large mustache. Murray figured he better get on with it.

"Sprechen Sie Deutsch?" Murray asked.

The Russian Captain just stared at Murray. A harsh frown grew across his face.

Murray tried again, "Capite italiano?"

The soldier very slowly shook his head no.

"Parlez-vous français?

Nothing.

At this point, Murray turned to Sid Mayer.

'Sid, you have any ideas ?' Mayer shrugged his shoulders and shook his head.

Murray turned back to the Russian and figured he'd give it one last try. 'Farshteyst Yiddish ?' Murray asked.

The Russian soldier perked up. His eyes opened wide.

Murray repeated his question, 'Farshteyst Yiddish?'

The Captain began to smile. He then reached out and grabbed Murray by his arms and gave him a big bear hug.

Sid Mayer started laughing. He turned toward the XO and told him not to worry, the Russian soldier was Jewish. Murray had found a common language between east and west, and it was Yiddish.

After Murray's exchange with the Russian Captain, relations between the ship's crew and the Russian troops became easier. The Captain ordered his men to provide the Catoctin's XO with whatever supplies and support that was needed. A group of Russian soldiers were assigned to guide Navy escorts. The escorts were driving military and state department officials from the ship to the Livadia Palace.

The meetings at Yalta would run from February 4 – 11, 1945. Each of the world leaders at the conference had their own agenda of issues. The Russians were in a very strong bargaining position. The British and American troop progress in pushing through Italy and France had forced Germany to direct its forces west, leaving the eastern front with Russia with less resistance. The Germans had long lost the territorial gains they achieved in Russia. However, there was no forgetting or forgiving the nearly 25 million Russians killed defending their homeland. The Germans underestimated the strength and resolve of the Russian people. By the time of the Yalta conference, Russian troops were now only 40 miles from Berlin.

The British were keenly aware that Russia wanted to take back and control as much of Eastern Europe as possible. While the British would return to their small island, once Germany surrendered, Churchill feared the Russians would fill the power vacuum and seize control of countries bordering Germany. He believed fascism would be replaced by a Russian communist dictatorship.

But the Americans had a different set of issues on their plate. The war in Europe was virtually over, but the war with Japan still raged on with thousands of daily U.S. casualties. Roosevelt and his military advisors wanted the Russians to join its war with Japan and provide a second front. The Americans needed to end the war in the Pacific as quickly as possible. Roosevelt also wanted Russia's support to create the United Nations.

At the conclusion of Yalta, it would seem that everyone won something and lost something. Stalin gained support for his plan to help oversee countries in Eastern Europe after the war, though his true intentions for control wouldn't become clear until it was too late. Roosevelt gained a commitment from Russia to join its fight with Japan. But Roosevelt had to settle for Stalin's commitment without a timetable. Churchill was likely the most frustrated of the group, since he would return home unable to convince the Americans of the future threat posed by Russia.

It was obvious to everyone at Yalta that Roosevelt was very ill. His eyes were sunken and he lacked the vitality that he so often projected. His aides worked tirelessly to help Roosevelt, though they made certain their efforts were not readily visible to other conference participants.

Roosevelt was the only world leader allowed to stay at the Livadia Palace, where the Yalta discussions were held. Churchill chose to stay 20 minutes away at the Vorontzov Palace, a larger compound built in the mid-1800s and architecturally designed by an English man.

The Catoctin had prepared for Roosevelt's arrival on February 11th. On the bumpy three-hour drive from Yalta to Sevastopol, the President would occasionally stop to view the devastation of war. In the port city of Sevastopol only remnants of buildings could be found. There were miles and miles of ruins. Walls could be seen, but no single building was left intact.

As the President's car rounded the bend in the road, there stood the USS Catoctin. The ships full complement of sailors were dressed for the President's visit and stood along the ships rails to greet their Commander-in-Chief. The visit had been planned as a gesture by the President to rally the morale of sailors. However, the sailors on the Catoctin had a surprise of their own. Once the President's car reached the dock, the sailors unleashed a moment of uncharacteristic behavior. The cheering was deafening and a sea of waving white sailor hats dominated the landscape. The President was gaunt and clearly exhausted by the journey from Yalta, but the loud greeting buoyed his spirits. As he was helped from the car, he waved to the sailors. Everyone could see the famous Roosevelt smile.

A second wave of cheering followed. Finally, the PA system restored order and the sailors returned to their duties. The President was eventually brought aboard ship, up the long wooden ramp that had been built while the Catoctin was in port. The President was greeted by the ship's Commander, joined by a line of senior military officers.

Hours would pass before the gala dinner that was planned for President Roosevelt. After a week of Russian food, the President, his daughter Anna and other dignitaries were looking forward to a steak dinner aboard Catoctin. This dinner was no small undertaking.

The President had taken a brief tour, after boarding the ship. He met with the Commander of the Catoctin and completed several short meetings with his military and personal staff. At his daughter's insistence, the President then retired to his room for some rest before dinner.

The sailors on Catoctin were beyond jubilant. This was a day they would forever remember. No one really thought about the discussions at Yalta. For these men, many from very humble backgrounds, seeing the President was a story for the ages.

Murray Goldman was working down below ship, when he heard the all-too-familiar PA announcement, "Goldman to the quarterdeck. Goldman to the quarterdeck."

Murray was in his blue denim work shirt, but he didn't think it mattered. With a ship full of dignitaries, he assumed something was not working and it needed his attention.

It was near dinnertime, when Murray reached the quarterdeck. The XO greeted him and asked him to go to the Commander's private quarters. When he arrived, the Commander asked Murray to follow him. They were headed for the stateroom where President Roosevelt was staying. They were soon met by a personal detail of men protecting the President. Murray assumed something must be fixed. He hoped it was a new problem and not a repair they had fixed before.

The door to the cabin opened. The Commander directed Murray to enter. He then closed the door behind him and walked away. In the corner, Murray could see President Roosevelt. He was sitting in his wheelchair, under a small light in the corner of the room.

Murray had never felt this nervous in his whole life. Suddenly, the silence was broken, when the President began to speak.

"What's your name, son?" asked President Roosevelt. "And where are you from?"

"Murray Goldman, sir. I'm from Brooklyn."

"Well, Murray Goldman, I am told by your Commander that you are quite a talented fellow," President Roosevelt said.

"Thank you, sir," Murray replied.

"And I'm told that when you fix something on this ship, it stays fixed," Roosevelt commented.

"Yes, sir. I hope so, sir."

"Well, I wanted to personally thank you," Roosevelt said, as he pointed to the bathroom. "This chair makes things more difficult than they should be."

"I've also been told by your Commander that you helped save the ship when German pilots attacked. I hear you ran down into a fire on this ship, when most men were running the other way. I applaud your bravery."

Murray was taken aback by the President's remarks. He stood silent for a moment, then he stood straight up and looked at Roosevelt.

"Mr. President, may I speak plainly," Murray asked.

"Why certainly, son."

"Sir, what I did when our ship was attacked wasn't heroic. I was simply doing my job."

Murray pointed to the wheelchair, "However, what you deal with every-day for our country, well sir, that's real courage."

President Roosevelt paused and then slowly smiled. He had not expected this young sailor to speak so directly or with such conviction. The President was clearly touched by Murray's comments.

"Anna, would you do me a favor," as the President pointed to the dressing table?

Murray had hardly taken notice of Anna Roosevelt, sitting in the cabin with her father. She walked across the room and then handed the President a blue box.

"Mr. Goldman, I'd like you to have these," said Roosevelt, as he stretched out his arm and offered the box to him. Murray quickly moved toward the President and took the small box.

As he opened it, he could see it was a pair of cufflinks with the Presidential Seal. Murray was stunned. He stood silent for a moment. He put his head down and instinctively headed toward the door. He then stopped, turned and said,

"Thank you, Mr. President. I'm just a kid from the streets of New York. I was a fighter in the 1932 Golden gloves, which until today was the proudest moment of my life. Thank you for this great honor."

"Well, the honor has been mine Mr. Goldman. And thank you for taking such good care of me here on ship. Good luck to you," Roosevelt responded.

The exchange with President Roosevelt lasted only a few minutes, but Murray knew he would remember this day the rest of his life. He returned to his bunk and stared at the cufflinks for the longest time. How strange his life seemed to be. One minute he had faced death, the next he had met the President of the United States.

His thoughts soon drifted to thinking about home. He had written to his wife often during his time in the Navy. Usually, the letters described places he visited. He was always mindful that his letters would be censored. He was especially proud to write about the Jewish family that they had found alive in Toulon. He wasn't afraid to explain to Franny about the court martial and the loss in rank. If there was anyone who would understand what Murray did, it would be Franny.

Now, however, Murray had an amazing story to share. He had met the President. In his letters, he didn't mention his own act of bravery when the ship was attacked. And he realized he could not talk about building a bathroom and toilet on the ship for the President. But the story would be shared with Franny when he got home. How many guys from Brooklyn could make that claim?

CHAPTER 38
Heading Home

—————

After Yalta, the Catoctin was ordered back to the Philadelphia Navy Yard for an overhaul of equipment. The ship left Sevastopol mid-February 1945. It would make a short stop in Naples and Oran, on its long journey home.

The sailors were still talking about the President's visit weeks later. The rumors were confirmed that the ship was eventually headed to join the fleet in the Pacific, where the war with Japan continued to rage on.

As the ship docked in Naples, the crew loaded supplies required to get them home. While in port, the Commander was asked to take onboard two amphibious boats that were left after the invasion of southern France. These boats were used to shepherd men to the beach. It was unusual for the Catoctin to be retrieving equipment, but sailors figured the boats were needed in the Pacific islands.

Three teams of men set about the task to retrieve the boats. The motorized lift slowly brought the boat above the deck, where sailors pulled on long chains to bring the craft over to the docking area. Once secure, the men went back for the second boat. The lift had not been used since they stopped in Algiers. The motor kept grinding louder and louder, until smoke was noticed and the lift went silent.

Mechanics were called to the deck. After two hours, it was clear the motorized lift could not be fixed while the Catoctin was in Naples. The XO ordered the men to set up the manual lift so the second boat could be loaded. He asked for "all hands" on deck to help.

The manual lift looked like something out of the last century. A large wheel-like structure was moved into place on the deck. The wheel sat on a crankshaft and each of the six wooden spokes would be handled by two men. The manual lift had never been used on the Catoctin before.

Jack Selby was on the deck working with the crew pushing the wheel that slowly lifted the second boat. The chains and pulleys connected to the boat grew tight and the task of the 12 men became tougher. Soon more men were called up, including Murray and Buster Johnson. Each wheel spoke now had three or four men pushing with all their strength. The sweat poured off the men, but they were determined to finish the job.

The boat was being lifted out of the water, about 25 feet up the side of the ship, when suddenly, they all heard the noise. The cracking sound of the spokes could be heard across the ship. The men started screaming. The boat lunged back toward the water, as the chains pulled up. The creaking of the wooden wheel stopped.

Jack Selby pulled the man next to him to safety. Buster jumped backward, as fast and as far as he could. Murray and the sailor next to him would not be so lucky. As the wooden spoke broke, the wheel spun backward at a high rate of speed pulled by the weight of the boat below. Murray and the sailor next to him were struck with such force, their bodies flew in the air 15 feet. The noise was over in a matter of seconds.

Jack, Buster and Tony Marano ran to him. He was laying on his side. The wheel had struck him in the face and head. The blood gushed from his mangled nose, eye and forehead. His friends tried to talk to him. He was unconscious. The second sailor was laying five feet away. He was dead.

A team of men rushed to Murray. He was carefully rolled onto a piece of canvas and carried to sickbay. He remained unconscious for days. The XO would come down each morning and ask the doctor about Goldman, but there was not much more to do except wait. The doctor could not tell if there was any swelling of the brain. He told the XO there was a possibility that Goldman might not wake up.

Murray's team mulled around the first two days, each of them taking turns to visit sickbay and check on their friend. Everyone on the ship had heard about the accident. They were shocked to think a sailor had died, while in port. Those on the work crew that day felt so lucky more men did not get hurt.

The XO launched an investigation. He was very aware of how valuable Goldman had been on the ship, since leaving Virginia. No one was taking the incident lightly.

Three days passed and he was still unconscious. It seemed to the XO and his friends that he was not getting better. As the Repair crew sat down at dinner that night, word circulated through the ship that he opened his eyes. The men left, racing through the ship to sickbay. By this time, Murray was sitting up in bed. His head and nose was bandaged. Ironically, he had no recollection of what happened or why he was in sickbay. He just complained that he had a whopper of a headache. The doctors would insist on keeping him another two days, but they could not see any other external side effects from this near disastrous turn of events.

The Catoctin had docked and left Naples before Murray regained consciousness. If he had any thoughts of seeing Cosima again, it was now a moot point. Later, he reckoned that it was meant to be this way.

The route home would take three to four weeks. The ship abandoned the effort to recover the amphibious boats. Two weeks after the accident, Murray started to experience seasickness. Was this caused by the injury? He had not been immune from getting motion sickness, especially in rough seas. But this time it seemed different. He could not stop vomiting and he could barely stand up. He was ordered to bed rest. After a few days, he was up and functioning again. Three days later, he was back in sickbay with another case of incapacitating seasickness.

By the time the ship reached Philadelphia, Murray had been in sickbay almost 15 days. A decision was made to send him to the Naval Hospital in Philadelphia. Once on shore, the seasickness seemed to subside. The hospital did a battery of tests on him, but nothing seemed to indicate an underlying cause. The hospital did not have access to medical records from the Catoctin. They were unaware that Murray had been hospitalized in October 1943, after a Navy boxing match. He knocked out his opponent in three rounds, but the fighting had been fierce. Murray had complained of headaches lasting three to four weeks following the fight. Medical tests, at that time, came back negative.

The Naval hospital did not have medical records from his injury on the ship in Naples. Murray told the doctors of his injury from the accident on the Catoctin. But he didn't think the accident was related to the seasickness, because his symptoms disappeared once he was on land.

After a month, the Navy doctors decided that he was no longer fit for sea duty. The war in Europe was over. He would be transferred to work at the Naval station in Shoemaker, California.

The rumors about Catoctin heading to the Pacific were true. Once the ship's equipment was overhauled, Catoctin left Philadelphia for Pearl Harbor and then sailed to Korea. By July, it was clear that the Japanese had lost the war. While the government of Japan quietly tried to negotiate a peace, Japan's generals continued to fight. The decision to drop the atomic bomb on August 6th and then, again, on August 8th hastened the end of the war. Ironically, Stalin's promise to Roosevelt at Yalta for Russia to declare war on Japan didn't happen until August 8, 1945.

Murray said his goodbyes before leaving the Catoctin. He regretted there wasn't more time to spend with his team of men. The past 27 months were an amazing journey.. No one dwelled on the horrors of war or the loss of life. Men survived by sticking together and looking out for one another. He felt enormous pride that his team had done their job well. Once again, he realized he was on his own.

The next three months, Murray worked in the Navy yard in California. Once the Japanese surrendered in mid-August, the war was officially over. There wasn't much work required of sailors. Everyone knew it was only a matter of time before they would be discharged and sent home. Murray was transferred one more time to Seattle, Washington, before his discharge in December 1945.

The trip home would take a week. It was a period of reflection. He had not seen his wife in two years. He would stare out the window of the train for hours without speaking. He knew the world had changed. He had changed. What about Franny? She had been on her own for so long. People change. He wondered if life with Franny would ever be the same again? He wanted to start a family. He thought about starting his own business. There was so much time to make up for, after the war.

The sounds of Brooklyn seemed so familiar to Murray. Taxi drivers were honking their horns, in the midday traffic. Two people stood on the corner arguing with each other. He could tell from the Brooklyn brogue, he was home again. As he passed the corner, the smell of neighborhood foods filled his senses. A big smile came to him. He was happy to be home again.

He carried his duffle bag on his shoulder as he walked from the train station. He passed Rosie's bar, where so much of his youth had been spent fighting to make a buck. His boxing days were now over, he told himself. As he climbed the stairs of his apartment building, he had decided it was time to turn his energy toward something new.

He paused at the second-floor landing of stairs, as he heard the saxophone. How he longed to hear that music again. How he longed to see her. He leaned against the wall and listened, until the song was over.

She had no idea when Murray might arrive. His letter from Seattle didn't give her a date, just the news of his return in the coming month. The knock on the door took her by surprise. She put her saxophone down. She was certain it must be Mrs. Lewis, down the hall. Her elderly neighbor would often come over to praise Franny's music. "No one could play that sax like you," she'd tell her.

He towered over her, as she opened the apartment door. His face was thinner than she remembered. His navy hat sat cocked forward over his forehead. His thick black hair had thinned out. She focused for a minute on his eyes. The tears came quickly to her. She jumped up into his arms. He held her tight. Her feet dangled off the floor. He pushed through the doorway. His foot kicking the door closed. As he set her down, Murray leaned down slowly and kissed her lips. Were they the only people in the world? At this moment, it was true.

CHAPTER 39
Starting Over

The homecoming lasted for months. Murray and Franny just couldn't get enough of each other. They were not alone. The whole country was celebrating, as waves and waves of men were coming back from Europe. Murray was in no rush to find a job. They spent their days like two kids, hopping subways, walking through parks, eating out and kissing under the streetlights.

During his absence, Franny worked at a food factory where they made cookies. She would tell him stories about working on an assembly line, with five other women, putting sugar on chocolate wafer cookies. It was difficult, at times, she explained. It wasn't unusual for a wife or girlfriend to hear they had lost someone in the war. The Army started to send soldiers to the plant, if the wife was not found at home.

The women pulled together during the war. If a death occurred, the women would stop their work at the factory. They would huddle close and hold onto each other. It was customary for the wife's friend to then leave the job and take the woman home. Those who lived nearby would bring food and visit. It was rare that a wife, who lost her husband, would be left on her own.

Murray was moved by these stories of loyalty and friendship. He pointed out to his wife that men aboard his ship never thought about how families were dealing with death and injury at home. "It's like you're in another time and place. You just have no idea what's happening in the world beyond your ship."

It took months before he told her about the attack on the Catoctin. He had mentioned the event in a letter, but he spent most of his time trying to reassure her that he was ok. When he finally did explain, his eyes stared off into space. His voice was calm. He could still see the young sailor who died in his arms, as if he was reliving the moment. "No one escapes the memory of war," he confided.

Nathan Weinberg had asked Murray to come back and work at Weinberg plumbing. With the war over, business was booming. Mr. Weinberg offered Murray a sizable raise and gave him a territory in Brooklyn to service. It was almost like running his own business. He worked long hours. He and Franny wanted to save money and start a family.

They never discussed her miscarriage before the war, even if the past haunted her. In 1946 and 1947, Franny would suffer two more miscarriages. The doctors could not find a medical explanation. Both miscarriages occurred early in her pregnancies. Franny didn't need the encouragement of doctors to keep trying. If she felt disappointment, she wouldn't let it control her. Neither Franny or Murray would live their lives looking over their shoulder.

A year later, she would surprise Murray with the news that she was pregnant again. They were both thrilled, but they refrained from talking about it. She would promise take good care of herself, to rest and eat right. This time would be different. And it was. By March of 1948, Alan Goldman was born 7 pounds, 6 ounces.

A bris was planned to fulfill the Jewish custom of circumcision. Both the Goldman and Sugar families joined together to celebrate their first-born son. Franny's brother, Ziggy, had married Berta. She had a daughter a year before Franny. But Alan would be the first boy born into the Goldman family. For Tonia and Isaac, the first grandson was a special blessing.

As an infant, Alan Goldman was a good baby, very alert. He ate well, slept well and was always curious about his surroundings. The apartment in Brooklyn became small overnight. They talked about finding a larger place to live, but they could not agree on where to move. Franny finally convinced Murray she had wanted to move to New Jersey, where they could buy a home and the children would have a yard to play in. She was also determined that her children not grow up with a Brooklyn accent, like the rest of the family. The two of them talked for months about the idea of moving.

After returning from the war, Murray wanted to start his own business. He decided to try his skill at opening a small luncheonette in Brooklyn. He left Weinberg's Plumbing, once Franny got pregnant. After two years, the luncheonette business was doing extremely well. He convinced Franny he didn't mind driving into the city, so they went ahead with plans to buy a home. The Goldmans had been settled in their small home in Paramus, New Jersey for almost six months, when the phone woke them in the middle of the night.

Franny answered the phone, "Murray, it's for you." As he took the phone, a New York firefighter told him the luncheonette was on fire; the whole building was ablaze. After a short pause, Murray responded, "Well, what do you want me to do about that?" He hung up the phone and went back to bed. "What was that about," she asked him. "It's ok," he responded, "let's go to bed."

The next day, he traveled into Brooklyn to survey the damage. He took one look at the rubble that remained and shook his head. It was not in his nature to dwell on things he could not control. He called Franny from New York and told her it was time to start a new career. His commuting days were over. He turned to what he knew best. Murray's plumbing business was born that day.

Franny greeted the news with enthusiasm. She promised to help him. He could start his plumbing business from their home. She would handle calls from customers and keep track of invoices. She encouraged him to seize the moment. The town of Paramus was young and growing. As a former sailor in the Navy, he got some assistance from the bank to help buy a small Cape Cod style home. The house was small, but it stood in a new development on a corner with a large yard.

It was not easy for Murray, at first. The town of Paramus was largely made up of people from German and Italian heritage. At times, the phone might not ring for days. Murray began to wonder if he was experiencing discrimination.

One night, Murray stopped at a local bar. He had just finished installing a new boiler for an elderly couple on Haase Avenue in Paramus. Bob O'Brien was sitting at the bar, when he arrived. Bob was struggling to start his own real estate business. He wanted to air his frustrations. He insisted on buying him a drink.

A former war veteran, Bob had served in the Army at the Battle of the Bulge. Nearly, 90,000 were injured and 20,000 were killed, as the Allies defended against the German attack. The battleground spread across Belgium, France and Luxembourg. "We were so lucky," O'Brien told Murray, "The Germans completely surprised us. Well, maybe not completely, but our intelligence was wrong."

The German attack was planned in November 1944, but fortunately didn't launch until mid-December. "They figured the weather would stop U.S. air support and it did. But the bad weather also slowed the German advance in the north. That was really key. Later on, the weather eased up in France to the South. General Patton's Third Army drove north toward the action and helped the Allies derail Hitler's plans."

Bob liked his scotch. He and Murray talked for more than an hour about their war experiences and the challenges of starting a new business. "I just don't understand," O'Brien said to him. "I grew up in Boston. In our neighborhoods, we had Italians, Scandinavians, Germans and Jews. Everybody got along. Everybody did business with one another. I've had nothing but aggravation since I came to Paramus. The Italian community won't even talk to me."

Murray was surprised by O'Brien's comments. He had just bought a house and moved his family to Paramus. He could not afford to fail in starting his business. He listened to O'Brien's stories about real estate deals he didn't get or those he lost, because he was Irish.

He listened quietly for the longest time. "Are you ok?" Bob asked.

"Yes, I'm ok," he replied. "But tomorrow, I want you to meet me at 9 a.m., at the corner of Forrest and Haase Avenue. Bring your business cards and wear your walking shoes."

Bob O'Brien sat scratching his head, as Murray left the bar. Bob instinctively felt his new friend was not someone who fooled around. He knew tomorrow something important was likely to happen. He smiled. He shook his head. Set his drink down and headed home.

The morning air was crisp. Spring was coming. Murray was wearing his plumbing uniform, a gray shirt and pants, which would become his trademark. In his shirt pocket, he carried a stack of business cards.

Robert "Bob" O'Brien arrived at 9 a.m., as promised. He wore a sports coat, white shirt and gray slacks. He, too, carried a stack of business cards for Robert O'Brien, President, Shamrock Realty Company..."where dreams come true."

Murray greeted Bob and handed him a business card. On one side, the card said, Murray's Plumbing and Heating, with his home address and business phone number. As he turned the card over, Bob found Murray's slogan, "Your shit is my bread and butter." He laughed. This was a friendship Bob O'Brien knew would last.

The two men spent the next three hours knocking on doors in the neighborhood. Each of them would introduce themselves and give the homeowner a business card. Murray would promise new customers to give them a 50% discount on plumbing jobs. Bob would offer to reduce his commission on selling a home. "We promise to do the job better and cheaper than anyone else," Murray would assure folks they met.

They were surprised at how polite everyone seemed to be. Only two houses closed the door on them. They agreed the effort was worthwhile. Over the next two weeks, Bob and Murray met every Tuesday and covered a good portion of town going door to door. Every morning they would meet for coffee and then spend two hours introducing themselves.

It would be nearly a month before anyone called to hire them, but slowly the business did start to come. The phone in Murray's house would ring off the hook. Franny would take messages and schedule the work. He was out of the house by 6 am and he wouldn't normally get home until 7 p.m.

O'Brien's Realty and Murray's Plumbing and Heating soon turned up as sponsors of little league baseball teams. Within six months, both businesses were becoming more recognized in the community. O'Brien was chosen to handle a brand-new housing development in Paramus. He would recommend Murray's plumbing to builders and town officials he met. Murray handed out O'Brien's business cards to every homeowner or business that hired him. To keep up with the work, Murray hired and trained two young men as assistants.

After a year, Bob O'Brien and Murray Goldman met at the same local bar to celebrate their slow, but growing success. They had overcome some of the reluctance and bias in Paramus, through sheer perseverance.

"I don't think we've seen the end of this," said Bob. "But Murray, I can't imagine anyone holding us back." The two men toasted and laughed. They each had found someone to lean on for advice and friendship.

By the time Franny was pregnant again, the plumbing business was in full throttle. She had a desk and three phones in the house. Alan crawled around on the floor. The Cape Cod house was small. Murray kept most plumbing supplies in a shed next to the house. Franny wondered at times how he found time for her, with the long hours. He had not disappointed her. In everything he did, he was disciplined and focused.

In the fall of 1950, Franny stayed by her parents in New York, until the second baby was born. Everyday, she'd take Alan for a ride in his stroller. It was Franny's chance to exercise and think about her growing family.

The contractions started on a sunny morning in September. She returned home and then was taken to Brooklyn Jewish Hospital. It would be impossible to reach Murray, who was working. She was not afraid. She had been here before. Giving birth was no picnic, but she took a deep breath and pushed with all her might. By 2 a.m., a small cry could be heard down the hall of the hospital. Zachary Goldman was born 7 pounds 1 ounce.

CHAPTER 40
Growing the Business and a Family

By 1952, Murray Goldman's plumbing business was thriving. He owned two trucks and had four men working for him. Franny juggled phone lines to handle customer calls, often holding Zach Goldman on her hip.

Murray used his own station wagon to also handle jobs. His morning always included a stop at Pop's donut shop on Route 17. Pop's real name was Richard Alberto. He was in his 70s and ran this small shop for over 20 years.

Behind the counter, in the corner, was a large vat of oil where Pop cooked the donuts.

Pop lived in little Italy in New York growing up. He and Pop would trade stories about the old neighborhood. Murray loved hearing about the "good old days."

When Murray arrived, Pop knew the order. He'd set out a fresh cup of coffee. He'd then take three eggs and put them in boiling water. Soft-boiled eggs were usually done in two minutes. Pop would put them in a special glass so the eggs stood up. Murray would crack the egg's shell carefully, removing the top and then scooping out the nearly raw egg white and yolk into a small bowl. His toasted bagel always arrived just on time. He would dunk the hot bagel into the egg. Life was good. A second cup of coffee and he was ready for the day.

Murray had the trucks and men meet him on Route 4 in the morning to get their work assignments. The noise of the trucks in the morning was too much for his neighbors, so the house had to stop being used for this purpose. Handing out assignments wasn't a quiet routine. Murray always talked to his workers about the quality of their work and not having to go back to fix a plumbing job once they completed it.

He knew the time had come for find a home for the plumbing business. The house was filled with supplies strewn across the dining room table and floor. Franny struggled to keep up, but with a third child on its way it was time to make a move.

He spent months driving around searching for a building to rent. He finally decided it would be better if he bought a piece of property. After looking in Hackensack, New Jersey, along Route 4, he finally settled on a vacant strip of land in Paramus. Behind the property was a swamp, but that made the asking price more affordable. The main highway, Route 17, was still young. Murray knew the area would grow, which would increase the value of his property. He asked his real estate friend Bob O'Brien to weigh-in before he put a deposit down. O'Brien not only liked the location, he asked Murray to rent space in the building for his real estate office.

It was nerve-wracking, at first. He knew Franny would be anxious about using all of their savings to buy the land and then pay for the construction. With the new baby on the way, it was a difficult thing to ask of her. But ask he did. She didn't really know what to say. He told her he planned to build his own building. Renting office space would help pay the mortgage on the property. She looked at him and then to make light of the situation sarcastically asked, "Does this mean I can stop answering phone calls?" Murray said, "Yes, we'll move the phones to the shop."

By the fall of 1952, a two-story brick building was completed. On the first floor, a large sign identified Murray's Plumbing and Heating. O'Brien's

Realty was located on the second floor. In addition, Murray had two other tenants, Charles "Chick" Steubens and a small accounting office. Chick owned a sheet metal company, where they fabricated vents and duck work for homes. Murray and Chick had met while working in several housing developments. After Chick moved in to the new building, their relationship grew as they collaborated on jobs and referred business to each other.

Franny finally agreed to a third child. She was hesitant at first. She felt blessed that after waiting almost a decade to have children, the Goldmans had two healthy boys. But one dream nagged at her. She wanted a daughter in the worst way. She wanted a someone to teach handball. If only she could have a street-smart girl who enjoyed playing a violin or saxophone.

Like Murray, she could be very focused on having her way. Once she got word about the third pregnancy, she shopped for three months. Everything for the new baby was red or pink. Even the baby's room in the house, she had painted pink for a girl.

In August, Franny received her surprise. She arrived at Hackensack hospital in to have her third child. She cried tears of joy as the nurses handed the baby to her. It turned out to be another boy.

Franny was exhausted by the labor and not about to give the baby back. She knew it would take time to let go of her dream for a daughter, but grateful her child had all his fingers and toes. She would grow to accept that life often has a different plan from the one we envision. It's not the destination, it's the journey. The new Goldman boy was small and delicate, a little over 6 pounds. She felt especially protective. But a week would go by without naming the child. Each day the nurses would visit her and ask what she wanted to call the baby. Finally, the head nurse told her it was hospital policy. She could not take the baby home without a name.

Franny was unprepared. She had a kept a list of girl names, Emily, Eli, Emma, but this was no longer relevant. "Can I have a book of names?" she asked. As she flipped through the book and stopped on page 13, the day her baby was born. "Ok, it's Gary," she told the nurse, "Gary Harrison Goldman." She had not followed the Jewish custom of naming the child after someone in the family or a close friend you admired, who had passed away. Each of her children would get a new name and a fresh start.

Hours later, Murray would come by to visit her and see the new baby. "Mr. Goldman, please come and meet your son, Gary," said the nurse. He scratched his head, as he looked through the nursery glass window. He wondered where the name Gary came from? He greeted the news with a big grin and a great deal of pride. He realized, he didn't go through labor of pushing that baby out of his body. He respected this was Franny's decision to make.

He spread the news to his family back in Brooklyn. He would kid talking with his brothers, Asher and Sammy, that this was proof he was a good plumber. He had three sons. Asher and Sammy both pushed back. They were no slouches. They also had sons, actually, four sons each. Only Berta, their sister, had the daughters in the family.

Over the next three years, his plumbing business continued to grow and so did the family. The parking lot around the building became quite crowded, as he and Chick kept adding trucks and men. Murray tried to keep the parking spaces in the front available for Bob O'Brien's customers. When it came to a friend, he would bend over backward to help them. However, there were times when friendships would be tested.

During the summer of 1952, Murray had words with Walter Schmidt, one of O'Brien real estate agents. He asked all the real estate agents not to park in the side driveway leading to the back of the building, so Chick and Murray could get their trucks behind the building. Walter was known, at times, to be a difficult person to deal with. He also had a habit of parking and blocking the side driveway.

It was a very hot day when Murray pulled up and saw his men trying to get their truck around Schmidt's car. Agitated, he got out of his station wagon, his sleeves rolled up and a cigar between his fingers. "Hold up," he yelled to his men. He was not looking for trouble and he didn't want the car damaged. He told the men to wait while he went upstairs to O'Brien's office.

Over the years, Murray had put on some weight. His hairline was receding, but he stood solid as an oak tree. If anything, his hands had grown thicker and stronger from working plumbing jobs. As he walked into O'Brien's realty office, he could see Bob was away with a customer. He called out to the agents that a blue car was blocking the driveway. "Move it, or lose it," he yelled across the room. Several agents in front of him waived their hands, indicating it was not their vehicle. Suddenly, he heard a voice behind him, "Look, you fucking Jew bastard, that's my car and you better leave it where it is."

It was easy to recognize Schmidt's voice. He was nearly six foot five inches tall, with a large build. He knew Murray owned the building, but he didn't respect him. It was never clear if Schmidt respected anyone. If he didn't have such strong ties in the community, Bob O'Brien would not likely have hired someone who didn't think they were accountable to anyone.

As Murray turned, he never said a word. His right fist hit Schmidt with such force that everyone in the office could hear the crack. Schmidt's jaw was broken in two places. His body fell backward until he hit the floor. He lay there unconscious. Murray matter-of-factly stepped back and walked out the office. No one—*no one*—was going to make an anti-Semitic comment to him and walk away.

By the time the police and ambulance arrived, he had gone down to the office and called his wife. "Look honey, I just hit someone. You better call Seymour, our lawyer, and have him meet me at the police station." Murray was well-known and had many friends on the Paramus police force. He had never been in trouble with the law. He was also known as a generous contributor to the Police Benevolence Association, which helped injured officers and sponsored programs for kids. He had to be arrested, but he rode to the police station in the front seat of the patrol car. He was later released without posting any bail.

For all the years they knew each other, Franny never questioned or thought of her husband as a hot head. Yes, he could be a rough guy, but never reckless. She realized long ago that there's something about fighters, they never go looking for a fight. Franny didn't know the whole story. She didn't know what Schmidt said to Murray. What she did know is that Murray would always walk away, unless he felt he couldn't.

The weeks and months ahead were not easy for Murray. Schmidt was in the hospital for several days, after the doctors wired his jaw shut. O'Brien made a deal with Schmidt that he could keep his job if he didn't press criminal charges. But he couldn't stop Schmidt from suing Murray. Franny feared the worst. The business was booming. Would they lose their savings?

Seymour Ginsberg, Murray's attorney, was a very capable and well-known lawyer in northern New Jersey. He contacted Schmidt's attorneys. After a couple of lunches and drinks near the courthouse in Hackensack, Ginsberg negotiated a settlement. It would not be cheap. But from where Murray's point of view, it was a cost he was willing to pay. He would not suffer fools and he would not tolerate a bigot.

Several months later, Schmidt returned to work at O'Brien's real estate office. He had been paid a sizable sum of money, but he never gloated. And he never parked his car in the driveway again.

CHAPTER 41

Tremors – An Uncertain Future

It was early spring in 1955 that Murray first noticed a tremor and weakness in his left hand. He was on a job with Lou Piasecki, one of his favorite workers. At five foot ten inches and 300 pounds, Lou was every bit Murray's equal in strength. A diligent worker. He didn't talk much, which his boss valued. They were renovating a building in the industrial park. Some of the pipes were over 30 years old. The job required them to remove and replace an entire floor of pipe. Murray and Lou each had a three-foot and four-foot wrench, respectively, and positioned themselves to pull in opposite directions.

They had already removed five of the six major pipes. They worked in sleeveless T-shirts, the sweat pouring off the men.

As they pulled on the final piece of pipe with all their strength, he suddenly felt the numbness shoot down his forearm. He winced in pain. The wrench fell to the floor. At first, he thought he hurt his elbow, but the numbness remained. Murray walked away.

Lou knew something must be wrong. He worked for Murray several years. He was the kind of boss who jumped into a ditch or rolled up his sleeves. He never asked his men to do anything he wasn't willing to do himself. They could see he enjoyed the physical labor. The men respected him.

It was not in Lou's nature to make a big deal of something, especially when it concerned the boss. He called over another member of the team to finish the work. He didn't ask Murray what happened and the boss didn't say.

Murray had been experiencing a certain feeling of numbness in his arm and leg for some time. He had also been waking up with terrible headaches. He'd gobble down a half-dozen aspirin and go back to bed. At first, he figured they were migraines. When the dizziness started to follow the headaches, he thought back to his final months in the Navy. No, he was not at sea, but on occasion he still lost his balance for several minutes.

Eventually, the numbness would pass and he returned to work with the men. Franny was aware he experienced headaches, but he didn't tell her about the other symptoms. He didn't think much of it. It wasn't in his nature to complain. He also didn't want to worry her.

In a few weeks, Murray planned a short vacation to the Catskill mountains with the family.. He figured maybe he just needed to rest, from the 12-14-hour days at work. Franny knew he would never leave the business for more than four days, so she settled for a long weekend. She felt some fresh air and rest would give them both the break they needed.

Alan, Zach and Gary scrambled into the back seat of the family station wagon. They left at the crack of dawn on Friday morning, so the kids would soon fall back to sleep. The Catskill resort was spread over several acres, with woods and a large lake. She could let the kids wander on their own, though always keeping them where she could see them. Murray delighted in swimming with the kids.

Only Alan actually knew how to swim, but it didn't stop Murray from picking each of them up and tossing them in the water. Gary was only three years old, so Murray never really let go of him. He would throw Gary in the air, holding his hand as he hit the water. Gary laughed on the way up, but showed signs of pure terror as his little body landed in the lake. All the children loved playing with their dad, though they greeted the cold water with shrieks of fear and delight.

By evening the children were fast asleep. Murray and Franny walked outside. The air was cool and the black sky was filled with stars. It was like standing at the end of the universe. Murray couldn't help but think about how lucky he was. The business had really grown. He couldn't be happier with his family. "I remember when we first came up this way," he said. "It was after our wedding. You were so beautiful."

"So, you're saying I've changed?" she asked.

He smiled, "No, you haven't changed. You are still the most amazing woman I've ever met."

He spun her around and then kissed her hard on her mouth. He then paused a moment, pulled his head back and looked into her eyes, "I love you. If I don't tell you every day, I hope you know." He leaned down again and, this time, kissed her very softly.

They walked hand-in-hand back to their room. Franny's thoughts drifted off. She, too, thought how lucky they were. She could almost let go of her fears. The Depression and war had scarred a generation. No one took life for granted anymore. She was grateful for the children. She dreamed of having a child for so long, and now there were three. He was making money and they were saving for the future.

Franny made love to Murray that night with a freedom and abandon she had not felt before. She realized how easy it is to get caught up in worrying about things in life. She wanted to make certain he knew how special he was to her. They fell asleep wrapped in each other's arms.

It was near three in the morning when she woke. The noise of Murray throwing up in the bathroom could be heard down the hall. At first, she sat up in bed and waited for him to return. Did he eat something that made him sick, she wondered? He so rarely got sick.

As he walked back toward the bed in the dark, Franny knew something wasn't right. He took two steps, spun around and collapsed on the floor. She ran to his side. His eyes were rolling back in his head and his body started to shake violently. She knew he was having a convulsion. She had seen this once before at the factory during the war. A woman on the assembly line collapsed suddenly. Someone had yelled, "Turn her on her side."

Franny tried to turn him with all her strength. She got him halfway there, though his legs lagged behind. Suddenly the convulsion stopped, as quickly as it started. She rolled him on his back. Murray laid on the floor. He stared at the ceiling. He seemed to be aware of where he was and slowly reached for her to help him sit up.

"Are you ok?" Franny asked several times. He nodded yes, as he leaned on his hands to get to his knees and stand up. "I think I bit my tongue," he told her.

"We're going home," she told him. "No discussion and no debate. You lay down on the bed. I'm going to get the children ready."

Within a half hour, she had the children dressed and in the car. It was still the middle of the night. She helped him into the car. He didn't argue about her driving home, which was so unlike her husband.

During the three-hour trip home, she was beside herself with fear. She stopped six times by the side of the road. Murray would stumble out of the car. He couldn't stop throwing up. Twice Franny had to help pull him from the hood of the car, where he held onto the bumper as he heaved his guts. The car lights illuminated his face. Fortunately, the children were oblivious. They slept the whole ride home.

By morning, they would be back in New Jersey. She took Murray directly to a local hospital. A young volunteer watched the children in the lobby so Franny could stay with him in the emergency room. Within the hour, the doctors gave him several injections and put him on an intravenous drip. His symptoms of dizziness and nausea soon subsided.

Franny sat in a chair next to his bed in the emergency room. She was relieved to see him sleeping. A young doctor came over and tapped her on the shoulder. She followed the doctor down the hall.

"Mrs. Goldman, I given your husband a pretty thorough exam. I've checked his eyes, his reflexes and his coordination. I don't know how to tell you this, but I believe your husband has a neurological problem," said the doctor.

She had trouble grasping what the doctor was saying.

"I'm guessing your husband has been experiencing symptoms for a period of time. He may not have understood the symptoms or he ignored them, but they have grown progressively worse."

"What can I do? I mean, what can we do to help him?" she asked.

"Well, we will run some further tests, but I'd recommend that you take Mr. Goldman to a specialist in New York. I'll speak to someone here at the hospital and get you a name.

The doctor's words hit Franny like a ton of bricks. "What?

What are you saying? I don't understand? What's actually wrong with him? Why New York? My husband is going to be fine."

The doctor put his arm around her shoulder. He could see she was tired and shaking like a leaf. He was not about to tell her what he really thought.

Franny would not take no for an answer. She must have called the specialist in New York six times before the nurse would fit Murray into the doctor's schedule. It had only been four days since he left the hospital. He insisted on going to work. She sat by the telephone for hours, worried she'd get a call.

She drove Murray into New York. She held his hand as they sat in the doctor's waiting room.

Dr. Robert Marks was considered one of the best brain surgeons in the country. There weren't a ton of doctors in this field. Cutting off the top of someone's skull and poking around in the brain was not entirely new, but few had the insight and skill to succeed in this area of medicine.

Franny was taken aback when Dr. Marks came out personally to greet them in the waiting room. He stood six foot, a rather thin man, with large glasses and greying hair. He seemed brusk, at first, as if he had some place to go. He asked them to follow him into the exam room. Murray was put through a battery of tests, touching his feet, standing on one foot, squeezing the doctor's hand. The doctor read the hospital report, as the Goldmans sat quietly in the room.

Dr. Marks asked Murray questions about symptoms he was experiencing. Franny sat stunned as he described several instances where he had sudden numbness and loss of strength in his arms. He also described the headaches he experienced the past two months.

More questions followed about his medical history, including his boxing career and the accident on the Navy ship, which left him unconscious for 72 hours. When the doctor was finished, he asked him to get dressed and meet him in his office down the hall.

Dr. Mark's showed more warmth of personality, as he motioned to Murray and Franny to take a seat. "Mr. Goldman, I believe you have a tumor growing in the front of your head. This may not be the news you wanted to hear, but I don't believe in sugarcoating the truth. I'd like to do a test, where we'll inject dye into your neck, so I can confirm the diagnosis. The X-rays from the test will also guide us, when we conduct the surgery."

"Surgery?" she asked. "Doctor, I don't understand."

"Mrs. Goldman, your husband's life is at risk. I'm surprised he has functioned this long without a more significant event."

Murray sat stoically, as tears rolled down Franny's face.

"How soon should we return for the test?" he asked.

"Mr. Goldman, you're not going anywhere. I will make arrangements to check you into the hospital here in New York.

We will do the test in the morning."

As the Goldmans left the doctor's office, they did not speak. Franny went with Murray to check into the hospital. Once settled, she would have to leave him to get home for the children.

"Franny, I'm not worried. I've been hit harder than this in my life and I still got up," he told her.

She could not put her thoughts into words. He was the only man she ever loved.

The next morning, Murray was woken up at 6 a.m. for the test. He was brought to an exam room. The X-ray machine took up almost the entire space.

The nurses had him lay down on a bed at the entrance to the X-ray machine. They then gave him a mild sedative to relax him. He soon realized the nurses had tied his wrists to the side of the bed. He was too groggy to resist.

Dr. Marks entered the room and greeted him. "Good morning, Mr. Goldman. The test we're doing today will inject dye directly into the artery leading to your brain. I won't kid you, this is going to hurt like hell. Are you ready?"

Murray nodded, though he didn't really understand what was about to happen. Dr. Marks asked him to lay perfectly still and to turn his head slightly to the left. When the needle entered his neck, he was certain they were cutting his head off. The pain was excruciating. He gripped the bars on the side of the bed. His face contorted with pain, as the doctor injected the dye. His chest heaved upward from the bed. His back arched. Two nurses attempted to hold his shoulders steady, while a third nurse held his legs.

"Hold him steady," Doctor Marks ordered the nurses.

The injection took less than a few seconds. They were seconds Murray would never forget.

Franny arrived at the hospital by early afternoon. She made arrangement with neighbors to watch the children. He was lying in bed. When she entered his room, his eyes welled up with tears. She could see where his neck was bandaged. Murray spared her the details of the test. He had never experienced pain like that. As she bent over the bed to hug him, he held on to her for just a minute longer. She knew. The invincible man she knew was suddenly vulnerable.

Within 35 minutes, the nurses came into the room to let them know Dr. Marks was on his way.

Dr. Marks entered the room with two associates, Dr. Charleton and Dr. Bailey. "Well, Murray the test confirms a brain tumor," he said in a calm, low voice. "I just didn't realize how large. It looks like it's almost the size of a grapefruit. The tumor is sitting in the front of your head and pressing against your brain. This is very serious and urgent. A surgery to remove a tumor of this size will be difficult."

Dr. Marks paused for a moment. He looked at Franny and then turned to Murray. "Let me be honest, there is a chance you might not survive the surgery. It's very complex. I suggest we tackle this as soon as possible, perhaps tomorrow. I will clear my schedule."

Murray sat motionless and silent. Dr. Marks outlined the procedure and the roles his associates would play during the surgery. The operation would last 4-6 hours.

"When I say the surgery is complex, let me explain. Removing a tumor of this size will require cutting away some brain tissue."

He went on to describe the possible side effects, following surgery. "It's likely that you'll have paralysis on your left side of your body. You may have impairment of your speech. We won't know exactly, until we can actually see how the tumor is attaching to the brain."

Without hesitation, he then looked up, "Dr. Marks, I trust you. Let's schedule the surgery."

Dr. Marks was surprised at Murray's composure.

"Do you have questions," Dr. Marks asked Murray and Franny?

He sat there in bed and shook his head, "No".

Franny was not about to ask anything in front of Murray. She asked Dr. Marks if they could step outside.

"Dr. Marks, as you can see, my husband doesn't seem to be afraid." With that said, Franny broke down and began to cry.

"Please tell me if I'm going to lose him? He's only 40 years old. We have three children."

"Mrs. Goldman, I always hope for the best in these situations. But I won't lie, there is a 50-50 chance he might not survive the operation. I'd suggest you get all of his personal affairs and papers in order. If needed, we can wait a day to perform the surgery."

Her eyes filled with tears again. "Yes, I'd like time to bring the children to see their father."

Dr. Marks reached out and put his arm around her shoulder. He turned out to be a very compassionate man, she thought. He took her hands into his and looked her in the eyes, through his glasses.

"I know what I'm telling you may sound grim, but I promise you...I promise you, I will do everything in my power to save him."

Franny shook her head yes. She would hold on to that promise, with all her strength. Murray Goldman would not quit on life and neither would she.

On Wednesday, Franny sat the children down before they left for New York. She explained to them that "daddy was very sick" and "he needed an operation". "Daddy injured his head. The doctors are going to try and fix him, so he can come home to us. It is a very dangerous operation. When you see your father today, please hug him and let him know you love him."

Franny doubted Zach at 5 years old and Gary, who was 3 really understood the situation, but Alan did. He began to cry uncontrollably. She let Alan go for several minutes. She knew the fear he was experiencing. Soon, she stepped in. "Ok Alan. You have to get control. At 7 1/2 years old, you have to help your mom, you're the big brother." Alan slowly calmed down. He liked being the oldest brother. He did not argue or protest. He rallied Zach and Gary to listen to their mom. He then helped her get his siblings in the car. He explained to them that there was no running around in the hospital. They should be very quiet and give their dad a hug.

At the hospital, Zach and Gary scrambled onto Murray's lap. He was sitting in a big chair, in the lounge on his floor. Franny brought him a beautiful navy-blue silk robe to wear over his hospital gown. "Daddy, we love you. Please get well and come home," Zach told him as he hugged his father's arm. Alan stood back until Murray pulled him into a collective hug with his boys.

It was always so easy for him, with his long arms, to scoop the boys up. He didn't talk about the operation. He just hugged them and told them to be good to their mother. "Don't worry dad, I'll help mom with my brothers. I'm the oldest. We just need you to ...." Alan's voice trailed off, as he began to cry. Murray put Zach and Gary down. He held Alan with both arms and kissed his forehead. "I'll be home soon Alan. Dad will not let you down." Neither Franny nor Murray talked about the surgery in front of the children. The afternoon was spent quietly. After their initial greeting, the boys played by themselves in the lounge area. Franny was grateful they made little noise and there was no fighting. She, too, sat holding Murray's hand without commenting on the operation. She refused to consider the idea that this could be the last time the boys would see him.

By 4 p.m., she was headed home with the boys. She asked each son to kiss his father. She wanted the children to remember this day. No one ever really knows when their time is up. How could she know if there would be days to follow? She paused at the hospital room door to catch her breath. The boys ran down the hall ahead of her. She turned around and walked over to kiss Murray. "I'll be here first thing in the morning." As she turned to leave, he held onto her arm. He did not want this moment to end. His hand slowly released her arm, sliding down to her hand. He pulled her back closer to him and gently kissed her hand before she left.

It would be a long night. He could not shake the concern he had about his family's future. He had done well starting his plumbing business, but he had not anticipated if he was not around to earn an income. He promised himself, if he survived, he would find a way to secure his family.

The night passed slowly. Both Franny and Murray kept waking up and looking at the clock. The minutes and hours ticked by. You know the night must end at some point, but it never does. Life has a way of twisting you inside out, when you face the inevitable questions about death. Is this it? Why was I here in the first place? Is there nothing more? What will happen to those I love?

Ironically, you fall asleep just as morning comes. By 5 a.m., the nurses were in his room. He had finally drifted into a deep sleep.

"Mr. Goldman, I'm sorry, but we have to check all your vitals.

Alice also has to give you a quick shave, as we prep you for surgery." He kept thinking it was the best sleep he had in a long time. He was groggy, but he smiled at the nurses and followed their instructions.

Franny arrived at the hospital before 6 a.m. There was very little traffic on the roads. She, too, had fallen into a deep sleep by morning. The alarm clock rang so suddenly, she sat straight up in bed. She could not calm herself. She quickly kissed the children and she was gone. Janice, a teenager from next door, was asleep on the living room couch. Janice would stay with the children, until she came home.

As she closed the front door behind her, she was resolved. She needed to see Murray. There would be no regrets today. She could be as stubborn and willful as her husband. Today, she would summon all her strength and give it to him.

Franny and Murray would not have much time, once she arrived at his room. Brain surgeries could go on for hours, so the doctors always started very early in the morning. He was wearing a cap on his head. She could see they had shaved his beautiful mane of hair. She made small talk about the children for 10-15 minutes, until the nurses told them it was time.

Franny leaned over the guardrail on the bed. She ran her hand gently across Murray's face. Her voice was soft.

"Murray, you've never let me down. You've always fought back, even when you were hurt. I need you to go in there and come back to me. I mean it. I'm not taking no for an answer."

He looked at Franny's curly brown hair, which spread across her shoulders and down her back. You never know in life how long you will love or be loved. He was thankful for what he saw in her eyes. He nodded and smiled.

"Franny, you don't have to worry. I'm not going anywhere. You married a fighter. No matter what they do to me, I won't quit on you."

His words were not reassuring to her. Was he telling her the truth or just saying what she wanted to hear? She held on to one thought. He had never gone back on his promise.

"Look, I brought you your ring," Franny said.

A smile came to Murray. She had bought him a diamond horse-shoe ring for their anniversary. He loved it. He never took the ring off his finger, except when he came to the hospital.

"I wanted you to have it for good luck."

One of the nurses entered the room. She saw him put the ring on his finger. "I'm sorry Mr. Goldman, but you cannot wear jewelry in surgery."

Franny sprung to her feet. No, was not an option. The nurses could see it in her look. "I want my husband to wear this ring for good luck." Mrs. Collins, the head nurse, could see tears well up in her eyes. As she left the room, Mrs. Collins, a wife and mother herself, realized some accommodation would have to be made. After several minutes, she returned with a roll of adhesive tape.

Two nurses helped him onto the gurney taking him for surgery. After a brief discussion with Franny, Mrs. Collins taped the ring to the plastic identification bracelet patients wear at the hospital. Mrs. Collins promised her she would personally take her husband downstairs and make certain the ring was not cut off.

Murray and Franny were never melodramatic with each other. She rode the elevator down to the surgery wing. She held onto his hand. A brief pause at the door, where they kissed several times, and he was rolled into surgery.

When the threat of death passes, you hope for a moment of relief. Reality, however, often grabs you by the shirt collar and it rarely lets go. The difference between life and death is often the suffering that lingers choking oxygen from the room. Your loved one has been changed forever and you are all that separates them from anguish and despair.

After six hours, the surgery was over. Murray survived. But as Dr. Marks predicted, he had paralysis on one side of his body. His vision and speech were impacted, but the doctors would need more time to fully assess the damage.

Several hours would pass, after he returned to his room. Franny sat by his bed waiting. She had no idea what to expect. Suddenly, she could see him slowly open his eyes. She could see the near terror come across his face. He struggled to form words, but they would not come. "You're ok," she tried to assure him. He looked frantically at the nurses who came in to check his vital signs and change the intravenous bottles next to his bed. What had they done to him, he asked himself. He pulled at the side of the bed with his right hand. His voice let out a loud moan.

"Murray, calm down. You're alive," Franny told him. "You're alive, nothing else matters. We'll get through this. Please lay still and rest. Close your eyes. I won't leave you."

He struggled for several minutes. The nurses gave him an injection and the drugs took over. Soon he was asleep. Franny stood next to the bed. She looked at his chiseled face and bandaged head. What had they done to my husband, she wondered? She could not bear to think he'd never be the same again. What would she tell the children? What would happen to them, if he could not work? Through her tears, she knew she had to be strong.

The day seemed like an eternity. Franny left the hospital by midnight to return home and check on the children. She asked Janice to stay at the house for several days, so she could go back and forth to the hospital. She promised Janice an extra $50 if she would help out until school vacation was over.

It was 3 a.m. when Murray woke again. Franny was gone. His head felt like it was coming off. He called out for the nurse, but all that came out was a muffled groan. He tried to yell louder. The door to his room was half open, so he waved his right arm in an effort to get the nurse's attention. Several nurses walked up and down the hallway, but no one looked in to see his flailing hand.

He then realized, he had no control on the left side of his body. His vision was blurry. He struggled for several minutes to make noise. His head hurt terribly. Panic started to overtake him, as he laid helplessly in bed. Nobody was coming. He tried to get up, but couldn't move his left leg. He was locked in his own body.

As he lay in bed, Murray thoughts drifted off. He could hear the crowd during his boxing match with Ritchie O'Brien. That was more than 20 years ago. He remembered the pain he felt when O'Brien broke his nose and knocked him down. He wasn't certain if he could get up. Slowly, he began to take deep breaths through his mouth to calm his nerves and rid his body of pain. By the referee's count of seven, he would get back on his feet. He took more deep breaths. Soon the fog cleared and Moe Fields did what he knew best. He won.

Murray lay trapped in his bed. He was afraid, but he would not feel sorry for himself. These were the cards he was dealt. He was glad to be alive. He closed his eyes and took some deep breaths. More would follow. Slowly, his body eased. His head still hurt, but the breathing helped him relax until he drifted off to sleep.

The days in the hospital following surgery turned into weeks. Dr. Marks came to check on Murray often. He told him and Franny that his brain's recovery from the surgery was quite remarkable. He had not expected any improvement in his motor function for some time. However, Murray was already able to use his hand. His leg was also responding to physical therapy. Franny was very pleased to hear the news. Dr. Marks, obviously, didn't know her husband the way she did. She reached over and grabbed his hand. He promised Murray that regaining his speech and use of his left side would return, if he worked hard during his rehabilitation. The doctor's words were not lost on him.

Dr. Marks had sized up his patient quite well. In truth, he wasn't certain how much body function Murray might fully regain. His brain tumor was one of the largest he had ever removed. The doctor used great care during the surgery. However, so little was known about the brain. The doctor could only hope that Murray had the will to overcome the side effects. He gave him the most important challenge of his life.

When the rehab nurse finished working with Murray each day, he'd motion for Franny. She knew he wanted more. He wanted as much exercise as his mind and body would tolerate. At times, he would get frustrated with the lack of progress. He'd raise his good hand in a fist. But she knew his anger would motivate him even more. "Ok, are you going to punch someone or do more exercise?" she would ask him. Her sarcasm and toughness always brought a calm to Murray's face. She was always in his corner, pushing and routing for him. However, Franny worried at times if the doctor was too optimistic. But she would not share her fears with him.

After three weeks, Murray still sat in a wheelchair with limited mobility. Franny would help him in and out of bed. She'd dress him. She comforted him and she cajoled him. And she would remind him that inside, Moe Fields still lived. "The man I know," she would tell him, "doesn't know how to back away from a fight. The man I married is fearless. Look at me Murray. Are you that man? I'm asking you," she said loudly, Are you that man?" She never doubted he would rise to her challenge. His words were slurred, but his actions spoke volumes.

Eventually, Dr. Marks let Murray go home. He told Franny that being home with the children might be good for him. There were days when the doctor could see he was depressed. "He's an unusual man," the doctor told her. "I've not met anyone who pushes themselves like him, but the recovery can be frustrating. I know he's depressed when he tells the nurses he's tired and refuses physical therapy. I'm hoping your children will help his spirits." Regular visits were scheduled with the doctor and his associates to keep up with his progress.

Franny did her best to try and prepare the children. The sight of their father struggling physically to move around the house they accepted. His slurred speech and his difficulty communicating with the children, however, scared them. He tried when he arrived home. He couldn't form the words. Alan backed away quickly. This was not his father. Zach began to cry. Murray could see the shock in their eyes. The harder he tried to speak, the more frustrated he became. He wanted to assure the boys dad was going to be ok. One-by-one the boys ran from their father.

She settled Murray in bed to rest after the long day. She found the boys playing in the den. Each child was engaged in separate activities, but they wanted to stay together. Franny called for a tribal discussion. She didn't sugar coat their dad's circumstance. "Alan, when you split your chin open....or Zach, when Alan hit you with the pole in your face, who was there to help you? Your father has always taken care of all of us. Now, it's our turn. Your dad needs us now. If we want him to get better, each of you has to do your part.

Dad's speech will get better. If you don't understand him, don't be afraid — and don't run away. Make believe you understand him and his talking will get easier. Remember, your father needs your support — and your love."

The boys took turns holding dad's hand, as he limped down the hallway with his leg dragging behind. Alan and Zach could not support or steady Murray's gait, once his body was in motion. However, their tiny hands squeezed his fingers. Gary was the sweetest. He talked non-stop walking with dad.

Franny could see what a positive impact the children had on their father. If he felt off balance, he'd lean against the wall in the hallway. He made a point to let each son know how much he valued their help. He had a special way of caressing their face with his large hands. Dad's touch was always special.

Once home, Murray and Franny became full-time partners, a virtual tag-team, in the race to regain his life. They would work several hours a day doing his rehabilitation exercises. And after he was totally exhausted, she would simply lay him on the floor and roll him around. It wasn't your classic physical therapy. Franny was tough. She'd pull and push on his left arm and leg until he tried to push back. Lifting him took all of her strength. She used these situations to challenge Murray's ego, "c'mon help me get your ass off the floor". When he finally landed in the chair or on the bed, it was not unusual for her to pause and laugh out loud. For her, it was a way of making light of the handicaps he struggled to overcome. Soon he would join in the laughter. He was starting to find his voice again.

While Murray worried about the business, Franny took charge. She arranged for the office phones to ring at the house. Lou Piasecki would serve as the manager of his plumbing crew, while he was recuperating. Lou would stop at the house almost daily to review jobs and work schedules. He was patient listening to Murray's instructions. His physical struggles did not interfere with Murray's business acumen.

When the phones weren't ringing, she helped him with exercises to regain his strength and coordination. Twice a week, he worked with a speech therapist. At times, he would get upset with his progress, but no one tried harder than him.

Dr. Marks would not guess at how much movement he might recover. He did, however, try to seed in Murray's heart that he could overcome limits, if he worked at it.

The children remained a huge inspiration for him. It wasn't anything they did or say. Like most boys, they jumped and ran through the house with reckless abandon. Sometimes they would be screaming so loudly that Franny had to intervene. Soon, Murray became one of them. He imitated them. His speech slurred, but he could easily make the grunts and groans mimicking the children.

"Oh, great, now I have four kids to take care," Franny would yell out from the kitchen.

She could see they boosted his spirits. "Boys will be boys," she'd say with a shrug, as she tackled baskets of laundry. As time went on, his walking improved, though his left leg still dragged. "It's a monster," Alan would yell to his brothers. Murray played along, raising his right arm and chasing them around the dining room table.

By five months, the impossible started to become possible again. He regained coordination in his arm and leg. He walked with barely a limp. He squeezed a tennis ball all day long. His speech had a slight slur, but he could be understood when he spoke to his men. As he saw it, the time had come to go back to work.

Franny refused to let on how nervous she was about him leaving the house. Dr. Marks warned him that any blow to his head could kill him. Murray was a tough S.O.B, but he was not stupid. He moved back into the shop.

Instead of going out on jobs with the men, he barked orders and made use of the telephone to keep tabs and give instructions.

Murray would keep the promise he made to himself. It wasn't enough to grow his plumbing business, he wanted to financially secure his family. The brain operation had not hurt his natural abilities in math or his keen sense of business. As a plumber, he could walk into a room or a warehouse and predict within inches how much pipe was needed to do the job. He could estimate and add the numbers in a contract faster than his secretary could total the costs using an adding machine.

At work, Murray still negotiated by telephone, when he bought three new Dodge trucks. He would always wait until the last day of the month and, where possible, the last day of a quarter. He understood the need for a car salesman to reach certain sales quotas. If the car dealer tried to charge him the sticker price on the vehicle, Murray would ask him if he was serious about making a deal. "Charlie, let's stop the bullshit. Show me the dealer's invoice," he demanded, "I'll pay you $200 above your list price. If you stop screwing around, I'm giving you the chance to sell three trucks today." The voice on the phone went silent. "Well, is it a deal or do I buy the trucks from Donovan Chevrolet?" The negotiation was completed in 15 minutes. He would drive to the dealer, sign the paperwork and the trucks were delivered to his shop in three days.

During his recovery, Murray read the financial section of the newspapers every day. He opened a brokerage account and began buying and selling stocks. He rarely held the stock for a long period, preferring to turn it over for a quick profit. He earned hundreds of dollars each week in the stock market, which he gave to Franny for groceries or buying the children clothes.

CHAPTER 42
Turning to Family

___

In 1958, Murray launched his long-held plan to build the family a new home. The Goldmans were living in Paramus for almost a decade. They started out in a small Cape Cod house, which was more than adequate when the children were very young. Their second home on Wedgewood Drive was larger. The children could walk to the Ridge Ranch Elementary school. This split-level home had a detached garage, where Murray could keep tools and the Goldman station wagon.

The kids loved the Wedgewood Drive home. Murray had placed a large boulder on the grass in the front yard, between the curb and the sidewalk. This was a favorite place for the children, who frequently sat or climbed onto that rock. Perhaps all children ever need is a vantage point from which they can become conquerors of their land. Very simply, the rock signaled they were home. Standing on the rock became a rite of passage. As youngsters, they would take turns. They could spend hours playing near the rock, on the rock or just sitting there and watching the neighbors.

Their other favorite place was the family garage, which was not connected to the house. The garage had a flat roof, where the children could walk. In the wintertime, Zach would scramble up the side of the garage and onto the roof. He would coach Gary to climb on a wooden horse, where Zach could reach down and pull him up. If the snow was deep enough, Zach and Gary would jump off the roof into 3-foot snow drifts.

Alan preferred throwing broomstick handles, like a spear, into the drifts. It was during one of these wild escapades that Alan's broomstick accidently hit Zach square in his face. Zach had climbed down from the roof., He sat on an old bicycle stuck in the snow. Alan tried too hard to throw his broomstick with force. His body twisted as he let go and the stick veered to the right. Zach's screams could be heard down the street. The snow quickly turned crimson, as the trail of blood led to the house.

Zach was lucky. The accident happened on the weekend, when dad was home. Franny was well-equipped to manage her three sons. But with blood gushing everywhere, she was grateful dad took charge. Murray was calm. He turned Zach's head upward. He put a towel in his mouth to stem the bleeding. He locked the bathroom door so he could determine the damage without distraction. Franny would nervously pace and knock periodically to get an update on him.

Murray could see Zach's teeth were not damaged, but the lip inside of his upper lip was torn away from where it connected to his gums. He didn't believe Zach could get stitches in such a sensitive area of his mouth. He reasoned, it was just like when Alan fell and split his chin as a three-year-old. The trauma of a doctor putting in stitches would be worse than taping the wound shut. At the time, Murray taped Alan's chin with ugly grey duck-tape. Unlike stitches, the tape did not leave a scar.

He gently packed Zach's mouth with soft tissues to stop any further bleeding. He called to Franny for ice, which he wrapped in a clean towel. Zach's fat lip remained for almost a week. But his father's intervention would calm the boy within minutes. Murray never coddled the boys when they were injured. He always seemed to instantly know what to do in a crisis. His calmness instinctively gave the boys confidence. Whatever their dad asked them to do, they trusted him.

As the business grew, Murray dreamed of building a large ranch-style home. It took him more than a year to find the right location. Initially, he thought of Alpine Drive. This street already was a growing development of upscale housing in Paramus. The street was a Who's Who of businessmen and "rich folks." Franny described the custom-built homes as mini-mansions. She didn't want her boys growing up in a neighborhood where everyone was "competing with the Joneses," on who had—and who could spend—more money.

He asked Bob O'Brien to search for land in new undeveloped areas of Paramus. Only two custom built homes had been constructed on Koman Drive, near the edge of town. The rest of the street, on one side, consisted of dirt lots, cleared of trees and marked off for 20 new homes. Across the street was a wooded area. Koman Drive started at the top of the hill, off Linwood Drive, and ended at a cul-de-sac. Murray bought two lots and hired a contractor to execute his plan. His men would install all of the plumbing and central air conditioning.

The new home was the longest house on the street. It would only have 3 modest sized bedrooms, but a very large living room, dining room, kitchen and den with a white marble fireplace. The Goldmans didn't care to show off their growing wealth with family or friends, but he wanted a home where Franny had space to entertain. Gary and Zach were going on 7 and 9 years old respectively. They would share a bedroom. Alan was near 12 years old and would have his own room. The master bedroom and bath were quite sizable, even though the Goldmans spent little time there.

Murray also volunteered with a small group to help build a Jewish Community Center (JCC) in Paramus, starting in 1958. This large building included the first synagogue in town. Having been one of the early Jewish families in town, he hoped the JCC would encourage others to follow. Before this, the small Jewish community used a multi-purpose room at a local bank for several years, to hold religious services. A Committee of 12 would serve as fundraisers to help acquire the land and pay for the construction. Building the Synagogue would be the first priority, followed by Hebrew school classrooms and, finally, a large room for community events.

He embraced his fundraising responsibilities for the JCC with enthusiasm. He made a sizable personal contribution and he volunteered to complete all of the plumbing and heating required for the building. Franny also got involved, working with a group of women who would host various fundraising dinners and events. The JCC effort was a huge success. The Goldmans hoped Alan would be among the children Bar Mitzvahed in this new Synagogue, followed by his brothers. The JCC would become part of Murray's many giving back opportunities to his community.

By this point in his career, he had a certain amount of clout with local building and plumbing inspectors in the northern part of New Jersey.

He adopted a business strategy of contributing to both the Republican and Democratic party, so he didn't have to worry about each election. As the Mayors and City Council members changed, everyone knew Murray Goldman as an honest and hardworking tradesman, with no political axe to grind. Most elected officials were on a first name basis with him. He was someone they respected and his friendship was valued.

Murray's agnostic approach to politics also extended to the Police and Fire department. His reputation was that he could always be counted on to generously contribute to those front-line folks who served their communities. He never abused these relationships or looked to bend the rules. He believed in the words, "honest--and hard working." He would tell his realtor friend, Bob O'Brien, that his good name meant more to him than any business deal. "I don't believe in gambling and I won't risk my reputation. It's just not worth it."

That said, he did on occasion bend rules. He'd get permission from the local police to break-in his new car on a vacant stretch of highway. The common wisdom, at the time, was that driving a new car at high speeds would tighten the transmission and improve performance. Murray was not reckless, but he would take the car up to 80 or 90 miles an hour on newly built sections of the Garden State Parkway. He would only go out on an unused stretch of road. After 15 or 20 minutes, he'd be satisfied and head home.

The police and firemen had regular contact with Murray, as he completed jobs in almost every building along the two major arteries in Paramus, Route 17 and Route 4. Sometimes he'd meet them at Pops, in the morning over breakfast. But wherever he'd run into these folks, the contact often led to jobs he would offer to complete at a discounted price for the men and women in uniform. He always had a soft spot for those who served, and he didn't think it was appropriate to make money helping them. Maybe this was his Depression upbringing coming through or maybe it was just his character.

As the house on Koman Drive was completed, it would take months to get a final Certificate of Occupancy (CO) approval so the family could move in. Murray knew the school year would be starting in September. He told Franny the move would be completed in time for the children. The CO approval, however, was delayed. He decided to go ahead and move the family into the house, so the family was settled. He cloaked the move in secrecy, instructing the moving trucks to arrive late in the day. He told the children they could not be running around outside for the next two weeks. Franny was suspicious, but followed Murray's lead. She knew it was like him to sometimes break rules. The children took their father literally, hiding in their bedrooms when the building inspector stopped by to speak to him.

He expected the town to issue fines, because the Goldmans did not wait for a final CO inspection. Murray was surprised when the Inspector handed him a signed CO and waived off going through the home.

The house received final approval two days before school started. The children were excited about their new home. The woods across the street became their new playground. Zach would take Gary hunting for frogs, snakes or almost anything else that moved. They couldn't quite climb the trees, since few of the birch trees had limbs. Zach loved the woods and exploring. He fancied himself a hunter. They discovered that Alan was not someone who enjoyed nature. Gary and Zach found their new-found power over Alan, when they brought home frogs. Alan, the oldest brother, screamed and ran to escape. But the brothers cornered him by the family garage door. It was here that the younger Goldman brothers made their stand—and commanded Alan's respect. Overnight, Gary and Zach had developed super powers.

Murray wanted to be a good father, but following his brain tumor he became even more obsessed with growing his business and investing his money in stock and real estate. He often worked six days a week. He was gone by 6 a.m., before anyone in the family was awake. He rarely got home before 6:30 or 7 p.m. Franny tried her best to make the children wait for dinner, so they could eat together as a family.

Eventually, to compensate, he decided to start bringing his sons to work with him during school vacations. Alan and Zach were old enough, though it was not unusual by afternoon to find Zach napping in a tub that sat in the display window of the shop. Customers would drive up and see a little boy curled up in the window. It made for good conversation.

When they traveled with their dad, the boys always thought they were in a Charlie Chan movie. Murray would introduce each son, "oh, this is my Number One son or this is my Number Two son." Rarely, would he use their name at work. "Number Two, can you go sit over there, while I talk to Mr. Gardner about this job?"

In time, Alan and Zach began to wonder if dad had forgotten their names. Gary Goldman was much younger, nearly four years younger than Alan, so at five or six years old, he didn't get to travel to work that often with his dad. Nevertheless, when he was taken along, he too, had become "my Number Three son." The boys would watch Charlie Chan movies on TV and argue with each other. There was jealousy that "Number One Son" always seemed to be present at critical moments in the story, when Charlie Chan figured out who committed the crime.

Eventually, Murray's names for the boys became a badge of honor. When the opportunity presented itself, they preferred to introduce themselves, "hi, I'm Number Two Son." The boys would beam. Their father would also look on with pride.

The routine of going to work with dad was pretty straight forward. They'd stop at his shop on Route 17 in Paramus, where his plumbing business was located. Assignments were given out to the men. By 8 a.m., the trucks pulled out and he would head to Pop's on Route 17 for breakfast.

The boys never knew the man's real name. They'd describe Pops as a small hole-in-the-wall place dad took them for breakfast. From the outside, it looked rundown. There were two men running the place. The owner was Pop. He was bald on top with white hair on the sides of his head. Murray had been coming to Pops, since he started his plumbing business. He was not alone. The food was always fresh. In the far corner, Pop cooked fresh donuts each day. No one who ate at Pops left empty handed.

Pop would greet each of Murray's boys with the same question, "and which number are you?" Zach would reply, with a smile, "I'm Number Two." After breakfast, customers would leave with a small bag of jelly donuts.

Back at the building, Murray would be on the phone for hours talking with builders and customers about new jobs. Cigar smoke billowed from the door to his office. On more than a few occasions, the boys could hear their dad's voice get louder. They weren't certain what all the words meant, but they knew, if repeated at home, mom would be washing their mouths out with soap. No cursing was allowed in the Goldman home, but dad seemed to make up for that rule while at work.

Zach and Gary loved hanging out at dad's shop. In the back of the shop there were wooden bins built up the wall. Each bin was filled with different sized plumbing fixtures. The boys would climb the bins. Zach was fearless, climbing to the top of the wall. Gary didn't like heights. Instead, he'd grab several plumbing fixtures and he would play with them on the ground. Gary was always trying to see how he could connect the fixtures and then take them apart.

Behind Murray's shop was Chick's sheet metal business. The boys could find pieces of metal scraps all over the ground. If they got bored climbing the bins for plumbing fixtures, they'd collect handfuls of scrap metal to build their own buildings on the ground. The process kept them busy for hours, while dad finished his business on the phone.

By mid-morning, Murray loaded up his son or sons into his station wagon. They'd visit the work sites to check on the men. If Alan was alone with him, his son took the point, bounding out of the car and walking straight up to the building site ahead of his dad. His presence signaled to the men that the boss wasn't far behind. Zach, on the other hand, was initially shy at the work site. He'd wait for his father and follow him. At the job, he would hide behind Murray's leg, which seemed like two redwood trees. He would reach back with his large hand and gently grab Zach's face from underneath, as if holding up his chin. "It's ok Number Two, you can come out now."

For all of their dad's loving nature and gentleness with his boys, he could also be a tough disciplinarian. Like his father, before him, he did not believe in "sparing the rod". Alan, Zach and Gary learned early on that dad never said something more than once. If you didn't pay attention, you did so at your own peril. Those hands, that were so incredibly quick in the boxing ring, could appear out of nowhere. Alan and Zach could hear the crack and the hand disappear, before the pain registered in their brain.

The scary part for the boys was that their dad often didn't realize his own strength. After the brain surgery, his large six-foot two-inch frame weighed 245 pounds. His arms had regained their strength from exercise and plumbing work. Murray never really stopped working at jobs. He didn't tell Franny, since she worried that he might get injured.

On several occasions her fears were not misplaced. A worker slipped with a pipe and hit him. Another day, he banged his head on a wood beam. Any of these injuries should have sent him to the hospital, but Murray would not have it. He sat down to settle the dizziness that quickly overwhelmed him. After 10 minutes the symptoms subsided and he pushed on with his day. Franny never knew, except the one time he gashed his forehead on an exposed pipe.

The Goldman boys never really knew when dad might get angry with them. For three boys, who could be wild and reckless at times, their fear of dad was often used by Franny to deter bad behavior. "Wait til your father comes home," would send chills down their spine.

One day, while mom went shopping, the boys ran through the house chasing each other. It was not unusual for the boys to be left alone, when mom went out. They were, mom thought, old enough to look out for each other. Franny never wanted perfect children, who would sit quietly and watch TV. Both she and Murray came from larger families, where children were often loudly heard running and arguing in very tight living quarters in Brooklyn. But the Goldman boys had enough space in their home for two or three New York families. In the back of her mind, she knew her home was an open invitation when the boys wanted to be wild.

Gary was often feisty and determined to get back at his older brothers. He couldn't even remember what they had done to him, but his mind filled with excitement as he chased Alan and Zach across the living room. The older brothers thought they had crossed into the "safe zone." The living room was off-limits to the boys. All fighting would stop if the boys crossed the line, from the hallway, kitchen or dining room. It was ok to resume the chase or wrestle each other, once they left the living room. However, Gary didn't care and didn't understand the danger.

His arm wound back and he arched his back. With all the strength he could summon in his little body, he let loose the small plastic pail that would doom them all. As his brothers scrambled to avoid being hit, the pail missed Gary's intended target and destroyed mom's favorite glass vase. The boys froze in their tracks. Not a word was spoken. No recriminations for Gary. Alan and Zach knew they'd all suffer equally.

The house got quiet quickly. Pieces of glass were everywhere. Would plastic save them? This was after all the 1950s. It was common for the furniture to be protected by plastic covers. Until this moment, the boys would joke about mom's obsession with the boundary lines.

The living room couch, the floor, pieces of glass had reached all the way to the dining room. The boys were doing their best to clean up the mess, when the front door opened. No one ever thinks of their mom as the angel of doom, but the Goldman boys knew their pleas of regret would not save them. Mom's favorite vase was broken. She paid almost $10 for that vase, but it wasn't just the money. In her mind, the boys needed to learn there were consequences.

She ordered the boys to their room. They were instructed not to leave until Dad came home from work. "You just wait. Your father is going to teach you boys that you can't wreck our home. You just wait!"

Nothing in life is more tortuous for a young child than the waiting. You sit idle for hours knowing you are doomed. For the Goldman boys, the waiting was worse than the pain they expected to experience. Would dad crack them with his hand? Would he take off that two-inch thick belt, they had seen—and felt—before? Locked in a room together for two hours, they would all soon forget why they ran through the house and the havoc they had caused. Faced with a common enemy, they would soon be playing quietly. It was so quiet, mom would get worried and peek in to see what they were doing. She couldn't believe the silence that came over these children.

Unknown to her, Murray had had an especially rough day at work. Anger and frustration had followed him like a shadow from job site to job site. The last thing he expected was conflict at home. By evening, he was just too weary. He walked through the door, just hoping for a quiet dinner with the family. But Franny would not have it. Her voice got louder and louder, as he opened and closed the front door behind him, "Do you know what those boys did today? They destroyed by favorite vase. There was glass everywhere in the living room. They're waiting in their bedrooms. I want you to go in there and beat those kids."

He looked at her with his eyes fixed steely on her every word. "Beat those kids," was not to be taken literally. She just wanted them to know there were limits on what would be tolerated in the Goldman home. For Murray, however, this was not the evening he had planned on his way home. He knew that he could not ignore his wife's demands for recompense. He was resigned to his task. He handed her his jacket and started down the long hallway to the bedroom, where pain and suffering waited.

The boys were holed up in the 2nd bedroom, which Zach and Gary shared. Their necks stiffened and they sat up straight, when they heard the front door open. They could hear mom yelling, even if they couldn't make out what she was telling dad. Doom would soon be upon them. They huddled together on the bed, as if they might cushion the pain as a group rather than submit to it individually. Hysteria swept the room as they heard dad's footsteps coming down the hallway.

The door swung open and his large frame entered. He repeated the story mom told him. He asked the boys if mom was right to punish them. Tears flowed quickly from the boys, as they pleaded their case. Murray slowly reached down to pull his belt from his pants. Terror was everywhere. The boys were openly crying, "Please dad, please don't hit us. We didn't mean to break mom's vase. It was an accident."

He quickly took note that while the boys pleaded their case, none of them tried to pass the blame on the others. He could see them backing up across the bed toward the wall. There would be no escape, as dad raised the folded belt in his hands.

The boys were now crying uncontrollably. "Please don't hit us!" Suddenly, Murray raised his finger to his lips. "Shush, shush, shush" he told the boys. "When I hit the bed, I want you to scream at the top of your lungs." The boys were paralyzed with fear. They expected the wrath of god to come down on them. They did not understand what dad was doing, but they knew better at this moment than to ask questions.

"Ready?" He smacked the bed twice with his belt. The boys let out screams like no one had heard before. And each time the belt came down on the bed, the boys' blood curdling screams grew even louder. By the third strike, the bedroom door swung open. "Murray, what the hell are you doing? I told you to beat them, I didn't tell you to kill them. Stop this right now. Just stop."

Franny's anger had quickly turned to sympathy. She insisted Murray leave the bedroom and come to the dinner table. She then turned and left the room. The boys sat stunned by their life altering good fortune. He slowly put his belt back on. He stopped long enough at the bedroom door to look back at the boys and smile. Order had been restored at the Goldman home.

On Sundays, Murray would wake one of the boys to go with him. They would drive to Teaneck, New Jersey, where he would buy bagels and lox. He'd stop at Butterflake bakery for chocolate babka or marble sponge cake and cookies for the children. After, he'd walk down to the corner five and dime store to buy the Sunday New York Times. This was a ritual in the Goldman home. Dad had no particular rationale or favorite in deciding who he'd wake up to go with him. None of the boys, however, would ever refuse getting up to be with their father.

However, Zach could be a pain in the ass. Murray would always treat each child to candy, for getting up so early. Zach would insist his father also buy candy for his brothers.

"Your brothers didn't come today, so we're only buying candy for you."

"Well, if I can't get for my brothers, I don't want any."

"Ok, let's go then," he would finally tell his son.

This test of wills ended at the door. Murray paid for the newspaper and started to leave. Zach stood his ground. "One for all and all for one," he would tell himself. Zach took seriously the lessons his mom taught the boys about sticking together. Murray could see the determination in his face as he looked down at Zach. His arms were folded across his chest. Shaking his head, he said, "I don't understand. Your brothers don't buy you candy when they come with me." Zach looked up at his father, with a steely resolve his dad recognized. "Ok, ok," he finally gave in, "Go pick out candy for your brothers." His father never told Zach, but he admired his stubbornness.

Sunday breakfast was a family tradition at the Goldman home. Afterward, Murray would read the newspaper for a couple of hours. The children ran around the house or went outside to play in the backyard. By 1 p.m., the Goldman boys were summoned for a nap. He marched the boys into his bedroom. The next 20 minutes were pure bliss, as their dad wrestled with the boys. He could now pick up a son with each arm. He'd toss the boys across the bed, until they bounced from the bed onto the floor. They always scrambled back for more. "No rough housing," Franny would yell down the hall.

Eventually, she walked into the room and told Murray when to settle down. The boys always protested, until he wrapped his long arms around them and held them close. Alan was the only one who regularly tried to crawl off the bed and sneak out of the room. He would almost reach the door, when his father reached down along the side of the bed. He threw a slipper at Alan. "Get back here," he'd yell half-smiling. Soon the Goldman boys were fast asleep next to him.

Franny would check on them. She'd shake her head, with a big smile on her face. There her husband laid fast asleep with his three little soldiers. If only the house were this quiet all the time. She headed back down the hallway. It was mom's turn to relax and watch TV.

CHAPTER 43

Broken Bonds

With the surgery a year behind him, Dr. Marks was truly amazed at Murray's recovery. His speech was normal. His gait while walking was normal. Only a thinning hairline and glasses gave Murray a distinct new look. He also noticed a new habit. His patient was smoking cigars.

Dr. Marks and Murray formed a friendship. They talked freely about the shared experiences of saving a life and being saved. He still had Brooklyn blood running through his veins. Dr. Marks, a more educated and refined man, nonetheless admired his patient's tenacity and his success. Murray looked forward to seeing Dr. Marks for regular six-month checkups. He would always value the second chance in life this skilled brain surgeon had given him.

Murray and Franny shared one major disappointment in their lives. Neither one of them had a close relationship with their family. Lifelong jealousies and selfishness robbed them of maintaining close bonds with brothers and sisters.

While Murray's sister Berta married Franny's brother Ziggy, the years were not always kind. Ziggy worked in the garment industry in New York, what they called the "Schmata business". Berta worked in an office. They had three daughters and struggled at times. Murray's mother, Tonia, had already passed away. But when his father Isaac died, the siblings were surprised to find their dad did not gamble away all of his money.

Berta and her brother Asher Goldman found the family will dividing the estate equally among the four children. They decided together to hide the papers from their siblings.

Asher Goldman worked at the post office to support his wife, Esther and four sons. Three of the boys experienced intellectual disabilities. After the first child, the doctors had warned Asher not to have more children. They believed there must be something genetic between the couple that impacted the baby. But Esther, his wife, wanted to keep trying. Their fourth son, Jared, was the only child born without a handicap.

Asher was a terrific father, always making time to help and play with his children. He was patient and committed to working with each child. He wanted them to be self-sufficient by the time they reached adulthood.

Murray was proud of his younger brother. He admired that Asher's self-absorbed nature had changed as he became an adult. He showed such compassion with his children. Asher's job gave him lots of flexibility, but he didn't have much income.

He remained closest with Samuel Goldman, or Sammy, as he was called. Murray taught Sammy how to be a plumber. After the War, he helped Sammy start his own plumbing business in Brooklyn. Sammy had two sons with his first wife, though she tragically died very young. Sammy remarried and they had two more boys. Like his older brother, Sammy always worked hard. He had ambition. He was gone before his children woke up and arrived home after they went to sleep. While not as tall as his brother, Sammy was equally as strong by middle age. He also had a great sense of humor, always joking with Murray's children when he'd come to visit.

It's not unusual for all families to fight over money. In these situations, siblings lose sight of how these battles forever rip relationships apart. At what cost? Is the money ever really worth it? Does anyone ever consider how these conflicts will impact the relationships among the next generation? Perhaps the children of the Depression feared more than others about money. Whether or not that was true, the battle among the Goldman children would be fierce and unforgiving.

Isaac Goldman surprised everyone at his death. He had squirreled away $300,000 from gambling. While he gave his wife Tonia money to support the family, no one ever suspected he had saved so much money.

Isaac had grown miserly as he got older. He remained in the small apartment he rented in Brooklyn in the 1930s. The building and the apartment were run down, but Isaac only needed a bed to sleep on. He never forgot how he came to this apartment and the separation from his family.

The fight among the Goldman children over Isaac's money broke out even before the will was discovered. Sammy knew from his father that he had a will. He was certain his siblings were hiding it. Berta had told Asher that they should get Isaac's money. She argued that Murray and Sammy had successful businesses and didn't need the money. She convinced Asher that he should get more money to help care for his handicapped kids. She wanted the money to make her life with Ziggy easier. They had both worked their whole lives and had so little to show for it.

Sammy didn't trust Berta. He lived closer to his siblings in Brooklyn, whereas Murray was off in New Jersey running his business. Sammy would talk to Asher regularly. He soon came away with an instinctive feeling that his older sister was trying to steal the old man's money.

He called Murray to intervene. His older brother was reluctant to get in the middle of a fight over money. He was grateful that his own plumbing business was doing so well—and he was grateful his life had been spared by the brain tumor. But Sammy did not want to confront Asher and Berta alone. While Sammy had a successful business, he felt it was his right to share in whatever money his father left behind. He also had four sons to think about. He hoped Murray could help reason with their siblings and the father's money was divided equally.

Murray arrived at Berta's apartment building the next week. He asked for a meeting among the siblings to discuss their father's will. He asked Berta to make certain the will was available for them to read together. Berta resented his involvement, but she was afraid to confront him.

When he showed up, Sammy was arguing with Asher in the street. Asher was much taller than Sammy, but Sammy was yelling and cursing at his older brother. "You crook, you lying bastard. Do you and Berta really believe that I should not get some of dad's money?" Murray separated the brothers, before they started swinging at each other.

The police sirens could be heard in the distance. None of the brothers thought the sirens had anything to do with them. But they underestimated Berta's resolve to keep their father's money. The police jumped from their cars as a crowd gathered. Berta ran to the officers and pointed out Murray and Sammy. "They're the ones who started the fight. Arrest them. Arrest those two." Murray could not believe his ears. His own sister was having him arrested. He did not care about the money. How could this situation get so out-of-hand?

As they approached the Goldman brothers, the police could see the arguing had not turned violent. This was clearly a family dispute. They still had to take Sammy and Murray down to the station. Berta had signed a complaint. "I'm ashamed of you," Murray told his sister as he was placed in handcuffs. "How could you do this? How could you be so greedy?" He stood shaking his head.

The call to Franny was very difficult for him. He needed her to drive out to Brooklyn and post bail. If she ever had concerns about Berta being sneaky and selfish, her disgust now turned to rage as she drove along the highway with her children in the back seat. Murray was spared on the ride home by her silence. He would not defend his sister. He regretted trying to help Sammy. He knew, aside from major family events, the days of visits to Goldman relatives were over. Franny had drawn a line in the sand. It was one that would not be crossed again.

Sammy never saw any of his father's money. Family bonds were torn apart that day. Murray was philosophical. He had a thriving business and didn't care to fight over his father's will. He regretted, however, that Berta and Asher had so lost their way.

By 1959, Murray was a more diversified businessman than Franny realized. He invested in several properties along key highways in northern New Jersey. He expanded the number of plumbing licenses to 70 towns in northern New Jersey and parts of New York bordering Jersey. His crew expanded to six trucks and 15 men. Chick, with his sheet metal business, and Murray leveraged their respective business dealings. Murray also partnered with a backhoe company to expand into the excavation business, which allowed them to install municipal water pipe systems.

He had kept the promise he made to himself. His business was projected to be worth $1 million in a year. This did not include his real estate investments, which provided additional financial security for the future. At 43, Murray was well on his way to achieving financial independence.

Franny Goldman had her own set of issues with family. The jealousies of childhood still influenced her siblings. She lived her life in a low-key, understated fashion. Even as Murray did well in business, Franny never flouted his success with her friends or her family. She didn't wear fancy jewelry or buy expensive clothes. She couldn't believe it, when Murray surprised her on their anniversary with a mink stole. She made him take it back. Largess was not in Franny's dictionary. Going out to dinner with friends was a rarity for the Goldman clan. Her priorities would always be her boys and cooking at home.

Ironically, Family meant everything to her. This included her own family—and helping her siblings, where possible. She tried to help her sister, Myrna (nicknamed Micky). Micky was the youngest in the Sugar family. Her husband, Ira, was a mailman. Ira earned a steady income, though the dollars could only stretch so far to support Micky and four daughters. Ira was a good man, a devoted father. Unfortunately, he suffered his whole life with eczema and psoriasis. The skin on his arms, face and scalp were always inflamed, flaky, red and, at times, bleeding. When Ira was not working, he'd often remain at home and out of sight. His arms would be wrapped in gauze up to his elbows.

Micky's girls shared clothes to help the family save money. The apartment where they lived in Brooklyn was in a very old building. In the early years, when the Goldman boys were young, they'd visit their aunt Micky. It was not uncommon to find cockroaches climbing the walls. The boys loved their cousins, but visiting could also be terrifying. None of her siblings in the Sugar family completed more than a grade school education. Micky was no exception. But she was a happy and loving sister to Franny. In contrast, Rachel (Boots) was always jealous of Franny. Micky admired her sister's athletic ability and her musical talents.

Franny loved her youngest sister. She looked for ways to help her. Franny would periodically change the furniture in her house, so she could bring the slightly used stuff to her sister. "Look, Micky, I can't keep all of these dressers in my house. If you don't take this dresser—or couch—it's just going to the garbage dump." In her heart, Micky knew better. Whatever she sent to her looked brand new. Micky knew Ira was too proud to have her sister buy them furniture, but the story from her was always the same, "it's you or the garbage dump." Micky was forever grateful.

Meir Sugar, Franny's younger brother, was in trouble by 1959. He lived in Detroit and his marriage was crumbling. Meir worked in a retail store, selling men's suits. At 38-years old, his two sons were nearly teenagers. Franny and Meir talked often by phone. The Goldman family had driven out to Detroit the year before for Meir's oldest son's Bar Mitzvah.

The infamous Zach Goldman story occurred during this first visit. Meir and his wife, Dorothy, joined Murray and Franny for dinner one night, leaving the five boys alone with a teenage baby sitter.

As the evening wore on, the boys got rowdier. The baby sitter chased the boys through the house. Zach came out the darkness with a plastic garbage can on his head. The baby sitter flipped over young Zach and a large porcelain statute on the end table was quickly destroyed. Panic set in, when the boys realized the damage. This would not be something that escaped punishment by their father. The next morning, Murray lined up the three boys. Like a Marx Brothers movie, one long slap would sweep across three faces. To the boys, however, they were convinced he hit them all at the same time. Dad had big hands.

Six months later, Meir came to live with the Goldman family in NJ. There was no saving his marriage. The Goldman boys doubled up in one room, so Meir had a room to himself. Murray helped Meir find a job at a local supermarket. He completed the plumbing at the Safeway market, which saved the owner thousands of dollars. At this juncture in his life, he could hardly drive on Route 17 or Route 4, the two main arteries in Paramus, without having done the plumbing in virtually every building he passed.

It would be nine months at the Goldman home before Meir could get on his feet, earn enough money to send support for his kids and find a place to live. He would move to the town of Fair Lawn, which was next door to Paramus. Murray guaranteed to the landlord that Meir's rent would be paid. He went out of his way, because he knew how important Meir was to Franny.

The idea of family is often very different from the reality. We'd like to believe everyone growing up together in the same home will share the same, common values. But the prism through which we see the world is not the same. Franny Sugar grew up in the Depression. Her most valued possession was her saxophone, and later on, a clarinet that she also mastered. She never second guessed her responsibility to help her family, whether by bringing home the money she earned as a musician or her refusal to ask her parents for anything. She didn't care about getting new clothes or shoes. In looks, Micky like Franny had long curly hair stretching down her back, though Micky's hair was black. Franny was simple. She was satisfied using rubber bands to tie her hair back. She was never a girly girl.

Franny was always ready to sacrifice her own needs and dreams, if it meant others in her family would benefit. These lessons from her early life would underscore the values she would try to teach her own children. "Look away, when you can," She taught Alan and Zach. "Life isn't just about material things. You boys must learn to look out for each other. At the end of the day, you need to stick together. No one else will be there. You have to be there to help one another."

How could siblings be so different from each other? Franny's oldest brother Lennie had been a surrogate father. A musical prodigy, he taught each child in the Sugar family how to play an instrument. He hoped they could then work and help support the family. But Lennie never took a real interest in the lives of his siblings. He was totally self-absorbed. He had overcome near poverty. And though he lacked a college education, he was certain his life as a band leader was far superior to what his siblings or their spouses might achieve.

Franny never spoke of her husband's success in business. She was grateful he was so driven and ambitious, but she saw no point in senseless comparisons with the lives of her brothers and sisters. "That's just not the way we should behave in life," she would say. "If we can't help or encourage each other as siblings, we shouldn't say anything."

Her sister, Rachel (Boots), however, could be sharp tongued and even mean spirited at times. She lived near Franny in New Milford, New Jersey, but never invited her sister and her family to dinner. Aunt Boots, as the Goldman boys called her, would insist they play in the backyard when their mom visited. She didn't want those Goldman boys in her home. Boots had two boys of her own, but they were older by 5 or 6 years. No one could measure up to her children. Sadly, she looked down on Franny's boys.

Boots could never let go of the envy she felt toward her sister. Boots coveted the attention she got from Lennie, the family patriarch. She learned to play the trumpet by ear, to impress him. Lennie was a terrific trumpet player. But Franny always overshadowed Boots, with her natural talents. She was the only Sugar sibling, other than Lennie, that learned to read music. She could pick up any piece of sheet music and immediately play in an orchestra. On the handball court, no one could beat her. Lennie was also athletic. He excelled at tennis. Franny came closest to Lennie's strengths, and she also had a more open and loving heart.

Franny never harbored jealousy or ill will toward her brothers and sisters. She had her own dreams and aspirations for the Goldman boys. Yes, she wanted them to learn instruments, as she did growing up. But she wanted more for her children. Her dream was for her children to go to college. No one in her family or Murray's had gone beyond a grade school education. She was not competing with her siblings. She just wanted Alan, Zach and Gary to reach for the stars.

CHAPTER 44
The Boys

———

The Goldman boys were growing and they couldn't be more different.
Alan was born to success. He was the oldest and clearly his parent's favorite child. He finally showed up in 1948, almost two years after Murray came home from the Navy. His parents had waited almost a decade to have a child, through the War and after three miscarriages. It's true most first-born children carry the heaviest burden of hope and parental aspirations.

Alan worked very hard to live up to his parent's affection. The seeds of success were sown early. He was an avid reader and a good student in school. Murray loved to take his oldest son with him to work or to run errands. With encouragement from mom, Alan would also become the first and best musician in the family. He learned to play the accordion by 10 years old. Later, he switched to playing the saxophone. Franny was determined to have each child play an instrument. The lessons of the Depression years would be passed down to her children. "If you can play an instrument, you'll always find a job," she told her children.

Alan started playing little league baseball at eight years old. By 10, his determination to win each time his team was on the field was not lost on his proud father. His parents didn't teach him to be competitive. It seems this came naturally. There was no such thing as second place for Alan Goldman, whether in school, sports or life. He could be his own worst critic, if his hitting or fielding did not meet his own high standards. His dad and Bob O'Brien both sponsored baseball teams. Alan wore his "Murray's Plumbing" uniform with a special brand of pride.

Zach Goldman was a very different child. Murray and Franny had already been married 13 years, when Zach was born in 1950. In some ways, he escaped the high expectations placed on his older brother. Free to explore and find his own way, Zach was both curious about the world—and rebellious. He was quick to challenge common wisdom. He was not as book smart as Alan, but he had an uncanny instinct about people. His dad could identify with Zach, with what he considered his "street smarts." Zach could be a tough competitor, when he wanted to be. At other times, he could be drawn by his imagination in new directions.

At school, Zach was not a top student, but he was always one of the teacher's favorites. In second grade, for Zach's school project, he went up to the front of the class. He proceeded to tap dance as he sang his favorite song, "You are my Sunshine." His teacher couldn't get over his poise and confidence. However, teachers were equally impressed with the insightful questions he'd ask. Mrs. Levine would tell Franny during teacher conferences that Zach was "her little man." He had empathy for other students and things going on in the world. He also wasn't afraid to speak his mind or to tell his teacher she was being unfair, if he felt wronged.

Like Alan, Franny would insist Zach learn an instrument. At 8, he began playing the trumpet. He loved music. Franny thought he might be the most gifted musician in the family, with a natural lip for the horn. As a child, he could hit the highest notes. After school, both Alan and Zach were required to practice their instruments. It was not unusual for their mom to be yelling to the boys upstairs, when they hit the wrong note on the music scales. For Zach, hitting the wrong note wasn't always by accident. He was a rebel at heart, not afraid to provoke or challenge the status quo.

Zach also scared his mom by running through the house doing somersaults and landing on his back on the wood floor in the den. Yelling at Zach wasn't a solution. He had a fierce determination, much like his father. For her own peace of mind, she decided to sign Zach up for classes in acrobatics and tap dancing. She knew Zach loved to dance. Whenever the family went out for dinner at Tony's Italian restaurant in Lodi, Zach would ask his dad for a quarter to put in the jukebox. As Bobby Darin sang "Mack the Knife," everyone in the restaurant would turn their heads to see Zach dancing and doing cartwheels.

As a young boy, Zach idolized his older brother, Alan. It was this bond that often brought out Zach's combative and protective instincts. In third grade, Zach was standing at the end of the school playground, when he saw three boys pushing and punching Alan. Zach could hear the anti-Semitic words, "C'mon Jew boy, fight back. C'mon you little kike."

Alan was not afraid to fight back. He was just out numbered. Zach would see the commotion. No one was going to gang up on his brother. They were older and bigger, but he wasn't fearful. He ran as fast as he could, hitting one boy from behind and tackling another boy nearby. "No one is going to hurt my brother," he told his mom, when she was called to pick him up from the school Principal's office. "I'm not afraid of them."

The anti-Semitic comments at school were not new to Alan or Zach. The Goldman's were one of the first Jewish families to move into Paramus. The boys didn't really understand why other kids started fights with them. "We don't look or act differently than anyone else at school," Alan would tell his mom, "so why do they hate us?"

That night, Murray Goldman would sit Alan, Zach and Gary down and talk about anti-Semitism. He explained how children learn these things from parents or friends. They don't really understand hate. They grow into it. He talked about World War II and how many Jews were killed, just because they were Jewish. He told the boys that fighting wasn't the answer. "You may knock someone down, but that doesn't change the way they think," he explained.

Zach and Alan looked at each other. They were confused. "I think I did the right thing," said Zach, defiantly to his father. "Yes, you did do the right thing. As your mom always teaches you, you need to stick up for each other. You need to look out for each other," he responded.

"There will be times when you can't walk away, where the other guy just won't stop picking on you. Always try to avoid fighting," Murray pleaded with his sons. "But if you can't walk away—aim for his nose." Both Zach and Alan looked at each other. "Did you just tell us to hit someone?" Alan asked.

"Yes," he said. "If someone doesn't let you walk away from a fight, then, Yes, I want you to just punch him right in the nose." His dad pointed to Zach's nose and demonstrated a right cross with his huge hand. "He'll start to bleed, and then he'll never bother you again."

Murray Goldman was not a pacifist. He was careful to teach the boys restraint, which was important to Franny. "There's too much anger and fighting in the world," she would tell him. "The boys need to learn how to solve issues by talking and reasoning with people." Her motto was to look for compromise. On the other hand, Murray wanted his sons to push back if they were pushed too far. He taught them how to shake hands and how to throw a right cross. "Never, never, never, never look for a fight," he would say, "because there will always be someone out there who is stronger or faster than you.

At the same time, never run from a fight you can't avoid. If you stand up for yourself, people will respect you — and they will think twice before crossing the line. Remember, let people judge you by what you're willing to fight for."

Gary Goldman sat and listened to his father lecture his brothers. He was still young. He may not have understood the conversation, but Murray wanted him there. The youngest Goldman adored his father and loved being included.

Gary was born in 1952. The doctors and nurses had Franny convinced she was finally having a daughter she always wanted.

Murray and Franny couldn't have been happier with their tribe. It was not her nature to dwell on things she couldn't change. But she could never forget the miscarriages. Pregnancy became sheer torture for her. The doctors couldn't explain why she lost the babies. She refused to give up. Alan and Zach were her special blessings. She would consider a third child the icing on the cake of blessings in her life.

Bob O'Brien and Murray met for a drink to celebrate Gary's birth. He had actually missed seeing the delivery, but he could hear his wife down the hall. He laughed as he told O'Brien that his sister, Berta, had children, but they were all girls. "The plumbers in the family," Murray explained, "did their job well. Asher, Sammy and I, all produced boys."

As he joked, he knew in his heart how much a girl would have meant to Franny. He, too, prayed for a little girl.

O'Brien at this point in life had two children of his own. The two men drank and expressed gratitude—and pride. They had worked tirelessly to succeed in business, but they were especially thankful for their families.

Gary gave Franny her greatest challenges as a mom. He was a colicky baby, crying half the night. By day, she had to keep up with Alan and Zach racing around the house. The business phones rang off the hook. Gary would have bursts of non-stop crying during the day, but it was at night when exhaustion overtook Franny. Murray was also exhausted from work. But he never heard Gary crying at night. She couldn't bring herself to ask him for help. Nothing prepares a mom for this type of challenge. It can, over time, bring depression. Franny tried to look past the sleeplessness and noise. She just kept thinking about how much her children relied on her. This focus on the children, instead of herself, gave her strength and added resolve.

The first three or four months passed and Gary's colicky period ended. For the most part, Gary became a happy child. He played with Zach more often than Alan. Alan was always off on his own. Zach liked having a younger brother. He would look after him, making certain he didn't get hurt.

Zach loved the idea of going on adventures with Gary. They would explore the woods, looking for frogs under rocks. He hated playing games, but did so periodically to keep him happy. Zach could see that his brother, at times, was a sickly child. He was near two years old, when he was taken to the hospital for an emergency hernia repair. Gary was never as active and wild like him or Alan. He was happy to sit for hours playing with a toy, watching TV or trying to build with his wooden blocks.

The motivation and influences in a child's life are always clearer in hindsight. The early years shape the future, without anyone ever knowing why. How ironic that we don't really stop to consciously observe and think about a child's development. Do we ever ask ourselves whether their early experiences and foundation are strong enough to weather the life ahead of us?

For Alan, Zach and Gary, though they lived in the same home, they each experienced a different world. Each of them were shaped by their own view of life as a Goldman.

As the boys grew, they found that their mom could be a tougher disciplinarian than their father. It was her will power which made a lasting difference in their lives. She taught the boys proper behavior and to dress appropriately. Franny Goldman came from little in the Depression, but her travel as a musician in the Catskills had instilled a keen sense of dress and a determination to look your best. She would harp on the boys about "first impressions being lasting ones." And she could be ruthless in trying to shape their attitudes.

The twice-a-year visit to Bloomingdale's to buy new clothes was always a tug-of-war. In August, there was a ritual shopping for the new school year and the Jewish holidays. Even at 8 and 10 years old, the boys would be required to wear a sports coat to Synagogue. Alan loved getting new clothes. He and Gary were pretty compliant in trying on outfits, even when their mom couldn't decide what she liked best on the boys.

Zach was different. His protests grew louder as the shopping went on past an hour. "Please try this on," she would ask him. "I don't want to try it on," he responded. "Try this on," she instructed. Twice more, he would refuse. "Crack!" Franny's hand landed across his face. The back and forth would continue for several minutes. "Crack, crack," from left to right, she was not taking any backtalk. The tears rolled down Zach's face. By the third slap, he was ready—and willing to try on clothes.

Spring shopping was easier. She was keen to find matching outfits for them. The boys would get shirts in red and blue, with pants in white or blue. Franny bought Perry Como jackets to match with their outfits. Each of the boys could wear their choice of clothes, but they were unmistakenly connected to her tribe. In time, the Goldman boys came to appreciate her lessons on haircuts, dress and overall appearance. She was preparing them for a world, which she hoped for, as they grew from children to young men.

CHAPTER 45
Alan's Bar Mitzvah

Alan Goldman's Bar Mitzvah was planned in early spring 1961. As part of his coming of age, the 13-year-old would be called to read from the Torah for the first time. The Torah scrolls cover the Old Testament found in the Bible. In addition to the Ten Commandments handed down to Moses, the Torah includes a total of 613 commandments to guide the conduct of a Jewish life before God.

Studying for the Bar Mitzvah teaches children that they are not alone in the world, and they have responsibility to god, their family and all mankind to care for the rights of others and to do "mitzvahs" or good deeds. Alan learned from his studies with Rabbi Michael Rackowitz that he was no longer a child. After his Bar Mitzvah, he would stand before the whole congregation as an adult.

He studied every day, learning to read the Hebrew required to lead the Haftorah service in Synagogue, the Musaf service and to reading his portion of the Torah reading. Not every Bar Mitzvah boy reads so much during the Saturday Sabbath service. Alan insisted that he wanted to conduct the entire service. The Rabbi was impressed by his student's commitment to study and master his part. He also wrote his own speeches explaining his Torah reading to the audience in the Synagogue and separate remarks thanking his parents on this special day.

The Goldmans were so excited that their first son would be Bar Mitzvahed. Instead of a small family celebration at home, by the 1960s, the Bar Mitzvah party competed with weddings in size and cost. Their friends would joke that in the United States, the catering industry had taken over this solemn occasion. Within one generation of Jewish immigration coming to the U.S. from Europe, the Bar Mitzvah had become both a rite of passage and a cultural sign of financial success.

Murray booked the largest catering hall in northern New Jersey. The "Rounders" restaurant and catering hall on Route 17, less than a mile from his plumbing business, could handle more than 300 guests. Franny shared her husband's enthusiasm, but she restricted their list to 225 guests. "I don't want a circus," she told him. "Let's have some dignity."

Every uncle, aunt, cousin and friend, from back in Brooklyn to their homes in New Jersey would be on the invite list. Franny finally gave in to her husband on his insistence they include his brothers and sister. He argued with his wife that they both had siblings who were less than loving and supportive. "It not really about them," he told her. "This party is about the Goldmans. Look at what we have accomplished." His face beamed with pride. "Franny, you and me," he said waving his hand around the house. "We did all of this on our own. We shared a dream for us and the kids. I want all of them to see how small they are. We don't really need their approval. We did it ourselves."

After sleeping on the conversation, Franny decided he was right. She would focus on the celebration. They had left Brooklyn for a different kind of life with their children. At the very least, Alan, Zach and Gary didn't talk with the same Brooklyn accent as their cousins. Their world view and their future of going to college had been decided for them, before they were born.

The blessing over the wine at the Bar Mitzvah would be given to Saul Sugar, Franny's father. Saul was a tailor. He was never seen without a suit jacket and tie. He never told his children the story of coming to America. Decades later, in his twenties, Zach Goldman would learn about his grandfather while visiting cousins in London. When he returned home, he shared the story with his mom, though she thought the whole thing seemed preposterous. His grandfather was not the quiet-spoken person Franny grew up with. He kept to himself, going and coming from work. On weekends, he could sit quietly for hours reading the Jewish Daily Forward newspaper in Yiddish. Zach found it odd that his mother knew so little about her father—and she never asked questions. "Was this just Depression era children," he wondered, "who learned not to ask questions? Or is it just that children tend not to focus on their parent's history until they are gone? At that point, all the good stories about their lives are lost." Zach had so many questions for Franny, after meeting his London cousins—but, in truth, he had many good stories to share with her.

Saul Sugar had fled Russia in the early 1900s. He had been a young activist passing out leaflets against the Czar. He was arrested twice. He ran away when his friends and fellow revolutionaries told him he was in danger. After a few arrests, it was not uncommon for leftist revolutionaries to be taken out and shot. Saul's extended family had talked about leaving Russia, once the pogroms started and Jews were being killed by Cossacks. Families fled west. Saul's cousins, the Solomon family, stopped on their way to America in the United Kingdom and decided to stay. Saul wanted to reach America, where his friends waited to help him in New York.

"My father a revolutionary," Franny would say to him. "I don't believe it. My father read the newspaper every day. He never spoke out about politics." However, Zach knew differently. The Solomons were closer in age to his grandfather. They knew stuff his mom might never know. These stories must be true.

He told his mom how her father told their cousins about his experience entering the country and going through U.S. Customs. The man ahead of him was rejected from entering the U.S.. At the time, Saul didn't speak much English. As best he could tell, he attributed the man's circumstance to his torn T-shirt and dirty clothes. Saul beamed, as his application for entry into the U.S. was stamped approved. He had made his own suit in Russia, before leaving the country. He was certain this made all the difference for someone coming to America. Whether this was true is anyone's guess, but this lesson would stay with him the rest of his life. His one surprise, as he left Customs, was his name was changed. He could no longer be Guric. This Russian name "Guric" would fade in memory. His papers now said Sugar. Saul was happy to have the name Sugar. He had made it to America.

The Bar Mitzvah was a huge success. Aside from family, the Mayor of Paramus and many notable businessmen attended the event. As a founding member of the Paramus Jewish Community Center, the entire executive board of the Synagogue attended the party.

Franny and Murray remained true to themselves. There was no gloating or showing off. In their typical low-key fashion, they walked the banquet hall greeting guests, hugging family and thanking everyone who attended. It was a glitzy affair without "too much glitz". Franny just wanted everyone to have a good time.

For a family of musicians, she knew how important it was to hire an exceptional band. The mini-orchestra had at least a dozen instruments and an exceptional drummer. This was the 1960s. Rock n Roll was storming the country. Guests were dancing the Lindy, the Twist. No one sat down for even a minute, while the music roared. Zach was only ten years old, but he was quite a dancer. He also did cartwheels, splits and handsprings, thrown in to impress the crowd.

His brothers were no slouches on the dance floor. Alan was an excellent dancer, though he was initially shy to get up when the music started. Before grabbing the prettiest girl, however, he walked across the floor and asked his mom to dance the "Cha Cha" with him. For Alan, mom would always have the first dance. He practiced with her for over a month dancing in the kitchen. Back and forth, side to side, he was a perfectionist and it showed. Franny beamed. She was so happy.

As usual, Gary also surprised everyone. Like his brother, he was not shy getting on the dance floor. He also wasn't afraid of asking older girls to dance and then impress them as he did the "Twist."

After the dancing slowed down, Murray went over to the band and made his request. He asked for a minute to find his wife, pulling her away from small talk with neighbors in Paramus. The band leader could see he was ready and the music began. A woman singer stepped to the microphone. Her voice was haunting. She began to sing his favorite song, Autumn Leaves, first in English and then she switched into French,

"The falling leaves drift by the window
The autumn leaves of red and gold
I see your lips, the summer kisses
The sun-burned hands I used to hold….."

This proud moment would not be lost on him. He was grateful to have such a wonderful family. But most of all, he was in love with his wife. He held her hand and looked down into her eyes, as her head tilted back.

"Franny, have I told you how much I love you today?"
Franny Goldman smiled. "I know."

Depuis que tu es parti, les jours s'allongent
Et bientôt j'entendrai la vieille chanson de l'hiver
Mais tu me manques surtout ma chérie
Quand les feuilles d'automne commencent à tomber

The music continued as he pulled her close in his arms. The noise of the crowd gave way to a brief moment of solitude. In this moment, the Goldmans celebrated each other.

The dance had ended when the Manager of the Rounder's catering hall tapped Murray on his shoulder. There must have been 15 boys attending the Bar Mitzvah. And boys will be boys, except this time they went too far. In their boredom, as the dinner dragged on, the boys went outside the restaurant. It was March. Snow covered the parking lot. The boys started throwing snowballs as the trucks and buses passed the catering hall on Route 17.

Carefree fun became more serious, when one of the boys molded a snowball with a rock inside. At he hurled the snowball, all of the boys could hear the crash of glass on the bus window as it passed. Luckily, no one was on the bus, but the driver was livid as he pulled over and looked at the damage. The boys ran inside, thinking the driver couldn't tell where the snowballs came from. They underestimated the situation. Within 15 minutes, the bus had circled back along the highway and pulled into the Rounder's.

The Manager found Murray quickly, when the driver threatened to call the police. He was cursing up a storm, as Alan's dad came outside. . He was not happy. He could not imagine what possessed the boys to carry on like this? He called Alan outside. He was an adult now. Wasn't that the whole idea behind the Bar Mitzvah? He asked him for an explanation. Alan started telling his father he didn't know his friends were throwing snowballs with rocks inside. He quickly put up his hand, as if to stop his son from talking.

"Don't tell me son. I want you to go over to the driver and tell him. I want you to apologize. I want you to tell him it was stupid to throw snowballs and you realize someone could have gotten hurt. If you can convince him of your sincerity, I'll let you off the hook."

Alan stood silent as his father spoke. He knew his dad rarely gave instructions more than once. As a child, if you didn't respond—and respond quickly, the next experience was the back of his large hand. Alan and Zach often told stories about being hit so hard you flew across the room, landing upside down against the wall. That was hyperbole. But for the Goldman boys it wasn't the fear of pain that drove their behavior, it's that feeling that they disappointed their father.

The bus driver was red in the face, talking to the restaurant manager. However, he was taken aback, as Alan approached him. He did as his father instructed. He did not put his head down. He looked the bus driver straight in the eye, as he spoke. A part of him thought if his dad was watching, he wanted him to see that he owned his mistakes. Alan was certain this wouldn't be the only one he made in his life, but the lesson of taking responsibility would stay with him always.

As he finished his apology, Murray came over to speak with the bus driver. He motioned for his son to go back inside. The incident was over and it was time to resume the celebration. He joined in apologizing to the bus driver. He reached out to shake the driver's hand. When the man opened his hand, he found two crisp $100 bills. "Nothing excuses what happened here," he said. "I trust my son has learned something today. But maybe this will help express my regret. I'm also happy to pay the company for any damage to the bus. You have my business card."

The bus driver calmed down. He thanked Murray. He walked back to the bus, as Murray turned to the Manager of the Rounders, "I guess I've entered a new period of uncertainty...teenagers." With that, he smiled and headed back to the party.

The Goldmans were almost giddy at how well the Bar Mitzvah party came off. Franny's phone didn't stop ringing for days, with friends congratulating her. Not surprisingly, only Micky and Mair called their sister to offer kind words. If she wanted to hear from her brother Lennie, she would have to call him. She was also certain her sister Boots wouldn't call. Whether it was sibling jealousy, Boots couldn't help herself. Franny took it in stride. She didn't worry about that sort of stuff.

The plumbing business had grown to cover more than 70 towns in northern New Jersey and stretched into neighboring towns in New York. He had expanded the business to 15 men and 6 trucks. The partnership he created with Jim Rossmor Excavation, allowed them to offer new capabilities, like installing pipes for municipal water systems. Rossmor owned the bulldozers and large-scale excavating equipment. Murray was able to provide manpower and market their services through the network of contacts he established. He build a good reputation with elected officials and local businessmen, having installed plumbing for many commercial buildings along major highways in Bergen County.

Whatever health issues he faced were in the rearview mirror. His penny stock portfolio provided extra weekly income. He enjoyed reading and investing, though ironically, he never saw the buying/selling of stock as a form of gambling. For him, the exercise was an escape from the daily rigors of the plumbing business. He made a conscious decision that he would never take risk by investing in major stocks. The frequent buying and selling of small stocks satisfied his hobby.

However, real estate was another matter. He liked the idea of buying tangible assets that could be sold if an emergency required him to do so. After his brain tumor, these investments represented the security he promised to create for himself and his family. The doctors did not promise him threats to his health were behind him. While he didn't think a second brain tumor was likely, he remained aware there were no guarantees regarding his general health.

At 46, Murray bought real estate wherever he could find commercial property along major highways. He strategically looked for highways that were still young and in various stages of development. In some cases, he just bought the land and held it for years. He had confidence that as long as the land sat on a major highway, the development and increased value would follow. Real estate became Murray's annuity.

Alan's Bar Mitzvah in March was the first of two major family events in 1961. Zach Goldman was preparing for a dance and gymnastics show, which was scheduled for late July. Franny had enrolled Zach in classes at the Fred Kelly's dance studio in Oradell, New Jersey. Franny wanted him to stop doing somersaults and landing on his back in the family's home. The Kelly school taught acrobatics, in addition to jazz and tap dance.

The owner, Fred Kelly was a famous tap dancer, choreographer and teacher. It was Fred who taught his older brother, Gene to tap dance, so he could earn money for college. Fred grew up the youngest of five children. Few knew the Kelly children all started out as performers in the 1920s. Gene Kelly's dancing and acting brought fame. Fred was equally famous, but most of his career was behind the scenes as a choreographer. The brothers were close and collaborated throughout their careers. Gene and Fred Kelly were featured dancing together in three movies. Fred was portlier, but considered a better dancer. Franny could recall seeing the Kelly brothers on screen in the 1940s.

Mrs. Kelly, Fred's mom had started a dance school near Pittsburgh in the 1920s, which morphed into the Gene Kelly School of Dance. They had multiple locations across several states. Franny met Fred Kelly in the late 1950s. Semi-retired, he opened his own dance studio in Bergen County New Jersey to teach kids.

Zach started attending Fred Kelly's school at 10 years old. In those years, they taught tumbling or acrobatics. This was not a pathway to formal gymnastics training like the Olympics. Franny just wanted Zach to have fun, not get hurt—and perhaps to land on his feet one day. Ironically, her son never had that problem. He had natural agility, strength and rhythm, whether doing flips one after the other or tap dancing.

She dropped Zach off on a Saturday morning. From acrobatics to tap dancing, the day grew longer attending more and more classes. He'd walk two stores down from the studio to get lunch and then return for afternoon lessons. One of the dance teachers wanted Zach to take some ballet classes, but he didn't like being in classes that were all girls.

The Kelly dance school's annual show for parents and relatives was scheduled for Thursday, July 27, 1961. Zach was asked to perform in five segments of the show, which included both acrobatics and some group tap dancing numbers. This involved more performances than any other student in the school. Typical of Zach, when he wanted to accomplish something, nothing could stand in his way. His dad had never seen Zach dance at the school. Saturdays were still a work day for him. He'd hear about his son's accomplishments from his mom's excited descriptions.

Participating in five segments of the dance recital would require Franny to buy or make costumes. Luckily, Zach already had a blue blazer which he'd use for the tap dancing number, which involved singing with a line of boys and a shuffle hopping to the song, "Hey, Look me Over. Lend me an ear. Fresh out of clover. Mortgage up to here. But don't pass the plate, folks. Don't pass the cup. I figure whenever you're down and out, the only way is up...." He'd practice singing and memorizing the lines for hours at home.

Franny thought this was the cutest number, which she saw only once in rehearsal. None of the boys were in-tune or in-step. She told her husband it was a work in progress. She'd laugh as the boys would mistakenly go in opposite directions. "Mr. Kelly and the teachers," she said, "had their work cut out for them."

For her part, she called upon her long unused skills to sew three outfits that her son would need. His uniform for the acrobatic numbers had to be loose enough for him to move without ripping apart. She took this task quite seriously and worked long hours at home, while the children were at school.

It struck Franny how three boys could be living in the same house together and be nearly oblivious to each other. Alan and Gary knew Zach had a dance show coming up, but they could care less. As close as she wanted her children to be with each other, there would always be a gap in how they saw their life—and how they experienced the world. Maybe that's just true for all kids, she thought. We can travel the same road together, but we can never fully understand the uniqueness of someone else's experience.

She knew how different her children could be. She recalled when Zach at 9 years was playing baseball. He was pitching on a minor-league team in the Paramus recreational baseball league. His coach recommended Zach be given a chance to move up and play in the major league, with 10 and 11-year olds. Almost overnight, Zach found himself on "Murray's Plumbing", the same team his older brother Alan played on. They rarely spoke on the field to each other or yelled encouragement when they got in the batter's box. "They each were so competitive," she asked herself? "But competitive with each other or within themselves? Did their presence on the same team make each try harder to make their father proud of them"?

Franny knew something about competition, with a rivalry among four siblings for her brother Lennie's approval. The work on Zach's costumes gave her many hours to think about her children. Like an army sergeant, she drilled her kids to be true to themselves, their values and their own individual view of the world. But she also refused to permit jealousy to interfere with her defi-nition of family. "Whenever you disagree, always remember you are family. You stick up for each. You stand with each other. When you need someone badly, make certain you are there to help each other." These are lessons Franny prayed would be her lasting legacy.

CHAPTER 46
It All Comes Undone

The Plumbers' Convention June 15-18, 1961 in Atlantic City was a great excuse for Murray and Franny to get away for a long weekend. School was almost over. They both thought it might be fun to take the children. The hotel in Atlantic City had a pool and they were a block from the beach and boardwalk. For two weeks prior to the trip, they casually debated whether to bring the kids or steal away for some quiet time by themselves. Murray was pretty exhausted. He had started construction of a major new building on Route 23 near Wayne, New Jersey. Half of his plumbing crew was at the work site daily, which meant he had to be there as well.

They had been to the Plumber's Convention once before. These events could get raucous, as these working men drank and were entertained by half-naked girls. Wives attended major events and dinners, but the "boys will be boys" values were well in attendance at special sessions late in the evening.

The Goldmans decided to leave very early Thursday, for the nearly three-hour drive to Atlantic City. It was unusual for Franny to drive, but he gave in to her protests to simply relax and read the newspaper. Two days before the event, she decided to leave the children home. While they would likely sleep during the trip, she was concerned that her husband just have some peace and quiet.

She asked her cleaning lady, Georgie, to babysit for the children and to stay at their home until Sunday afternoon. Georgie was in her late 20s and welcomed the chance to earn some extra money. The Goldmans always treated Georgie well, like a member of their family. She was especially grateful Franny always offered her stuff, like clothes, dishes, toys which she could share with her family.

Murray talked with Franny for most of the drive. He told her about new jobs he had coming up and his purchase of a new property along Route 23. She raised the subject of the children going to day camp in the summer. Even though they lived in the New Jersey suburbs, she wanted them to go hiking in the woods, do arts and crafts and practice their swimming. She recalled how Zach had followed Alan, jumping in the pool one summer in the Catskills. "Remember Zach couldn't swim." He went straight to the bottom of the pool.

Murray and Franny laughed as they remembered the story. They both agreed the day camp was a good idea.

During the last half hour of the trip, as they drew closer to Atlantic City, Murray sat back and read his New York Times. He was turning the page, only two miles from the city, when his eyes glanced up to see a black object coming toward him. He instinctively put his hands up against the dash board.

The screech of tires and the sounds of metal crashing could be heard almost a mile away. Cars pulled over to the side of the road, as they witnessed the collision. The front of the station wagon looked like a crumpled accordion. Inside, two large indentations could be seen, where Murray had placed his hands to absorb the impact.

Franny Goldman's blood was everywhere in the car. Her lifeless body hung over the steering wheel. Her face was turned toward the side window. Blood flowed down her head, her arms and across the seat. And just as quickly as life had changed for her, the world around the accident fell silent.

It would be nearly ten minutes before an ambulance would arrive. Witnesses ran to Franny and Murray Goldman's car door to lend assistance. They opened her side. She was unconscious. "Are you ok?" the man yelled to Franny. The blood continued to cover her face. The man said to his friend, "I think this lady is dead." His friend ran to other side of the car.

The friend approached Murray's door just as a policeman arrived. Together, they pulled and pried open the car door. It was a sight they had never seen before. His eyes were open. "Hey, buddy," the policeman called out, "can you hear me?"

It was as if he had seen the whole accident as it happened. The policeman gently pulled on his arm. Murray didn't know it, but he had physically stopped the station wagon engine from coming into the front seat and killing him and Franny. His body fell toward the officer. His eyes were open, but he was definitely unconscious. The dents in the dashboard, where he placed his hands were clearly visible. "Either this guy has enormous strength," the witness told the officer, "or I'm seeing a miracle of some sort. The front of this car is caved in, but he stopped the engine. I've never seen anything like this before."

Another group of witnesses had run to the other car. It was a beat up black 1953 Cadillac sedan, which in those days weighed almost 5,000 pounds. One witness described it as looking like a tank. The car had clearly crossed over the double yellow line, before it hit the Goldman's 1959 Dodge station wagon head on. It looked like Franny's side the vehicle suffered the most damage.

The driver opened the Cadillac door and stumbled out. He was dressed in a sleeveless t-shirt. He limped a few steps, before losing his balance. They could smell the alcohol as they reached to stop him from falling. "This guy is drunk," a witness yelled back to the policeman at the Goldman station wagon. The witnesses helped the driver walk a few steps and sit on the curb. A second police officer had arrived and walked over to the Cadillac. He thanked the witnesses for helping the driver. The policeman shook his head at the thought that this drunk driver just plowed straight into the Goldman car—and maybe killed one or both of them. He told the driver he was under arrest. He eventually put him in the patrol car and headed to the station.

"Ironic," the cop told his fellow officer before driving off. "Why is it that the drunk guys never get injured"?

Franny and Murray were taken in separate ambulances to the hospital. The sirens screamed as they drove through the streets of Atlantic City. The ambulance para-medics worked on her the whole ride, trying to determine the source of all the blood. Great care was given not to move her too much. They feared internal injuries. Both she and Murray remained unconscious. The medics could not figure out why he was so unresponsive. They had no way of knowing about his prior medical condition.

Teams of doctors and medical personnel began working on the Goldmans as soon as they arrived. It would take hours before bloodwork and X-rays could be completed. They stitched up the large scalp laceration that cut across Franny head. The doctors were concerned about internal damage and the bones that were pushing through her skin. At times the nursing staff expressed gratitude that neither Franny or Murray were aware of what happened and might not feel the pain associated with their injuries.

Within the hour, a team of doctors met to review their conclusions on Franny. Her jaw was broken in three places from hitting the steering wheel and windshield. Her right arm was broken in two places and her left wrist bone was shattered. Both her legs and ankles were broken. The left side of her hip bone was shattered and posed an immediate threat. If chips of bone pressed internally against an artery, Franny would not make it. The doctors agreed they should cut her open and do an exploratory surgery. There was no way for them to determine if internal organs had been damaged.

The doctors had stopped the bleeding they found. They agreed not to wait before deciding on cutting Franny open. Two of the doctors wanted to tackle surgery immediately to stabilize her shattered hip. Another team was anxious to correct the multiple bone fractures in her legs and arm. The plastic surgeon on call at the hospital was pushing to proceed with performing surgery on Franny's jaw, which would have to be wired shut to hold the bones together.

The hospital staff couldn't remember such a large team of doctors being called in to oversee the well-being of one patient. The doctors worked pretty collaboratively. No one's ego got in the way of patient care.

By evening, a plan of action was well-underway. She had three surgeries before midnight. The doctors knew it was critical to stabilize Franny's hip and remove bone fragments that could rupture arteries. Surgical screws, rods and plates were used to try and piece her together. The doctors understood that half the patients with damage as extensive as Franny would die within 6 months of the surgery. And, if they survived, the likelihood of recovering their independence and function to walk was nil. At 44, Franny would never walk normally again.

In a separate surgery, intramedullary steel rods would be inserted to align her fractured left femur and the tibia bones in both legs. She would remain in the ICU. The doctors gave her one day of rest, before proceeding with four more surgeries. The doctors kept her heavily sedated to avoid the panic and pain they expected her to experience. Before the end of the following week, she had survived eleven surgeries.

In the meantime, Murray was still unconscious on the day following the accident. The doctors could see the scars on his scalp which was a clear sign of a previous brain surgery. But there were no external injuries the doctors could find from the car accident, except for bruised knees and a deep cut on his chin. Nurses tried calling the Goldman home, but Georgie was either out in the backyard with the boys or down the other end of the sprawling ranch home. Murray's vitals were stable. They conducted several examinations, looking in his eyes and checking his reflexes. There were no signs of internal injuries. The doctors decided to monitor him and to wait for him to wake up.

Meanwhile, Franny was still not out of the woods. First the accident and then multiple surgeries put her body into a state of shock and uncertainty. Her vitals would fluctuate wildly. The doctors understood that individually, the surgeries they performed might not be life threatening. However, few of the doctors could recall completing so many surgeries on one patient under the circumstances required by the extent of her injuries. The nurses were asked to keep a crash cart near her room, just in case her heart gave out.

Her last thought before the accident was planning summer day camp for her children. Murray was just taking a break from reading the business section of the Times, smiling at a stock he bought that had climbed 20 points. He didn't know if the profit on the stock would cover the cost of day camp, but he was pleased knowing it would help.

His athletic training and lightning reflexes kicked-in on Thursday, June 15, 1961. He was certainly long past his boxing days. Murray had turned 46 last December. His weight had climbed from 190 to 240 pounds. But the years of long and grueling labor, as a plumber, had also increased his strength. His arms and hands were even larger and more muscular than back in the days when he was a fighter. If he moved with lightning speed the day of the accident, he did so without thinking. Now he lay quietly in a hospital room, unaware of the accident and uncertain whether he had saved Franny and himself from certain death.

By the end of day two, following the accident, Murray opened his eyes. He seemed confused. "Where am I? What happened? How did I get here? Where is my wife?" The questions came rapidly, a good sign, the nurses thought. But he was also getting agitated. They tried their best, but they couldn't keep up with Murray or answer questions fast enough. The head nurse came into the room, "Look Mr. Goldman, I'm Sylvia Bloom, we're all here to help you. You and your wife have been in a car accident. If you'll settle down, I'll go get a doctor to fill you in on your wife. She is having a rough time, but she's alive and getting the best care we can give her."

Murray sat up in his bed. He was ready to go find Franny when a wave of dizziness forced him not to stand up. He sat quietly on the side of the bed for a minute, holding onto the bed rail. He closed his eyes and took a deep breath, but any sudden movement and the room began to spin.

Mrs. Bloom returned quickly with a doctor. "Mr. Goldman, I'm Doctor Richard Shivlin. Can you tell me how you're feeling?" Murray explained the dizziness. He answered another half dozen questions about his previous brain surgery. While the doctor listened and tried to assess his physical condition, he waved off further questions. "How is my wife? Where is my wife?" Dr. Shivlin paused for a minute. He didn't know Murray Goldman. He couldn't be certain if he might suffer from damage or unseen injuries. Was it safe to tell him? How could he give him any assurances, when the medical team wasn't certain Franny would survive? And how could he tell him more surgeries would be needed in the coming weeks?

The doctor decided to try and slow down the delivery of information. "Mr. Goldman, I don't know if you realize that you've been unconscious for two days. Do you recall anything about the accident?"

"I remember reading the newspaper. I was turning the page and saw something black. I don't know anything after that."

"Well, the police told us you braced your hands against the car's dashboard. It looks like you absorbed the full impact of the collision. They believe you saved your wife and yourself."

Murray tried to stand up. His legs felt wobbly. The doctor grabbed hold of his and asked him to sit back on the bed. "Mr. Goldman, I know this is difficult for you, but we need you to go slow and help us concentrate on your well-being. Your wife is sedated and sleeping. You'll be no help to her if you can't function or further injure yourself. Do you understand what I am saying to you?"

"Doctor, I will do whatever you ask, but I need to see my wife."

"Ok, Mr. Goldman. If you'll stay calm and rest a few more hours, I'll get a hospital orderly to take you up to the ICU area. You'll have to promise me you won't argue with us about using a wheelchair until we resolve the dizziness."

Murray did not realize it, but during the very short conversation with Dr. Shivlin he started to feel weak and tired. He lay back on the bed. The doctor ordered the nurse to give him an injection to relax him. The nurses came in to take blood and check his vital signs. He soon closed his eyes. He slept for several hours. When he woke up, a nurse insisted he try to eat some of the food they saved. It was long past dinner time. Murray sat up in bed. He drank the juice and ate the cold soup on the dinner tray. He nibbled at a cheese sandwich, but he had no appetite.

"Excuse me, nurse. Dr. Shivlin promised me I could see my wife."

"I know, he left instructions," the nurse replied. "Let me see if our orderly is around."

Murray could not explain the weak feeling in his body. He knew the dizziness was right at the edge of his bed, waiting for him to step off. It took fifteen minutes before a male orderly appeared at his room door.

"Mr. Goldman, my name is Nate Smoleck. I'm the orderly and I have a wheelchair to take you up to the ICU. I'll only ask that you take your time and be patient with me. I will get you upstairs to see your wife."

"Thank you," he replied. "I'll follow your lead. Just tell me what I need to do."

Nate took his time helping him get out of bed and into the wheelchair. The nurses had told Nate that their patient was still experiencing dizziness. Nate did not think he could lift the patient if he fell on the floor.

"Ready, Mr. Goldman?" Nate asked, as he pushed the wheelchair past the door of his hospital room. The ride up to ICU was uneventful. Nate tried his best not to share too much information. He had heard about the car accident and how the wife was in bad shape.

The door to Franny's room was open. Nate pushed past the nurse's station and brought Murray close to his wife's bed. His eyes opened wide in shock. The swelling of her face made her almost unrecognizable. She had multiple lacerations on her face. He could see her hair was cut short so the doctors could stitch the head gash that reached both sides of her.

Murray could see wires and tubes everywhere, going in and out of his wife. There was some sort of device holding her lower body in a single position, to prevent any turn or movement. Murray turned to Nate, "How long has she been like this?"

"Mr. Goldman, I'm not suppose to say anything." Nate could see the distress on his face. He couldn't imagine what Goldman must be thinking right now. "Look," Nate said, "I know she's had a half-dozen surgeries the past two days. They weren't certain she'd make it, but there she is. She's fighting as hard as anyone could expect of her."

"Could I have a minute with her?" he asked. "I promise not to move from the chair."

Nate was nervous. He was not supposed to leave his patient alone. Take him to ICU and bring him back, those were the doctor's instructions. "Ok, ok, but please Mr. Goldman," Nate motioned to the chair and slowly backed out of the room.

"Franny, what have they done to you?" he asked, as he sat looking at his wife. It was a rare occasion, when Murray showed emotion. He didn't have an easy time of it growing up in a broken home, going to war or facing the possibility of death from a brain tumor. But he was always calm and stoic in the face of danger. He never thought of it as false bravado. He just felt confident that he could summon all his will power to get past the pain, hurt and fear of death. As he quietly tried to speak and comfort his unconscious wife, he realized he had met his match.

He buried his head in his hands and wept. Nate had positioned himself right outside the door, in case he needed him. Nate heard the sobbing. He was not about to disturb this man, who clearly was agonized by the sight of his wife. Life had finally broken Murray Goldman. He thought he could handle anything thrown at him, but why Franny? She didn't deserve to be laying in this hospital broken and near death.

He gave in to his tears. He let it all out. Then he raised his head. He leaned forward from his wheelchair and kissed her hand. At this moment when so much seemed lost, he began to pray. He asked God to spare his wife. He believed she shared his determination to overcome obstacles and shape the course of their lives. He prayed for her to come back to him. He had no conditions or expectations. Finally, he pulled closer to the bed and whispered, "I love you Franny Goldman. Don't quit on me. Please, please, don't quit on me. Come back to the boys. I will not leave this hospital without you."

Nate could hear Murray murmuring. "The man deserved his privacy," Nate said to himself. He sat in the room with his wife for almost an hour. Most of the time was spent in silence. At one point, he sat back looking at her and thought about their early courtship and dating. She had the most amazing smile. Nate came into the room. It was getting very late and the nurses would give him static. He promised his patient he could return the next day. "If no one is around to take you, I will stop by before I go home tomorrow." Murray nodded his appreciation to Nate. Here was this complete stranger offering to go out of his way for him. At this moment in time, Nate was the most important person in his life.

Dr. Shevlin came in to examine Murray the next day. It must have been near 7 a.m. He was joined by a neurosurgeon. Dr. Shevlin asked his colleague to consult in assessing Mr. Goldman. While his blood pressure was slightly elevated, the doctors could not find anything else suggesting an underlying problem. The Neurosurgeon put him through a series of exercises and movements, including touching his toes. Two nurses stood along-side. Murray felt fine as he bent forward. However, as he tried to stand again, his body trembled and his legs started to give out. Both doctors joined with the nurses to help him back onto the bed. They could see he was very dizzy. The pupils in his eyes twitched back and forth.

A nurse stayed in the room with him. She tried to make him comfortable, pushing extra pillows behind his back. The doctors spoke for ten minutes outside of Murray's room. The Neurosurgeon thought for certain there was brain trauma. But they could not detect any bleeding in the brain, It's possible, the impact he absorbed during the accident had caused a whiplash effect in his brain. Too soon for them to know if Murray needed medical intervention. The doctors agreed to give him time to simply rest—and see if the symptoms got worse or went away on their own.

Dr. Shevlin came back in the room to brief him on their assessment. He was very straightforward in telling Murray that the medical team could not say when the dizziness would go away. "Doctor, you've been very up front with me. I appreciate your candor. What I'd appreciate now is for you to tell me about my wife."

"Mr. Goldman, at this stage of things, it is doubtful that your wife will ever walk again."

The doctor paused for several minutes. He then spoke slowly, to hopefully let the message sink in with him. Franny was only 44 years old. They had just danced with such joy at their son's Bar Mitzvah three months earlier. Why was this doctor telling him his wife would be crippled for the rest of their lives?

Dr. Shevlin did not want to sound cruel. But he had sized Murray up as someone who was very strongminded. If he could not cope with his wife's reality, how could he possibly help her overcome the shock when she woke up? . Murray looked up to the ceiling, then down at the floor. He shook his head twice, left to right. He finally looked Dr. Shevlin in the eye. "I don't think you know Franny Sugar."

"Mr. Goldman, it's not my intention to upset you. Both you and your wife has been through an incredible ordeal. She's still looking at several surgeries, before we can let her go home. But the underlying damage will still be there."

"I hear what you're telling me doctor. But if you think I'm strong willed, you haven't met my wife. I've been knocked down several times in my life, both as a young boxer and following brain surgery. This woman lying in your ICU is the toughest person I've ever met in my life. And I'm not about to let her accept the life you've defined."

Dr. Shevlin smiled. He reached out and patted him on the shoulder. "I have no doubt, Mr. Goldman, that you will give her the help and support she needs. As a doctor, I know my limitations. My view has always been that we are what we make of life—and anything is possible."

Murray sat for a period of time. The doctor and nurse had cleared out of his room. He glanced toward the window. He quietly wondered about the future. He prayed for his wife. Soon after, He closed his eyes and fell asleep.

Nate Smoleck was a man of his word. He showed up at Murray's door at 4 p.m. to take him up to the ICU Unit. This time, the dizziness did not hit him until he was in the wheelchair. He took some deep breaths to try and shake it off. He was not about to tell Nate, fearing he might not take him to see his wife.

Nate made small talk with Murray as they headed to the elevators. He could see his patient was somewhere else. Nate tried to give him a pep talk. When they reached Franny's room, he raised his hand to stop Nate. "Look, I don't know how to express this," he said, "but I want thank you for bringing me up here." A smile came across Nate's face. "Mr. Goldman, you do things in life, not because they are fun or easy to do, but because they are the right thing to do. You have to know that I am pulling for you and your wife to leave this hospital together."

Murray reached up and shook Nate's hand in gratitude.

As they entered the room with the wheelchair, he could see that Franny's eyes were open and she was awake. It was day 3, and the doctors couldn't keep her sedated much longer. She lay motionless, as her eyes saw Murray's face. The tears rolled down her cheeks. She could not speak. Her jaw was wired shut.

Murray reached over the bed rail to calm her, his hand reached out and gently wiped the tears from her face. Almost in a whisper, he told her, "If I knew you were awake, I would have come sooner. They have me down on the third floor. My friend Nate has been bringing me up to visit you. Franny, we were in a car accident. A drunk driver slammed into us, just outside of Atlantic City. You've been unconscious for 3 days. The doctors have done several surgeries. Your jaw was fractured, so they had to wire it shut." And then with some sarcasm, he said "I guess you won't be yelling at me for a few weeks."

Her tears came faster at this point. Murray's comment was funny, but she could not laugh or let go of the pain. She felt trapped in her body. She wanted in the worst way to talk to him. She was so afraid. He could see her eyes widen. He knew that look. He tried several times to calm her down.

"You have to give yourself time now," he told Franny. "We've been through challenges before, remember? You always told me, quitting was not an option. Well, I listened to you then. I trusted you. You inspired me. It's my turn now. I need you to trust me. I told the doctor, you were the toughest woman I ever met. Please. I need you to hang in there. Don't give in to the pain and don't give up. We have a life ahead of us. We have three sons who need their mom to guide them."

Franny blinked her eyes repeatedly. She tried to speak, but her words were muddled. Murray realized he had mentioned the children. They had no idea about what had happened to their parents. The weekend was almost over. The cleaning woman, Georgie, would be returning home and to her daily jobs. He hit a nerve. "Franny, I have not told the children. I will call them today, before Georgie goes home. I'll have them reach out to your sister, Boots and your brother, Maier to help keep an eye on them.

There was little she could do. She accepted his assurances to tell the kids and arrange for help. The school year was over, so getting them off every morning was not an issue. She knew Zach would have to attend more practice sessions for the dance and acrobatic show. She hoped her brother could find a parent at the school to take Zach to practice.

The nurses came in to see Franny. It was time to check her vitals, take blood and give her more painkillers so she'd sleep. Nate was asked to take Murray back to his room. He could come again tomorrow. He reached out to touch her hand one more time, before he was whisked away. Nate grabbed the handles on the wheelchair. Murray raised his hand up to slow the orderly down. He put his hand on her arm through the bars on the bed, "I love you Franny. Be that girl... you know, that girl. The one I fell in love with. I'll be back tomorrow."

She knew what her husband meant, when he said, "be that girl." He had used this expression so many times, and over so many years ago. The first time was when she challenged him at the handball court. Her mind drifted off, as the nurses worked on her. There are moments like this, between two people, that only they own or understand. Murray was acknowledging to Franny, she was always his equal as a competitor. He was throwing down the gauntlet, "be that girl", at a time when he feared it might all be over. When you hit bottom, what's left?

In the days and weeks that followed, he would visit her regularly. Often he'd just sit in his wheelchair staring at her, as she slept. His mind wandered. He thought about the struggles she would face. At times, depression set in for Murray. His eyes filled with tears, but he fought back from letting his emotions out. He didn't care about his own pain, only that he would do whatever was necessary to help his wife. Nate dropped him off at his wife's room in the morning. He'd periodically go back and check on his patient. By mid-day, he'd find him sleeping in his wheelchair next to Franny's bed. His hand held the bed railing, hoping she'd open her eyes so he could hold her hand. He'd resist, if Nate tried to take him back to his room. He belonged with his wife. When she'd wake, he had to be there. He had to assure her. He looked past her swollen face and body. Her eyes energized him. Somewhere inside was Franny Sugar. He was not giving in to his fear about the future.

CHAPTER 47
Abandoned and Alone

"Alan, this is your father. Listen, your mom and I were in a car accident near Atlantic City. Mom is in really bad shape. I need you to take charge, son. I just spoke to Georgie. She can't stay to watch you and your brothers. She has to go to work tomorrow. I want you to call your Uncle Maier and Aunt Boots. Tell them what happened. Ask them to stop by to check on the three of you this week. I will try to call you again, as soon as I can. Do you understand?"

Alan Goldman had been wrestling on his parent's bed with Zach and Gary when Georgie called him to the phone. For the first time in his life, he heard fear in his dad's voice. This didn't seem possible. Alan realized the situation must be really bad. His father's assurances that everything would be ok fell on deaf ears. He wanted to go to the hospital and see for himself.

Murray tried to explain that mom still required more surgery. He hoped Boots and Maier would come to the house, but he doubted they would volunteer to drive Alan, Zach and Gary three hours to Atlantic City.

Alan asked as many questions as he could fit in the time his father stayed on the phone. He knew his brothers would want to understand. He promised his father he would call mom's brother and sister. "Dad, please don't worry about us. Tell mom, not to worry. We will look after each other. We will be ok. Please let mom know we want you both to come home to us."

The call could not have lasted more than 10 minutes. He had to use a public phone in the hallway. The hospital did not have a phone in a patient's room. The nurses helped find coins for him. When the coins ran out, the call ended.

Alan called his brothers from their parent's bedroom. They gathered around the kitchen table, where he broke the news. Zach began with questions about how the accident happened? Why wasn't dad coming home? Couldn't mom be brought to a hospital closer to home? Why had mom not talked to Alan? When could the boys go visit their parents in the hospital? Who could they call to get someone to drive them to Atlantic City? "If we don't look after them," Zach asked, "who will?"

He was not surprised his brother asked many of the same questions he had asked himself. Alan explained to his brothers, they were on their own. He would call his aunt and uncle who lived in New Milford and Fair Lawn, towns next door to Paramus. But if they weren't willing to help, the boys would have to look out for themselves.

Gary started to cry. He feared his mom was never coming home. Alan and Zach had the same fear, but this was not the time to dwell on things they didn't know or couldn't control. The boys drew up a plan of action. Georgie was leaving for home. Alan would make the calls to their aunt and uncle. The next morning, Zach would walk down the hill to the supermarket and buy essential food items, like milk, eggs and bread.. They made up a list, which included Oreo cookies. They all knew this was Gary's favorite. Alan rummaged through the drawers where his parents kept cash. They were not without some food. Their mom always kept the kitchen and freezer well stocked.

Over the next two hours, the boys congregated in the kitchen to consider what they had to do next. Alan insisted the boys needed to keep to themselves and avoid attracting attention from the neighbors. "We don't know how long it will take before dad comes home. If neighbors see we're alone, I'm worried the town may come and take us away where there's supervision. I don't know if that means they would split us up and have us live with strangers until our parents come home."

Zach understood and agreed with his big brother. But in the coming months, none of them could imagine how isolated and alone they would feel. Their world was slowly coming undone. Without their parents, all the safety they felt at home would be lost. Each Goldman child would experience the loss differently. None of them would come away unscathed. The sadness and melancholy from this period lingered the rest of their lives; like dust on their clothes. Even in moments of sheer delight; their first kiss, a victory in sports, they'd anxiously wonder when the next shoe would drop. Franny had been their teacher. She provided them with a moral compass. She drilled them on the value of family, a love of learning; and of reaching beyond circumstance. But in this darkest period of their lives, their father's lessons reminded them of the need to find inner strength. His life was filled with stories of perseverance. The children clung to their father's understated directness about life. "Always try to walk away from a fight. But if they won't let you, punch him in the nose so he'll bleed. We all get knocked down, the challenge is to get up and never, never, never give in."

Later, toward evening, Alan would call his aunt and uncle. The relatives both expressed shock at the news. You can always tell in a crisis, the folks who make the most noise are usually the ones who will look for excuses not to help. Alan could sense that despite their promises, the boys were unlikely to see Boots or Maier anytime soon. Being young does not mean a child doesn't have an intuitive sense of the world around them. Family members in these situations speak in code, but their words are transparent, "Well, keep me posted when you hear from your dad. Let us know if they tell you how long they'll be kept in the hospital. See if your dad wants to have the cleaning lady come back and stay at the house with you. We can call her for you."

A 13-year old boy is not prepared to talk back to family elders. At least that was the way Franny had raised her children. But neither of the family members living in the town next door said, "I'll be right over. I'm so sorry about your parents. Don't worry, we will help you. I'll take you to see them tomorrow." The only concession Alan managed to get from Franny's siblings, was to let others in the family know what happened. These siblings living in Brooklyn were much further away, but Alan hoped that someone in the family might take responsibility to help the Goldman boys.

Both Zach and Gary stayed in the room with Alan during these calls. They wanted to hear the conversations. It was a moment in their lives none of them would ever forget. Franny had impressed on them the importance of family, starting at an early age. But they were without the support of family. Whatever they feared most, they would face it alone.

What does it mean to be alone? As adults, we often experience the feeling. A spouse travels on business. Perhaps, a divorce or even the death of someone we love. That empty feeling seems like it will last forever. As an adult, however, we find ways to distract ourselves or compensate. We have resources, knowledge, and usually a car to take you wherever being alone no longer applies. Unless hopelessly trapped in your own mind, an adult can— and will look for the door marked exit, from loneliness. Yes, at times, it lingers like a wet shirt that is cold and clinging. But humans, for the most part, are optimistic. They will entertain themselves with friends or movies, going out to eat—and even, at times, sitting with strangers to share conversation and company.

However, when seen through the eyes of a child, after just two weeks, it is near impossible to fully understand the impact of feeling alone and isolated. The Goldman boys each experienced this trauma in their own way. It would shape their relationships and world view for the rest of their lives. The seeds of despair were never visible. When the mail man stopped at the house, the boys made quick and friendly conversation. "Good face" they called it. Wear it whenever it is needed. Their interactions with neighbors, who slowly heard about the accident, were kept brief. When necessary, they'd tell neighbors that Georgie was staying with them until their parents came home. Fear crept into their daily lives. They worried all the time about the possibilities the boys might be split up and taken from their home.

The Goldman home became their solitary refuge. There was little fighting among the boys. An unspoken bond had formed, in the long hours and weeks that followed. Each day gave them confidence of the days ahead. They never gave up hope, even when at night the fear overcame them. Each of them weathered the loneliness and sense of abandonment in their own way. Alan could be terribly moody and withdrawn. Zach and Gary were younger. They expressed fear differently. Often, at night, Zach would bury his head in a pillow and cry himself to sleep. "Nobody loves me," he'd say over and over again. How do you measure the trauma in a ten-year-old? His happy go-lucky personality turned serious. He would never be carefree or a child ever again.

Gary struggled as well to understand the impact the accident might have on their family. He refused to be alone. He followed his brothers around the house day and night, like a lost puppy.

The weeks slowly turned into a month, without knowing when or if their parents would be coming home. Alan tried to give his brothers a turn on the phone to hear their father's voice and encouragement. Dad tried to call twice a week. Mom had 3 more surgeries to set and correct her broken bones. Dad experienced two seizures while trying to recover in the hospital. The doctors had no answers and no treatment, other than to try various medicines with Murray's regimen of pills he regularly took after his brain tumor.

As time wore on, the boys eventually came to an agreement on how they would run the Goldman home. At 13, Alan was the oldest. He would assume responsibility for all financial matters, including paying bills and making phone calls on behalf of his parents. Murray had coached Alan by phone, where to find his checkbook and how to keep on top of family decisions. Zach was good at cooking simple dinners like spaghetti, hot dogs and beans and frozen TV-dinners. "Ah, Swanson's Turkey TV-dinner," was the backup food of choice, when no one wanted to cook at home. Franny kept a supply of frozen food for her active and demanding family.

Zach would get Gary to help him collect and wash the laundry. They carefully followed the soap detergent instructions, though Zach insisted on using less than what was required on the box. "Gary, we can't have any accidents. We don't need repairmen coming to the house."

All the boys shared a concern that no one in the neighborhood know they lived without parental supervision. If the boys were outside playing, neighbors would ask about their parents. Alan and Zach would provide updates, though they didn't have much information themselves. However, each would make a point of mentioning Georgie staying in the house and the family relatives who regularly stopped by at night to check on them—and bring food. Lying was frowned upon in the Goldman home, but it became a tool the boys used to protect themselves from outsiders. "We have to stick together," Alan would tell his brothers, "and look out for each other. That's what mom would want us to do."

Dinners were quiet rituals. Zach called Alan and Gary. They'd assemble at the kitchen table, without much discussion. To an outsider, they each seemed locked in their own world. No one could see the raw emotion eating at the Goldman boys. Alan would report on his efforts to find someone in the family to take them to Atlantic City. Their uncle Sammy, Murray's younger brother, would call periodically to check on the boys. He was the only family member to do so. But Sammy worked 6 days a week and lived far out in Brooklyn.

Gary helped clear the dishes, while Zach washed. The TV was left on in the den, to keep them all company at night. It was rare for them to fight anymore over what programs they'd watch. The boys often gave in to Gary, as the youngest. He had first choice on the TV. Fortunately, Gary was more than willing to follow his brothers lead. The favorite consensus usually was a cowboy show.

The word spread through the Jewish community in Paramus. The Goldmans were founders of the Paramus Jewish Community Center (JCC). Franny was a very active member of the JCC's Women's League. From a neighbor on Koman Drive, the news of the accident reached the JCC. One of Franny's closest friends, Diane Shulman began calling to check on the Goldman boys. Diane was not convinced by Alan's assurances that the boys were fine. Alan told her that Georgie, the cleaning woman was staying at their home.

Diane had two children. She was not about to leave Franny's kids alone. It was already summer time. Zach needed someone to step in and take him to the Fred Kelly dance classes. Zach had all but written off attending the school any longer and performing in the upcoming show. The costumes Franny made were still sitting on the washing machine, untouched since the car accident. Diane saw her opportunity and made a point of taking Zach to the practice sessions in Oradell. "Zach Goldman, your mom would be very disappointed if you don't perform in this show. She never stopped talking about you doing handsprings and cartwheels across the stage. You have to go, so you can tell her the story when she comes home."

Diane was a bright light to the Goldman boys,. She had no idea how bad Franny was or when she might come home. But Diane's positive "can-do" energy filled the room. She was the first adult to give the Goldman boys hope. Even Alan, who stayed by himself most days, could not ignore Diane's growing influence. When she stopped by to drop off food, occasionally, the boys increasingly grew comfortable trusting her with whatever information they could glean during their calls with dad.

Zach Goldman would have his day in the sun. The Fred Kelly School of Dance held their show in late July. Zach performed in 5 different segments. For two hours, Zach forgot about the accident. The music lifted him up. His tumbling reached new heights. His dancing steps were crisp. His smile was not practiced. He wore his costumes with pride. This is what his mom would have seen, he said to himself, if she were not laying in a hospital. He stood in line with other kids at the end of the show, as the audience cheered.

Diane came back stage and hugged Zach. "You are such a special boy, Zach Goldman. Your mom will be so happy to hear about your performance. I can't wait to tell her." The words hung in the air for Zach. (I can't wait to tell her.) But he had been so caught up in the moment, Zach stopped thinking about his mom. Suddenly, his mind came racing back to her. She had spent months sewing his costumes. He realized she would hear about the performance, but she never got to see him. "Would she ever be coming back?" he asked Diane. Did he dare think about his life without his mom in it. His eyes filled up. A sense of guilt overwhelmed him. How could he not be thinking about his mom every minute of the day? Diane saw the tears flow down Zach's cheek. Victories are empty without those we love. She pulled him close to comfort him. But she understood that for this child there was no way to fill the void.

Diane Shulman became more than a friend. As she came to understand the challenges facing the Goldman boys, she became their strongest advocate. She spread the word at the Synagogue about the accident. Some of the moms in the JCC Women's League took turns once a week to drop off a cooked meal for the children. Diane was careful not to mention the boys were home without adult supervision. She would keep their secret.

The story reached Rabbi Michael Rackowitz, who knew the Goldman family very well. No one fit the image of a Rabbi more than Rackowitz. He stood well over six foot two inches, with dark black hair and beard. His booming bass voice could be heard at the back of the Synagogue. To the children it sounded as if the heavens above had opened. Rabbi Rackowitz led a conservative Jewish synagogue, but he identified strongly with many orthodox customs. The Rabbi was good natured and a very kind man. Though he had a studious reserve as a Rabbi, he always communicated a down to earth feeling to his congregants. He could care less about synagogue politics and the pettiness that frequents many houses of worship.

Rabbi Rackowitz had an especially warm feeling for the Goldmans. Franny made a point of calling the Rabbi's wife, Sylvia, as soon as they arrived in Paramus. As challenging as it may be for a Rabbi to get comfortable in a new community, it's even harder for the wife. Franny visited Sylvia frequently, mindful to bring Kosher food and bakery goods.

She drove her around Paramus and to neighboring towns, where Sylvia might go and shop for her family. Franny was very private about helping Sylvia. She did not believe promoting a social connection with the Rabbi's wife was appropriate. She wanted to be a true friend, who cared only that Sylvia felt comfortable in her new community. This discrete outreach meant so much to Mrs. Rackowitz, and it meant even more to the Rabbi. It was clear to the Goldmans that the Rabbi felt relieved that his wife was happy in the new and larger congregation he was taking on.

Alan's call to the Rabbi took Rackowitz by surprise. He had studied with him for his Bar Mitzvah for nearly six months. He knew and trusted the Rabbi. But the phone call was not expected, even after knowing about the accident. Alan spoke slowly. He told the Rabbi that nearly 5 or 6 weeks had gone by, without seeing his parents. The Rabbi was shocked to hear the boys were living on their own at the Goldman home. He promised him not to report their situation, after numerous pleas—and assurances by Alan that the boys were managing well. "Rabbi, we have all become what our parents wanted us to be. Maybe it came sooner than we wanted or planned, but my brothers and I have learned to take charge."

The Rabbi listened, as Alan told him the sad news that family members would not take the boys to Atlantic City. It was a shocking story to hear the excuses being given, when the Rabbi was quite aware of the support Franny and Murray Goldman had extended to their family.

At a certain point, the Rabbi could hear the silence. The voice at the other end quivered and broke apart. He could not contain himself any longer. He told the Rabbi he didn't know what else to do. His brothers could be heard crying at night. They needed to see their parents.

As he tried to recover his composure, there was a long silence at the other end of the phone. Alan had hoped the Rabbi might find someone at the synagogue—a congregant--willing to help the boys.

"I will take you," the Rabbi said slowly. "Today, is Tuesday. I will pick you up tomorrow morning at 7 a.m. We will drive to Atlantic City. You will see your parents."

The silence was deafening. "Alan, did you hear what I said?" the Rabbi asked. It took Rabbi Rackowitz a few moments to realize, Alan Goldman was crying at the other end of the phone. The Rabbi asked him if his brothers would be ok by themselves? After a few minutes, he told the Rabbi he would ask Diane Shulman to take Zach and Gary to the town pool. He was certain Zach and Gary could be home alone, but he didn't want to say that to the Rabbi. He also thought to himself that a day away might distract the boys until he came home with a report.

Alan's mood was almost giddy. He had no idea the Rabbi would volunteer himself to drive nearly 6 hours in one day. He was not certain this day would ever come. There was no way to reach his father. He paused for several minutes wondering if his dad would be angry with him for asking the Rabbi, or for coming to Atlantic City without his permission, or leaving his brothers at home by themselves.

The giddiness gave way to somber thoughts. He had not expected to find a solution. None of his uncles or aunts had made any effort to take the children to see their parents, even after a month in the hospital. They didn't call to check on the boys. No one even brought food. How could they all be so callous? But the Rabbi's gesture made Alan think about his mom. How bad was she? Would he be able to handle seeing his mom disfigured and broken? While the oldest, he was never good at seeing someone injured. When Zach got hit with the broom stick in the face, Alan's first reaction to the gush of blood was to puke. He began to think about the challenge he would face seeing mom. He so desperately wanted to go — and to see his parents were ok, but could he avoid having his parents see the reaction on his face?

Alan sat alone on the bed in his parent's bedroom. The room was dark, except for the sunlight that was coming through the ends of the window shades. He still wrestled with issues in his mind. Why hasn't dad come home? What about the business? Dad left someone in charge, but that couldn't last forever. Alan's head began to hurt. He could not grasp the future . It's odd at times like this, when a crisis hits a family. No one can predict the outcome or the impact. The Goldman children kept telling themselves to take one day at a time. We view the world in this way, perhaps more out of ignorance than from clear, dispassionate thought. Alan thought to himself, "The hardest battle had already been won. Mom and dad were alive." He and his brothers were ready to accept whatever hardships might follow.

Alan planned to bring his brothers an upbeat and hopeful report, when he returned from his visit to Atlantic City. He was determined to do so, even if he lied. There was plenty of time to make the adjustments in their lives. What he saw was not as important as convincing his brothers that mom and dad would be coming home.

The Rabbi drove an old car. Alan had never thought about it, but he realized the man who mastered such knowledge of Talmud didn't make a lot of money. Yes, it was true. The Rabbi, perhaps all Rabbis, don't make a lot of money. Or, perhaps, the Rabbi simply didn't think it was important to spend money on cars? This had never occurred to Alan Goldman. Even as a boy, he was quite aware of material things in life. He didn't judge too harshly, but he always took note of what people owned or could buy.

As the Rabbi headed down the Garden State Parkway, he engaged Alan in a long conversation about school and his future. He was certain the Rabbi wanted to distract him from thinking about his mission. He explained to Alan how important it would be for him to one day go to college. I've talked to your mom about this subject many times. "Your parents never had that opportunity," the Rabbi explained.

I don't think you know this, the Rabbi told him, "but in ancient times the first-born son was supposed to become a Rabbi. By custom, your life should have been dedicated to the study of Torah. This practice underscored the expectation that the first born would help lead the Jewish people, through education and teaching God's law.

"Alan, it is important that you be the first one going to college, so your brothers will follow your example. In your family, you must lead."

Alan told the Rabbi about Diane Shulman and what a good friend she had been to his mom. She volunteered many times to take his brothers to the Paramus community pool. The pool would be crowded with other families and many of their school friends. Zach would likely cause Diane some breathless moments, since he often did somersaults off the 10-foot diving board. Diane had boys of her own, but she knew from Franny the Goldman boys could be an exceptional challenge. Zach, like his father, didn't fear much. Gary, like his father, could assemble or disassemble almost any toy, object or machine. He had an innate sense of how things worked. And, Alan, like his father, had a determination to succeed.

Fortunately, Diane only had to worry about Zach and Gary. This was often more than enough to keep her busy. She tried to keep the boys in the pool or at the playground nearby.

It was late morning, when Alan Goldman walked into his father's room. He had not expected that his son would find a way to visit in Atlantic City. Murray greeted Rabbi Rackowitz and his son with a big smile. There was a mixture of pride in seeing Alan's persistence, but he felt terrible that the Rabbi was the only person the children could find to make the journey.

From what Alan could tell, his father seemed ok with a cut still healing on his chin. He took back his assessment, as his father tried to stand up from the lounge chair. He quickly grabbed onto his son for balance and then sat back down. The Rabbi pulled a chair over and sat next to Murray. He asked Alan if he could find some water for his dad. While out of the room, the Rabbi asked about Franny. Murray's eyes welled up with tears. He explained the doctors weren't certain Franny would ever walk again. "My strong and beautiful wife," he said, "has been broken almost beyond repair." He warned the Rabbi her jaw was wired shut, so she would have great difficulty talking. He listened to Murray. He understood from the conversation that he and Alan might be shocked when they see her during their visit.

After a half-hour, the nurses called for an orderly to take Murray up to Franny's room. She had been moved from the ICU, but remained on that floor. Murray's new friend, Nate Smoleck, had a day off, so a different orderly showed up to escort the visitors.

The door was slightly open, when Alan walked into the room. His mom was laying straight on her back. There was some sort of device keeping her legs from moving. As she turned her head toward the door, her son began to cry. Her head and face were swollen, with one eye almost completely shut.

Her hair was cut on one side of her head, where doctors had shaved the scalp to put in stitches. He promised his father he would not excite his mom, but she could see the terror on his face. Franny began to cry. She stared at the ceiling, uncertain how to calm her son. She then motioned with her good arm for Alan to come closer. At this moment, Franny realized how grateful she was to still be alive. He walked slowly to right side of her bed. He leaned down, crying and carefully hugged and kissed his mom.

"We all miss you so much," he told her. "You would be proud of us, how my brothers and I have pulled together, as you taught us. Each of us has taken charge. And all of us are looking out for each other. The Rabbi has done something for us today, which no one else was willing to do."

As her son spoke, Franny realized she had missed seeing the third person who entered her room. The Rabbi stepped from the shadows near the door. Now, she began to cry again. Her modesty overwhelmed her. Alan telling his mom the Rabbi drove him to Atlantic City had not fully registered in her mind. She wanted so badly to thank him, but her words came out muddled. Rabbi Rackowitz approached the bed. He reached over the bedrail to hold her hand.

"Franny" he said in that rich bass voice, "I am without words to tell you how sorry I am. When your son called me, I couldn't get over that only 3 months ago we all stood at the Bhīma for his Bar Mitzvah. You can be very proud. I was moved by your son's resolve. You have raised 3 strong boys, who share their father's will and their mother's generous and gracious heart."

The tears continued to flow. A Rabbi often has a way of speaking to the soul. Franny squeezed his hand and she clung to his words. This was a rare moment for her. While Franny and Murray were raised in religious homes, they led very secular lives. Rabbi Rackowitz spoke with such authority. At times it felt as if he speaking for God.

The Rabbi paused for a few minutes, so Franny could regain her composure. "Now comes the most difficult challenge you have ever faced," he told her. At times like this, we may feel abandoned by God. We may wonder if God cares about us. You Franny Goldman are not alone. God has not abandoned you.

"I cannot say why some of us face such insurmountable odds or suffer. The Talmud teaches us that even righteous people can suffer. In the Bible, when Moses says to God, 'Let me know your ways,' he is asking God to help him understand and gain insight from the creator. But as human beings, God tells Moses, we will never understand the mysteries of nature and the universe.

"We praise God, even as we suffer, because we trust that there is a purpose to someone's life that transcends us. This may not make much sense right now, but God has given us three precious gifts to guide and inspire us: The Torah, the land of Israel (a homeland) and a Future (the World to Come).

"Franny, your body may be broken, but your mind is free. You must think about 'the world to come.' Your children and your husband need you. You must persevere and work to overcome this tragedy. Let your Voice and your love continue to be their moral compass. My Sylvia sends you her love and she wanted me to tell you how much you mean to us—and to your family."

The Rabbi then leaned down and did something she had never seen before. He gently hugged her—and kissed her forehead. A Rabbi touching a woman, other than his wife, was almost unheard of in her life's experience. Rabbis were so formal, they seemed distant and aloof. They taught lessons and told stories from the Talmud, but rarely was there this type of human connection.

She heard the Rabbi say something quietly in Hebrew, when he leaned down to hug her. He was giving her a blessing. She no longer wondered during her pain if God had deserted her. The Rabbi had come to see her. He restored her faith. She held onto his words. She still had a purpose in life to fulfill.

Her son stood quietly next to his father during the Rabbi's conversation with Franny. His bond with the Rabbi could never be broken after this day. His visit to the hospital had taught him more about God, and about this Rabbi, than in the six months he spent preparing for his Bar Mitzvah.

On the ride home, he broke the silence only once to thank the Rabbi for encouraging his mom. "Rabbi, my brothers and I are no longer children. The days of running around, playing sports or just being carefree are over. I believe we understand this, even if we don't openly talk about it. We are grateful that our parents are alive. We will do everything we can now to take care of them.

"I will share what you told my mom, with my brothers. I know they will work hard at making a difference."

CHAPTER 48
The Road Back

After almost two months, the Goldman boys heard from their father. He asked them to prepare the house. Mom would soon be coming home. Alan's visit to Atlantic City with the Rabbi was followed by a second visit, with Zach and Gary. Once the word had spread that Rabbi Rackowitz drove to the hospital, several members of the Synagogue wanted to follow his example. The boys couldn't get over that they now had a host of volunteer drivers.

Diane Shulman was their obvious first choice. She had not only been Franny's closest friend, she became their friend as well during this difficult period.

Diane showing up at the hospital with the boys gave their mom a real morale boost. The wire had been removed from her jaws. She still spoke with difficulty. Her face was no longer swollen. The bandages on her head were removed. Franny's body was still immobilized. A final surgery on her shattered wrist was bandaged. Diane came in the room like a bolt of lightning. She had a great poker face. She was not going to let Franny see her reactions. Diane only talked about her friend coming home. She promised to find Franny someone to live-in and help take care of the house.

The hospital made arrangements to have medical equipment delivered to the Goldman home. The boys had decided, with Diane's help, to put a hospital bed for Franny in the larger, second bedroom. Zach and Gary would share the master bedroom with their father.

Their mother would arrive in a full body cast, stretching from her chest to her feet. This cast would remain for almost six months to allow the multiple bone fractures and hip to heal. A section of the cast was cut out in the back, which would allow Franny to use a bed pan. Since help would not be available when she arrived, the boys initially agreed to share responsibility for bringing the bed pan; wiping and bathing their mom. However, when the time came, Zach took over for his brothers. He became very adept at getting the bed pan under his mom, without causing her too much pain.

Murray Goldman would remain in Atlantic City for a period of time, after Franny was sent home. The doctors were still trying different drugs to stem the dizziness he experienced. He was also given a regular regime of physical therapy to try and restore strength to his arms and legs. At the time of the accident, he was strong in appearance. It was almost as if the accident had sapped this strength. He was a shell of the man who drove in the car to Atlantic City. The damage he appeared to experience also affected his short-term memory. The doctors worked to relieve symptoms, though none of the medical team were certain how long it might take to restore Murray to his old self.

Franny arrived at the Goldman home by ambulance in August 1961. The boys had worked together to remove beds and furniture. The medical supply company had delivered and set up a special hospital bed. Other provisions were made for a food tray, a cabinet for medicines and an IV stand (to use, if needed, for pain management).

Mom was exhausted from the long trip. The ambulance drivers got her into the bed, checked her vitals; gave instructions to Alan on her medications—and then left. Diane Shulman stopped by the house for a short visit, soon after Franny had arrived. Mom was out cold. Diane reviewed the instructions on the medications with Alan, so she was certain he knew what to do.

She promised the boys they would have live-in help in three weeks, which put their minds at ease. The new school year was fast approaching. The Goldman boys could not skip school without being noticed.

For several days, the boys stood vigil around the clock near Franny's bed. It was not uncommon for them to fall asleep on the floor. But they never slept too soundly, jumping up as soon as they heard their mom cry out in pain. Alan set aside pills each night to give their mom, if she woke up. Every activity required support. Mom's right hand was still bandaged. She needed a straw to drink water. The boys had to help push the pills in her mouth. And if the bed pan was needed, they either woke Zach or tried fending for themselves.

During the day, the boys rotated to watch Franny and do their chores. Someone had to be with mom at all times. "We cannot leave her alone," Zach would tell his brothers. "We have to be there, when she needs us." Gary would gather dirty clothes and bring them down to the den, where the washing machines were located. Zach worked in the kitchen to get meals ready for dinner. Franny would ask Alan about mail and bills and give him instructions. The boys would help her with the phone so she could call to check on Murray's business. She did her best to explain their dad's condition, but she couldn't be certain if they fully understood.

The school year would be starting soon. Zach Goldman would turn 11 years old in September. Even at that young age, he showed maturity and empathy. Now, it was Zach who stepped in to play a hands-on role in taking care of his mom. He coached Gary on helping feed their mom, mindful that she had difficulty chewing while her jaw healed. While Alan called the shots on giving mom medication, Zach watched her intensely to assess her mood and pain threshold.

Alan could not bear the responsibility of helping his mom use the bed pan. He was older, soon to be 14-years old. Maybe, he was too self-aware. He had a growing curiosity and interest in girls. He was overly self-conscious at this stage of his life. The smell of poop made him feel ill. Zach wasn't necessarily stronger than Alan. He approached his task stoically and tried to disassociate his mission from the person he was helping. While one might assume Zach was more impressionable, his self-awareness had already been shaped by his father. You just do it.

Franny was mortified to think of her children having to help her go to the bathroom. The mix of growing up a tom-boy, knowing only one man in her life and being governed by an internal sense of modesty confronted her with her worst nightmare. How do you explain any of these feelings to someone? Worse, how do you begin to tell your children? She had become a prisoner in her own body. While the alternative to the accident could have been death, Franny did not want to lose her dignity.

When the bed pan was needed, the children did not know how long their mom suffered or tried to hold back calling for their help. It was sheer agony for her to lay in a body cast, unable to fend for herself. Her only saving grace was her children's refusal to leave her alone. When the pressure had all but stolen her will power, she gave in to having Zach bring her the bed pan. He would try to angle the metal pan under her from the right side.

She would ask Zach to standby as she struggled with her left hand to wipe herself after urinating. He would pull the bed pan from beneath her body, so she could deposit the toilet paper. When the dreaded moment came for her to poop, he was ready. Franny would turn her head to the left and look out the window, as Zach reached with his little hands to wipe her rear end. He did his best, but often his hands came back with brown excrement across his fingers. He would go wash his hands and then return with a warm wash cloth to clean his mom.

Both Franny and Zach accepted a sort of suspended animation when bodily functions required him to gently reach under mom's body cast and wipe or bath her. The task could take 15 minutes, with Zach running back and forth to the bathroom. When the initial work was done, he would take the bed pan to the bathroom to empty and wash it. His mom was fastidious about cleanliness and personal hygiene. The bed pan had to be as clean as the tooth brush, or so he thought, fearing his mom might not use it.

She apologized to her son each time she called for him. She could not imagine his fear or disgust. But she never realized that for Zach it was not a job, but a purpose he did not resent. He loved his mother beyond words. He was ready to do whatever was required of him, if it meant his mother would get well.

Nearly three weeks passed before Murray Goldman was finally allowed to come home. The doctors had stemmed the dizziness he experienced with a regimen of drugs. There would likely be side effects from the drugs, but Murray didn't care. He wanted to get home to his family—and to his business.

The boys were at school, when he arrived. Diane Shulman had kept her word and found someone to help take care of Franny. Effie Johnson greeted him at the door. She was a very large black woman. He thought to himself, she must weigh close to 300 pounds. She wore a yellow bandanna wrapped around her full head of hair. Effie was very warm and friendly. She welcomed him home with a big smile. He could plainly see one of her front teeth was capped in gold.

Murray walked down the long hallway to where Franny was lying in bed. Her face lit up at the sight of her husband. She knew he was coming home, but his presence gave her renewed confidence that life at the Goldman's might return to normal. She hid her pain and motioned for him to give her a hug. His arms wrapped around her so gently. He kissed her cheek, forehead and just held her for the longest time without speaking. As he set her back in the bed, he could see the tears roll down her face. He knew what she was thinking. He knew she was now facing the reality of life that she might not walk again.

He distracted her, asking a range of questions about the children and if Effie Johnson was helping her. She gave Effie high praise. "She's very strong," she explained, "and she works hard to help me turn so I don't get bed sores. She washes me, so the children get a break. She's taken over some of the cooking, which allows me to press the children on their homework."

Her husband listened attentively. He was pleased to know she felt good about the support she had at home. After an hour, he excused himself. He wanted to drive to the shop and check on the men, as they came back from work later in the day. Franny knew it would be futile to ask him to wait a few days. He promised to be home by dinner and spend time with the children.

The smell of plumbing supplies greeted Murray, as he entered his office. For him, the smell was better than roses. He was so anxious to get back to work. Just sitting in his office, with the smell of left-over cigars gave him a feeling of normalcy that he longed for. His secretary, Dorothy 'Dottie' Gleeson came in to give him a big hug. She brought him a hot cup of black coffee. Dottie was in her mid-50s, maybe 5-6 years older than Murray. She was a caricature of 1940's blond bombshell, with ruby red lipstick, large breasts and a rapidly expanding bottom. Dottie's husband left her and her kids long ago. She had few skills and struggled for years. Murray needed someone to manage the phones while he was traveling to jobs or meeting with new customers. Dottie was perfect, and she proved herself good at keeping track of supply orders and filing.

He sat and talked to Dottie for well over an hour. He answered her questions about the accident. She filled him in on the business. He had put Jamie Finnegan in charge. Jamie was a decent plumber, seemed conscientious and had experience supervising men on various jobs. His one weakness was that on occasion, Jamie drank too much. At the time of the car accident, Murray didn't have many options.

Dottie confirmed Murray's instincts. The business had slowed down, while he was in the hospital. The current schedule of jobs was light and the future schedule was almost non-existent. Dottie brought in the financial ledgers, so he could look at the books and understand the cash flow. He spent several hours, until he had a fuller picture. The news was not good.

The Goldman children were waiting at the door when he returned home. They could no longer expect dad to sweep them up in his arms, but they all held onto him. He tried to hug each child. For them, however, one hug would never be enough. How odd it is that children can go about their daily activities for hours without ever thinking about their father. It's as if knowing he's around, somewhere close, is enough to encourage them. So, what's the lesson,

Murray wondered? Is having an actual father as critical as simply the idea that a father exists somewhere? Where does reality balance with storytelling?

Effie stood by the kitchen entrance and watched the boys circling their father. When the uproar calmed down, Zach, Alan and Gary took their turn walking up to Effie and greeting her. She had become a surrogate mother to the boys. She hugged them in the morning and when they came home. She confessed her lack of schooling prevented her from helping them with homework, but she excelled at consoling each child when they suffered a setback or cried over their mom. Effie had arms and enough love in her heart for the entire neighborhood. The boys came to trust and rely on her.

Murray was surprised by the affection they showed Effie. He trusted the childrens' judgement of character. Something strange had also happened while he was away. His children no longer seemed to be children. There were few arguments in the Goldman home. The boys functioned like a team, sharing and taking ownership of responsibilities. He could not see their scars. If the boys suffered from being home alone, it wasn't apparent or talked about.

By mid-November, Franny's personal physician, Dr. Bernie (Bernard) Schwartz arranged for her to be taken to Bergen Pines Hospital. Dr. Schwartz knew the Goldman family since they first came to Paramus. He visited Franny weekly during her recovery at home and kept in close contact with Dr. Shivlin from Atlantic City. The hospital would complete a series of X-rays on her hip and legs. The test results would tell the doctors when it was ok to remove the body cast. This was the second trip to the hospital and Dr. Schwartz was satisfied with the results. A medical technician went to work on her almost immediately. She could hear the buzz of the saw slowly cut away the cast, starting at her chest. The effort took almost an hour as the staff used great care not to cut her skin. Her face showed anxiety as she tried to lay perfectly still, but she felt growing excitement to sit up or get out of bed.

Orders were given to begin rehabilitation exercises within days. The doctors cautioned her to go very slow. A fall could cause serious damage and put her back in the hospital. She would be kept at the hospital's rehabilitation wing to begin strengthening her body. Once the doctors had confidence she could keep her balance and sit in a wheelchair, she could return home. Dr. Schwartz understood it would take many months to achieve progress, but his goal was to get her started on the long journey to recovery. His priority was to get her home after she learned an exercise routine. Then she could go home, where her family could work with her and encourage her. The doctor released her after three weeks.

However, the next month at home was hellish for Franny. Getting in and out of bed was a huge undertaking. Effie was a terrific help during the day, almost lifting her by herself into and out of the wheelchair. In the afternoon, Effie would come in to rub her legs with body lotion.

All of the muscles in her body had atrophied, especially in her calves and legs. The physical therapist who came to the house was a drill sergeant. She worked with her three days a week. The therapist lacked the compassion one would expect, for someone who had suffered and struggled like Franny. She made her exercise almost 2 hours a day. Even Murray would become queasy, when he stopped home to check on her and heard his wife yell out in pain during a therapy session. But he held back his instinct to intervene. While she often ended each session in tears, he knew she needed to be pushed by someone at this point in life. Her will power was only half there. The therapist calmly and directly told her to push harder, even when she was ready to quit. Over time, the struggle got easier.

If the therapy wasn't enough of a challenge, sleeping through the night was a nightmare. The hospital bed was gone in the house. Murray put a thick sheet of plywood under her bedroom mattress to give Franny added support. But frequently, severe muscle cramps would wake her up. The drugs the doctors gave Murray for dizziness knocked him out at night. Zach could hear his mother cry out in pain. He would pull himself out of bed. He'd wander into his parent's bedroom. "Mom, are you ok?" he'd ask. Her failure to answer spoke volumes. He would sit at the edge of her bed. His small hands would rub her calves and lower legs. He'd squeeze her muscles until his hands hurt. In the morning, he could often be found fast asleep at the foot of Franny's bed.

While the Goldman boys were at school, Effie would take over. She'd help bath Franny and regularly rub her legs with cream. This was perhaps the happiest part of her day. At night, Effie lived at the other end of the Goldman's ranch style home. It was a small bedroom near the rear of the house. She could not hear anything.

The doctors tried different medicines to help Franny get through the muscle pain at night. But nothing and no one could accomplish more than the 11-year old Zach Goldman's magic hands. Often, he would wake in the morning, right before daylight, and return to his bed. If not, Effie would come in to Franny's bedroom and shake the boy so he could get ready for school.

Murray was returning to a normal life. He worked long hours trying to save the business. There's a certain momentum a service business requires, to ensure there's adequate cash flow to pay the workers. He tried to restore the rhythm, reaching out to new customers and pushing the men to complete jobs faster.

But he had one preoccupation. He wanted to be certain his wife would be able to walk again. He spent hours on the phone with Dr. Schwartz, Dr. Shevlin and with orthopedic specialists they recommended. Most of them told him that there might be a limit to Franny's recovery and she would require the use of a wheelchair. This news was never received well. A few of the specialists felt that if she continued to strengthen her body, she might reach a point where she could walk with crutches. The doctors gave no guarantees. They told Murray to reach this goal, she would require almost round-the-clock therapy. Some recommended a warmer climate might be helpful, along with regular swimming exercise.

There are times in life when you wonder how to shape the next day. For Murray Goldman, he wanted to shape the next 20 years. Seeing his wife in a wheel chair was not acceptable. This was the tomboy who wore short shorts and had enough speed to beat him on the handball court. He had been a man of the world, before he fell in love with her. A physical guy, who loved boxing as much as he loved coffee, he could have almost any girl he wanted, and he often did. His tall frame and jet-black hair gave added strength to his high forehead and sharp hazel green eyes.

But beneath the worldly guy, he never compared Franny to the any of the women he had known. She was different. They shared a common struggle in life during the Depression. They also shared a determination to dream big and make their dreams come true. Franny won his heart. These shared a purpose and set of values that would endure.

Murray was badly depressed after the accident. "We had it all," he often thought. "How could it go so wrong? Why did it have to be her? Why does she have to suffer so much? I'd gladly switch places to spare her this struggle."

Alan Goldman still volunteered going to work with his father. Their routine didn't change much, except Murray spent more time in the office on the phone rather than driving around to check on the men. It was late Fall 1961 and schools were closed for a week.

Alan would be 14 years old the following March. He was already chasing girls. He could be found with girls on occasion at the house, making out in the garage. But he had great difficulty with his little brother always hanging around. The incident with Sally Tilson became Gary's favorite story in the Goldman home. Gary was looking for something to do in the garage one afternoon, when he heard noise coming from the small supply room at the rear of the house. The supply room had a door leading to the garage and a door existing to the backyard. It was unusual for anyone to be down in the supply room. Gary quietly approached the door in the garage. He definitely was hearing noise. As he cupped his hands to look through the glass on the door, he could see his brother Alan kissing Sally. Gary just stood there, not certain what was happening. Before he knew it, Alan had pulled her shirt off and was kissing her naked chest. Sally had reasonably decent sized breasts for a young teenager. His brother moved from kissing her neck to her breasts. He got on his knees to continue kissing Sally down to her stomach, when all hell broke loose.

She had kept her eyes closed or looked toward the ceiling. But as Alan reached her stomach, Sally opened her eyes. She saw Gary at the door. His cupped hands and nose were pressed against the glass. Sally screamed and grabbed for her shirt. Alan, who had been facing the opposite way turned to see Gary's handprints leaving the glass. He could hear Gary yell as he ran to exit the garage, "I'm going to tell mom." He ran to catch up and stop his little brother. Sally ran out the back door of the supply room.

"Mom....mom, Alan has a naked girl in the garage." The words rang out, as Gary ran down the hallway to his parents' bedroom. Alan stopped dead in his tracks. He could hear Gary repeating the whole story. He was not going to follow his brother down the hallway. He left the house and didn't return for hours. He wanted to clobber Gary, when he came back. But Franny never raised the subject with him. He'd never hear about the incident again. Gary didn't say anything. Had he really gotten away with it, Alan wondered, or was his mom respecting his privacy?

Alan had entered his awkward teenage years. He thought constantly about Sally Tilson and a handful of other girls at school. He felt both guilt and desire. He was less mindful of any emotional connection. His obsession was the kissing and touching a girl in places he never expected to find.

While he enjoyed the time he spent with his dad, he got bored easily and often. The year was coming up on December, so school was off for two weeks. Alan had been hanging out at the back of the shop, when he decided to ask dad about going for lunch. As he approached the back door to dad's office, he could see Dottie Gleeson sitting on his dad's lap and giving him a hug. He stepped back from the glass window on the door. Twice he stepped back and twice he stared in to see Dottie.

He ran from the shop. Fear gripped his body. He wanted to barge into his father's office and confront him. His head began to pound with disgust. How could so much be lost so quickly? His idol in life, his inspiration, had failed him. He walked over to the Great Eastern Mills department store. He milled around inside the store for more than an hour. His thoughts raced, but they had no destination. The store was just down the highway, on the other side of the golf range from Murray's building. He didn't mind the children walking over to the department store. The area was back from the highway and a short distance. Usually, the children would bring a dollar from home and buy a small toy to keep them busy. Almost always the children were required to tell their dad where they were going.

After looking for Alan for 20 minutes, Murray figured his son must have gone to the store. He didn't return, which was unusual. It was way past lunch hour. Alan eventually come back and got in the car to go with his father. He never mentioned Dottie or asked his dad what was going on. He sat quietly. He didn't talk during lunch. When they got home that evening, Alan went to his room and declined joining his brothers for dinner.

The incident was never mentioned, but Alan felt betrayed by his father. He grew angrier in the days ahead, thinking about his dad's behavior while his mom was crippled lying in bed. "How could he do this to her," he kept asking himself. "How could he do this to all of us"? For a long time, Alan hid his resentment. Only on occasion would there be an outburst of emotion. Neither Franny nor Murray would know why Alan could be so moody. "You wouldn't understand," Alan would respond, when asked by his mom.

Through the eyes of a child, the world can seem black and white. When and why do children grow to hate their parents? Alan's worldview had changed, even before he became an adult. He hated his father now, with a passion he could not let go of. How unforgiving a child can become. But is it really hate or is it love? At the opposite end of the spectrum of love is a sense of abandonment which for a child can lead to despair, disrespect and hate. Finding the way back is never easy.

CHAPTER 49
Seeking Warm Weather

Early in 1962, Murray waited for the family to assemble around the kitchen table to make his announcement. Effie had brought Franny in with her wheelchair. While she could stand up and take a few steps with assistance, she was far from the goal of walking.

He told the family they would be moving to Florida next month. "Next month?" Alan asked. "How is that possible? We still have to finish the school year.

His dad explained he had been working with Bob O'Brien to locate and buy a home near Hollywood. The house was being built and it would have a swimming pool in the backyard for Franny. The home in Paramus would be rented for two years, leaving the family the option to return one day.

"What about your business," his oldest son asked? Murray paused. He looked at Franny and for the first time confided, "Dad's plumbing business cannot continue. While your mom and I were hospitalized, the fella I put in charge did not take good care of the business." The children sat stunned.

He would later explain to his wife in great detail how Jim Finnegan, his manager, had squandered his cash line with the bank and mismanaged several major projects. It's possible that Finnegan was even stealing money, but Murray didn't have proof. He told her that he asked Seymour Ginsberg, their lawyer, to salvage and sell whatever assets he could to protect the Goldmans from remaining creditors and the bank. Unfortunately, Murray's Plumbing was headed toward bankruptcy.

Franny knew her husband would not have reached this decision, if there were other options. She found comfort that his real estate properties had been kept separately from the business and were not at risk. The lawyer had taken steps to wall off these assets.

At the dinner table, as dad broke the news on moving to Florida, the boys were not about to question their father. They each shared anxiety and concern over leaving new friends at school. The boys had just been through a traumatic time, following the accident. Each of them had a million questions, but their fears faded away as their father spoke. "I know this change won't be easy for any of us," he said, "but the only priority in this family right now is to see your mother walk again."

Silence swept the room. The boys sat quietly. They felt guilty about their reaction to the news. How could they be so selfish? A few month ago, they weren't certain if their parents would ever return. No one could appreciate mom's suffering more than her children. How many nights did they sleep at the side or foot of her bed, hearing her waking up in pain. None of them really thought about their mom walking again, until dad stated his goal.

He had worked through the details, including moving their belongings and having the children transfer to new schools. Later that night, Franny spoke to her husband about the move. He had not consulted her, because he feared she would do what was best for the family rather than herself. She worried about disrupting the children. They had been through too much already. She also asked Murray why his brother Sammy couldn't take over the business. "Sammy is the most loyal family member you have. He adores you. You can trust him."

"Franny, I can't ask Sammy to take on a failing business. It's too late at this point. Besides, he can't give up his own plumbing business in Brooklyn. He can't just uproot his family and come to New Jersey. What would he do, if he gave up on Brooklyn and the business in New Jersey fails?"

For Murray Goldman, he had learned some very basic lessons in his life. He never backed away from a challenge. And he never spent time worrying about the unknown.

He made several trips to Florida over the next month, to check on the house construction. He took Alan with him on the last trip. The Goldmans had good friends who lived in a town nearby the new home. He would leave his son with this family for a few weeks, while he drove down with a car load of their possessions from New Jersey. Zach and Gary would keep Murray company on the drive. Franny would fly down, once the boys and Murray were settled. A moving company handled the rest of their belongings.

Zach and Gary enjoyed the adventure. As they got closer to South Carolina, they would count the number of signs for a tourist stop called South of the Border. They were convinced there were more than a hundred signs.

South of the Border was huge, with bright colors and a Mexican theme, including large sombrero signs that decorated the highway for miles. Dad had planned to stay over one night with the boys, since Dillon South Carolina was a midway point on their journey; about 10 hours from Paramus and 9.5 hours to Hollywood Florida.

The complex had a hotel, general store, restaurant, video arcade and gas station. The boys couldn't believe they found fireworks being sold in the general store. They had never seen fireworks before. Murray entertained the boys by setting off firecrackers in the parking lot. After dinner, he was tired and headed back to their room. He gave the boys time to wander around the complex on their own, but instructed them to return to their room in an hour.

The boys had no idea they were about to learn one of those special Murray Goldman lessons, when they stopped in South of the Border's video arcade. Clearly, they were excited. Zach had a pocket filled with coins. He took Gary over to play the pinball machines. The Goldman boys had never seen so many pinball machines in one place. Everything was blinking color and bright lights. The machines also made noise and played music. A few quarters could go a long way in the video arcade and it was easy for the boys to lose track of time.

They never knew how strongly their dad felt about gambling. Murray's parents split up, because his father Isaac often lost his weekly income playing cards. During the Depression, this was especially hard on the family.

The boys were still playing at the pinball machine, when their dad came up from behind them. He never said a word. His foot booted Zach in the rear-end and he levitated for several seconds. The pain did not actually register in his brain, until his feet returned to the ground. "No gambling. Now get back to the room," he told the boys. They took off like jack rabbits. This was a day the Goldman boys would remember. Dad did not like gambling—and in his world, gambling included pinball machines.

By morning, all was forgiven. Their dad did not revisit the events or scold the boys. He made his point. A foot or hand could not be mistaken or confused by anyone. They drove off after breakfast. Zach occasionally reached back to rub his bottom, which was sore for two days.

After leaving South of the Border, the boys laughed for miles as they drove on, only to see signs saying, "Ooops! You passed South of the Border. Turn around."

The year in Florida went very quickly. Murray's goal to see his wife walk again began to pay off. He flew north several times. By the spring of 1962, he met with his attorney, Seymour Ginsberg, to sign all the documents to close the business down. Most importantly, there were no lingering debts. His business reputation remained.

How does one put into words the inner conflict? He had given his all, building one of the largest plumbing business in northern New Jersey. He was well on his way to becoming a millionaire within a few years. The long hours working six days a week. The dangers he shrugged off, as he climbed in a ditch or walked the upper floors of buildings under construction. He wrestled with the consequences of simply walking away. But he knew in his head, it was too late. Time and money can be your friend—and it could be your worst enemy. The accident had robbed the Goldmans of a life they dreamed of. Like the luncheonette he owned in Brooklyn after the war, he could not control these events. Murray knew his real estate properties would still protect and secure his wife and the boys. Now was the time to focus on the future—and his future was to help Franny Goldman.

The Goldman boys were only too happy to be swimming in February, in a pool that covered the length of the backyard . Alan and Zach would help their mom into the swimming pool every day after school. Once in the pool, she kept her elbow crutches to help steady herself. The boys would take turns walking next to her back and forth in the water. They held onto her as if their lives depended on it. The water supported her, but the boys felt neurotic about making certain mom did not slip or fall. Each move in and out of the pool was filled with high tension. Her exercise routine would last an hour or more, until she was too tired to continue. Gary was not much of a swimmer, but he'd walk along side of the pool trying to give his mom encouragement. "C'mon, you can do it mom. Don't give up. If you stop now, my brothers are likely to drown you by accident." Gary was quickly becoming the family comedian.

When they were done, the three boys would work together to help mom out of the pool and into her wheelchair. If there was ever a coming together among the boys, they worked seamlessly as a team to ensure mom was safe. Once in her wheelchair, she'd sit resting while the boys swam like fish in the water. This was a special part of the day for Gary. He would sit with his mom and have her full attention. He looked forward to not having to compete with his older brothers.

Murray had moved through two different jobs during the first six months in Florida. He tried working for a plumbing contractor on a large-scale apartment building project, where most of the workers were half his age. He hoped his experience would be valued. However, the contractor was more concerned about the speed of completing the buildings and less worried when it came to the quality of work being done. He struggled physically, as well as mentally. He did not have the same strength. He quit the job after several months.

No one back in Paramus would have ever thought it was likely. Murray took a job as hourly security guard for a retail store in Hollywood Florida. He was a proud man, but at the same time he understood the value of having a job—any job. He'd leave the house every day, wearing his blue security shirt with a shield like a policeman wears covering the pocket. The sacrifice was now complete. He came home at night thrilled to hear the boys talk about mom's progress walking in the pool. But his smile hid from the family the depression he began to experience. The medicine he took helped with the dizzy symptoms from the car accident. When they reappeared, he never told Franny. The boys never focused in on their dad's physical limitations. He was guiding them and he was succeeding in nurturing their mom back to health.

The boys all shared a natural curiosity and thirst for learning, but home-work and test taking were secondary in importance to supporting their mom. Grades at school were passing, but each Goldman child knew they could do better.

The school environment in Florida seemed like something out of an old movie. Zach and Gary attended an elementary school that still had dirt floors in the class room. Florida would always seem to be a strange backward place, a world away from New Jersey. Alan was attending the Junior High School, which had a modern building. While Paramus had long ago changed from his childhood memories, in Florida he still ran into anti-Semitism at school. Sometimes, fights would follow a harsh exchange of words, but he was with-out his younger brother to help him when he was bullied by a group of boys. Alan remembered his father's boxing instructions, which proved useful at times. However, in Florida he also learned new lessons. He was surrounded by several boys at a school dance. When he put his fists up, one boy stepped forward from the group and kicked him in the groin. He fell against the school locker and slid to the floor. He had never experienced this type of pain before. He was ashen color. Once he was finally able to stand on his feet, a teacher helped him to the boy's room and washed his face with cold water, before sending him home. Alan realized if he was going to survive in this new envi-ronment, his feet had to be as quick as his fists.

By early June 1962, Franny surprised the family, taking her first walk with a pair of elbow crutches. The boys had been making dinner. Dad had come home early. They were all in the kitchen, when they heard a clanking sound and saw mom in the hallway. "Get back," she told them. "I can do this without your help."

She had been practicing for days in her bedroom. The exercise in the swimming pool had renewed her leg strength. The rest came from Franny's internal competitiveness and drive. It took several days just to stand up, next to the wall for balance. She would stand in the one spot, until she felt steady enough to take one step forward and then one step back. She was surprised— and happy—not to feel weak or out of breath. In the pool, she began to spend more time in the shallow end where her feet could touch the bottom. She had the boys bring her crutches into the water.

The Goldmans celebrated one of their happiest moments that night, as their mom slowly walked to the dinner table. The boys cheered and clapped for mom. Murray had the biggest smile on his face. The boys danced back and forth as they brought food to the table. Everyone had hoped for the impossible—and now it had arrived. She smiled through the tears. Mom was back! From this point foward, she was convinced it could only get better. That would not be true, but it gave her hope.

The month ahead still revolved around Franny's progress. Daily swimming was followed by walking in the street near their home. The boys took turns walking with mom, which gave each of them time alone with her. After dinner, it was still daylight outside. Murray would try to get home early enough one day a week to hold Franny's arm as they walked together. It was during one of these walks in August that she started to see the strain he was feeling. Her husband was never much of a talker, but he now seemed distracted and distant. He didn't even realize they had walked two blocks without stopping to give her a rest. "Let's stay here a minute," she told him. "You need to tell me what's going on."

He waited for months to tell her the legal steps he took to close the business. He explained he was able to keep the building, but all the equipment, trucks and income from last year was taken over by the bank. Franny stood with her crutches in the middle of the street that night and cried. He tried hugging her, but she became inconsolable. How could she not realize? Why hadn't she asked him, all these months? She cried thinking how much she let her husband down. She had been living in her own little bubble. "I'm so so sorry," she told him, "you've been dealing with this terrible burden on your own." Murray would not have it.

"It's not your fault. It's not my fault. This time, we're just a victim of circumstance. Neither one of us wanted to lose the business. We both worked very hard to create a future for our family. The business may be lost, but you're still standing. We can't go through life looking over your shoulder," he told her. "There are no guarantees. As long as we don't give up on each other, or on ourselves, we'll figure it out."

Over the next week, she insisted he spend more time with her. She was desperate that he let go and unburden himself over the decisions he was forced to make. He was a strong man, but this setback for him was at the heart of their dreams. He had been careful to keep his personal assets and investments separate from the business. "We'll still get some income from the rent folks pay in the building," he told her. "However, I fully expect some creditors will come after us. Seymour will handle that." He shared with his wife how stressed he felt over all the workers that would lose their jobs, including his secretary Dottie.

Franny also began to see the struggle Murray was finding, living and working in Florida. He had hidden so much from her—or was she blinded by her own challenges? As she grew stronger, walking with the crutches, she grew more aware that moving south had been horribly wrong for the rest of the family. Those who loved her most had also suffered the most. The children were falling seriously behind in school. They didn't even seem to care about school any longer. And her husband still suffered bouts of dizziness. More importantly, he lost some of his dignity, as he stood at the entrance to a retail store in some stupid blue uniform. He was too proud to complain or refuse to work. He had never been afraid of doing whatever it took to make a living.

By August 1962, Franny could walk almost the whole neighborhood. The elbow crutches helped her keep her balance and she had become independent of her children. She felt strongly that the point had come for her to take charge of the family. This time it was her turn to gather them at the dinner table. "You have all sacrificed to help me this year, but there will be no debate on this subject. It's time to go home." She realized a move north would be even more difficult. There was less income to fund the relocation. Their home in Paramus was being rented until the end of the following year. They would have to rent an apartment before getting the house back. She told her husband, the children they needed to do better at school. She expressed fear that Florida would not give them the discipline and education they required to get into college. She made up the excuse that she was also too far away from her doctors in New Jersey.

Each day, thereafter, brought a new story from Franny and a new rationale for moving north. But her biggest reason for moving north was not discussed. She could look at her husband and know he needed to be anywhere but Florida. He was not the same healthy guy from before. More and more, she began to see the toll the accident had taken on him. He was slower, weaker and had aged in ways she had not realized. Murray would soon turn 47 years old, but seemed almost a decade older.

Franny finally convinced Murray to make the move, by stating her wish that he start up the plumbing business, once again. "We'll start over," she told him. "I can handle the phone calls from home, just like when we first came to Paramus."

The thought of starting over energized him. It sparked a new purpose in his life. She knew her husband always rose to challenges, even when they seemed insurmountable. His depression soon gave way to thinking through the myriad of details associated with getting the business up and running again. She knew she was making progress, when her husband started asking her opinion on his plans.

CHAPTER 50
Starting the Business Again

There is truth to the adage that you can't go home again. Or better put, you can't expect home will ever be the same. The world spins, things change. Murray could hardly recognize the challenges a new business would face only two short years after the car accident. His body moved slower, but he was not daunted by this. Even at this stage of life, the voice inside his head instinctively knew the importance of forward momentum. Never let them see you are hurt. Never back up. Victories could always be won with heart—and a forward momentum.

The family landed in Fair Lawn, New Jersey. The children were enrolled in new schools. Franny began to keep a tight leash on them. She reminded the boys of her expectations, when she asked to see their homework each day. The children often longed for Florida, where the pool gave them an excuse to play. However, in time, they made new friends. Fair Lawn was more to their liking. They welcomed having structure and accountability. For too long the Goldman children were on their own, making their own rules. She knew it would take a long time, but she was determined to get some goal-setting back in their lives. She pushed the boys to get involved in sports, so they could use up some their endless energy. Alan played recreational basketball and he joined the Fairlawn High football team. Zach went to a gym near home to practice his tumbling. Money was tight for the family so Zach couldn't take formal lessons. His mom paid a few dollars for a membership and Zach simply went for exercise. He loved the smell of the gym. He would spend hours practicing handsprings and flips. Gary was not inclined to exercise. She tried to encourage him, but he was happy to be at home building a plastic model car.

Murray picked up the boys from home on Wednesday, for the weekly trip to McDonald's. Alan always had an excuse for not joining his brothers. A dinner out with dad gave their mom a break from worrying about who would cook. Zach had become the chief cook in the house following the accident. Franny would now try to share responsibility for making dinner, though she needed her sons to help her reach pots or bring food to the stove.

Dad drove the boys in his new Econoline van, which he bought to start up the plumbing business. For the boys, it was like a house on wheels. Zach and Gary would take turns sitting in the front and back seat. They had finished their burgers and fries, when dad signaled it was time to go home. As he slowly backed out of the parking spot, the van gently tapped the parked car behind him. Murray was confident he didn't cause any damage, but he jumped out to check the vehicle. No damage. Suddenly, as he got back in the van, he heard someone yelling and cursing at the top of their lungs. He was sitting in the driver's seat, but could see two men approaching the car behind him. The men were eating their food as they returned to their vehicle.

He waited for the men to inspect their car and see there was no damage. He then pulled forward to leave the parking lot, but the young driver of the car kept cursing and screaming at him. Zach and Gary sat quietly in their seats. Then it happened. The boys would never really understand. Their dad could be so calm and then the light switch was moved. The second man was older. He tried to quiet down his son from behaving badly. As much as he wanted to avoid a confrontation, Murray could no longer tolerate the loud abusive language.

He pulled forward several feet and put the van into park. Slowly, he opened the door and got out. The Goldman boys scrambled out on the other side of the van. They were scared. They did not want their dad to get hurt. By this time, the two men had each moved to their side of the car. The sight of him getting out of the van caused the younger man to get even louder, hurling more curse words. The young man was six foot tall, but thin. Murray walked directly up to him, without saying a word. He grabbed the young man by the throat and lifted him in the air against the car.

Zach and Gary would repeat the story many times to their friends. For them, it was something out of a movie. "As my dad grabbed the man by the throat, in slow motion, the French fries he was holding flew into the air. Dad cocked his right hand back." The second older man started to yell, "Don't you hit him, don't you hurt him." At this point, the young man fell silent. Terror gripped his eyes. He had clearly yelled at the wrong guy. Again, Murray said nothing. He let the young man down. He shook his finger at him, as if to say, "Shame on you". He then turned away and walked back to the van. The boys scrambled back into the van. As he drove away, he turned to his sons and paused at a traffic light: "Don't tell your mom." The boys were all smiles.

Alan Goldman hit his teenage years with a vengeance. He resented anyone who tried to tell him what to do. While he held his anger toward his father in check, he didn't hesitate to express his feelings with his brothers. The episode with Dottie sitting on his father's lap while mom was still recovering revolted him. How could his father be so disloyal? He hated his father. Both Gary and Zach did not understand his behavior. He never told his brothers of the detail of the incident. He just would call his father a bum. "He never loved us. He never loved mom."

Zach would jump to his father's defense. This often led to strong words between brothers, followed by Alan beating on him. He'd hit him like a punching bag. Sometimes, he'd double over his younger brother with a blow to the stomach. Once, he lost his breath from a punch square in his back. He lay on the floor gasping for air. Alan had grown taller and gained weight. Zach did his best to try and avoid these confrontations, but he would not accept his brother bad mouthing dad. Alan was determined to vent his anger on someone, anyone. The "one for all" mantra of childhood gave way to the rebellious teen years, where bonds of brotherly love are often destroyed for life. There is a fine line between animosity among siblings and Zach sitting up at night hoping one day to grow taller and strong enough to beat the tar out of Alan.

These fights went on for more than a year, and Zach would never forget or forgive his brother. The car accident gave the children no option but to rely on each other and stick together while their parents were in jeopardy. Beyond those "bonds born of crisis," Zach would see his brother as self-absorbed. Those words didn't find their way into his vocabulary until years later. The unspoken hurt and estrangement would always be there. Gary could not understand Alan's behavior. He watched with horror, while he beat him. How could he be so mean to his kid brother. Gary started out idolizing his oldest brother. Over time, he lost respect. Their closest moments as they grew older came only when one of their parents faced the prospect of death.

One wonders why siblings fight or don't get along? Sometimes they can spend a lifetime not having a clue where the car left the road. They hate each other. They harm each other by indifference. They create distance, because they simply can't handle their own pain. They stop talking or caring, and no one takes responsibility for fixing what was broken. How often do these issues have something to do with the shock of seeing, as Alan did, an incident and having no way of righting a perceived wrong? And what if the wrong is not real? What if what Alan saw was not what he believed at the time? As siblings, our actions have consequences. Alan craved the admiration and respect of his brothers. While they acknowledged his accomplishments, they no longer looked up to or idolized their brother.

Murray worked hard at trying to restart his plumbing business. He would never regain the size or momentum he had with "Murray's Plumbing and Heating." His ability to leverage his resources, the banks' resources and the network of contacts he had created were now gone. Two years can be a lifetime in the business world. Everyone is a friend, when you have something to offer in return. Your network of contacts are glad to help you, when there is a symbiosis and sharing of benefits. But it's near impossible to get a business launched without a sizable amount of capital or a critical mass of customers ready to call you for service. Contractors and trade union folks that he had helped along the way, were quick to forget how they struggled. Some had businesses that had grown so large that they couldn't give piece meal projects to small vendors or start-up plumbing business.

The new plumbing business started from scratch. Eventually, he was able to hire a helper to give him some added muscle on the job. Murray could be stubborn at times. He was a proud man, who had always exceeded expectations. Even a brain tumor couldn't diminish his drive to succeed or his keen mind for business. But now it was different. Even he realized his new limitations following the accident. His life experiences and skills taught him to adapt rather than resist what he could not change. He spent even longer hours working small jobs to make up for the business he might have done, if he had six trucks and 15 men. His plan of attack was to improvise. When your strength and speed start to ebb, you move slower and with greater purpose in each step.

Eventually, this lesson in life would not go unnoticed by the Goldman children. They grew up learning about self-reliance and taking control of events that would shape their lives. Their dad wore a grey shirt and pants, which were often soiled from jobs he had completed. The days of cigar smoke flowing from his office and barking orders on the phone were gone. But dad never gave in, and he remained their role model. The trauma of the car accident; the feelings of abandonment experienced by the boys during the long absence in the hospital and the subsequent loss of childhood freedom did not deter the Goldman children. Even Alan's anger at his father gave way eventually to admiring his father's single-mindedness in trying to shape the world he lived in.

Murray's first thought when he arrived home was to check on Franny's progress walking with the elbow crutches. The Goldmans were not in a position to hire help to work in the home and support her. The boys would each have chores to keep the house in order. Alan continued to help her with paperwork, sitting and learning how to keep a checkbook and going with mom to the bank. Zach cooked two nights a week. He helped mom prepare meals and he did the food shopping. Gary collected laundry around the apartment. He and his brother would take the clothes to machines in the apartment complex once a week. Franny would fold clothes when they returned.

By the spring of 1963, the Goldmans confronted something they didn't think was likely. Encouraged by her husband, Franny decided it was time to get back in a car and drive. They had been through an ordeal unlike anyone they knew. She might never be her full self again, but Murray desperately wanted her to reclaim her independence.

One Sunday afternoon, he took Franny to a large industrial park. He initially promised her a quiet drive in the country. She couldn't figure out why he pulled off the main road. As they entered the huge parking lot, she could see several buildings in the distance. "What's going on?" she asked. "Why did you pull in here? I thought we were going to the lake?"

Her husband pulled the car over. He got out and walked to the passenger side. "Franny, I need you to step out of the car. Please, I have your crutches." She couldn't imagine what was going on, but she did as her husband asked.

After taking a few steps, he held her arm for support and walked her to the driver's side of the vehicle. "Please get in," he instructed.

Franny was beyond nervous sitting behind the wheel. She sat frozen for several minutes, her hands squeezing the steering wheel. Her husband threw the crutches in the back seat and casually walked to the passenger side of the car. "Look, you don't forget how to ride a bike," he said. "You don't forget how to drive a car. Just turn the key and let's go." Franny's hands clutched the wheel. She started to panic.

Murray reached across and put his hand on the wheel. "Franny, it's not in your nature to fear anything. I know you can do this. I need you to do this! Now, drive. Don't be a schmendrick."

A smile came to her, but it was filled with nervous energy. It wasn't often her husband used Yiddish expressions. She turned the key. The engine hummed. She put the car in gear and began to drive. For 15 minutes, the car was coasting more than being driven. Again, she squeezed the wheel afraid to take her eyes off of the parking lot roadway ahead of her. Her head was bent low as she concentrated. His demeanor was calm, but resolute. He was not giving up. He sat and waited. Ever so slowly, Franny's confidence began to show itself. The car never got faster than 25 miles per hour, as she drove for 20 minutes. At the end, she pulled over. She was exhausted. Murray got out and helped her return to the passenger seat.

Over the next month, every Sunday he would take Franny to drive in a parking lot. Eventually, he took her on a country road. In time, he decided it was time for her to fly solo. She couldn't believe it, when she woke one Sunday to find a new car sitting in the parking lot near their apartment. He walked her to the door. "That new car out there is yours." Sitting in the lot was a 1963 dark blue Dodge Dart. "Here's the keys," Murray told her.

The Goldman boys heard their father and ran to the door. They helped their mom walk down the apartment steps and over to the car. The boys scrambled in the back seat, as mom opened the driver's door. "C'mon, Franny. I know it's early, but we have to keep with our tradition," said Murray. "The boys are expecting us to take them for ice cream to celebrate getting a new car." This was indeed the family tradition on so many occasions when their dad bought a new car, before the accident.

"Are you crazy?" she asked. "It's not even 11 a.m." "Look," he responded, "by the time we get to the ice cream parlor, they will be open. We'll take the long route along the Parkway."

Franny froze. Driving on country roads was certainly not as demanding as Route 4 or the New Jersey Garden State Parkway. She wasn't certain how her nerves would hold up. And to drive with the children in the car was sheer folly to her. But her husband was having none of it. He asked the boys to keep the noise down in the back seat, while mom drove. The boys were so excited, they could hardly contain themselves. Gary kept yelling out, "let's go, let's go."

As the new car reached Route 4 in Fair Lawn, you could see the wave of traffic heading toward New York City. This was Sunday in Paramus, so all the stores were closed. But this meant the usual congested, slow moving traffic conditions during the week would be moving faster. Franny would have to drive several miles on Route 4 to reach the intersection with Route 17 heading toward Paramus. Murray made a point to take Route 17 to reach a short cut on the Parkway. This would force the issue of driving on a major highway with his wife.

While initially driving at 35 miles per hour, Franny's comfort level began to take hold. On Route 4, she slowly built up her speed to 45 miles per hour. At the Parkway, she got nervous again, coming to a full stop at the entrance where the yield sign permitted her to jump into the traffic. On a Sunday morning, the Parkway traffic was light. Everyone in the car was silent when she hit the brakes and stopped. She turned toward Murray, who looked straight ahead. It was now or never.

Seeing no alternative, she stepped on the gas—and they were off. During the short ride on the Parkway, she hit 60 miles per hour. More importantly, she found her confidence again. At 45 years old, she was crippled and needed elbow crutches to walk. Her husband felt strongly that her disability did not have to hold her back any longer. She could reclaim her freedom to take the children, to go shopping or simply to go out and enjoy her friends. The boys waited patiently at the ice cream parlor for more than a half hour, until it opened. It turned out to be the best Sunday and the best ice cream they could recall.

CHAPTER 51
Military School

Zach Goldman would begin studying for his Bar Mitzvah in the spring of 1963. He was at a significant disadvantage. While his older brother had gone to Hebrew school for nearly five years, Zach only completed one year before the family car accident. He could barely recognize Hebrew letters and he read with great difficulty.

Franny went to visit Rabbi Rackowitz and his wife Sylvia. She thanked the Rabbi again and again for bringing Alan to the hospital. The Rabbi could barely believe his eyes as he watched her walk with crutches and then, get in and out of the car. Sylvia served tea and they talked about their children. After an hour, she explained her concerns about her son preparing for his Bar Mitzvah in the fall. He would not be capable of reading the Torah, the Haftorah or leading the service in Synagogue. "Franny, each child in our congregation is different," the Rabbi pointed out. "We shouldn't judge them on their ability to read, but on whether they have a feeling for their religion—and the special responsibility that comes with being Jewish.

During the many months of your recuperation, I've had the opportunity to spend time with your children perhaps more than most kids in the temple. Diane Shulman brought the children to several events. Your middle child is very special. He told me stories of standing in the back of the synagogue and listening to the Cantor sing. He shared with me many of the bible stories he learned in the 'Aleph' class. So many of our children study for Bar and Bat Mitzvah, but see it as a chore to be met...and soon forgotten. Zach is guided by something he feels deeply. He's more aware of others around him. He talks about injustice in the world. I believe he's certain that he has a one-on-one relationship with God. That's more than we can teach in Bar Mitzvah lessons."

Franny was stunned to hear the Rabbi describe her child. Was this the boy, who like his father, didn't seem to fear anything? The daredevil who at 6-years old did flips landing on his back in the den, or the child who dove into a 12-foot swimming pool in the Catskills not knowing how to swim? Was he the kid that climbed a 10-foot diving board and did somersaults into a pool in Florida? He nearly killed his brother Alan, who tried to copy him and landed with a huge belly flop. Yes, he was a wild child. But she also paused to think about the child who slept at the foot of her bed, rubbing her legs when in pain. Who was this boy, and why had she not seen the young man he was becoming?

The Rabbi assured Franny that whether Zach led the entire Saturday morning service or read two prayers, he would be ready for his Bar Mitzvah. He told her he would ask Rabbi Barry Discoll, head of the Hebrew School, to work on tutoring him on his Hebrew over the summer months.

Franny confided to Sylvia and the Rabbi, the doctors wanted her to have additional surgery to stabilize her hip. She had seen an orthopedic surgeon in New Jersey who specialized in something called "hip replacement." Essentially, the doctors would open her up, cut the top of her left leg off and then insert a metal shaft into her bone. A piece of metal would then be glued to her hip bone, creating a new joint. The doctors described the surgery as new and potentially dangerous, but it would give her greater mobility and the chance to stay on her feet longer without pain.

But it would be impossible to be in the hospital and rehab for months after the surgery, with three near teenage boys in the house. Sylvia was taken aback when Franny told her of the plan to send Zach to military school. Her husband was working so hard to bring the plumbing business back to life.

They couldn't afford to have help in the house. She had met with a recruiter from Riverside Military Academy, an older man called Colonel Robert Burns. He convinced her that the school was an excellent choice to guide young boys into manhood.

"But why Zach?" Sylvia asked.

"Well, the school starts at 8th grade, so Gary is still too young. And I need Alan to help me manage the family financial affairs. Most importantly, we can use the money we've saved for a Bar Mitzvah party, to help pay the tuition for the school."

Rabbi Rackowitz had never heard of a Jewish family sending their child to a military school. He was doubly shocked when he heard this school was located in the deep south, with its history of racism and anti-Semitism. He wondered if Franny had any understanding of what this environment might be like for Zach in the mid-1960s? The Rabbi feared for the young boy. He tried to ask if the Goldmans had explored other options. Whoever Colonel Burns was it appeared he had done his sales job well.

His mom had spent time with Zach telling him about the military school. At first, it wasn't clear if he understood that he would be living away from his family. He had met Colonel Burns, when he came to the house for the school applications and tuition payment. Zach seemed ok with his parents' decision. He knew his mom needed the hip surgery. He wasn't certain what it would be like being so far from home.

Preparing for the Bar Mitzvah was sheer torture for Zach. Rabbi Driscoll reduced the number of prayers he had to read. He read the "Barachu" prayer, at the beginning of the Aliyah. He would practice three lines from the Torah, though he never did understand the "tropes". His Haftorah was the shortest Rabbi Driscoll could find. He wrote his speech, thanking his parents on becoming a Bar Mitzvah. He added in lines, thanking God for allowing his parents to reach this day of celebration. Rabbi Driscoll was quite surprised and delighted to read his remarks. It was short and hand written on a folded piece of paper. He had never had a "Bar" or "Bat" Mitzvah boy or girl express their gratitude to God. Rabbi Driscoll became more forgiving with the child who struggled to read Hebrew, but nevertheless wanted to thank God.

The Bar Mitzvah ceremony on Saturday, in September 1963, was a blur for young Zach. Unlike his older brother, Zach was not nervous. He got up and read the prayers, as he was taught. If he stressed over his pronunciation of Hebrew words, it was not apparent to the congregation or his family. The only emotional moment was clearly evident when he stood on the Bimah (stage) by himself and read his Bar Mitzvah speech. Half way through, he paused for a minute and looked out at the Synagogue. He wrote the sentence "thanking God," while thinking about his family. His voice cracked, as he looked down at his mother and father. The tears flowed down his cheeks. Many families in the congregation knew about the horrible car accident, but they did not expect this open expression of love from a child. Zach would never be ashamed of showing his emotions. He finished his speech. He looked down again at his parents, with pride and a smile on his face. He wiped the tears away with the back of his hand and the sleeve of his sports coat. He took a deep breath and walked to his seat next to Rabbi Rackowitz.

Unlike the huge celebration for Alan, there would be no party for Zach Goldman's Bar Mitzvah. The Goldmans took the boys for dinner at the Suburban Diner on Rte. 17. It was a quiet family dinner. His parents heaped praise on their second child.

Since the Goldmans had only moved north a few months prior, Zach had few friends to attend a Bar Mitzvah party. His mom made a big deal about his going off to military school. He'd had so much fun. Most importantly, he wouldn't have to worry when mom had her hip surgery. She explained to Zach how hard his parents worked at setting aside the money to pay for the military school tuition. He didn't pay much attention to the dinner discussion. He did wonder why no one had ever asked him whether he wanted a party? He was relieved, however, he could see the Bar Mitzvah ceremony in the rear-view mirror. Zach was happy to just enjoy his roast beef, mashed potatoes and gravy.

On the Thursday, following his Bar Mitzvah, the Goldmans drove Zach to the train station in Newark, New Jersey. He boarded the train by himself with one footlocker. Franny packed clothes inside following the guidelines provided by the military school. Zach looked out the window, as his brothers and parents waved good bye. At this point he asked himself, "Why me? Why was I being sent away?"

His mom had worried if Zach would get upset or emotional leaving home. She watched from the train platform, as he lifted his hand and waved back. Zach was expressionless. His face did not show fear. He didn't know what awaited him. He was about to embark on an adventure, unlike any he had ever experienced. The train pulled out. And then he was gone.

Zach sat on the train alone for 17 hours. As the train pulled in to Gainesville, Georgia, about 16 miles from Atlanta, he could see two yellow school buses. He was certain some of the boys he saw on the train, many of them with parents, must be headed to the same place. He had eaten the sandwiches and fruit his mom had given him for the trip. It was morning and he was hungry.

Next to the school bus was a man in a brown military uniform barking orders as the boys exited the train. The grownups at the military school were mostly faculty or school administrators. It wasn't clear if any of them had actually served in the military, but the uniforms sent a message of authority.

The buses drove a half-hour into the middle of nowhere. Zach was among the youngest. He was entering 8th grade. Some of the boys on the bus were much older, perhaps juniors and seniors in high school. Most of the older boys wore their military school uniforms, with blue coats, gold buttons and grey pants. The newbies, as Zach was labeled, sat quietly the whole ride to the school. When they arrived, the adult in uniform began yelling again. The boys quickly dragged their footlockers to a common area, next to the mess hall. They were told to stand at attention, if they wanted to eat.

After a few minutes of chaos, the newbies stood at attention and then were organized into lines of ten students to enter the main building. They picked up a metal mess hall tray and walked down the cafeteria line, where school employees slopped food down. The flat sausage patties looked over-cooked, like hockey pucks. The biscuits were toasted well done and hard as rocks. Zach didn't recognize the gooey white stuff on his tray, but another boy called them grits. He asked if he could eat his portion. Zach could swear the grits had no taste. Once he ate breakfast, he wondered if his appetite would ever return.

An announcement was made for the boys to reassemble in 15 minutes on the promenade. The boys were given 25 minutes to eat. Two older cadets at the school cautioned Zach's table not to be late for roll call. The promenade was a large square area in front of the main building, where nearly 600 students would march until their military company was called to enter the mess hall. Since school would not start for two days, the promenade was empty. Again, the adult, Colonel Jones, began barking orders for the newbies to line up and raise their hand when their name was called.

After roll call, the boys were marched over to the Riverside Military Exchange Hall. Each cadet entered the Hall. Gray uniforms including shirts, trousers and two black clip on ties were handed out. A line meandered through the building. First, they were told to hold out their arms. A supply clerk made a judgment on their size and handed them uniforms. Next, the boys walked through the barber shop, where crew cuts were the dominant hair style. The shoe shop followed. Each cadet was given a pair of black shoes, shoe polish, buffing rags and quick instructions on how to "spit shine" their shoes. Few would remember the instructions, but the older boys would teach them once they were assigned a room. At the last stop, a cadet was given his uniform brass with instructions on polishing and placing the insignias on their uniform. As the cadet finished his trip through the Exchange Hall, he was given a map and assigned a barracks and room number. The boys would return to the main square to pick up their foot locker and carry or drag it to their room. This was Riverside Military Academy, there would be no hand holding. Find your room or go home, the choice was yours.

Zach had made it through the Hall without difficulty and found his room in a half-hour on the far side of campus, facing a main road. He was assigned to "F" company, one of six companies of cadets at the school. A company had about 100 boys, each platoon had about 30 cadets and there were three squads in each platoon. Each company was led by 3-4 seniors in high school, with ranks like Captain, First Lieutenant (Lt.) or Second Lieutenant. Platoon and Squad leaders were also Seniors or Juniors in high school. At 5'3", Zach Goldman was among the youngest and smallest cadets in F company.

After the first week at the school, Zach and his suite mates were visited by Lieutenant (Lt.) Robert Aldridge. Each room had four cadets sleeping on two bunk beds and the two rooms shared a common toilet and shower. The footlockers fit snuggly into a small closet area, where each student could hang their jackets and uniforms. Zach figured Lt. Aldridge must have been working his way down the hallway to meet the newbies. He had a very distinct "Southern drawl" accent.

"When an officer comes into your room, you boys have to learn to stand at attention," Aldridge yelled as he entered the room. "Respect is the first lesson y'all better figure out quickly." Aldridge summoned all the boys into Zach's room.

"Now, I know y'all think you're pretty special, but I'm here to set you straight." As Aldridge finished his sentence, he raised his left leg and gave Zach a side kick to his chest. The Lt. obviously had learned Karate. Zach landed on a foot locker in one of the closets. He was smart enough to stay there. The Lt. turned and hit the cadet opposite him with the back of his hand. He moved quickly with a front kick to another boy who hit the bed and fell to the floor. Another side kick brought one more boy to the wall, where he slid down and sat riddled with fear. The last four cadets were spared, but everyone got the message about who was in charge. The Lt. was starting the year off with a lesson about respect, following orders and taking the chain of command seriously. This was a military school. This was not summer camp. And mom and dad were almost a thousand miles away.

Lt. Aldridge left the room almost as quickly as he arrived. There were other cadets to visit that day. These cadet orientation meetings, if they took place in other Companies, had to be completed before school classes began. Zach crawled out of the closet, rubbing his chest where he had been kicked. The boys didn't really talk about the visit. Each licked their wounds and worked on preparing their uniforms and polishing their shoes.

Sargent (Sgt.) Miguel 'Tico' Torres, their Squad leader, stopped by the room about a half-hour after the Lt's visit. "Everyone ok in here?" he asked. Torres was a Junior in high school. He had attended Riverside Military Academy since 8th grade. His family lived in Texas. He was shorter than most of the older cadets, maybe 5'6" but with broad shoulders, dark hair and a quick smile. If you were looking for someone to coach you, Sgt. Torres was a good guy. He never mentioned Lt. Aldridge, but he knew the drill. He tried to follow the "cadet meetings" with some lessons of his own. "Look, don't talk unless you're asked a direct question," he told the boys. "Keep your mouth shut...that's what's expected of you. Follow orders as they're given, no back talk. Salute officers, as they enter your room or walk past you on the school campus. The environment here is like the real military. If you don't want a visit in the middle of the night from a group of cadets enforcing the rules: sit up, stand up and don't screw up."

The room was silent, as Sgt. Torres spoke. He could see their eyes almost popping out of their heads, as the boys listened. Lt. Aldridge had made his point. Sgt. Torres' job was to guide the new cadets on making their beds with hospital corners, how to wear their brass insignias and polishing the brass on their belt and uniform, and the techniques for spit shining your shoes. None of the boys had ever polished shoes before. Sgt. Torres explained the routine of morning inspections by Lt. Aldridge, where every cadet stood by their bed. If the hospital corners on the bed were not exactly at a 45-degree angle or the sheet and blanket weren't tight and crisp, the inspecting officer would rip the blanket off the bed. It would not be uncommon for Lt. Aldridge or another officer to try bouncing a quarter on the bed. If the sheet and blanket were loose, the quarter just fell silent and the bed was ripped apart.

"If your brass isn't polished, the inspecting officer will give you demerits or points which add up over time and result in punishment. Too many demerits and a cadet walks the main square, while everyone else has free time after school classes. If your inspecting officer can't see a reflection in your shoe shine, he will politely step on your foot and grind his shoe on yours. This will destroy the spit shine you worked a week to create, so your shoes better be properly polished.

"Any questions," Sgt. Torres asked? The boys sat silent. No one dared speak, after the visit from Lt. Aldridge. After several minutes, there is always someone in the group who will muster the courage or is just too stupid to stay quiet. Finally, Richard Menendez raised his hand. "Yes, what's your question," Sgt. Torres called out. "What does any of this have to do with my school work?"

"Nothing. It has nothing to do with your school work," Torres responded. "But these lessons are equally important to school. These are life lessons about discipline, respecting leadership and paying attention to the details that in the real military can make the difference between life and death. Here at Riverside, you will learn and practice these lessons. You will master these lessons. You will be aware of these responsibilities every waking hour of every day. Follow the rules and you'll be ok. Got it?"

Sgt. Torres ended his instruction period, after the question from cadet Menendez. He figured some of the boys might have other questions, but he was not looking to parent these new cadets. They would have to learn to fend for themselves.

The next two weeks were mind altering for the newbies. Often, the students stumbled out of bed. They tried to leave enough time to wash, get dressed and make their bed. No one could be certain which door Lt. Aldridge would enter. "Attention," one of the boys would yell, which was the signal to run and stand next to their bed. It wasn't unusual for boys to be in the bathroom, brushing their teeth or half dressed. But when the Lt. entered the room, dressed or naked you better be at that bed post for inspection. Being out of uniform or half-dressed resulted in demerits. Some students set alarm clocks to get up an hour early, to avoid not being ready for inspection.

The morning inspection did not take long, but the results could be devastating. When the Lt. ripped your bed apart, everything was left on the floor in a pile. You didn't dare speak or ask what you did wrong. You were told to stand straight with eyes looking ahead. You were asking for trouble, if you glanced to see what the Lt. was doing.

Lt. Aldridge was usually followed by Second Lieutenant Hanley and Sgt. Torres. Every infraction was recorded by the Second Lt., so they could hand out demerits and penalties. If the bed was ripped apart, the Lt. often felt that it was punishment enough and did not assign demerits. Zach had figured out a strategy to help him get ready for these morning inspections. First, he took the top bunk, which wasn't as easy to see as the bottom one. Also, he never slept under the covers on his bed. He would climb to the top and cover himself with an extra blanket from his footlocker. In the morning, he'd pull the bedding tight and return his blanket to the closet.

Polishing the brass on your belt and the school insignias, along with spit shining shoes was usually the last activity before bed time. All cadets were required to sit 2 hours after dinner at their desk, which was the designated study period. An officer patrolled up and down the hallway to ensure cadets were sitting at the desk. No one could force you to study, but they did give you structured time to sit with a book open.

Students were also aware that every week, a progress report (post card) was mailed home. This card recorded your grades in every subject, along with a grade average for the week. Your parents were not allowed to send you money. Funds were sent and kept in a school account. If you received an "A" grade average for the week, you could collect $5 at the Bursar's office; a "B" average would get you $4; a "C" average got $3. These were the only funds you'd have access to during the week. This was a powerful motivator, when you wanted to eat a snack at the Canteen before marching practice for the weekly school parade.

Zach Goldman was quick to admit he had a number of $3 weeks. At the canteen, he learned to pour half a bottle of Catsup on his French fries to hold his hunger through parade practice.

Lights out in the dorm rooms was at about 10 p.m. The Officers would shut the hallway lights in the dorms, which signaled it was time for bed. The cadets had to shut the lights in their rooms or they'd get demerits. However, it was not unusual for students to stay up until 11 or even midnight, using flashlights to polish their brass or shine their shoes. One of the best lessons of military school was learning how to navigate rules—and survive.

About three weeks into the school semester is when Zach received his first lesson in military life. He returned to his room after class. As he opened the door, he could see his bed had been torn apart. At first, he figured it was a prank someone played on the newbies. He hadn't yet closed the door behind him, when he felt the blanket thrown over his head. The boys had to be older, because they seemed so much bigger to him. A half dozen punches were thrown, hitting Zach in the back and stomach. While he tried to protect himself, he could hear one of the boys yelling out, "We don't like Jews here in the South. It's time to go home Jew-boy."

Zach slumped to the floor in pain. The blanket still covered him, as he heard the boys close the door behind them. He slowly pulled the blanket off his head. His lip was bleeding. Of all the changes he anticipated at the military school, this was not one of them. What happened to order and discipline? After several minutes, he lifted himself off the floor and washed his face. He did not know who attacked him. He was not about to run to his Sgt. or to the Lt. and report what happened. If it was a fight they wanted, he was ready to defend himself. He was not afraid.

Two more weeks went by, before the incident repeated itself. This time, it was at night, after the "Lights out" announcement was made. The boys in his room were drifting off to sleep when the door opened. There were at least three boys who ran straight to Zach's bed. Again, they threw the blanket over him and started punching. "Kill the Jew," one boy yelled. The others laughed as they hit him. Zach reached for the edge of the blanket and started throwing fists of his own. He wasn't certain if he hit anyone, but he was going to try. "C'mon, Jew boy, you can do better than that."

Robert Rountree, his roommate, heard the noise and jumped out his bed. He began yelling at the boys, who quickly turned and fled the room. Zach got down from his bunk and ran out the door after the boys, but they were gone. "What the hell was that about," Robert asked him? "Was that the first time they attacked you"? Robert had been sent to Riverside, while his father worked in Indonesia as an airline pilot. He was farther away from family than anyone at the military school.

Zach confided in Robert about the previous beating, but he asked him not to report what happened. The Rountree family had traveled the world, following his father's career. Robert had seen prejudice of all types in countries, between Hindus and Muslims, Christians and Muslims, Christians and Jews, etc. He explained to Zach that while he was spiritual, he could not accept the amount of "hate in the name of God" that he saw in the world. After a half-hour or so, the boys became sleepy and returned to their bunks.

Several days would go by, before David Stoddard, Captain of "F" Company heard about the beatings Zach received. His roommate, Robert, refused to sit by and ignore what was going on. He knew silence was not an option. The attacks would continue, unless someone stopped them. He told Sgt. Torres, who promised not to let anyone know he reported what happened. Captain Stoddard had attended Riverside Military Academy since 8th grade. He thought he had heard and seen it all, but was shocked to hear what happened to one of his cadets. He called a meeting of his officers. He did not want to confront the behavior head-on. Stoddard knew that singling out a cadet might cause more problems. The Captain grew up in Boston, and he understood the racial and religious issues in the South were not that different than South Boston.

Captain Stoddard decided on a strategy to help cadet Goldman. He informed his officers what happened. He asked them to keep their eyes open. He also asked his officers to spread a story in F Company that Zach was the kid brother of his best friend, Scotty Goldman. At Riverside Military Academy, there were only six companies and the Captains of each company were a close knit group. Almost all of them had been in school together for four years. They came up the ranks together and they looked out for each other. David Stoddard was smart enough to know that once the story was circulated, no one would bother him again. Whether the cadets who attacked him came from F-Company or another Company, you did not want to take on the cadet leaders at the school.

Zach was never told about the story Captain Stoddard had spread around the school. He shrugged when the Captain asked him at Company formation near the mess hall about Scotty Goldman. The question was asked in a public setting, where other cadets could hear the conversation. At one point, Zach believed the Captain thought he looked like a boy back home, named Scotty. Other Officers would sometimes call out, "Hey, Scotty, how are you?" His name tag on his shirt said, ZS Goldman, which stood for Zachary Samuel. He figured folks were getting the initials mixed up. He would always wonder why the visits from students who hated Jews stopped? He was grateful. But he was always guarded when he walked the campus that students might attack him.

Most cadets received "care packages" from home. Parents were told not to send cash, but they were allowed to send a large box filled with cookies, cakes, candy bars, etc. Unfortunately, students on a hallway always knew when a care package arrived. A white card was taped to their room door, to pick up the package at the campus post office. By the time they got back to the room, you could see at least 10-12 faces looking through the window…and waiting for the cadet to open the package. The timing had to be precise. As the box was opened, the crowd would run into the room screaming to distract the cadet. Everyone would reach in and grab some candy or cookies and run for the door. By the time the group left, half the package of food was gone.

Zach was lucky. He never cared much for sweets, except for Baby Ruth bars. He sent word to his parents requesting a limited list of food items. When his turn came, the cadets ran into the room and began pulling his box apart. Suddenly, boys stopped in their tracks to look at their ill-gotten gains. "What the heck are bread sticks?" one boy asked. Another boy ripped open a bag of Kosher soup nuts and gagged, "This stuff tastes like saw dust," he yelled. He put the bag back in the care package and rummaged around for something better. "Ritz crackers, who sends Ritz crackers?" After several minutes, the roar of the crowd died down. Most items from the care package were put back, opened but uneaten. They would not find Oreo cookies or candy of any type. Only one bag of sour hard candy was missing. Zach figured he could live with that. Word spread that this kid from New Jersey didn't get cookies or sweets. As a result, he rarely faced any future attacks on his care packages. When the box was brought to his room, he'd see the faces at the window and smile. The cadets were always ready to pounce, if they saw something good to eat. "Scavengers," he would say to himself.

Getting extra food and supplies were big challenges for cadets living at the military school. Each student would be limited to a monthly allotment of soap, tooth paste, toilet paper, etc. If you used up your supply, you looked for creative ways to address your needs. Zach's roommate, Richard Menendez was the first to discover the meaning of "black ass." The boys had heard older cadets talk about it, but weren't certain where it came from. Richard was in the bathroom often, too often. His roommates decided it was time for each of the boys to bring their own roll of toilet paper to the bathroom, so Richard didn't use up everyone's supply. And when Richard didn't have toilet paper, someone coached him to scrunch and ball up newspaper until it was soft enough to wipe his butt. Richard was getting ready to shower one day, when his suite mates started to laugh and yell out," Look, it's black ass; Richie has black ass." They all came running to see that black ink from the newspaper had come off when Richie wiped himself. Half his ass was literally black in color. The cadets were falling out with laughter. For the newbies, the mystery of where "black ass" came from was solved.

The school classes at Riverside were not easy. The good news for parents was the class size. They consisted of 13 to 15 students, unlike the 25-30 students per class in public school. At Riverside, a student could not hide if they hadn't done their homework. Students were regularly called upon to answer questions. Zach paid attention in class and completed his homework, but he rarely studied for tests. He had spent nearly three years ignoring school, to help his mom and family. He liked the structure and escape that a school class room provided, but in the larger scheme of things he was focused more intently on whether his mom needed him.

Those $3 of allowance he often received based on grades became increasingly difficult. The boys finished classes at 2:30 p.m. They had a one-hour break before they were due to attend practice for the school parade conducted once a week on the football field. Folks from town would come to see the students in full military dress uniforms march up and down the field. Marching for an hour on an empty stomach was sheer torture. Zach had to find a way to earn some money.

As the weather got cooler in late fall, the dress uniforms included wool pants. As a favor, Zach volunteered to help Sgt. Torres steam press his wool trousers. Franny had taught him how to take a wet pillow case and cover the pants, while ironing. This created a crisp crease in the pants without burning the wool. Word of his special skill reached Lt. Aldridge and Captain Stoddard. Without soliciting, he quickly found a new and budding business in F Company steam pressing wool pants for all the officers at $.75 per pair. Soon he had enough money to buy French fries after class. And, once a month, he would go with roommates to downtown Gainesville, Georgia, where a hotel offered an "all you can eat" brunch on Sundays. Zach didn't mind the nights he spent pressing pants, for the feast of roast beef or turkey, mashed potatoes, green beans and gravy he ate on Sundays.

He worked hard at military school to get back his discipline and study skills. It would take months, but he periodically got his grade to a 'B' average on his report card. There was no one to push him on his grades, so it was up to him and the internal competitive voice telling him to try harder. Aside from school work and marching practice, one day a week the cadets had a physical training (PT) program. In PT, the boys would be required to learn a callisthenic exercise program. Sgt. Torres would supervise his squad while they were in the gym. He was a nice guy and supportive to the boys in his squad, but during exercise he fit the true definition of a "Drill Sergeant."

The gym was quite large and could accommodate more than 100 boys during an exercise session. Gym mats covered about 3/4th of the floor surface. It was during one of these sessions that Zach started fooling around. The gym felt like an area where he could let go and be himself. As he waited for his turn to do pushups, he ran down the mat and did a cartwheel handspring, handspring and a third handspring. His roommates, Rountree and Menendez watched in shock. "Goldman," a voice called out. Sgt. Torres motioned to

Zach from the other side of the gym. Anxiety started to overtake Zach. He broke the rules. What rule did he break?

As he reached the Sgt., Zach stopped and stood at attention. Torres smiled and told him to relax. "Can you do that again," he asked him? "Yes, sir," he replied. "Go ahead, I want to see that one more time." Zach turned and took a long run across the mat. This time he added a fourth handspring. The Sgt. signaled for him to return. "How long have you been doing gymnastics," Torres asked him? "Sir, I think since I was 7 or 8 years old."

Sgt. Torres explained to him that Riverside had a school gymnastic team. He invited him to attend the team's practices during a cadet's free time on Saturday afternoons. Zach learned, for the first time, his squad leader was also a gymnast. Sgt. Torres specialized on the rings, which started to make sense to him looking at the Sgt.'s broad shoulders.

While Zach was anxious about the anti-Jewish sentiment among some at the military school and the challenges to improve his grades, joining the cadet gym team rebalanced the equation. He had found his place and purpose, almost 1,000 miles from home. The gym was his favorite place to hang out. Here he found freedom to express himself and use his boundless energy. Sgt. Torres told him to use his nickname, "Tico," in the gym. He taught him some basic exercises on the rings, which helped strengthen his upper body.

Tico also introduced him to the York brothers. Gerhard "Jerry" York was a senior in high school. Jerry was a monster, at least 6'2" 190 pounds of sheer muscle. He specialized in the parallel bars and the rings. He did hand-stands and walked the length of the parallel bars effortlessly. His younger brother Daniel "Danny" York was a sophomore. He was a miniature of his older brother in build and skills. He could walk the entire gym floor on his hands. His specialty was the parallel bars and the high bar. He was lighter than Jerry, so he had the agility and strength to swing into a hand stand on the high bar and complete double flip dismounts.

In the months ahead, Zach became a more rounded gymnast. At the Kelly dance studio, he only learned tumbling or acrobatics, as it was called. At military school he found other types of gymnastic equipment and students who would teach him. Sgt. Torres gave Zach lead responsibility for teaching other cadets acrobatics. Most of the students could barely do a somersault. The goal was to prepare a select group of 15 cadets to perform at a school gymnastic show in the spring. During this period, he also learned from the York brothers to perform on the parallel bars and to complete a back flip. He had always been scared to tackle back flips, but the York brothers tied ropes to his waist to help him build confidence. If he didn't jump high enough, Danny York could pull on the rope and prevent him from hitting his head on the ground. Zach's confidence grew and he perfected doing round offs, back handsprings and back flips.

Sgt. Torres may not have realized it, but Zach's job of teaching other students brought out his natural leadership skills. He coached cadets on how to do dive rolls. He stood on his head, spread his legs and let cadets do dive rolls, landing on the mat. If a student messed up, he never criticized. He would encourage and show patience, which is the way he learned. In time, he had a line of cadets who excelled at dive rolls. He moved on to teaching cartwheels and back rolls.

Tico was proud of him. However, once they left the gym, Sgt. Torres was still his commanding officer. There would be no favoritism in F-company's third platoon. During the week, every cadet would stop at the armory and pick up their M-1 rifle for drill practice. Riverside had a supply of M-1 combat rifles used during World War II. The rifles were heavy, over 9 pounds each, and students had to learn how to break down the rifle, clean the parts and put the rifle back together. Closing the bolt of the rifle required a student to press down with their thumb or index finger, and to clear their fingers before the bolt slammed shut. One cadet in the third platoon lost the tip of his finger, when he didn't pull his hand out fast enough. This was not an uncommon experience.

Some of the 8th grade cadets, like Zach, were still too little to parade for over an hour carrying a 9 lb. rifle. Some tried, but due to heat or exhaustion the cadet would pass out on the parade field. Commanding officers would make judgments and those cadets deemed to be too small would be issued "toy rifles" for parade practice. While somewhat humiliating, none of the boys complained about the arrangements. They could march for an hour without falling down or being excused from the exercise.

Before parade practice began, non-officers marched cadets around the football field for 30 minutes. During the drilling, Sergeants in the Company would improvise their drill commands, always remaining in marching cadence, "Hup 2, 3, 4.... I don't know what you've been told, but winter in Georgia is awfully cold...sound off, 1,2....sound off, 3, 4.....cadence count 1, 2, 3, 4." The younger students did not really understand the Sgt.'s drill commands, but they followed the older boys. To a bunch of kids, these improvised marching orders kept them entertained and engaged. The cadets didn't have to be prompted to call out the numbers.

Captain Stoddard and other company Captains took up command of the Battalion parade practice halfway through the exercise. Stoddard led F Company with his sword drawn. There was no humor as the company marched in unison. Lt. Aldridge would take over yelling out the cadence, "Hup 2, 3, 4....left, right, left, right." The Lt. would yell "you have to get off on your left," and the Company would reply in unison, "your right." This marching cadence would continue, until the Riverside band reached the football field.

As the band began to play, the energy of the "National Emblem March" would ripple across the entire Battalion of 600 cadets. From a group of kids marching independently to the commands of their Company officers, the music snapped the disparate groups into a unified and focused military Battalion. The music provided discipline and definition to their steps. The band would start mid-way through the song, with the trumpets slowly building toward a faster tempo, "Dah...ta,ta,ta,dah..dah, ta,dah,dah...dah,ta dah". The National Emblem was written in 1902, by Edwin Bagley from Vermont. The story goes that Bagley wrote the music while touring with his family's band. Ironically, he discarded the song in the trash, believing it wasn't strong enough.. His bandmates found his sheet music and began playing the march at public performances. The song is ranked as one of the greatest pieces of marching music ever written, by someone other than John Philip Sousa.

The cadets would not recall the name of this marching music, but it remained with them the rest of their lives. Whether a doctor, lawyer, construction worker or teacher, before you recognized the music being played by a military band your feet would be keeping the cadence. The trumpets were your best friend. They inspired you, when you were tired. The sounds of the band filled your head, long after the marching stopped.

The Company would complete one full tour of the football field. As F Company approached the viewing stand, Captain Stoddard would yell, "Eyes right." The Captain and all cadets would turn their heads toward the stand. Officers would salute. The Captain's sword would salute.

It was rare that parade practice was ever cancelled, even if the weather was "iffy." A light drizzle of rain would not keep cadets off the football field. Each cadet had been issued a white plastic cover for their military parade hats, which they would wear along with their blue wool jackets (to keep warm). However, parade practice was cancelled on Friday, November 22, 1963, as the world turned upside down.

Classes ended early on Fridays. Zach couldn't wait to head to the canteen to eat something before he had to report for parade practice. As he walked into the canteen, the first thing to catch his eye was the lady working there, stood behind the counter crying like a baby. A small TV was sitting on a shelf behind her. The voice of Walter Cronkite was distinct. He could hear him say something about "the motorcade entered Dealey Plaza at 12:10 p.m., when the shots rang out." Zach froze in his tracks along with 10 other boys, as Cronkite reported, "President Kennedy was declared dead at 1 p.m."

As he told the TV audience that JFK was dead, Cronkite lifted the heavy black framed glasses from his head and wiped tears from his eyes with the back of his hand. All of the boys who stood to the right of the canteen were motionless and dumbfounded. The women behind the counter continued to cry. Suddenly, you could hear boys clapping and cheering the news from the left side of the canteen. At first, Zach assumed these cadets must not be paying attention. Perhaps they were busy horsing around. But as he walked toward the noise, he could distinctly hear the boys commenting, "Good. They finally got him. It's about time."

Zach kept trying to figure out and process the news. His head started to pound. He couldn't shake his headache. Soon, his anxiety turned to anger. He was angry at the stupidity. Why would anyone want the President of our country to be killed? The most important leader in the world had been killed. We had lost something that could never be recovered: our innocence.

A week passed before he fully understood why some of his fellow cadets hated JFK. He was advocating for civil rights. This was the South in the mid-1960s and blacks were not equal or welcomed. Zach knew these cadets who cheered for JFK's death weren't born with hate, they learned it at home.

Murray Goldman was a plumber, not a political person. He did not teach his children racial hatred, because he didn't accept it. He'd tell his children stories to make his points, "As a boxer, it didn't matter the color of your skin…just the size of your heart." He talked about the Golden Gloves and his friendship with Reggie Peterson. The boys could see his smile, when he told the stories about fighting Reggie. In those moments, the boys learned from their dad. He taught his sons to look for the good in people and recognize there was beauty in all religions and cultures. The Goldman boys didn't need convincing. Life itself is often the best teacher. The boys could never forget Effie Johnson living with them and helping take care of them, following the car accident. The boys hugged and kissed her, because she loved them. To the boys Effie wasn't black. Love has no color.

For months following the assassination of John F. Kennedy, a cloud of grief and anxiety hung over the country—and most of the cadets at Riverside Military Academy.

Like so many, Zach was shaken by this event. This death awakened in him an awareness about race in America. He was certain the boys who stood in the canteen clapping and laughing would never change. He didn't believe he was anymore accepted by these students, because he was Jewish. He had always defended himself, if threatened. But it wasn't until this moment that he began to realize there were values worth fighting for. Silence would never be an option any longer.

The Christmas break defused tensions, as cadets returned home to see their families. Zach would board the train back to New Jersey with several boys. One of the boys, Gil, a sophomore, had his own small private room, where he could sleep. Gil invited Zach and Jeff, a red-haired boy from Teaneck, New Jersey to hang out in his room.

Zach and Jeff had met at school and realized they lived one town away. They both had seats in the fourth car of the train. Gil came from New York and his family obviously had money. Gil ordered snacks for the boys to eat while they traveled north. They all fell asleep, as the train chugged along into the night. Jeff woke first, when he heard muffled noise in the room. He quickly elbowed Zach awake. Gil was sitting across them masturbating. His eyes were closed and his head looked up toward the ceiling. Jeff and Zach were 8th graders. They had no idea what Gil was doing. He had the largest dick they had ever seen. Gil was moaning for a minute or more, and then he came all over his uniform. It was time to go. Jeff and Zach quietly got up and exited the room. Neither Jeff or Zach had the courage to ask questions or discuss the incident. They returned to their seats closer to the front of the train.

As the train reached Washington D.C., a number of train cars were being disconnected to join a second train headed to Chicago. The boys were eating in the dining car, five cars back from their seats, when they realized their train car and their suitcases might be heading to Chicago. These 13-year old boys had never traveled. They scrambled as quickly as they could back to their suitcases. The conductor directed the cadets to exit the train. Panicked, the boys ran along the platform to the front of the train. Jumping back onto the train, the boys were determined to get their luggage. The train blew its horn, signaling they were getting ready to leave the station for Chicago. The boys got off just in time. After boarding the back part of the train that would continue to Newark, New Jersey, they sat down to catch their breath. This was a trip they would not soon forget.

Two weeks at home flew by quickly. Alan walked over to meet his brother in the train station, while their mom waited in the car. Zach was wearing his grey school uniform, with his clip-on tie, a dark blue peacoat and military hat. Alan never understood why his parents sent him away to a military school. The two didn't talk much, as they walked to the car. The gap between the brothers was filled with hard feelings. Alan felt guilty over his past behavior toward Zach. He wanted his brother to be home. His older brother offered, but Zach insisted on carrying his own bag.

He was happy to see his parents. He was surprised to learn that his mom had still not scheduled her hip surgery. He was certain the operation would be completed by Christmas time. Murray called Zach his little soldier. He was pleased to see how well he adjusted to being away. His dad missed him beyond words, but he wanted all his sons to grow up with a sense of independence.

Zach didn't share many stories with his parents when he got home. He didn't want to spend his vacation talking about Riverside. However, he did thank his mom for teaching him to steam press wool pants. She enjoyed knowing he figured out how to make some money. He also told his family about his experience in the canteen, when JFK was killed. The revelation that students actually cheered over JFK's death shocked the entire Goldman family.

Gary Goldman was so happy to see his older brother. He had a million questions to ask. Zach didn't mind telling some of these stories. He talked about marching on the football field. And he delighted in describing to his brother the roast beef and mashed potatoes he enjoyed every other Sunday in Gainesville. Gary loved mashed potatoes, except he preferred catsup to brown gravy. His brother had strange eating habits, often cutting up his hamburger, mashed potatoes and spaghetti and mixing it all together on the plate. It looked disgusting, but if Gary was happy…that's just the way it was.

The Goldman household seemed quieter while Zach was away. A certain vibrancy returned during his short break from school. His mom had found greater freedom now that she was driving again. She took the boys for pizza and to watch Alan play football. Zach and Gary went for walks in the woods near the apartment where they lived in Fair Lawn. He was always trying to find frogs, snakes or anything that moved. Gary followed along, content to hang out with his older brother.

After several days, he finally asked his mom if she had seen the doctor. She had been to two different surgeons, but each had a different opinion. The hip surgery would be very invasive and dangerous. Zach wondered if she was getting cold feet. She knew there were limits on her mobility without the surgery. He figured she preferred the status quo over the chance she might not survive the surgery. He resigned himself to support his mom, whatever her decision. He told her, if she needed him to stay at the military school another year for the recovery, he would do it.

Franny could always feel her son's love. All her sons were devoted to her, but Zach often showed a tender side. During his visit home, it occurred to her how difficult it must be for her son to be so far from the family. Only now, did she second guess her decision to send him off to military school.

Before heading back to school, Franny sat her son down and had words with him about sending her to the post office. It seems his only act of defiance and rebellion about military school came when cadets were told to write their parents every two weeks. Money was always tight for him. He resisted the notion that he should spend his resources on postage stamps. After all, he was the one sent away. He learned from another cadet how to handle the situation. He'd write his letter home. He'd address the envelope. And then, in the upper right-hand corner of the envelope Zach would draw a small image of a man. Real stamps had a photo of Abraham Lincoln. He did his best to draw a likeness of Lincoln and underneath he'd write, "C.O.D". He was told that the letters stood for "cash on delivery." What the hell, he thought to himself. If this doesn't work, the letter will never reach home…and his cadet Officers at school would never know. If the trick did work, his parents could pay for the stamps when the letter arrived.

Zach felt guilty. He had no idea that each time a letter arrived, "C.O.D.", his mom would be required to drive to the post office, pay for the stamp and pick up the letter. He couldn't help himself. A mischievous smile crossed his face. "Don't you smile, Zach Goldman," she scolded. "Your mother doesn't need to drive across town to pick up a letter. I will give you stamps to take back to school. Use them!" She could tell he got the message, but she wasn't pleased he kept shaking his head and smiling.

He was packing to go back to military school two weeks later, when an overwhelming feeling of loneliness gripped him. The Goldman boys had endured the trauma of the family car accident. Zach was affable and seemed as if he adjusted faster to the family challenges than his brothers, but beneath the surface he still carried scars. He would experience these feelings of melancholy for many years. If someone didn't know his history, they'd never know what to look for. He was good at shaking off and hiding the baggage he carried around. He could always focus on the here and now, when needed. Yet, at the strangest times, the anxiety could overtake him. At times, he could be surrounded by his friends at school or in the gym and suddenly grow quiet and withdrawn. In private moments, he sometimes cried to release these tensions. He always held fast until the loneliness subsided, but he was careful not to scratch the surface.

Cadets flew to Hollywood, Florida, after the Christmas holidays, where Riverside had a winter campus. They were happy to arrive in Florida and the warm weather. The cadets knew all too well that in Georgia the school didn't have heat. Zach thought it was ironic to be back in Florida, only a few miles away from where the Goldman family lived. He had to figure out new ways of earning money, since he could no longer steam press wool pants. Yet while he lost his source of income ironing pants, he gained more freedom to use the school's outdoor gym. He learned to compensate by stealing away food from the cafeteria. Three days a week he had free time after classes to go workout on the gymnastics equipment. The York brothers taught him to fill a bottle containing a concoction of baby oil, iodine and Wildroot hair cream. They convinced Zach this would yield a deep tan, exercising in the sun. He looked up to the York brothers and so he was willing to try their prescription.

Cadets periodically took a bus to the beach in Hollywood or to downtown stores. The campus sat in the middle of three very large traffic circles. Sometimes, kids from town would ride the traffic circle late at night, cursing, throwing bottles and beeping horns. While the noise caused concern among cadets, no confrontations ever occurred.

In spring, Riverside held a large gymnastic show on a Sunday in March. This exhibition substituted for the weekly cadet parade. Gym equipment was moved to the parade area and almost 500 people came from town to see the performance. Zach had grown taller during his time at military school, but he still seemed small next to the nearly 15 older cadets who followed his instructions for the floor exercise demonstration. As they practiced for several months, he walked out to the field leading his squad of boys. He walked onto the mat and stood on his head, as the cadets completed dive rolls through his legs. He was relieved none of the boys messed up. The crowd applauded. He then led the squad through cartwheels and 2 cadets took turns with him to sprint down the long row of mats and complete handsprings, round-offs and back handsprings. The attention then moved to the York brothers on the parallel bars and finally, to Tico on the high bar. Spotters were stationed at each event to ensure none of the cadets were injured. Several days later, the local newspaper published a photo and short story about the show. Zach was able to send a copy home to his family.

The memories of Riverside would stay with Zach for the rest of his life. He was reminded of the influence of military school when he responded to strangers. Even as an adult, he found himself always saying, "Yes, sir. No, ma'am." And the sound of a marching band always changed his cadence. He grew comfortable in a military-like environment, with its sense of discipline and rules. The school made him feel more independent. He liked being on his own, even if sometimes he missed his family. A part of him felt it would be easy to become a soldier and have a career in the military. Fortunately, this feeling didn't stay with him, once he returned home.

As the school year came to an end, the cadets were all given year books to commemorate their time at Riverside. Cadets exchanged books and signed. Zach didn't think it was likely he'd see any of these boys again, but they all wrote wishing each other "good luck". He never sat and read all of the remarks until many years later. Almost everyone wrote compliments to the "good kid", "great gymnast", but some included comments that surprised him. "Zach, great knowing you. You're a good guy, (for a Jew)." Another wrote, "You know, Zach, you're the first Jew I've ever met." "Are all Jews like you? Raise hell this summer." For almost the entire year, he was certain he might be the only Jewish student at this Southern military school, but there it was in black n' white from a history classmate in C Company, "To a great kid. Good knowing you. Mat Weinstein (Jew)."

The road back to civilian life would take time. Alan wanted his brother to fit in, as he entered 9th grade at the junior high school. He insisted on taking him shopping for new clothes, with his mom's blessing and cash. Alan had perfected the "collegiate look." He bought his brother gray and blue wool slacks, with cuffs on the pants. His shirts were white, blue and several colorful Madras shirts. The outfits were complemented by penny loafers and matching belts, both in black and cordovan color. His brother wasn't known for acts of kindness, but this clothes shopping adventure would shape Zach's clothing style through to adult life.

In many ways, he admired his older brother. But the gulf between them would remain. They had a different view on life—and on their father. There were fewer outbursts in the Goldman home. Alan refrained from the regular verbal confrontations he had with his parents, while his brother was away at military school. Alan saw what he saw. His father was fooling around with his blonde secretary, even as his mother struggled at home following the car accident. Zach never accepted his brother's view of what happened or his negative opinions of their father. He didn't believe any of the Goldman children had a right to judge their parents. He'd tell Alan, "No one really understands what goes on between two people. How do you know what you saw was really what happened?"

If there were differences in the way Alan and Zach behaved toward each other, it was influenced by the physical changes everyone noticed in Zach. He had grown several inches in height and his frame had filled out from all the gymnastics exercise. His shoulders were broader. His forearms and biceps bulged from his work on the parallel bars. Alan still remained taller, but he couldn't ignore his younger brother's strength. It seemed it was only a matter of time that words would be exchanged and the conflict over their dad would resume.

Franny was resting in the den on Saturday, when Zach came in to talk with her. As usual, Murray Goldman was working. Alan had joined the conversation. It didn't take long for the subject matter to change. Alan's words got heated. His mom scolded him for the foul language he used. He didn't start out planning to go on a tirade about his father, but his mom said something and he couldn't let it go. He had never actually said anything to his mom about Dottie Gleeson. The source of Alan's anger toward his father was never clear to her.

But on this day, Alan spoke plainly and in great detail about his father's sins, in his eyes. "Mom, don't blame me. My father was fucking his secretary, while you suffered in that hospital bed."

He could not believe his ears. How could he dare speak to his mother this way? The hurt was tearing him apart. He couldn't hold back any longer. Franny slowly smiled and told her son to calm down. Before this outburst, she didn't understand what he had experienced. However, she knew he was mistaken. In Alan's eyes, his father had shown the ultimate disloyalty. At this point, he was jumping up and down yelling in disbelief, "don't you get it mom? My father didn't love you. He was having an affair with that bitch."

Zach stepped between where Alan stood and his mom. He tried to get his brother to calm down. After all, why was he yelling at his mom? It was in Alan's nature to fight when he was challenged. He pushed Zach. He then grabbed him from behind. He wrapped his arm around Zach's neck and he was choking him. He was not afraid. Franny got excited and started yelling at him to stop. She remembered how these fights always ended up with her son being seriously hurt. Zach squared off his feet and leaned back into Alan. He quickly grabbed his brother's right elbow. He turned swiftly to his left and flipped Alan over his body. His older brother landed hard on the floor.

He landed two blows to Alan's back. His brother hunched down hoping to avoid more pain. Just as suddenly, Zach stopped hitting him. The confrontation ended as quickly as it had begun. He had taken him by surprise, fighting back. Alan realized, at that moment, the days of taking his anger out on his brother were over. Zach was no longer intimidated by his brother's size or how loudly he spoke. A message had been given. His brother was fully prepared to fight, if necessary. He would no longer be a victim to Alan's anger. Franny sat speechless, as Alan scrambled to his feet and ran out of the den. Zach could see she was upset. He apologized that the two brothers had fought. He left the den and walked out of the house to cool off. Almost an hour went by before Alan returned. He, too, came in to apologize to his mom. She counted herself lucky to have sons who worried about her all the time. He continued to grumble about his dad, "It wasn't right, mom. I saw it. I was standing outside his office. I saw her sitting on his lap. I'm old enough to know what men do with women. I've kept this inside of me for so long. I never wanted to tell you. I didn't want to hurt you. You've suffered so much already. How much can a person endure?"

And with that, Alan's eyes welled up and he began to cry. In a moment of anger, he had unburdened his heart. How could he have been so reckless, as to cause his mother more pain? He ran to Franny's side. He got down on his knees and hugged her, as he lost control of his emotions. His voice cracked. He begged his mom to forgive him for telling her his long-held secret. He began to cough, as he struggled to swallow the saliva caught in his throat.

His mom sat patiently and let Alan cry himself out. She held him in her arms. She rubbed her hands across his forehead and kissed him. "It's ok, it's ok." she would tell him. After 15 minutes, he finally started to calm down. "Alan, please sit up. I think it's time for us to talk." Alan sat next to Franny. He took deep breaths to regain his composure. Rubbing tears from his eyes, his body trembled from the exhaustion.

She began, "Alan, I know you saw something, but not everything is always as it seems in life. Your father has been the love of my life. And I'm his. Your father was very sophisticated as a young man. He had the looks of a movie star and the physical presence to get any woman he wanted. I don't doubt that he had many opportunities in those years. I was not so worldly. I really only dated two men in my life. The one your father chased away--and your dad.

Our bond cannot be broken. We came from the same place. We grew up during a very difficult time. We shared so many sacrifices, trying to survive or help our families survive. Our lives together was born from these early years. It was tested by war. It's not just a love affair, we have a friendship and partnership that transcends time. The accident has broken both our bodies—and, at times, our spirit. But the test of love," she explained, "is really when all seems lost. I pray you and your brothers never have to struggle as we have."

Franny quietly told her son stories he might never have heard about his parent's love for each other. She explained how tortured her life had been before he was born, with three miscarriages. "Alan, when I had the first miscarriage, I was bleeding uncontrollably. It was raining that night. Your dad worried I might die. He carried me in his arms for six or seven blocks until he could flag down a cab and get me to the hospital. He sat in the waiting room for hours, hoping the doctors could save me. Once he knew I was ok, his only thought was to convince me the loss of this child would not stop us from having a family.

I was devastated. I cried nearly nine months before you were born, because I feared having three miscarriages. Your dad has always been there for me. We waited almost a decade before and after the war to have a child. He didn't give up on us and he never let me lose hope. Your father loves you more than he will ever be able to express.

In the same way, when he had the brain tumor, I was determined to help him fight against all odds. You were all so young. I don't know what you recall, but I lifted that man, rolled him on the floor and loved him back to health.

Now, you were not with us at the hospital after the accident. You did not see how your father sat in a wheelchair next to my bed for weeks. Your dad would not leave my side and fought the nurses when they tried to remove him. My eyes may have been swollen shut, but I could still see his hazy face and I could hear him crying. When in your life have you ever seen your father cry? He's made differently than you or me. He didn't cry when the doctors told him to settle his affairs before brain surgery. Your father doesn't fear death. But when it comes to me, I could hear your father sitting near my bed asking God to take him instead. He offered his own life, if God would spare my suffering. Alan, love is the hard stuff. You will learn as you get older, love is about weathering the things we lose overtime and still valuing what you have left."

"But mom," Alan said, "I saw that woman sitting on dad. I know he was having sex with her."

Franny smiled, "Alan, whenever you think you know the answers in life, is when you should question yourself the most.

I don't know if Dottie was consoling your dad. He was so emotional during our time at the hospital and when I got home. But you need to understand and this may shock you. After your dad's brain tumor operation, he couldn't have sex. I want you to think about a man as physical as your dad. He lost his ability to have sex at 40 years old. I didn't love him less. And since the accident, your father has only loved me more.

Have you ever stopped to think that your father gave up everything, his livelihood, his business…..everything he had built for us, when he moved our family to Florida? Your dad didn't hesitate to think about the consequences. He only cared that the person he loved would get a second chance at life, after the car accident. I'm walking today, because your father wanted me to overcome the damage to my body. His will was stronger than mine."

Alan sat silently as Franny spoke. He was shocked at how openly his mom talked to him. There are things children never learn about their parents. Now that he knew, the feelings of guilt started to overtake him. How could he have hated a father, who sacrificed so much for his family. He had behaved like a child. His view of the world was black and white. He was so quick to judge that it blinded him to the truth. He had never confronted his father, but he felt wronged for such a long period of time. His brother was right about never knowing what goes on between a man and a woman. Alan should have talked about his fears sooner. He wondered if he could ever forgive himself for hating his dad.

"I am sorry you have struggled with these feelings for so long. If I had the slightest idea, I would have had this conversation sooner. I love that you care about me as much as you do. But, you never have to doubt your father. We are two Depression era kids, cut from the same cloth. He loves me and I love him. Remember this about life: Sex may allow you to express yourself, but it is not the definition of love. The bonds forged between two people transcend the physical. We shared a dream—and that dream is you and your brothers.

Your father's example should guide you. He's the best role model you'll ever find. Try to be happy now. Try to be forgiving with your parents. We are here. We are together. And we are alive, which is the best blessing you could ask for."

Franny could see Alan was confused. It would take time for him to fully understand. She had given him the insight and knowledge. What would he do now? This brave and bright child of hers had suffered, thinking he was defending her honor. She pulled him close and hugged him. She was so proud of him. How could he ever understand the depth of her feelings; how long she had waited to have him or the meaning he gave to her life. "Alan, I'm counting on you to make peace with your brothers. You have to be the one who keeps the family together."

The gulf between Zach and Alan would not close. There was so much history there. But Alan did his best to avoid further conflict with his brother. He would not tell Zach what he and his mom discussed. It was not his place. He decided the best way to make up for this angry period in his life was to honor his mother's wishes. He would strive to "keep the family together."

Zach had made his statement about being bullied. Tossing his older brother to the floor drew a new line in the sand, not to be crossed. He refused to be a victim. He grew tired of his brother's rants about his dad. Instinctively, he knew better. He would continue to be guarded dealing with his older brother. But he also had his own issues to resolve.

The rationale for him going to military school was the surgery and rehab his mom had to complete. A year later, Zach was home and mom had not had the surgery. What was that about? Why was he sent away? He could not understand his mother's motives. He realized she feared another operation. Anyone who went through her experience might do the same. She stalled until there was no more room for excuses. He told himself his time away gave him a break from the daily support his mom needed. He never spoke of the beatings he endured at military school from older students who didn't like Jews. He didn't let on to his parents or siblings the periods of loneliness students would experience being so far from their families.

Zach tried to wrap himself in the good memories of practicing gymnastics outdoors in Florida. He'd share with his brothers what it was like to march in a parade. The music still rang in his ears. He happily embraced that he had grown larger and stronger than before he left home. And he didn't complain, when Franny finally went for hip replacement surgery and once again required his help at home. It wasn't that Zach was blind to decisions impacting his life. In cases, he had a rebellious side and questioned the common wisdom. Yet he was growing up. It was always in him to look for a way to find balance and harmony. There would be no answers for why he went to military school. The year would fade in everyone's memory, except for Zach Goldman.

CHAPTER 52

Gary Goldman

———

It's likely that Gary Goldman never had a fair opportunity in life. He would tell you that, if you asked. Perhaps that's true for many who are born last. Last to arrive, always left out of family discussions and often not consulted on decisions impacting his life, "He's too young to understand."

He was only three years old when his father had his brain tumor surgery. He was only eight years old when his folks were in the car accident. Gary would experience all the tumult and uncertainty, but never at an age where he had the reasoning skills or insight to cope with the world around him.

Gary would argue as he got older that he suffered more than his brothers. After the accident, each of the brothers felt isolated and alone, with no adult in their lives to guide them for two months. Could these events have been toughest on the last of the litter?

"A sickly child" is how Franny fondly described him. She doted on him more than his brothers, but she had cause. At 18 months, he had pneumonia and high fevers which nearly cost him his life. At three, he required a hernia repair surgery. While Gary wanted to join the "wild ones," as Alan and Zach were called, he more often sat quietly on the couch. He watched from the sidelines, but wanted in the worst way to be part of the action.

Ironically, Gary never saw himself that way. Children never do. He wasn't ready to accept limits, whether physical or mental. Children want to be part of whatever is going on around them. He looked up to Zach, because he always looked to include him. Whether Zach was hunting for frogs, running through the house or playing music on the record player, he had patience to teach his kid brother whatever he wanted to learn. Alan followed his mom's instructions to protect Gary. He adored his little brother, but he set limits on what he was allowed to do. He couldn't bear the responsibility if Gary got injured. Alan didn't realize his desire to love and protect his younger brother would, in time, might be seen as holding him back in life.

Gary resisted constraints. He withdrew into his own world to find his answers. He looked to build things in his room, in the family garage or at the plumbing shop when he went with his dad. No one would see how amazingly talented he was when he worked with tools. His dad was too busy to focus on him. His brothers lacked his aptitude so they didn't really care.

Everyone knew Gary was around, but his interests and talents were taken for granted. The expression was often used, "seen but not heard from." However, by his early teens, he began to change that perception. He became invaluable to his mom, because he could fix anything in the house. In some ways, he was more like his father than his brothers. He had Murray's ability to see mechanical relationships, without measuring or studying directions. But he did not have his father's physical strength. He was not an athlete like his brothers. This frustrated Gary, as he struggled for recognition.

During the spring of 1965, Franny would finally have hip replacement surgery. The first experiments in using metal parts to replace broken hips were conducted in 1940, but medical mainstreaming of the procedure didn't begin until 1960. The operation was invasive, and patients faced threats from lengthy exposure to anesthesia and subsequent infections.

The doctors could not assure her she'd survive. The best odds were 50-50 on coming through the surgery and overcoming any subsequent infections. The operation required doctors to cut her open, from her hip to half way down her left leg. They then sawed off the top part of her leg bone, drill a hole into the bone, forced a metal shaft into the leg and then anchored a metal cup to her hip bone with glue. And after all of that, the new artificial hip lasted only 10-12 years.

Franny trusted Dr. Richard Katzenstein. He was an experienced orthopedic surgeon, who had treated her following the car accident. He was among the leading group of doctors who were performing and perfecting the techniques for hip replacements. However, she thought the doctor looked more like a butcher than a highly trained surgeon. He was tall, on the heavy side and had large arms and very strong hands. Dr. Katzenstein would often be seen wearing surgical scrubs, as he met with patients. This allowed him to quickly move between his office and the hospital. He was a very hairy man. The scrubs showed more skin and chest hair than any patient cared to see.

Following surgery, Franny stayed in the hospital for nearly three weeks. The Goldman boys would not leave her side. Each of the boys took turns sleeping on a chair in her room or on a couch in the Community room. Murray would come every night after work. He'd pick up and drop off the boys during his visits. She insisted, after the surgery was over, that Murray keep busy. She was sore and had pain following the operation, but she thought it would be worse. Her only frame of reference was the agonizing pain she had after the car accident. They drugged her so much, it was like living in a haze. This time around, the doctors and nurses were in her room by the third day, insisting she stand up on her legs. Alan and Zach Goldman stood off to the side, while two strong orderlies held their mom, under her arms.

Franny screamed twice, as she put weight on her foot. The doctor ordered the exercise be completed twice more that day. The doctors predicted she still needed the elbow crutches to walk. Her left leg bone had been shortened by the surgery, by one or two inches. Special shoes were ordered to increase the height of the sole and left heel. The goal was not to eliminate the crutches. Each visit by the orderlies was greeted with anxiety, but she gained more stability when on her feet. Dr. Katzenstein promised her the surgery would improve her quality of life. She would walk with greater certainty, for longer distances and with less pain.

The world had changed in the few short years between the car accident and the hip surgery. Patients were no longer allowed to lay in bed. Dr. Katzenstein believed you should be on your feet almost immediately to strengthen muscles connecting the leg and hip, and to avoid the potential for joint dislocation. The doctor explained to Murray that if a patient stayed in bed for any length of time, the risk of the implant slipping out of the hip socket increased 25-30 percent. Patients might have residual pain from the surgical incision, but getting Franny walking was a higher priority. By the end of the first week, the Goldman boys would take turns helping Franny with her walker down the hospital corridor. Their fears of maybe losing their mom during surgery were gone now. They shared moments of joy and pride, as they helped her exercise. Mom was back!

After two weeks, Franny came home. The boys could not get over how different mom's recovery was compared to the car accident. There would be no body cast. No need to bring mom a bed pan to urinate. She was able to sleep in her own bed, though she had to avoid laying on her side. The boys continued taking turns sleeping on the floor next to her bed, for the first 10 days, to be there if she needed them. They also took turns following her around the house. Even though she followed the doctor's orders to walk slowly with the walker or her elbow crutches, the boys wanted to ensure she did not slip or fall. Dr. Katzenstein met with the family and cautioned them not to let her bend over, to avoid a hip dislocation. No lifting. Be careful on wet floors, going in and out of the shower. No reaching. "Keep to these rules," the doctor told Murray and the boys, and "Franny will grow stronger and more self-reliant."

Months went by and Franny Goldman began to feel like the woman she was before the car accident. She would never walk again without the elbow crutches, but she now had more stamina. She couldn't sit still. She ventured out on her own more often and tackled a variety of social and family activities that had previously been ignored. When she started cooking dinner by herself, the boys felt a normalcy they had not experienced in years.

Gary was the last Goldman boy to have a Bar Mitzvah, in the fall of 1965. Alan vocally protested the idea of having a party, since he felt the boys had been abandoned by the Sugar and Goldman families following the car accident. He hated his aunts and uncles for failing to show any of the "values of family" the Goldman boys had been taught by their mom. Both Zach and Gary chimed in agreeing with Alan. Nothing united the Goldman clan faster than their disdain for their extended family. Franny realized she could not change their feelings, but she wanted Gary to have his moment.

Murray came home that evening with a surprise of his own. The family would soon be able to move back to Paramus earlier than planned. It seemed the renters decided to relocate sooner than originally scheduled. This move would give the Goldman family time to clean and have painters give the walls a clean coat. Franny was thrilled with the idea of the Bar Mitzvah party being held in the finished basement of their large ranch home. The family no longer had the financial resources to rent a venue like they did for Alan. However, Franny was still committed to celebrating. She would hire caterers to bring food, tables, and chairs. She did not want her husband to do more than show up for the event. Alan would help her fill out all the invitations. He also kept track of the paperwork and checklists.

Returning to Paramus resolved the issue of whether Gary could have his Bar Mitzvah at the family Synagogue. As Murray outlined his plans, Alan protested leaving Fair Lawn. He had been chosen for the Junior Varsity football team at the high school. The Bergen County high school football rules would disqualify him playing for two years, if he changed schools. Driving him to Fair Lawn everyday was out of the question. Alan was always quick on his feet. He proposed living with a friend. He had no idea if he could get someone to volunteer, but it was the best he could think of at the time. After a lengthy discussion, Murray and Franny agreed to let him live with Joel Fishbine's family. This was assuming Joel's parents agreed.

Franny set about having Gary take lessons with the Rabbi and she started planning his party. Ironically, this was the one time that Gary didn't mind getting less than his brothers. He had virtually no Hebrew school training. And he feared having an audience in synagogue to see that he couldn't read Hebrew.

The summer months of 1965 became a tug of war between Gary and his mom. While he hungered for recognition from the family, he was not keen to get on the Bema in the Synagogue and read to the congregation. He only softened his resistance, when the Rabbi suggested he have his Bar Mitzvah on a Monday morning. This was highly irregular, since the Saturday service at the Synagogue was so well attended. "Gary," the Rabbi pointed out, "I'll be happy if we get 10 men to have a minion for the Bar Mitzvah." It didn't take him long to figure out that his dad, his brothers and the Rabbi would likely represent half the number of people attending Monday service. If Murray's brother, Uncle Sammy, showed up from Brooklyn, with his cousin Morty (Martin), he'd only have to worry about four strangers in the synagogue.

The Rabbi slowly put Gary's mind at ease. It also helped that his Torah reading was about one to two sentences long and his Haftorah was one paragraph. He was given an English phonetic translation of the Haftorah to read. Like his brothers, he would rise to the challenge, if he felt certain he could reach the goal posts.

The summer raced by. Franny still insisted her teenage boys get new clothes for Gary's Bar Mitzvah and the upcoming Jewish holidays. She didn't care if there were 10 people in the Synagogue or 150 attending services. By this point in their lives, the boys no longer protested "clothes shopping." In fact, Alan had become somewhat of a clothes hound, always wanting to buy the latest and best-looking outfits. His tastes grew more expensive, as he got older. And whatever differences the brothers had, Zach clearly had been influenced by his older brother when it came to clothes.

The trip to the Garden State Shopping Mall in Paramus turned into an unexpected surprise for Franny. Her sons were excited to go shopping with mom. Murray's business was helping the family get by, but the glory days of a good income for the Goldmans was gone. Their mom tried her best to keep spending to a minimum. So, it was odd the tables had turned. The boys were pushing their mom to buy clothes for Synagogue and the upcoming school year, in sharp contrast to the early years when trying on and buying clothes was an ordeal. "Mom," Gary told her, "you created a monster—wait, three monsters. I remember we fought with you, every time you took us shopping. You insisted we dress and look proper. You didn't care about how much it cost. You wanted us to have standards and to value the importance of first impressions. Now, we still fight with you, but we're the ones asking you to buy us more clothes than we'll ever need. That's just so funny to us."

"Ok," she replied, "I get the humor. But you can start by putting back the shirts you and your brothers have picked out. We are staying within the budget: one suit, two shirts and one sweater each. You'll have to get a job, like Alan and Zach, if you want to buy more clothes." Franny wasn't angry. She replied to him with a wry smile on her face. Yes, she had created three monsters, but she lingered on that thought with great satisfaction.

At the Bar Mitzvah, Gary felt vindicated and relieved. He was certain he performed his reading of the Torah flawlessly, even if he was alone in this assessment. No one was going to critique him on this special day. When his dad came up to read an Aliyah, he reached out his long arm and held onto his son's shoulder. Gary's spirit would forever be lifted by the pride his father showed in him that day.

He emerged from the Synagogue feeling victorious. The performance bar was not set very high, but Rabbi Rackowitz knew the importance of this day. Not every child would master the skills to conduct the entire service on Saturday morning. However, his goal was to have each child walk away with a stronger connection to their faith. To stand on the Bema and read from the Torah, whether a full passage or one line, stood the test of generations and their relationship with God. Rabbi Rackowitz was a unique and special person, because he never lost sight of the goal. Gary, the least understood youngest sibling and the child with little Jewish education, nonetheless found a purpose and a bond with his heritage. His Bar Mitzvah would inspire his confidence and bind his faith.

The Bar Mitzvah party back at the house, went on for hours. At times like this, Franny and Murray let go of their heartfelt disappointments with their respective family members. They did their best to fill the basement, so Gary would feel special. There are so many times in life, when parents try so hard to do the right thing for their children. How different it might have been, if they simply asked him what he wanted. The boys finally went along with the party idea, believing this was a chance for all of them to show the Goldmans persevered and their mom had regained her footing. The boys could care less about the extended family. They would be polite to their uncles and aunts. They would be friendly and engaged with their cousins. But none of them could forgive relatives who came to eat the Bar Mitzvah food, yet were nowhere to be found when they were needed.

Zach and Gary would walk back and forth in the house; hanging in the kitchen to grab food before it was officially served and visiting tables in the basement to greet cousins. Their priority was doing whatever it took, so their mom felt the party was a success. And then it was over.

CHAPTER 53
Finding Jobs

His mom's comments about finding a job to help the family pay for stuff was not lost on Alan. The Goldmans' future was no longer financially secure. At 15, Alan made a point of finding a job in Fair Lawn when his brother left for military school. Near the apartments where the Goldmans lived was a small strip mall. The boys would go on errands—or just to hangout. Alan was a regular visitor at Petak's Deli, picking up food for the family. He'd bring home corn beef, pastrami, roast beef and sides of potatoe salad and cole slaw. Mom would also insist he pick up a piece of halavah, his dad's favorite treat. On Sundays, Murray no longer drove to Teaneck to pick up lox, herring and sable. Alan took over the task, walking up to Petaks.

He was well liked by the Glick Brothers, who owned the deli. They enjoyed his quick responses and his sarcastic humor. In time, Marty Glick gladly hired Alan to sweep and help clean up the store after school and on the weekends. Alan had a good work ethic and found ways to make himself be useful. Within a year, he was slowly moving up the ranks of jobs at the Deli. By 17, he worked as a server, handling customers on his own.

Marty looked after Alan and mentored him. He'd listen to family stories and encouraged him on playing football at the high school. Marty often chided Alan about his pre-occupation with girls. He had grown to 6 feet and his weight training filled out his upper body to 200 lbs. Next to the Glick brothers, it was hard not to notice Alan's blond hair and hazel blue eyes. Marty was short and balding. His brother, Lennie was taller but carried a huge donut around his waist. The Glick brothers all had dark hair and skin complexions. They considered themselves Ashkenazi Jews (from Eastern Europe), but most folks thought they were Sephardic (from Spain or Italy). Lennie's son, Steven, at 25 was the largest of the three men. Like his dad, Steven was nice looking and very friendly. He was just very overweight.

He told Alan he had his father's swagger. Alan liked that idea. His opinion of his dad had changed and matured. The stories his mom shared of the young Murray Goldman stayed with him. "He could have any women," she recalled. Alan understood, as he got older. His experiences taught him not to judge others. He had finally gained perspective. His quick wit and the sarcastic side of his personality caught the eye of women twice his age. Marty didn't mind the flirting. It was not uncommon for middle age women to ask for him, when they came in the Deli.

It was also normal for women to request food deliveries to their homes. Alan received an early education during these deliveries. He was mindful of Marty's coaching not to stay too long at someone's house or he might regret running into a husband. He always had an eye on the clock. Only once did he run late, leaving Rose Gottleib's kitchen by the backdoor as her husband's car pulled into the driveway. Rose always insisted Alan fool around with her, any place but in the bedroom. The living room couch near the front window, the floor in the entry way and her favorite included the washing machine, which was noisy and vibrated. He was convinced Mrs. Gottleib must have spent days thinking up new places to have sex. She taught him things he never knew about women. And when he left, his favorite delivery of the day always gave him a good tip.

His last year of high school, working at Petaks, was the most satisfying and educational period of his life. He could never quite figure out why these married women were so anxious to have sex. None of them were bashful, once he was alone with them. At times, their physical expectations of him could exceed his energy and skill, but he never gave up. He never talked about the customers to Marty or any of his friends, but he often wondered if he'd like to work at the Deli forever.

Zach Goldman followed his brother's example. He also went out to find a job at 15. His mom would have to sign special work permit papers. The Goldman family moved back to Paramus by this time. Zach would take any job and hope to increase his responsibilities over time. He was hired to be a busboy to clean tables at the Fireplace restaurant on Rte. 17. He would hitchhike nearly three miles to get to work, sometimes walking when he couldn't find a ride. He often jogged halfway, if he was late for work.

The Fireplace was a favorite for local businesses, families and high school students to get hamburgers, steak sandwiches and French fries. The food was cooked on an open grill, like you'd find at a cookout. You ordered in the front of the restaurant and then went to find seats in the large dining halls to the left and right of the entrance. The restaurant was largely run by kids, either college students who attended classes at odd hours or high school students who worked after school. The manager was maybe 30 years old. The place was a gold mine; overrun with business during lunch and dinner. The busboys couldn't clean the tables fast enough. It was that busy. Zach didn't mind the hustle cleaning tables. He liked that he could eat anything he wanted, when it was time to take a break from work.

He had continued to grow in height and weight. He still visited a nearby gym to work out on the gymnastic equipment and practice his floor exercises. By the time he reached sophomore year in high school, he decided to join the wrestling team. He had tried many sports in military school and in junior high school. The one major drawback was his need to wear glasses. His nearsightedness was discovered in third grade. Initially, the teacher thought he was a discipline problem because he would never answer questions she wrote on the blackboard. The teacher insisted he move to a desk at the front, where she discovered he couldn't see properly. He was only six feet away, but he couldn't make out the writing. She reported her discovery to his mom. Zach was soon wearing a thick pair of glasses. He also had answers, the teacher never expected him to provide.

He played half back on the Riverside football team, but was limited to running up the sidelines. He was very fast. But without glasses, he couldn't see the ball being passed in the air. He later tried basketball. He was very quick with his hands, stealing the ball from opponents. However, he lacked the relaxed nature and liquid movement to shoot a basket. Zach was solid muscle from the years of gymnastics. He threw a basketball as if he was shooting a gun. There was no finesse.

A wrestling career suited him well. He was quick and comfortable moving on a mat. At the Fireplace restaurant, he was able to eat two steak sandwiches, fries and milk shakes. He rarely put on weight because he was so active.

The Goldman work ethic was always evident. Like his brothers, Zach was ready and willing to do any job. The Fireplace would test him in new ways. He was asked to fill in for Peter, who didn't show up for work one day. Peter's task was to fill up the condiment stands inside the restaurant. Zach would open numerous commercial-sized cans of pickles and then fill the four pickle buckets on both sides of the Fireplace. However, he then had to fill up the onion bowls. He'd slice-up several large bags of raw onions. The restaurant didn't have slicing machines. He stood at a work station in the back with a carving knife. His eyes started to tear after cutting the fifth or sixth onion, but the quota for the lunch crowd would be 40-50 onions. Eventually, one of the college students suggested if he drank chocolate milk it would cut down the eye irritation and tears. It didn't work 100%, but it did calm the tears and Zach was grateful.

No one ever complained about their work at the Fireplace. If they did, they'd win the assignment of cleaning the bathrooms. The customer traffic was so frequent, no one wanted to grapple with the smell or the mess left behind. After working with his dad, Zach wasn't put off by the bathroom smells. But he lucked out from that assignment. He preferred his other jobs, because they gave him more time to see and interact with customers.

Unlike Alan, Zach Goldman never got the girl he wanted. That's not to say he didn't attract lots of girls, but the girls he liked seem to be looking elsewhere.

Perhaps he was too shy. He grew up next door to Angela Tommaso. Angela had been the love of his life since they were children. She was the middle child in a strict Italian Catholic family. The kids played together for years, both before and after the family car accident. He looked for her every day from the window of their home and ran out to be with her. Her smile brightened his world. Zach always felt Angela was the "real deal," with such a good heart and loving nature about her. He didn't care that Angela's dad didn't want her hanging out with the Jewish boy next door. The two of them could talk for hours. However, whether it was his shyness or his respect for Angela's dad, he never told her how he felt. As he reached his teen years, he dreamed of kissing Angela one day. Eventually, he did. It was a kiss he'd remember. He thought it was amazing that a song on the radio was written for him. He'd walk around singing to himself Frankie Valli's, "Can't Take My Eyes Off of You," still thinking of Angela. This music haunted him, even after they went their separate ways in college:

Oh, pretty baby
Don't bring me down I pray
Oh pretty baby
Now that I've found you stay
And let me love you, baby
Let me love you

You're just too good to be true
I can't take my eyes off you....

Zach's problem was that he never wanted to chase girls. It was not in his nature to throw out one-liners like Alan or be aggressive like Gary. He believed relationships should have a natural flow. He loved kissing girls... and being kissed. Yet he had an introspective side to him. Perhaps he thought too much about stuff. By high school, he was reading the Harrad Experiment, by Robert Rimmer, and The Art of Loving, by Erich Fromm. The 1970s were almost upon him. These books began to shape his views on love.

In Paramus High, he learned about "courtly love" from Shakespeare's Romeo and Juliet. True love, in his worldview, had to be unconditional. He rejected the idea that you should only care about someone if they reciprocate. He felt most of his guy friends wanted to own girls, like a piece of property. And he was confused by girls who wanted to be with guys who treated them badly.

He embraced the idea of unrequited love. If the girl didn't like him, he could accept this. He gave up the idea of having expectations when it came to dating girls. If they liked him, fine. He'd put on record albums and danced with the girl. If she wanted to kiss him, he'd kiss her with an abundance of passion. He felt less pressure this way, when he met a girl. Unlike his older brother, he wasn't in such a hurry to have sex. He still had to figure this out. He took seriously the books he read. He wanted to be certain his first sexual encounter wasn't a one-way street to happiness. He didn't know, what he didn't know.

Once Zach got his driver's license, at 17, he took a new job working at a gas station on Rte. 17 a few miles from the Goldman home. The job paid much more than he was getting at the Fireplace. He didn't mind pumping gas, except on Saturday night when drivers would stop after drinking at the local bars. One night, a big yellow Cadillac Eldorado pulled in near 10 pm. This was the biggest and brightest colored car he had ever seen. The gas station was on the New York bound side of the highway. The driver and passenger were loudly arguing with each other. The radio music was blasting away.

"Fill it up," the driver yelled out the window. Zach followed his normal routine, putting the gas hose into the car and setting the catch on the trigger so he could service a second car. As he walked toward the second car, he heard a loud clicking sound. The hose had jumped out of the Cadillac's tank. The hose was twisting wildly like a snake on the ground, with gas spewing out. Zach ran to grab the hose, as it moved away from him. Finally, he stepped on the hose and turned off the trigger. A sense of panic overwhelmed him as he considered how much gas was wasted on the ground. It may have been only a dollar of gas, but he feared the two grown men in the Cadillac would be furious. He ran to the driver's window. "I'm so sorry, I'm sorry," he kept repeating. There was a moment of silence, as the driver stepped out of the vehicle. He looked at the side of the car. No gas had spilled on the car. "Hey, look kid, don't sweat it. No harm done. Just some wasted gas." He'll never know why, but the two men weren't angry. They even gave him a $2 tip after he finished filling the car.

A week later, a middle-aged man pulled into the gas station in a beat up white 1959 Plymouth Fury. The back end of the car had a two-tone wing-like design, part white and part tan. It was obvious to him the man didn't drive into the station to get gas. He pulled the car over and parked on the side. The car was coughing and making strange noises. Zach could see smoke was coming from the radiator. The wheels were near bald. This car was on its last legs. The driver got out cursing up a storm. "I'm done. This f_cking car is a piece of shit."

Zach went over to see if he could help the man. "Hey, kid. I'm done with this car. I'm leaving it here. I refuse to have it breakdown on me again while I'm on the highway. Can I use your phone inside? I need to get a ride home? You want the car? I'll gladly give you this one."

At first he was leery of the stranger. Why would anyone just throw away a car? This seemed odd. When the man exited the gas station office, Zach ran inside. A lightning bolt hit him. He called home. "Gary, you're always fixing stuff. How would you like your very own car? A guy just drove a broken-down car into the station. He offered it to me, at no cost. I know you can't drive yet. If you're up for the challenge, I can tow the car to the house?"

The phone was silent at the other end. Then came a sudden burst of excitement, as Gary started thanking his older brother.

"Look, I need to figure out how I get this up Linwood Avenue and then down the hill on Koman Drive to the house. I gotta go."

The owner was sitting out front smoking a cigarette waiting for his ride home. Zach asked if he was serious about giving him the car. "You're looking at a lot of work to fix that car," the guy told him, "but let me get the papers in the glove compartment. I have no further use for this piece of crap."

Zach didn't realize that he had to have an ownership document signed over to him. Once he had the papers, he asked his boss if he could borrow some chains to tow the car home. He had no real idea how to tow a car, but the manager gave him some quick instructions and he was off. Dragging the car up the hill on Linwood Avenue was no big deal. He took his time, allowing most traffic to pass him. However, as he pulled off Linwood onto Koman Drive, he realized there was a problem. How was he going to brake the car he was towing as he went down the hill? He got out to try and adjust the chains as tight as he could to connect the two cars. It would take a half hour to creep down the hill. He allowed the old Plymouth to rub against the bumper of the Dodge Dart his father let him drive. He had to avoid any lasting damage to his car or dad would skin him alive. If he didn't keep his foot on the brakes as he went down the hill, the Plymouth would plow into him.

As he reached his family home, about six houses from the corner, Zach started beeping his horn and Gary came running out. No one had ever seen Gary so gleeful. He started jumping up and down. This was one of his happiest moments. His kid brother meant the world to him. He was never bothered hanging around with Gary. He wanted to teach, coach and encourage him, because "that's what brothers are supposed to do," Zach would tell his father. It didn't matter to him that Gary, at times, could be stubborn and wouldn't listen. "No one is perfect," he'd think to himself, "but my brother is a special kid and he has such potential."

Zach pulled the old car partly onto the driveway. Gary helped him unhook the chains and then the two brothers pushed the car all the way to the left. Zach wasn't worried his parents would object, as long as the broken-down car didn't block them. Mom's car was in the garage. Dad always left his van in the driveway. Gary hugged his older brother. He had already called his best friend, Robert 'Bob' Shiller. Bob shared his friend's interest in fixing things and he had experience working on cars with his older brother Gerry (Gerhard). Gary and Bob were not old enough to drive, but they agreed to repair the car over the next 18 months before they got their license. Gary did work after school. Fixing this broken-down car had given him a new mission in his life. He relished the challenge.

The boys spent hours each day working in the driveway. Gary would save money from odd jobs he completed for his parents and for neighbors, to help cover the costs of auto parts. Instead of gifts, his parents gave him cash. They had their doubts about whether the car could ever be brought back from the brink of the scrap yard. Yet they admired their son's drive and stubborn determination. After school and weekends were mostly filled with the clanging of metal and, sometimes, arguments that broke out between Bob and Gary. They worked well into the fall, until the cold temperatures forced them to take a break. It was in late October, when the boys had an accident. Gary closed the hood of the car and Bob lost the tip of his left index finger. There was blood everywhere. Zach drove the boys to Bergen Pines Hospital, where doctors stopped the bleeding and stitched the finger. Bob's mom met them at the hospital. The boys explained how the accident happened and that no one was really to blame. Neither one of them wanted to quit the project.

By the time Gary reached 17, the Plymouth Fury had new tires (a gift from his dad) and the engine had been overhauled. On occasion, Murray would check in on the boys and tell them stories of his experiences re-building Model-T Ford cars in the 1930s. The expression "like father, like son" was all Gary had to hear to stay motivated. The day he and Bob finally took the car out for a drive in 1969 was a proud moment. All their school friends recognized the car as they drove the white 1959 Plymouth with wings along East Ridgewood Avenue, to Bob's home, and then on Farview Avenue five miles to Paramus High School (PHS). They called everyone they knew. The friends waited for them to pass by and blow the horn. Driving in circles around the PHS parking lot, as sports teams practiced, was like a one car antique show.

Gary didn't follow his brothers into sports. His path in life would always be different. He had grown a bit taller than Alan and Zach. Working with his hands had also given him strength, like his father. He learned to fix almost anything, build almost anything and never be deterred by the labor involved. He had earned his brothers' respect. They didn't share his aptitude, but they began to realize their brother did have gifts they envied.

The Plymouth Fury was a point of liberation for Gary. Aside from the envy of family and friends, the car became his magnet for girls. Alan wasted no time in coming up with a snide comment. He nicknamed Gary, "hound dog." The characterization was not entirely true. Yes, his brothers often found him parked on the driveway after school, in the back seat with a girl—any girl. Zach was certain his brother did not have sex with girls. There was no parental supervision of the boys, so Gary was not held back by anything other than his own lack of knowledge and a willing partner. Alan likely projected his own prideful "hound dog" self-image, when he busted Gary's chops.

However, the baby in the family grew up quickly, as he began to sneak girls into the family basement. In his junior year of high school, he wanted more privacy and freedom. He convinced his parents that moving downstairs into the finished basement would allow him to listen to music or TV without bothering his parents. The Goldmans never suspected Gary had a steady harem of girls visiting him through the back door of the house. The basement ran almost the length of the large ranch house. Gary set up two twin beds, couches, a TV console with space for records and a tape player.

He rewired all the electronics, so they connected to a single switch box near his bed. He could turn off the security alarm when girls knocked on the back door at night. Zach started to agree with his older brother's assessment of Gary, after he came home from college for a visit. He was astounded seeing his brother's basement hideaway. He couldn't guess how many young women Gary had hosted, but he never seem to lack company.

Zach was a touch more romantic than his two brothers while dating girls in high school. He was curious as hell about sex, but he wasn't rushing anyone, including himself.

Yes, there was the incident in Fair Lawn at one of Alan's beer parties. Zach was just back from military school and had to be pulled off of Jane Nixon. She was exceptionally beautiful with strawberry blonde hair and bluer than blue eyes. At 14, Zach lost all inhibitions that night. Alan could see his younger brother was drunk. "He only drank three beers," his brother told his friend Joel shaking his head. Zach couldn't resist. He went to kiss Jane, who was three years older. She leaned away from him and they both fell onto the couch. He landed on top of Jane with no real plan in mind. As his body started to levitate off of Jane, Zach realized he was being lifted up by Alan and Joel. Jane escaped, narrowly. His brother was taken outside, where he sat for an hour until the booze started to wear off.

The incident with Jane was so out of character. Zach would feel embarrassed for the longest time. He never sought Jane out again, to apologize or to curry her favor.

By junior year in high school, Zach liked the idea of having a steady girlfriend. He was satisfied holding hands, having long make-out sessions and feeling a girl's body. But, most importantly, slow dancing to Johnny Mathis records.

He dated Daniele "Dani" Millstone for almost a year at PHS. Dani was perfect. She dressed exceptionally well. Like Zach, she wore collegiate clothes; round-neck sweaters with light colored blouses. Her hair was always done up every day in a "flip". She had a wonderful outgoing personality, enjoyed dancing and was a PHS cheerleader. Dani's father, Micky Millstone, worked for the Post Office and delivered the mail to the Goldman home every day. Franny thought Micky was the nicest person. Together, the parents would often talk about their children. When Zach and Dani started dating, they both expressed hope the kids might settle down together one day. They were way too young for anyone to seriously entertain such notions, but both parents were set on seeing their children marry someone Jewish.

While Zach felt strongly about his faith and his one-on-one relationship with God, he rarely followed the rules on Jewish holidays. Once he took Dani to the Suburban Diner during Passover. She was crazy about Zach. Being together on a Saturday night was so important. She didn't mind if he wanted to eat out, but she was definitely more observant of Jewish customs. She would not eat or drink anything that wasn't Kosher for the holiday. Zach had a solution. He ordered two deserts. He drank the chocolate milk shake on his side of the table and afterward he'd switch his empty glass with an ice cream soda he ordered for Dani. She was always such a good sport. The two teens would talk and laugh all night together.

There were many nights when the young couple would hang out in the Goldman home. They'd listen to records in the den, talk about their friends, dance and sit on the floor near the couch and kiss for hours. "She was the best kisser," Zach would tell himself.

He was always trying to figure out what type of girl he would marry one day. There were also long conversations with his best friend, Mitch Moran, about being fathers. These were largely philosophical discussions about their view of life and what was going to be important to them when they grew up. Mitch would sit in his kitchen and pour catsup on his egg sandwich, which totally grossed out his friend. They would joke about having sons as the same time, so they could compare notes and learn from each other. Zach confided to his friend that Dani was the closest to his ideal of who he wanted to marry in the future. She had very strong values and a smile that could win his heart. But he knew it was too soon to settle down. He and Dani were headed off to college. Zach was going to a state college in NJ, while she was headed to Maryland. He didn't know if fate would bring them back together again, but Dani taught him what it meant to feel loved.

CHAPTER 54

The Bronx VA Hospital

As Zach Goldman swung open the door, the sun shined through the long basement hallway at the VA hospital. It was a beautiful spring day in 1968. Zach loved this time of year, when winter lost its hard edge.

He could feel his neck muscles tighten with first smell of the disinfectant that permeated the building. Zach had been to the Bronx Veterans hospital several times. He could not escape the tension and discomfort he felt.

From the parking lot, the hallway snaked through the bottom of the hospital like a long umbilical cord.

The more he thought about it, he realized he hated hospitals. All hospitals. Since he was young, he had seen both his parents close to death on so many occasions. For him, hospitals represented a threat to an otherwise normal life. And at that moment, he wished more than anything for a normal life. He could not bear the thought of losing his father.

But if Zach hated hospitals in general, he hated VA hospitals even more. He was keenly aware of the poor conditions. The buildings were old and not well kept. The hospital aides could care less about the patients. There were so many patients and few hospital staff. Even worse, many of the doctors were foreign born and could barely communicate with the patients in English. Zach had nothing against immigrants or doctors who studied overseas, but he lacked confidence veterans were getting the best treatment.

Young men were coming back from Vietnam and he couldn't believe hospital conditions and how poorly the nation's finest young men were treated. He wished the TV folks and politicians would tour these VA hospitals and see firsthand the severely injured young men laying in their own feces-filled beds. He was certain it would end the war in Vietnam sooner.

Once past the initial smell and institutional colors, the basement hallway would inevitably come to Ward-C.

As Zach reached the second bank of elevators, he saw the sign overhead, "C-ward." Sitting in the alcove near the elevator doors, he found three wheelchair bound boys. They did not seem much older than him, maybe 20 or 21. One had lost both legs below the knees. The stumps were exposed, though bandages covered the tips. The other boy had lost an arm. The third seemed to be paralyzed from the chest down.

The amputees started for the open elevator door. Zach could not control himself. "What about him?" he asked angrily, pointing to their paralyzed comrade, off to the side.

"Are you simply going to leave him here?" The amputees stopped and looked in silence, surprised by the stranger's anger.

"It's ok, it's ok," said a voice softly. His head was held tightly by a wire halo frame. "They will send someone down for me later. I like being down here by myself—it's quiet. I can think."

The others left, without responding to Zach's protest. This kid didn't get it. A soldier was on his own. Even if you escaped death in the jungles of Vietnam, no one was going to rescue you from the consequences of war. He stood silently for a moment staring at the boy. Zach's body was frozen. He could not hold back the tears that streamed down his face. He knew it could be him sitting in that chair, or one of his brothers. He could not even begin to imagine the experience of war or how this boy must feel.

"Hi, I'm Tom Hosford," a voice broke the silence. 'I'd get up, but around here someone might steal my chair."

He nervously smiled, in response. "Hi, I'm Zach Goldman. So, you're just hanging out down here?" he asked.

"This is a great place to pick up girls," said Tom. "You know? It has a romantic ambience. It's dimly lit and quiet. I'm just waiting for the right girl. Do you sing Zach? Occasionally...if the mood strikes me, I'll come down here and practice."

Then in a beautiful, tenor voice Tom started, "What's your name, what's your name, is it Mary or Sue? What's your name, what's your name, do I stand a chance with you......?"

Zach stood there motionless. Tom stopped and just stared off into space. The silence was a wall between them. Zach waited, and then asked, "Are you ok?"

"Yeah, I guess..." Tears welled up in Tom's eyes and ran down his face. Life as he knew it or the life he dreamed about was over. He had no clue what his purpose was any longer. He would only be a burden to his family. He would not marry. He would not have children. His mind was as paralyzed as his body.

Zach could not look away. He could feel Tom's pain like the jagged edge of a knife running across his arm. And yet, he could not think of anything to say. Finally, he walked over to Tom. He slowly bent over and gently hugged Tom around the wire cage that held his head. "Don't give up," Zach whispered to Tom, "Don't give up. You still got it inside, where it counts. And no fucking son-of-a-bitch can take that away."

As he leaned back, Tom had a smile on his face. The act of defiance in Zach's voice comforted him. This new friend shared a defiant and kindred spirit. Zach reached down and wiped Tom's eyes with his hand—and then he wiped his own.

"You want me to take you up?" he asked.

"No, I'll stay a while, until they come get me. I'm ok. Trust me, I'm going to be ok. Don't you have to visit someone?

"Yeah, I came to see my dad," Zach explained. "He has to have brain surgery. I guess this will prove whether he's got one in there."

Tom laughed. He enjoyed the sarcasm.

"Good luck to you," he said.

"You too," Zach replied, as he started down the hallway.

As he reached the next elevator bank, he looked back at Tom.

A single lightbulb hung down from an exposed wire above this paralyzed veteran, sitting at the basement gateway to Ward C.

He would look for his new friend later, as he was leaving for home. This would only be a one-time encounter that he had with this young man. However, that image of the young veteran in the basement hallway would stay with Zach.

At the third bank of elevators, Zach looked up for the familiar Ward D sign. He stepped off at the eighth floor and headed for room 825.

Murray Goldman lay sleeping in the far corner of the room. His large frame filled the bed, and there were those huge hands that so reminded the boys of their dad's fighting spirit.

Sitting next to the bed was Uncle Sammy, dad's youngest brother. Sammy visited often. For him, Murray was the best big brother. He looked after Sammy, when their parents divorced. He helped Sammy find jobs, taught him a trade. And no one in the neighborhood messed with Sammy, as long as his older brother was around.

He also dragged Sammy along to Synagogue. It was one of the contradictory notions, that the rough and worldly Murray Goldman had such a strong connection to his faith. In his deep Brooklyn accent, Sammy would joke about Murray breaking Jewish rules, as frequently as he broke noses. But his big brother could also stand in a Synagogue, without a prayer book and recite the entire service by heart. Sammy could never quite figure out how his older brother reconciled his lifestyle with his love of God, but he tried to follow his example.

Sammy smiled and got up, as he saw Zach come in. "How is he doing?" he asked.

"Fine."

The doctors came by and told him the operation would be done on Thursday.

"Did he seem upset?"

"Zach, you know your father. He wanted to know why the doctors couldn't do the surgery today. Your father told him, 'Look Doc, I'm a plumber. If I said to a customer your toilet is stuffed up, but I can't fix it until Thursday, what's he going to do? Crap in the backyard?'"

The thought of his father's plain-spoken approach brought a smile to his son's face. At the craziest moments, his dad could win over the toughest cynics and the doubters. He lived his life as if roadblocks were nothing more than new challenges. And he met challenges with a single-mindedness that Zach envied.

Once again, the brain tumor was large. Except this time the tumor was at the back of Murray's skull. It would be a long operation. The doctors would have to open up a significant part of his head. No one in the family believed that he could have a second brain tumor. Life at the Goldman home had finally returned to normal after Franny's hip replacement surgery. Dad worked six days a week. Mom drove the boys to and from sports practice or to their games on weekends. She cooked dinners. But the signs were all there: The numbness he experienced in his limbs; the periodic dizzy spells; the headaches that wouldn't go away. He hid his symptoms well from the family. He offered excuses for his irritable behavior, rather than burden Franny or the boys.

Gary had found his father after school one day. He was surprised to see dad's truck in the driveway. Dad never came home from work before 6:30 p.m. He went into the kitchen to get a snack. Mom must have been out food shopping. He sat at the kitchen table eating Oreo cookies, when he heard a mumbling sound. At first, he ignored the noise as he drank his milk. Soon the noise seemed louder to him. He put his glass down and walked toward the bedroom. He first saw his father's legs by foot of the bed. By the time he reached him, he could tell dad was having a seizure. Murray's body was shaking violently. Gary ran to the phone and called the police. He ran back to his father and gently put his hands on his chest, as if trying to calm him down.

Zach Goldman arrived home a few minutes before the police and ambulance. He could hear his brother calling out, as he entered the house. He tried to calm Gary. "Turn him," Zach instructed, as the two boys tried to roll their dad onto his side. Zach could see blood near his father's mouth. He must have bit his tongue badly, he told himself.

The rest of the day was a blur for the Goldman boys. The ambulance took their dad to the hospital. Zach insisted his brother stay behind and wait for mom to come home. Zach sat in the rear of the ambulance and watched as the medical technician tried to stabilize his father.

After several days in Bergen Pines Hospital, Murray was transferred to the Veterans hospital (VA) in the Bronx, New York. It took years and a ton of paperwork for Murray to press a claim over the injuries he suffered on his ship during the war. At first, the Navy could not locate his medical records. The Catoctin was at sea in the middle of fighting a war. No one ever expected to find, no less keep such accurate records. Eventually, however, the doctors reviewing his service record concluded the significant head injury he received contributed to the brain tumors Murray experienced. Almost two decades later, the Navy awarded him benefits, which included free medical care. The decision proved very timely. At this point in life, he no longer had the resources to cover a major surgery. Without benefits from the Navy, an operation could bankrupt the Goldman family.

Weeks after the seizure, doctors at the VA hospital concluded Murray had a new brain tumor in the back of his skull on the right side. They would have to remove a large section of skull to reach the tumor. The surgery would be challenging to avoid any impact on the brain tissue.

The boys shared visits and vigils at the hospital waiting for the scheduled surgery. Zach could not remember his father's first brain tumor. He was only five years old. His older brother, Alan would tell the story of how mom had to drive back from the Catskills. Every fifteen minutes, dad rolled out of the car heaving his guts up. An image of his father throwing up in the glare of car headlights stayed with Zach, but it wasn't clear if it was a real image or just the stories he had heard so frequently.

The first time was a haze for Zach. But Alan, at eight, could remember being told that his father needed an operation and might not live.

At the VA hospital, Murray Goldman opened his eyes as Zach and Uncle Sammy stood talking at the foot of his bed. He was happy to see Zach, "Hi, son." His father did not regularly say much, but the deep voice and soft inflection was always the same. To him it conveyed love. It was always special. Zach walked over, leaned down and kissed his father's forehead.

"Hi, dad. Sammy tells me the doctors were here. Are you ok?"

"Sure. Why shouldn't I be? They haven't done anything yet. I just wish the doctors in this place could speak English. It's so hard to figure out what they're telling me."

Zach turned to Sammy, who had a wide grin on his face and chuckled. "The doctor was Indian. Neither one of us could understand a word he was saying."

"Is he the surgeon?" Zach asked.

"No," said Sammy. "He was just explaining what would happen on Thursday. You know.....all the procedures. Maybe it's better they sent him down to explain." He couldn't ignore the humor of Sammy describing in his heavy Brooklyn brogue how the Indian doctor described Murray's surgery.

"Dad, I don't want you to worry. It is going to be fine. This is not 1955. I think things have changed since the last operation."

Murray Goldman was calm. He could not get over how much his middle son had grown. He was always the compassionate one. "Son, I'm not worried about anything. They ain't slowing me down with this thing."

It was the sort of defiant statement Zach had come to expect from this father. He wondered at times if his dad could be so strong minded that he could actually change reality? He felt certain that question would stay with him over the next few days. But whether or not he had an answer, he would follow his example. Zach would pray with all his might not to lose his dad.

"Well, if you're in that good a mood, why don't I take you and Uncle Sammy down to the canteen for coffee. I'll tell you about graduation."

Zach knew it would please his father to hear about his graduation from high school next month, and plans for college. Murray Goldman never finished high school. He made no apologies about it. But he and Franny shared a dream their children would all go to college......and be educated.

His older brother, Alan, had just finished his sophomore year at Temple University in Philadelphia. Alan was the only sibling that always had a clear goal. From 11 years of age, he wanted to be a lawyer...the best lawyer. And even though he excelled in high school athletics, He passed up two football scholarships at Universities to concentrate on his studies.

It wasn't as if Alan was some straight arrow jock. Quite the contrary. His high school days were littered with beer bashes, wild parties with girls and C and D grades. Alan worked hard to compensate for his lost childhood. But somehow, as wild as he got, he had a goal and he never lost sight of it.

To Zach, it was like his brother woke up after graduation day from high school. He put away the beer and began to skip the wild parties. From that point forward, nothing mattered except excelling in every college class. And Alan did. His success at college was scary--and intimidating. His brothers always felt he was a tough act to follow.

After an hour at the canteen, Zach returned to the room with his dad and said goodbye. He would be back early on Thursday, before the surgery.

He passed by the second bank of elevators on his way out through the basement corridor. He looked for the young veteran, Tom, but his new friend was gone. It was a long day. Zach couldn't let go of his feeling that life was capricious. He took a deep breath as he exited the hospital door. His head throbbed from the headache. He knew he'd feel better once he left the smell of the VA hospital.

Music blasted loudly on the radio as Zach raced across the George Washington Bridge to get out of New York City. The music had always been there for him. It was where he escaped. It was where he could hide from the tension and loneliness. He felt the music, like he wrote the words. It was as if he was on the radio singing the songs. And for those few moments Zach Goldman was gone.

At wrestling matches in high school, he'd go off by himself. No one could make out the mumbling, but up close you'd recognize the tune, "I never met a girl who made me feel the way that you do, you're all right. So, fee, fie, fo, fum, look out baby for here I come......"

While his teammates got psyched up for their matches grunting and groaning, Zach was rocking out to Smokey Robinson or the Temptations.

When he came out on the mat, he was sure-footed and fast. He surprised many opponents. He had been an acrobat since he was six--and later a gymnast. Unlike many wrestlers, he wasn't a weight lifter with bulging chest muscles. Most of his strength was in his back. Often opponents misjudged how naturally stronger a gymnast becomes walking on their hands or swinging on the parallel bars.

Zach was very serious about wrestling. He and Richie Gardner, his wrestling partner, would go to clinics at Lehigh University in the summer. Lehigh produced several national wrestling champions. For a week, the boys would attend classes and practice wrestling moves in the University gym. In the fall, he would run with his best friend, Mitch Moran, a long-distance competitor. Mitch would help him get in shape, though after 2-3 miles, he'd leave his friend at the high school and finish another 10-mile jog.

As a wrestler, Richie was built like a mini Mr. Olympiad, and competed one weight class heavier than him. There was a healthy respect between these two athletes. There was no question that Ritchie was stronger, but he was faster. Zach also excelled at countermoves. When they worked out together, the wrestling mat cleared off to avoid the flailing bodies and unyielding movement of these two animals. At the end, they would always come off the mat soaked in sweat.

Like many of his teammates, Zach was forced to lose weight. Wrestlers understood that if you went down one or two weight classes, you'd avoid facing an opponent who was bigger, stronger and naturally weighed 20 pounds more than you. His natural weight was around 160-165 pounds. If he stayed at the 165 pound weight class, he'd face wrestlers who naturally weighed 180 pounds. He starved himself to get down to 148 pounds. Losing weight balanced out the issue of strength. Zach would often go without eating or drinking for days to get down to his weight class. He'd sit in the cafeteria watching his friends at lunch. Sometimes he'd eat an apple and drink one glass of water.

The wrestling team had to weigh-in right before the actual match. As soon as your weight was checked by the referees, you'd run back to the locker room and drink pure honey or eat oranges to get some energy in your body. The weigh-in could be a tough and surprising event. His team Captain, Tommy Reynolds, had the most challenging time making weight at 105 pounds. Tommy's real weight was probably closer to 120 pounds. Zach was drinking honey, when he heard his team mates gathering to see if Tommy made weight. As he walked over to the weigh-in area, he could see his team mates close in a tight circle around him. While the referee was looking at the scale, Tommy put his hands behind his back. A wrestler on the team grabbed his hand and carefully lifted him up an inch. The boost from behind was just enough to help him clear weight on the scale. The process took less than 30 seconds. The referee never knew. PHS wrestlers won that day, when Tommy pinned his opponent to garner extra points.

As Zach reached New Jersey, the music drifted off. His escape, if only for a short time, had ended. His thoughts again returned to his father. What if his dad did not make it through the brain surgery on Thursday? He could not bear to think about this. He needed his dad.

Alan, Zach and Gary Goldman arrived at the VA hospital at 8:00 a.m. on Thursday. The operation was scheduled for 11:00 a.m. Franny waited down the hall in the visitation room, so the boys could have some private time with dad.

The three sons dutifully walked in and kissed their father. The boys never questioned the open displays of affection they showed Murray. Alan and Zach recalled seeing their father show that same affection for Grandpa Isaac, before he died. The image of a grown man kissing his elderly father, seemed only natural and appropriate to the boys.

Alan started with a quick question for his father, followed by a rapid succession of one liners. He was the most natural wanna-be lawyer around. His come back to comments from his brothers had always been very fast. It was never quite clear whether he was practicing a skill or driven by his fierce competitiveness for his father's love.

And oh, how Murray loved his eldest son. He lay there in bed and reveled at his quick wit, his hammer like approach and command of language. Alan surely had his father's ambition. He could smell the blood of his opponents, much in the same way that his dad could back in the boxing days. He knew just when to move in for the kill. Alan was a personality to be reckoned with, even at 21.

His dad remembered the one football game he attended. Most Saturdays were spent at his shop, tending to his plumbing business. Seeing his children compete at sporting events was just not possible. Running the business was his first priority. He had never seen Zach wrestle or play baseball as a youngster. Gary was not much interested in sports, but he did love cars. He always wondered if his dad realized they shared this gift. At least in Gary's case, his dad would stop when he came home to see the work his son completed on the car. His dad didn't pretend to understand what Gary was doing, but he made a point to compliment and encourage him.

Coming to see Alan play football was a very special occasion. Alan had only one or two more games left in his high school career, and what a career it had been. He was already being talked about as a shoe-in for the All County Football team honors in northern New Jersey, and a likely candidate for the All-State team.

He was surprised by his father's sudden interest in seeing him play. He had complained so often about his dad missing his football games, it seemed useless. But a week before the game, Murray told him he would be there. Alan tried not to think about it. He half expected that his dad would cancel last minute. He wanted this moment for so long.

He did not dare mention his swollen hand. During a game the week before, someone had stepped on his hand after a pile up on the field. By Wednesday, his teammate and friend Joel insisted he go to the doctor. A cast was put on his left hand and wrist to protect the fracture. Alan knew he would not keep it.

He had always been good at keeping secrets. This time he was intent on playing for his father, and nothing, nothing would stand in his way. By the time he came home that evening, the cast was cut off. He taped the hand and wore an Ace bandage. He told everyone it was just a sprained wrist.

At times, Alan had trouble reconciling his conflict about his dad. As a teenager, he hated his father....or so he thought. He could not erase the memory of that one time his dad had so disappointed him. He felt better after Franny talked to him. He understood and yet it took years for him to gain enough perspective about life that he could totally forgive him. Yet, his father's approval and love meant more to him than anything in the world.

He played that Saturday as if he were a moving wall. An offensive guard, it was his job to open the hole in the line for the running backs. At six foot and 210 pounds, he was not the biggest lineman. But on this day, he cleared a path that a truck could drive through. His teammates kidded on the sidelines that he seemed possessed. He was unstoppable.

He did not mention his hand, or the pain. He taped his hand tightly, but it throbbed. He would not give in to it. With the clock running down and less than a minute of playing time, the quarterback called a run off the right tackle. Alan's team had time for a field goal attempt, if they could just get ten yards closer to the goal. The game was tied at 14-14.

Murray watched from the fence along the sidelines as the ball was snapped. He didn't really understand football, except that someone gets the ball and runs "like his pants are on fire." His eyes could only focus on the white jerseys and the one with the red number 42.

Alan knocked the first defensive lineman on his ass, as Tony Nardo, the running back, moved through the hole with the ball. Alan was not finished. He chased after Tony. The linebacker was coming from the right. He did not see Alan until they met at mid-field. The crack of helmets could be heard above the roar of the crowd. Both of them went down. Tony continued up the field to thunderous applause, and with two defenders still in pursuit. They would not catch him before the goal line.

As the roar of the crowd died down, attention turned to the two downed athletes laying on the field. Coaches ran out on the field. For the next few minutes a soft murmur of voices waited and watched. Helmets were off. Slowly,

Alan and the linebacker got to their feet. The linebacker walked over to him and extended his hand, "Man, I ain't never been hit like that. What did you eat today?" Alan still dazed, shook his head and grinned. "My dad's here."

The sight of the two opponents coming off the field together brought the fans to their feet cheering. They were pleased both were not seriously injured. As Alan walked over to his bench, he could see his dad. Murray Goldman did not speak, but his son could see a smile that stretched from ear-to-ear. Alan's victory was complete. He could see how proud his father was that day.

Standing around Murray's hospital bed, Zach Goldman shook his head as his older brother dominated the conversation. He was not intimidated by Alan's aggressive behavior. Zach, at times, just chose not to compete with it.

Gary would throw in his own occasional one-liners. He had a wonderful off beat, earthy sense of humor, much like his father. But he knew he couldn't keep up, as long as Alan was around. He loved his older brother and looked up to him. At the same time, he resented the brow beating he often got from Alan.

He was never as slow, or awkward, or uncaring as Alan would claim. The four-and-a-half years in age between them often felt like 30 to Gary. He did not need or want a second father. For Alan, being tough on his brothers was just his way.

Murray lay in bed and proudly watched his three sons. Where did the time go? He was happy to have them there. How good it felt to have sons.

"Listen, I expect the three of you to look after your mother." The sudden interruption silenced the brothers. They looked at each other with added concern. "Wait, I'll get mom," Zach said.

From down the hall, you could hear Franny Goldman. Slowly, she walked toward her husband's room. Her crutches made a distinct clanking sound as she made her way, with Zach holding her arm. He was always nervous walking with his mom. What if she lost her balance? What if she slipped? Could he catch her in time? Could he protect her from struggling so much?

Franny did not pamper herself. She struggled to get out of bed and walk. She still experienced pain daily. However, she could be as tough as any situation required of her. It was no accident that she and Murray had made it this far. Brooklyn was not only their common bond, it was in their DNA.

The boys made room, as their mom moved toward their father's bed. She struggled, at first, to reach over the bed railing. Alan quickly reached out and lowered the railing. Gently, she leaned down to kiss Murray. The boys backed away to give their parents some privacy.

"Listen," she said looking into her husband's eyes, "We've been here before." Clearly, she was talking about Murray's first brain tumor. He was not expected to live. Back in 1955, brain surgery was not very sophisticated. He was only given a 50-50 chance of surviving. But he did survive. She didn't give up and he overcame the physical side effects. It was an unspoken part of their relationship. He gained everything back, in time, and life went on.

"I will be here waiting for you." She took his hand. "I know it hasn't always been easy for us, but I love you. I don't want you to worry. Be strong for me."

For a few moments there was silence. She pulled Murray's hand and pressed it to her face. She kissed his hand. She leaned down, struggling to reach across the bed and gave him a hug. She would not cry. She did not want him to see her fear. Gary and Alan rushed over to the bed and helped their mom regain her footing. She had a wonderful smile on her face. At 51, she was grateful to have reached this point in her life. She was so proud of her boys.

The nurse at the door told the boys it was time to go. Following the nurse were two orderlies with a stretcher. Franny motioned to her sons, "O.K., let's go. Murray, be good up there. The boys and I will be here when you get back."

"Boys, kiss your father and let's go." Alan was first. He hugged and kissed him, "I love you dad." Next came Zach. Usually, the more upbeat of the three, he was silent. The words just wouldn't come. "When do these epic moments of possibly losing a parent ever end," Zach asked himself? "When do we ever get to be just kids?" Gary followed his brother. He held on and hugged his father the longest. Maybe that was just the way it is being the youngest. He always wanted more time.

They all stood in the hallway until Murray was being wheeled away. The trip to the elevator was quiet. Another round of quick hugs and he was gone.

The family headed down to the canteen for coffee and the long wait until he finished with surgery. Zach made no apologies. When he was nervous, he had to eat. He bought two coffees, a roll and butter, and a piece of pound cake. Aside from being hungry, Zach had an insatiable curiosity about his father's life. "Mom," Zach started, "tell us about our dad. What was he like at our age? Did he really hop freight trains?"

"What are you talking about?" Gary asked.

"Your father started hopping freight trains at 15 years old," she said. "He would go down to the yard, wait for a train to start pulling out and run after it. After one hundred yards, he'd grab onto a side rail near an open car door. He would leave early and ride all the way to Philadelphia. After spending the day walking around, he would hop a train back to New York by night time."

"Didn't his folks raise hell?" Alan asked. "No," Franny responded, "it was different then. It was the Depression years. No one watched their kids back then, they were too busy trying to make a living and survive. Besides, things were not great at your dad's home."

The three sons sat and listened to their mom. They had heard parts of stories before, but mom was now telling them what they really hungered for. It was unusual for children to be so interested in knowing much about their parent's lives. Most never learn much at all about their parents. But the stories mom told did not seem to be about the same person they knew as their father.

The nurse entered the waiting room, where Uncle Sammy sat with Murray's three sons. Sammy had been telling stories for almost two hours. The boys immediately stood up. Their necks stiffened.

"The doctor asked me to stop in," she started, "they're still in surgery. It will probably take a few more hours."

Each of the Goldman boys stood motionless. They did not know how to interpret the news. Did it mean the tumor was worse than expected? Were they having difficulty with the surgery? Was their dad going to pull through? The nurse could not provide answers. She had dispensed the message and after a few polite, "I don't know," she left.

Sammy finally stood up. He walked past the boys to a coffee machine.

"Who's got a quarter? Alan, you have a quarter? Zach? Ahhh, it's o.k., I found one."

Sammy pulled the coffee out and sat down again. The boys were still standing. Alan and Zach began to pace about the room.

"Boys, boys, it's going to be fine. Aren't you listening to the stories I'm telling you about your father? Nothing could hold him down. Your father's going to be fine. C'mon, come sit back down. Trust me. C'mon, I haven't told you how your father and mother got together."

Sammy dove in once again, in a hearty Brooklyn accent to tell Moe's story. Sammy could see the hunger in their eyes to hear more about their father. They sat anxiously. They feared this might be their last opportunity. For Sammy, it was his way of dealing with his own fear—and his love, which he rarely expressed. He knew the boys were looking to him for comfort. He had to be strong. That's the way his brother would want him to be.

The doctor came into the waiting room still dressed in his surgical gown. His hands motioned to Murray's three sons to stay seated. It had been six hours, but the surgery was completed. Once again, Murray had beaten the odds. The boys smiled at the news, relieved that the ordeal was over. As Sammy joked with Zach and Gary, Alan walked over to the window. The tears welled up in his eyes. He stared straight ahead.

"It's ok," Zach told him as he put his arm around his big brother's shoulders. "You know dad wouldn't have it any other way. There's nothing that can stop that guy." He stood silently for ten minutes staring out the window with Alan. They knew it was over for now, but when would there be "a next time"? When would God smile down on the Goldman family, the boys wondered? Their memories haunted them. It had not been the first time that they faced the prospect of losing one of their parents. Each of the Goldman boys grew up with death stalking their family. And each in their own way had been changed by it.

Several hours would go by before Murray was expected to be back in his room. The Goldman family would not leave. The boys scattered in different directions. They clung to each other, when the world seemed uncertain. Each, however, had grown fiercely independent. They needed space and time to deal with their own emotions. Alan was very scared during the surgery, but that feeling would give way once the crisis had passed. Zach, on the other hand, was the calmest during the crisis, asking questions and trying to anticipate what came next. But after the crisis was over, he, too, struggled. Two days would go by before he welled up with tears, just thinking about his dad. Gary was less expressive. He shared the same stress and anxiety as his older siblings, yet he rarely showed it. Gary was a study in repressed anxiety and anger.

Sammy headed back to Brooklyn. He had not planned to stay through the entire operation. For him, it wasn't a matter of family pride that his older brother would pull through, he just couldn't see any other outcome.

By evening, Murray could be found in his room. He was asleep, when the boys returned. Their mom was sitting at his bed side. "Mom, what's with the bandages?" Zach asked.

She started to cry. "Look what they've done. They had to remove a large section of dad's skull to get to the tumor. It is unlikely they will be able to put the bone back."

None of the boys understood what that meant. "They couldn't put his skull back?" Gary asked. The questions nagged at them, but they accepted their mom's comment and were just happy to see dad back again.

Days, and then weeks, would pass before Murray started to feel like himself again. However, that would never be totally true. It take time before Franny noticed Murray forgetting things. She'd had conversations with him, but hours later he'd revisit the subject. Initially, she wanted to overlook the situation. Soon, the Goldman boys, started to notice as well.

Murray accepted he could not go back to work. He was missing almost a third of his skull. The bandages had all been removed. It looked like his skull had been caved in, on the right side in the back of his head. The skin looked stretched and tight, where the skull used to be. Everyone was keenly aware he had to move about with extreme caution. He was discharged from the hospital after three weeks. Zach and Gary took turns walking with their dad around the house or for short walks outdoors. Alan had to get back to his college classes in Philadelphia. A month after the surgery, Murray's gait seemed very slow and his balance was off. The boys would ask their mom if she thought this was a temporary effect from surgery.

The family returned to the VA Hospital with Murray for his post-surgery checkup, six weeks after the operation. The doctor explained to them the tumor was very large on the right side of his brain. The right brain can cause weakness on the body's left side, post-surgery. Doctors couldn't be certain if the symptoms the family noticed would be temporary or permanent. As they arrived home, Gary couldn't contain himself any longer, "What did they do to my father?" he asked. The question hung in the air like a thick cloud of smoke.

Zach's graduation from Paramus High School in 1968 was a welcomed celebration for his parents. Milestones are always significant, but often they are less so for the person being honored. While his dad never talked about his feelings before the surgery, he had them. Seeing another Goldman child finish high school and go off to college was about the most important thing in his life.

But how does a father put into words the hopes and dreams he may have for his children? And even if the thoughts come to him, why is it such a struggle to communicate them when they matter the most? Murray did not have words for his number two son. If there was a connection, it was unspoken. Zach felt his father's pride when he saw him smile, sometimes a wink of the eye—and when his dad grabbed the back of his head with his hand. Ironically, Zach had anxiety about moving on to college.

Franny had reservations whether Murray should attend his son's graduation ceremony. There would be over 550 students and the auditorium would be packed. She knew her husband had to be extra careful, missing almost half the skull on his head. His father wanted to see Zach cross the stage to get his diploma. As a compromise, Murray agreed the Goldmans could have dinner at home. Franny had arranged for a delivery of sloppy Joe's from Petaks. Alan skipped the graduation ceremony, but he volunteered to pick up the food.

The doctors in New York scheduled Murray for a second surgery six months later. He would be sent to the Philadelphia VA Hospital, which specialized in orthopedic surgeries. To replace the portion of skull he lost, doctors would cut him open and shave bone from both his hips. The bone would be inserted in his head to cover his unprotected brain. At that point, Alan left the meeting. The thought of his father having his hips cut open made him sick to his stomach. Zach peppered the doctor with questions about the surgery and the impact this might have on his dad. Franny's eyes glazed over. She was thankful he was ok, but for how long?

CHAPTER 55
Another Surgery

The drive to Philadelphia went smoothly. The hospital looked very modern, a far cry from the Bronx VA. Zach Goldman had started his first semester at Trenton State College (TSC). His father had given him his old car, as a high school graduation present. Alan was heading into his third year of college and still talked about going to law school. The dream his parents shared had come true. A first generation of Goldmans were going to college.

Murray's second brain surgery went smoothly. The doctors completed removing bone and shaped it to fit in his skull. Aside from the turban of bandages wrapped around his head, the whole procedure seemed like a non-event. Alan and Zach headed back to college. Gary drove mom back to Paramus. The family was looking forward to a few days off.

By Tuesday, of the following week, Zach got the call from Alan. "Come, as soon as you can. Dad has an infection. He has a fever. I just got here."

He left his apartment in Trenton immediately. He arrived at the VA Hospital in less than an hour. His brother was standing in the hallway, when he arrived.

"Look, they put him in this side bedroom by himself. His fever is very high and he sounds congested. There are only two nurses on this floor, with 80 patients."

Zach knew the drill. He and Alan would not leave their father alone. "Did you call mom?" Zach asked.

"Yes, but I didn't want to drag her down here again. There's nothing she could do. I promised her we'd give her an update each day."

The boys met with a nurse. Then they started demanding to see a doctor. After grilling the hospital staff, a test was scheduled later in the afternoon. The doctor came in with a rubber hose and plastic Emesis tray. He explained to Murray and his sons the need to get a sampling of mucus for the lab. There were no nurses to help the doctor. Alan and Zach stood on either side of their father, as the doctor pushed the rubber hose up their father's nose and down his throat. He inserted a syringe at one end of the hose and pumped a small amount of water into it. Murray immediately began to cough violently, while trying to sit up in bed. The boys grabbed him from behind his shoulders to lift his body into a sitting position. The doctor held the Emesis tray up to his mouth, until he brought up several coughs filled with phlegm. His face was red as a beet. He was obviously in distress, as the boys set him back down on the bed.

"Look, as you can see, we're pretty short staffed on this hospital floor," the doctor said matter-of-factly. "If you want your dad to survive the night, I'd encourage you to sit him up every hour and force him to cough up the phlegm. I suspect he has pneumonia, which the lab will confirm by dinner time. However, it will take 24-48 hours of heavy antibiotics to fight the infection. Your dad could drown from the fluids in his lungs. We need to help him clear his lungs and fight the fever."

The Goldman boys now had clarity. They immediately took charge. Their mission was clear. By dinner, the doctor came in to give Murray two injections: a strong dose of antibiotics and something else to help him expel the mucus. The boys continued to wake their dad each hour, physically pulling him up to a seated position. Zach held the Emesis tray, as they ordered their father to cough. He was not use to taking orders, especially from his children. But he was too weak to argue. It took him several coughs to get his body convulsing and expelling liquids. As the phlegm dripped from his mouth, Alan was visibly gagging. He tried turning his head toward the wall. He wasn't certain if it was the sight of phlegm spewing into the tray or the noise of dad coughing, but he could not get over being sick to his stomach.

Zach came to the rescue, as was usual in these circumstances. He set the Emesis tray down, while he wiped Murray's mouth with a wad of tissues. Alan helped settle his dad back in bed. His brother washed out the tray in the bathroom and set it down next to the bed, so they were ready for the hourly exercise. The boys could tell their dad's body temperature had hiked in the middle of the night. There would be no nurses to help them. They devised their own plan to soak wash rags from the bathroom in cold water and sponge their dad down. He was lying in bed with a sleeveless t-shirt, so washing his face, arms and upper chest was easier. He reacted to the cold water, shivering when they were done for 10 minutes. The boys would cover him up. He'd fall back to sleep, which gave them an hour to sleep before resuming their efforts.

Over the next three days, Alan and Zach refused to leave their father. They slept on the floor in his hospital room. They took turns going for food or the bathroom. The nurses began to check in on him. They knew his sons were in the room. This gave little comfort to the boys. By the second night, their dad woke up on his own, coughing phlegm from his congested chest.

They forced him to drink fluids and helped the nurses when it was time for him to swallow medicine. They called their mom three times each day, not to cause her any alarm, but to keep her informed on his condition. If they were going to err, it would be on the side of optimism. The boys did not want her to know how uncertain the whole situation had become. The surgery had gone well, but Murray might die from the pneumonia he contracted.

By the fourth day, he started to respond to the large doses of antibiotics. His fever finally broke. It shocked the boys to see two nurses struggling to treat so many male patients spread from one end of the floor to the other. Their dad was not the only patient put into a private room. However, with the volume of patients, the private rooms were "out of sight and out of mind." The Goldman boys could only wonder, how many of the patients tucked away in private rooms survived?

During their stay at the hospital, for the first time, Alan and Zach talked. The discussion started around their experiences in sports. Each of them shared their notions about training and competing. For Alan, it was running drills on a football field until half the team was puking or bleeding. For Zach, it was the starvation diet of not eating for almost two days to make weight. They laughed, as stories were shared and a stronger bond was struck. These boys had become men. Their own independent natures were readily apparent. The Goldman sons realized they both lost their childhoods, but they shared a common worldview. The events in their young lives had taught them to control and shape their reality. At times, they were not polite to the hospital personnel, if being nice interfered with getting a result. Neither one of them spent much time asking existential questions. The boys were battle-tested for over a decade now. The mission in Philadelphia was now over. They had won. Another test had been passed.

CHAPTER 56
Alicia, Gary, Alan & Grace

Gary Goldman announced his plans to get married in the fall of 1970. He was only 18 years old. He could not be persuaded to wait. His parents had hoped that he'd follow his brothers and go to college. But it was not easy to hold a Goldman boy back once he made a decision. Gary would marry his high school sweetheart. Both sets of parents opposed the idea of marrying so young, but they finally signed the legal papers giving their permission.

He had become indispensable to his parents, once his brothers left for college. He had Murray's sensibilities and skills to fix things around the house. His father now had difficulty keeping his balance and walking. His short-term memory grew worse. Gary could complete almost any construction or electrical work needed at home. He lived in the finished basement, but was there when his parents needed him. Before settling down with his girlfriend, Alicia, he had a regular stream of girls visiting the Goldman home. He would joke with his brothers how easily he could turn off the house alarm and sneak girls through the back door.

No one would ever guess their baby brother would become such a lady's man. The sickly child had grown up. He shared his father's swagger, his brother Alan's one-liner sense of humor and his preoccupation with girls that his friends suggested was part of the "Goldman DNA". In the teenage years, boys at school were often bitchy and rude with their girlfriends. Some girls loved being "shit-on", but that was not the Goldman way. Gary never pushed a girl away. Most guys played hard to get or obsessed with trying to see how far they could go with a girl. Gary won hearts by his attentiveness. He talked nice. He treated girls with respect. He'd bring little gifts or tokens. He was affectionate. He was focused on showing girls there was another type of guy they could date. In time, girls wanted him more than words--literally, more than words could say. These girls, valued being treated well. They would do anything to show Gary their love for him. It was easy to love this Goldman boy—and it was easy for him to fall in love.

Alan was perhaps the most notorious and complex of the Goldman clan. He also showed the sensitivity that girls liked, but could be bitchy as well. The oldest sibling of the family had seen the most in his lifetime. He sometimes lacked patience with girls who could not make up their minds. Intimacy for him was a form of escape. He, too, had his father's youthful swagger. Often, he would be described as mature beyond his years. His quick mind and verbal skills could be very attractive to women of any age.

At 17, he was surprised at the attention he received the summer he worked at a Catskill Hotel. He was waiting on tables. And married woman tried to pick up the blonde boy with blue hazel eyes. The women were more than twice his age, which unnerved him at first. A woman slipped him her room key and a twenty-dollar bill. By the end of summer, his education was more than complete. And these lessons served him well, when he returned to work at Petak's deli in the fall.

Taking a page from Alan's mocking nature, Zach affectionately began referring to his older brother as the "whoremeister". It never took Alan much time. Girls and women were drawn to him like a moth to the flame. He was never mean spirited. He treated girls respectfully, but he had no goal beyond the sex. He was not a romantic. He wanted as much physical contact as he could find. Zach was certain they all shared a need for intimacy as a form of escape. He didn't want to get too psycho-analytical. He understood the warmth of a girl's lips. And he valued the warmth of a young soft body.

Alan's world changed when he met Grace Manelli. She was strikingly beautiful with long black hair, dark eyes and a smile that took no prison-ers. Much to his brother's surprise, Grace saw something redeeming in him beyond the sarcasm and quick wit. Grace and Alan had shared high school classes in their senior year. She watched him for months, before making her move. Yes, it was Grace who would be the aggressor, introducing herself and asking for a date.

Zach and Alan only crossed paths in sports twice. Once, when Zach was brought up to the Majors baseball team at age 9, to pitch and play second base. Alan was not pleased to share the field with his younger brother. The second experience occurred in high school. Alan was asked to join the wrestling team in Fair Lawn, during his last year in high school. He still carried weight from football season and his school was desperate to find someone to compete as a heavyweight wrestler. He was not experienced in wrestling, and he knew it. The family had already moved back to Paramus. Zach wrestled junior varsity (JV) for PHS school at 141 lbs.

It was on this fateful night when the wrestling teams for Paramus and Fair Lawn competed—that Zach first met Grace Manelli. He was sitting in the stands, after the JV wrestling matches, when this tall girl walked the gym floor in front of the entire team. She stopped and pointed toward Zach,

"Are you Alan Goldman's brother?" she yelled.

"Yes," Zach replied, somewhat surprised.

"Well, I'm going to date your brother. You just watch."

Zach smiled, shaking his head in disbelief. This girl had chutzpah, he thought to himself. Beneath it all, he was kind of jealous. "How the hell does his older brother always attract such nice, pretty girls," he asked himself. He hoped his brother paid attention to this one. She was somehow different—a keeper.

As the night wore on, Alan did not acquit himself well on the wrestling mat. The Paramus heavy weight was 240lbs and had been wrestling since 9th grade. He was merely 210lbs, with little experience. Zach watched with angst and horror, as Tommy John pushed and threw his brother, at will, around the mat. Alan was bridging on his neck, trying to avoid getting pinned, when Zach couldn't contain himself. He didn't care that he was routing for the opposing team, it was his brother. "Don't you quit," he yelled at the top of his lungs. "Turn, turn, turn, move your butt," he screamed. As quickly as he screamed, Tommy did what he did best. He let the air out of his lungs and put his full weight on his brother's chest. In 15 seconds, Alan lay flat on the mat. The referee's hand slapped the mat. It was over.

His teammates were surprised by Zach's behavior, but he didn't care. Zach had won his match earlier that night. His team sat in silence, as he yelled commands. No one really worried that one match could change the team outcome. After the match, Zach looked for Grace. She was not in the gym. Two days later, his brother called home. He asked his brother if he had met this girl at the wrestling match. From the conversation, he knew his older brother had met his match with Grace, in more ways than he expected.

Alicia Dombrowski married Gary in fall of 1971. Her mother was yelling to her, "you can still change your mind," as Alicia walked down the aisle ahead of her. Gary knew it was more than just a concern about their age. Her Polish parents hated the idea that she was marrying a Jew. Anti-Semitism still ran deep in Paramus. Alicia laughed at her parents. She did not share their views. In fact, the marriage would be her escape from her family, where alcohol and bad tempers created a hostile environment for Alicia and her sisters. For Gary, getting married gave him a sense of purpose and certainty in life. He wasn't afraid of the responsibility. He had never really been a carefree child.

The wedding consisted of a small dinner with family at a local restaurant. Gary and Alicia would move to a small apartment. Gary got a job as store clerk in a retail store in Paramus. Alicia worked in a book keepers' office. Neither had wanted college, but they would soon learn how much that decision impacted their income—and their lives together.

During high school, Alan's grades and party behavior were out of control. It became unmistakably clear to his mom, the night the doorbell rang. His buddies carried their friend from the car and propped him up against the family front door. They rang the bell and took off in the car. He fell on the floor in the hallway, when his mom opened the door. He was laughing and obviously drunk. His mom tried to look away. She knew her kids had been through a lot.

Alan also snuck girls into the basement, sometimes into the back seat of the family car in the garage and, brazenly, late at night into his room across the hallway from his parents. His post-athletic career, after football and wrestling, was drinking six packs of beer or a bottle of scotch. His grades followed his drinking, which were in the toilet, after he puked. Increasingly, his mom was at a loss. She feared he would never get into a college.

However, his behavior masked Alan's innate intelligence. He scored high on the SAT college entrance exams. Few people in his mom's generation ever went to college. No one heard of the SATs, though the test had been around since the 1920s. In the 1950s, only 75,000 students took the SAT exam across the U.S. This number grew to more than a million in the 1960s. His high school grades might not get him access to college, but his guidance counselor knew Alan's SAT scores would definitely open the door. Alan would wait anxiously for months before colleges responded to his applications. He grew less confident, as applications were denied and the acceptance process dragged out. The wait forced him to begin thinking about his life decisions and his future. Many of his friends were being drafted into the Army and sent to the Vietnam War. Having been to the Bronx VA hospital with his brothers, this was not a reality that he wanted to face. He wanted more.

He was finally accepted at several universities. Life decisions for the Goldman children, however, would always consider the challenges faced by the family. Alan chose Temple University in Philadelphia, which kept him under two hours to reach home. While the awards he received for "All County" football tackle in high school earned him several scholarship offers, almost overnight, he had become a different person. All of the Goldman boys would need money to pay for college. Murray was no longer working. The family was on a tight budget. But Alan turned down the scholarship money to focus his full attention on school. If he had to work the summers or at night to help pay for tuition, he would do so. He had a goal. He would not be distracted. After two semesters at college, his grades were firmly established. He made honor roll at Temple. It was time for the next phase of his life.

All the Goldman boys would eventually get seed money to help with college expenses, based on the disabilities Murray suffered after the war. The Navy doctors concluded after a review of wartime records that the head injury, while at sea, was a major contributing factor to his brain tumors. The funds the boys received as educational assistance for tuition helped, but neither of them complained about working jobs to help pay room and board.

After reaching college, Alan had also finally decided to settle down. This was a welcomed move, from his mom's perspective. He was only 20 years old, but he had sowed his oats many times over. He knew one girl could keep him on track and remain his biggest booster. He proposed to Grace Manelli after his sophomore year in college. They would marry and soon begin a family.

Grace came from a very close-knit Italian family. Alan had gotten close to Grace's grandparents during the two years they dated. Their initial reservations were set aside about Grace marrying someone Jewish, because of the respect and warmth Alan showed the family. She was her father's favorite, compared with Julia, her older sister. Grace had her dad's inner strength and fortitude.

Like Murray, Grace's dad, Joe, had built a furniture business from scratch after the war. Both dads didn't talk much, but shared a strong commitment to family—and their children. Josephine 'Josie' Manelli, Grace's mom, expressed strong reservations about her daughter going out with Alan Goldman. It was never clear if she didn't like his ethnic background or just didn't like his strong, assertive personality. Joe was less apprehensive. He wanted a son-in-law with a backbone.

CHAPTER 57

Life Catches Up

Murray Goldman would never work again after the second brain tumor. At 54 years-old, the effects of surgery would sideline him. His movement and gait were slow, and at times, off-balance. He suffered from short-term memory loss, which could cause him to be impatient. How does anyone begin to understand the impact a physical loss can have with someone so defiantly independent as Murray Goldman? In truth, there are two types of people. Those who lead very active lives; soldiers; firemen; policemen (and women); construction workers; cowboys. Then there are intellectual types, who read books; consider rationales for making business decisions and generally are preoccupied with concepts, theory and research. That's certainly way too simplistic. There are many men and women who are hybrid models of these two essential types. Yes, there are men and woman CEOs who run the marathon. Yes, there are both intellectuals—and people who enjoy abusing their bodies in sports.

The point is that men and women who grow up being naturally physical from sports or doing jobs that require physical labor have great difficulty accepting limits later in life. Why does a fireman or policeman run to danger, even when their age has diminished their stamina and their skill? Out of breath, they struggle to perform because a voice inside pushes them beyond their boundaries. We believe these folks are either crazy or exceptional. Regardless, they garner our admiration and respect.

A gymnast notices the decline in his body's flexibility but refuses to stop doing handsprings or walking on their hands, until the pain covers them like a ragged blanket. The boxer learns at a young age how the universe conspires to impede their gifts over time, leaving them only the stubbornness of an athlete's heart to compete—and to win.

Everything in life changes around you, but what makes us so unique is what everyone sees. Brooklyn still lived in Murray; the days of his youth; the boxer; the guy who built a business empire from nothing.....the spark in his eyes and the broad smile that filled his face each time he sat with his sons. His physical prowess and determination had defined him.

Long before the loss of his plumbing business, he planned in great detail how to secure his family. He plowed money into his real estate investments. He kept investments separate from the business. When he started up the plumbing business again, after the car accident, he knew it would never be the same. It would be impossible to reach that scale of work again. And he knew, even if he wouldn't admit, that he didn't have the stamina. He still worked six days a week to provide cash flow for the family and to keep busy. He would explain to Franny what she needed to do with the real estate holdings, most of which were located in growing commercial areas on major highways in northern New Jersey. "Franny, these properties are our annuity. We can sell them and put the cash into certificates of deposit, which will give us income to live on."

The Goldman boys never let their father see their anxiety about his health. He was a proud man, the strongest willed man the boys would ever know. If pride is not the essence of a man, then what is? At the point he began to lose control of his bowels, the boys would outwardly show little emotion. His brain and his body were now at odds with each other. He could not anticipate when he might fail to function properly. The boys repressed their horror and resisted the new reality. He crapped in his pants more than once. He was not oblivious to the shame associated with these events. His mind was still sharp, but his body was failing him.

Alan and Zach would take turns helping their father stand in the bathroom, while the other one wiped him clean. His clothes had to be changed. The boys sponge bathed him with rags that were quickly thrown away, as if by disposing of the evidence they could hide the crime. Each held their breath. Their hands could not avoid being soiled or avoiding the stench. After getting him changed and sitting in a chair by the den, his sons would gather his clothes and spend 20 minutes washing their hands. They'd alternate using soap and disinfectant until the skin hurt. The silence during these clean up periods did not go unnoticed, but there wasn't anything to say that would make the time go by faster or less painfully.

The decisions about where to go to college was guided by their need to be proximate and capable of getting home on short notice. Franny held back, as long as she could. They each had their health issues, but the boys were gone now. Murray needed care beyond what she could provide at home. The Lyons VA hospital in New Jersey had nursing home-like facilities, where he could stay and still come home regularly to visit.

Franny and Murray talked for months about what to do. She tried in vain to have a woman take care of him at home, but no one could lift the big guy. Most times, she ignored comments or complaints from the nurses' aides, until they quit. The aides could not be with him 24/7 and he needed too much help from one person. He could see the stress on Franny, both physical and mental. One day, he sat her down and made the decision for her. "I am going to the VA nursing facility. I know we are both struggling. I will not be a burden on you. Sometimes you just have to do what you have to do. It's not anyone's fault, yours or mine. And I'm not worried. I don't doubt they'll treat me well." It had always been his way to try and use humor to lighten difficult moments.

Murray had just turned 56. "He was so young," she would tell herself over and over again. She cried for weeks. "How could life be so cruel?" she asked herself, over and over again. The Goldman boys came home to discuss the situation with their mom. They could see the stress on her. The family talked for several hours, as the boys wrestled with their guilt about what to do with dad. The questions ran deep. No child should ever have to choose which parent to protect, but then the need to make a choice never goes away. "Mom, you can't do this on your own anymore," they'd tell her. "And you can't afford to hire 2-3 aides to help dad. We are not giving up on him. If he goes to the Veteran's facility, you can count on one of us to visit him every weekend at the hospital. We will never abandon dad. We will bring him home for every holiday."

Alan, Zach and Gary kept their word. Franny just could not get over her grown children. Every weekend, one of the Goldman boys would drive to the Lyons VA facility to spend the day with their father. They never complained, even if it meant time away from girl-friends, wives or missing social events on weekends. If one had a conflict in their schedule or a commitment to keep, another son would volunteer to make the three or four-hour round-trip journey.

The visits to the VA hospital were stressful. Seeing their dad in a facility only reminded them daily of the suffering he had experienced in his life. They could never do enough, though they tried, to turn back time. The father who took them to Teaneck on Sunday mornings; the guy who held them in his arms when they took naps or who rescued them when they were injured and in pain—those moments were a distant reference point. Children are not immune from feeling powerless in the face of a changing reality, even as they grow into manhood. Feeling powerless is the way life teaches us humility.

It would never be easy for them to look away from the visible decline they saw in their father. They tried to hide their sadness until driving home afterward. Each had their own way of coping, whether blasting the music or crying in the car.

At the same time, through all the stress, the Goldman sons found new meaning. The visits to the VA nursing facility became more satisfying than they ever thought possible. Murray had serious health issues that would not get better, but during each visit, a son had private time with their dad to share their stories and gain insights from his comments about life.

He never lost his way with the boys. He might have worked six days a week, but his influence in their lives was ever present. He rarely had long talks or lectured his sons. He believed children learn by observing the values and people they experience.

Not every lesson in life is instructional. Murray could be very tough and strict with the boys. He also had a loving nature with his sons. His warmth, like sunshine, showered them with light to navigate huge challenges and overcome insurmountable odds. Even in the shadows of their darkest moments, the boys could find from his strength the ability to persevere in their own lives. A smile would come to their father, with each visit to the VA Hospital. The boys would tell him about school and their aspirations. Alan was finishing college with high honors and looking ahead to entering law school.

"Alan, I never doubted you. But if you're going to be a lawyer, make the decision to be the best lawyer. Don't let anyone think you have shit in your blood. Show folks you are willing and you have the skills to win." Holding up the bar of expectations was what Murray did best for his children. He used their love to inspire them and challenge them.

He knew, at times, Alan could be cocky, but this false bravado hid his inner struggle to find confidence. Murray never saw this as a weakness. Alan was smart enough to recognize what he didn't know. It wasn't blind arrogance that drove his son. He had a thirst for knowledge. He had a hunger to learn from others. In the end, his dad felt certain his son's confidence would grow, as he mastered the technical and substance required of his profession.

The years would pass. Murray's proudest moment was seeing his oldest graduate law school, "first in his class." The tough language from dad's conversations wasn't lost on him. "Just remember, Alan, don't take crap from anyone. Always look to surprise your opponent." None of the Goldman boys had a dad translator. "What did he really mean?" they'd ask themselves over and over. Each one found their own interpretation. Alan knew in his study of law that "surprising your opponent" was no easy task, with all the rules about evidence discovery. But he took from the conversation to prepare for his legal cases better than anyone. Ironically, he often did surprise opposing lawyers in court. He had mastered the techniques of interviewing witness on the stand and he could remember facts buried deep in hundreds of pages of transcripts. No one prepared as thoroughly as Alan Goldman. And that reputation made him someone to respect—and avoid—in a court of law.

CHAPTER 58

Zach and Nia

Zach was a middle child. Like many "middlings," he was the most loving and empathetic with both his parents, but he could also be the most rebellious. He was not quick to judge others, unlike his older brother. However, he could not accept or be silent when he perceived intolerance or injustice. His nature was to question things. Everything! Especially, those points of view and bias others might look past.

Franny's favorite story was when Zach told-off Rabbi Levine. He promised Zach extra points toward his Hebrew school grades for playing trumpet in the Synagogue band. The report card sent home never reflected his contributions to the band. He didn't hesitate to tell the Rabbi how wrong he was to forget his promise. "How could you do this?" his mom questioned her son, when she got a call from the Rabbi." "I don't care if he didn't remember to give you points, you can never question or talk back to a Rabbi. Tomorrow, you're going to march into that class room at the Jewish Center and apologize. This is not up for debate." Zach was not afraid to stand up for himself, but the line was drawn when his mom spoke. He did not agree with her. His sense of being wronged would not go away, but he marched in the next day and apologized to Rabbi Levine.

The behavior of students at military school, when JFK was killed, stayed with Zach. Even at that young age, he was connecting dots. He was gifted with an intuitive side, which always looked for answers to the larger questions of right and wrong. Effie, who lived with the Goldmans and helped take care of Franny, was like a second mother to the boys during the most difficult of times. The idea that Effie was black did not occur to Zach. When he hugged her coming home from school, he only knew Effie loved him—and he held on to that large sized woman with the gold tooth for as long as she'd let him. At 13, his experiences at military school opened his eyes to issues of race and religion.

By high school (PHS), Zach's rebellious side started to show itself. He joined with other students to protest the lack of racial diversity in the town of Paramus. In the 1950s and 60s, realtors in town rarely, if ever, showed homes for sale to Blacks, Hispanics or Asian families. A student group at PHS launched an effort in 1968 to start busing black students from Teaneck High, calling it a "cultural exchange" program. Zach was not afraid to speak up at the Student Council to ask fellow students to vote for the program. Students rallied and approved the busing idea, though the Paramus School Board would later reverse their decision.

Zach left for Trenton State College in the fall, which was just over an hour from home. He wanted his freedom, just as Alan found by going to college in Philadelphia. At the same time, he knew he could never venture too far from home. He loved being on his own. He moved into an apartment in the student ghetto on North Hermitage Avenue in Trenton. The street served as a dividing line in the city, with whites and blacks living on either side. Three blocks of apartments stood in the middle, some of them over store fronts. College students rented these apartments. This was the cheapest housing around.

Alan had given his younger brother one piece of advice when he left for college. "Act like you own the place. Don't walk around like you're some dumb, inexperienced freshman. The older students will eat you alive."

During his freshman orientation weekend, he met two girls at a dance: a tall beautiful girl with surfer-like long blonde hair and ocean blue eyes named Daryl Skagen and a second girl, somewhat shorter, with gorgeous brown eyes and a winning smile named Nia Williams. Daryl was less of a dancer than Nia, so it was only natural for Zach to spend most of the evening with her. When he came home the following weekend, he shared stories with his best friend, Mitch. Franny sat at the kitchen table, while the boys talked. He described the girls and what he liked about each. His mom was smiling and calm, until Zach got to the fact that Nia was black.

"You're kidding," Franny interrupted Zach, while Mitch stared down at the kitchen floor. "Look mom," he replied, "I didn't plan this. It just happened. I asked her to dance. She has a great personality. Relax, I just started college. I'm not Gary…and I'm not getting married."

"Well, just don't bring her home." Franny responded. "Mitchell, please talk to your friend. I believe people should be treated equally and race or religion should not matter. But, at the same time, my son has to realize that an interracial relationship just won't be accepted." Mitch decided it was time to stuff his mouth with Mallomar cookies. He finished the box before the conversation was over. It wasn't clear if the smile on Mitch's face was at his friend's crazy idea to date a black girl named Nia or that he finished a whole box of cookies without Franny yelling at him.

Back at college, Zach was shy, at first. He'd run into Nia at the student union. They'd talk and have coffee together. It took weeks before he finally summoned the courage to ask her out on a date. He wasn't certain if Nia or her family would have the same concerns about dating across racial lines. He asked her out to go see a movie. The two of them sat quietly in the movie theater, as Zach reached over to hold her hand. He had no idea what was about to happen. The movie, "Rachel, Rachel" was about a 35-year-old woman who had not married and struggled to find her purpose in life. Both Nia and Zach sat in shock, as a second actress reached over and started kissing Rachel. It was 1969. It may have been the first same sex kissing scene in a movie. How ironic the breaking of norms greeted them on their date. Neither of them were offended by the movie scene, but it gave them lots to talk about.

Both Zach and Nia were coming of age and trying to figure out their identity and their own sexuality. They talked about social norms of race and sexuality regularly. Each shared a growing interest in the protest movements of the 60s and the struggle for freedom and justice.

A week later, Zach would test his mother's resolve when he called from a local Paramus Diner. "Mom, we're at the Suburban Diner and I thought I'd stop by to see you." Franny was not pleased by the surprise call, but in spite of her reservation, she welcomed Nia when they arrived.

In time, Nia and Zach would become lovers. It was the first true relationship for both of them. It seemed they couldn't get enough of each other. They could spend hours talking about race relations. Other students were curious about the fact they were dating. Often, they sat in the Student Union and spent hours talking about current events. In the same way, they broke through the barriers of connecting physically. Their lovemaking had such passion and energy. Nia often stayed over at Zach's apartment. In the morning, they'd often start over where they left off the night before. Nia would go with him to see his mom in Paramus, where they could find privacy sleeping and making love in the basement. As Franny got to know Nia, they'd talk and eventually would become friends.

Nia was studying to become a nurse. Franny quickly grew to respect Nia's knowledge and advice. Zach would also visit and stay overnight at Nia's parents in Long Branch, New Jersey. He liked the Williams family. Her dad was not in good health. His arm had been injured years before in a factory accident. He had little movement in the arm. Her mom was a very joyful woman. She went to church regularly. Her faith gave her the strength to guide and take care of her family. Nia's parents were very quiet and reserved around Zach, but he always felt welcomed in their home.

Nia would take Zach to "Adele's," which was essentially a restaurant run in someone's home. Adele Richards was almost 75 years old and lived near the Long Branch High School. Local folks had been coming to "Adele's" for decades. The Victorian-style house was almost 100 years old, with a wrap-around porch where guests could sit drinking coffee or wine. When you walked in, Adele would greet you with her big smile and flowing gray head of hair. She'd point you toward the living room where visitors would find picnic tables lined up along the wall. The tables covered two adjoining walls. Guests started at one end of the line and walked the length of the tables. The two tables were filled with turkey, sliced steak and Adele's country-style fried chicken. Further down, guests could find mashed potatoes, gravy, corn bread, chitlins, black-eye peas, kale, corn and salads. Visitors were encouraged to take as much food as wanted. A return visit to the food tables was permitted. A dessert table with cakes and pies could be found in the hallway of the home. Guests could eat dessert where they sat or take it with them onto the porch. Before leaving, visitors would pay Adele for providing the food.

Zach thought the food was amazing. He loved Adele's chicken. He stayed away from anything he couldn't readily pronounce or found difficult to eat. Chitlins were not top of his list, once Nia explained where they came from. Adele's became one of his favorite places to go in Long Branch.

Going to Paramus on weekends was more low-key for Zach and Nia. They didn't mind, since the Goldman home afforded them lots of privacy. In Long Branch, there would always be less privacy and separate rooms. One weekend, Zach was sleeping upstairs when he heard Nia's high school friends come by the house, "Hi Mrs. Williams, we came to see the white boy. What's he like? Can we come in and meet him?" Zach was not fully awake, when four young women burst into the bedroom. He was pleased on this occasion to be wearing pajamas.

Zach was very laid back about being in public with Nia, even though it was the height of the "Black Power" movement in 1969. On campus, they participated together in many classroom discussions about race relations. The Black Student Association (BSA) sponsored dances, which Zach and a few other white students attended. Since he was active in student government on campus, many BSA members knew and welcomed him. At times, however, black students visiting Trenton State would vocally question why a white guy was allowed to date Nia. "White men have been taking our women all the way back to period of slavery. It's time these sisters embraced our history in this country. They should not be going out with honkies." On some occasions, the off-campus visitors backed off, when other BSA students assured them Zach was different.

If that wasn't enough, Nia and Zach would double date with another interracial couple. Jimmy Calvin was black, a former basketball player, who was dating Michelle Conyers, a very tall blonde and former volleyball player. Jimmy had a great mischievous sense of humor. If he felt the couples were attracting too much attention from whites at the local diner, he'd suggest the couples mix it up. Jimmy and Zach would then switch places. People in the diner didn't know what to think, once they changed the racial mix of the couples. What was even funnier, however, was to see how short Zach and Nia were next to their athletic friends.

But one day in spring Zach came out of class to find two flat tires on his car. He had to have the car towed to a gas station. When he met up with Nia, he finally had to deal with the undercurrent of racial animosity. This time is was from black students who didn't like the white guy. "Nia, I don't get it. Someone sliced the tires on my car, but no one ever says anything or confronts me directly."

"Zach," Nia responded, "Black students on campus resent the idea of seeing sisters dating white guys. I don't talk about it, but I also get push back from my sisters. They ask me why I can't find a black man to date. But you don't hear about that, because the word on campus is that some of the brothers are afraid of you. They say you look mean." Zach started to laugh. It seemed such a silly thing for someone to say. He then walked around to look in a mirror. "Mean? I look mean?" Zach could be very direct with people, but he never thought of himself as a "tough guy" or threatening to people.

Nia told him many black students liked him. He seemed like a very genuine guy to them. As a Freshman English major, he took a course on "Black Authors," which included Ralph Ellison, Richard Wright, James Baldwin, Amiri Baraka. But unlike the few white students in the class, Zach didn't just read these writers, he participated in the class dialogue. For black students, it was unusual to find "whites" talking at all in this class and shockingly, talking so openly about racism. He was seen as someone who understood or wanted to understand their perspective.

Nia thought he was accepted by her friends, because he always seemed comfortable at school functions. He talked and interacted with everyone. However, Nia made a point of not bringing Zach to places off-campus like concerts or dances, where a fight or violence could occur. This point was brought home a month later when she insisted they skip a concert in Asbury Park, New Jersey. A day after the concert, Nia heard from friends at home that an interracial couple were attacked. The white guy was beaten up and put in the hospital.

Zach and Nia would date almost the entire freshman year at college. But they were both too young to see themselves settling down. They decided to take a break and see other people, a month before classes ended in 1969. Zach had been working on the campaign to lower the voting age in New Jersey. The statewide effort would be decided in the fall, when voters had to approve a public referendum. Running around the state organizing a grassroots movement of nearly 10,000 students became a full-time job. Both he and Nia agreed to remain friends, which was a promise kept over the next 40 years.

CHAPTER 59
Figure it Out

Gary Goldman didn't visit his father as often as his brothers. At 20, he was working six days a week. He had a newborn son, Matthew, and more bills to pay then he ever thought possible. He had not thought his life could become so difficult. He was never afraid to work hard.

Gary believed if he had his father's drive, he could make a living. Alicia stayed home with Matthew, while he worked as a salesman at a clothing store. He later took a job selling shoes, where he'd earn more commission from his sales. Gary and Alicia lived in a rented trailer in New Egypt, New Jersey. The trailer community was only ten minutes from the military base at Fort Dix. A high school friend had joined the Army and was stationed near the base. The young couple were keenly aware they could not afford to live in Bergen County, near Paramus.

The trip to the Lyons VA hospital took him more than an hour. It required him to give up his one day off spending time with his family, to drive nearly three hours by himself. However, Gary didn't complain. He wanted to see his father in the worst way. The financial pressures on Gary were growing. If Alicia or Matthew were sick or needed his attention, he sometimes had to cancel the visit. He knew how much his father looked forward to seeing his sons.

He walked around with loads of nervous energy. He ate often to try and calm his nerves. While Gary was not athletic, he gained strength from working with his hands. At six foot two inches, he was skinny with long arms and tall like his dad. He may have been the youngest Goldman, but he'd often joke that he stood taller than both his brothers.

After arriving at the VA nursing facility, his favorite ritual was to take Murray down to the canteen. He'd buy his father coffee and a piece of cake. For himself, he would eat the most-unhealthy foods you could imagine. If he bought a hamburger and French fries, this was among his healthier choices. Gary wolfed down the food, while his dad slowly drank his coffee. His father would wait for a second cup, to eat a piece of coffee cake. Murray would sit and listen to Gary's update on his job. His father could hear in his voice the one thing he could not tolerate: fear.

Maybe it was fear of the unknown, or fear that he hadn't figured out a plan. He had been, at times, stubborn like his father. He was proud of this fact. He felt he was no different than his brothers. They didn't have their futures planned either. But, he on the other hand was working non-stop at jobs that hardly covered the month-to-month bills. Soon Alicia and Gary began arguing over money.

After 20 minutes, Murray began to wave his hand in the air. He was signaling to his son it was time to stop talking. "None of this sounds good," his dad said matter-of-factly. "It's time you start thinking differently about your decisions—and your direction."

Gary was taken by surprise at his father's bluntness. He could not recall ever having a discussion like this about his family—and his life. Now, his father was cutting him off to give unsolicited advice. This was not what he wanted or expected. He was always sensitive to his father's judgments.

"Number 3," Murray paused and looked into his sons eyes, "you have your father's skills to be a plumber or work with your hands. You can be successful at this type of career, if that's what you want? Or, you can turn back the clock and go to college, like your brothers, if you want a career wearing a shirt and tie?

Stop wasting time!

Figure it out!

The people in life who cannot see past where they are will be lost. Lift your eyes up and see what's possible. Use your energy to shape where you want to be. It seems to me, your greatest obstacle in this decision is you."

Murray didn't say more. He reached across the table and picked up the piece of cake his son bought. He sat quietly drinking his coffee and eating the cake. "What the hell was he talking about?" Gary asked himself. To him, Murray was speaking in code. How often are we close to truth, but we don't hear it? How often does the obvious get pointed out, yet we are so absorbed with our current circumstance that we just don't see it? Something important was being said. This much Gary understood. He wanted to ask more questions, but he could see Murray was finished. His dad was not a talker. He didn't feel a need to dwell on subjects.

It would take the Goldman children a lifetime to fully understand how the Depression shaped and influenced their parents. His father had no coach or teacher to guide him. He was a street kid, who had to run away from home to find answers. We find love through the eyes of another human being, who can see us for who we are—and still value us. We find our future by letting go of our fear of failure. Murray never asked for permission in his life.

The ride home that day was quiet. Gary kept the radio off. He would mull over and over his father words again and again. As frustrated as he could be, he knew his father couldn't give him all the answers. He had to figure it out on his own. His dad's comments were a gift in his life. If only he could "stop wasting time" as he was told, his world would set its own course.

Zach tried to encourage Gary to revisit his decision about college, even though his high school grades and SAT scores were not very good. "Look, we all had terrible grades," Zach would tell him, "but there was a reason for that. None of us are stupid. Our priorities were taking care of our parents. If you focus now on school, I think you'll surprise yourself."

Alan felt differently. One brother sees the glass as half empty and the other one sees it half full. He encouraged Gary to forget college and accept his career would be different from his or Zach's. There was nothing wrong with being a plumber or working a profession where his natural talents could help him succeed. He tried to guide Gary by telling him, "If Zach or I had your skills, we wouldn't hesitate to work with our hands."

Alan wasn't wrong. Zach knew it, too. But Allan's view of the world failed to consider the one intangible. Gary looked up to his older brothers. He wanted to be like them. He wanted to follow them. He wanted to succeed like them, even when their success seemed unclear. Alan could not see his younger brother. He was too quick to define the limits of his brother's future, before the butterfly had wings.

The conversations with his brothers were sporadic, over six months, before Gary found his way. He knew Zach would do almost anything to help him. Zach could be as strong willed as Alan, but he always showed great patience and compassion with his kid brother. He wanted for Gary, what Gary wanted. He just wanted, like his father, for it to happen faster.

Zach began working on a strategy to help Gary get accepted at Trenton State College as a "non-matriculated" student. This would allow him to avoid the SAT entrance exams or a pre-determined grade average from high school. Gary would be able to take 6-8 college credits. If he did well in those courses over two semesters, he could apply to become a full-time student. Zach knew his brother could not attend college full-time and hold a job to support his family. However, as a part-time student, he could take a reduced number of classes at night over each semester and over the summer months.

He didn't tell Gary about the plan, until he had all the details nailed down. The Assistant Registrar at Trenton State was very helpful once Zach explained the situation. He promised to work with Gary to fill out all the forms and guide him in picking courses to take. The road map was there now. There would be no more excuses. Much to his brother's delight, Gary decided to take on the challenge and soon showed a commitment to school that neither of his brothers had ever expected.

Going back to school put an enormous burden on him, juggling between his job selling shoes, attending classes at night and studying on weekends. He was only 20 when his son, Matthew, was born. He was a child with a child. He adored Matthew and tried his best to carve out time to play with him each morning. Like Alan, however, getting good grades in college became his number one job. He and Alicia moved from their trailer in New Egypt to a small apartment near the student ghetto in Trenton. This shortened his commute to school and to his job. He tried to work during the day, leaving by 4 or 4:30 pm to attend classes until 9 pm. He attended summer sessions at college to help speed up his getting sufficient school credits needed for graduation.

By his junior year, Gary had declared a major in criminal justice. He had always been interested in law enforcement issues. He was encouraged by his progress in college and began to seriously think about going on to law school. However, after learning about Zach's conversations with Alan, Gary wasn't ever going to tell anyone his interest in law school. With little fanfare, Gary signed up to take the LSATs (law school entrance exams). He spent a month in the college library preparing. When the scores came back, he was shocked to find his results qualified.

Alicia and Gary had always faced financial pressures in their marriage. Alicia, like Gary, had overlooked her own intelligence and ambition by marrying so young. She wanted more from the world. She could be very difficult when pressuring Gary to do earn more. She didn't consider or care that Gary needed to complete college. She only cared about her immediate circumstance. This young married couple were not a team—and over time they became adversaries.

Matthew was only 5 years old when Gary and Alicia separated. The parents of this lovely child had just turned 25. The tension and arguing between them had become increasingly caustic. Gary was nearing graduation from college. He made the decision not to pursue law school. His world could not wait for him any longer. He needed to get a decent good job, so he could pay Alicia child support. The two high school lovers had checked out on each other. There was too much conflict at too young an age. As much as they tried to avoid arguing in front of their son, the fighting could get out-of-hand.

Zach tried to keep tabs on his brother. He would volunteer to take Matthew to stay with him on weekends. He hoped the couple might try to work things out. Having time alone might give them some breathing room. But the separation did not provide a timeout. Gary and Alicia would leave Matthew and then go their own way on weekends.

Zach didn't care. He was thrilled spending time with Matthew. He was the only Goldman that was not married. He liked the idea of being a weekend dad. Matthew had his own room at Uncle Zach's home in Hamilton Township. Zach also had a new Weimaraner puppy, named Sammy.

Early Saturday morning, Zach would lift Matthew onto the bathroom counter near the sink. He'd squirt shaving cream in Matthew's hand and let him wipe it on his face. It was all over his face and sometimes he put it in his hair by accident. They would both laugh together, as they looked in the mirror. He adored this precious and happy boy. Children are always innocent, until grownups shape them otherwise. Zach taught Matthew how to use a hand comb as his make- believe razor. Shaving with his uncle was a special treat for him. Music played in the background on the radio. And the routine always included a warm wet towel to clean Matthew's face, followed by a dab of cologne.

Breakfast usually consisted of eggs and toasted bagels. On occasion, Uncle Zach would make Matthew pancakes. Again, his nephew would sit on the kitchen counter. He would always engage Matthew as his partner in crime….for whatever activity they planned together. Zach poured the mix into the frying pan. He made a special effort to shape an M with the pancake bat- ter. His nephew couldn't wait to eat those pancakes. In the afternoon, they'd take rides to the Princeton battle ground, a large open park area that dated back to the Revolutionary War. Sammy was just a puppy and he would chase Matthew across the field. As he tired out, Sammy would jump up to lick his face. Nothing in the world is more special than a child and their dog rolling on the grass together. These were days Matthew would remember.

Zach hoped one day to have a son or daughter like Matthew. He would get so animated trying to teach his nephew something new. He'd take him into the woods by a stream to hunt for salamanders or frogs. Whatever the activity, his uncle wanted him to feel safe and to have fun.

Whatever issues would follow from his parent's divorce, Zach wanted to nurture Matthew. Be a child, he'd tell himself before reality steals your innocence.

CHAPTER 60

Like Father like son?

The Goldman boys would begin to seize their future with grit and determination. They looked past obstacles, always searching for opportunity. Notwithstanding the illness and absence of parents for long periods of their young lives, Murray and Franny remained their inspiration. They were driven by the early expectations their parents set for them. Franny's schooling on dress, appearance and "respect for others" instilled in the boys a core set of values.

No one would be surprised if the trauma experienced by Alan, Zach and Gary had set them on a more self-destructive path. The 1970s were filled with drugs, drinking, sexual exploration and wild parties. But something held these boys back. They didn't talk about their childhood with friends—or with each other. While they certainly did their share of acting out or trying to let go, something always pulled them up short by the shirt collar. They never got to the edge of the cliff. Did they fear adding to their parent's "tsoris," by getting injured or in trouble with the law? It seemed life had given them some sort of internal "speed controls" to keep them focused on the road ahead?

Franny, without question, was the conscience for her sons. She stood on their shoulders like Jiminy Cricket, chiding them to think before they act. They identified with her pain—and her toughness as the enforcer of family values; the yardstick for honesty and the arbiter of the "golden rule." Murray's physical presence, however, filled the boys with a sense of size and perspective. He was their grit. The image of the boxer who wouldn't stay down dominated their lives. They admired his strength of character and resolve. Where did the expression "like father, like son" come from? The connection they felt with their father, the hunger to live up to his expectations and win his love became their North Star.

Alan never had any doubt that he would be one of the best trial lawyers in New Jersey. By the time he reached law school, he and Grace had two children. Sara was born first. She was the happiest baby and quickly took to running around the one-bedroom apartment where they lived in Fair Lawn. Grace and Alan were only 21 years old. Their son, Blake, would be born two years later. Both Sara and Blake were born on the same date, which no one in the family could believe.

After an hour of play time with the children each morning, Alan would disappear into the bathroom to study. He'd turn on the water in the bath tub just enough to drown out the noise, as the children played in the next room. His routine was consistent. He spent nearly six hours a day reading, highlighting text in his law books and preparing for the next exam. Alan was never a dawdler. His sharp mind and maturity kept him focused on his goal. When he spent time with Grace and the children, he was a 100% committed dad. Grace was a valuable partner, demanding his attention when needed, but protecting his solitary study time in the bathroom. He knew he could not achieve the success he sought without Grace. He certainly should have told her more often how important she was to him, but he didn't.

By the time he finished Rutgers University Law School, Alan graduated first in his class. It was a terrific moment, but even more special when he visited his father at Lyons VA hospital to share the news. He cherished seeing the grin on Murray's face. His son had done what he said he was going to do. "I never doubted you," a proud father told an even prouder son.

Graduating with highest honors opened doors for Alan. He applied and was chosen to clerk one-year for a New Jersey State Supreme Court judge. In his short life, he had already accomplished two of his more important goals. His sacrifice sitting on the bathroom floor studying for law school had given him the knowledge and skill he would need in the future. Grace had given him two children he would grow to cherish in his life.

By his senior year in college, Zach Goldman had become a "stringer" or part-time writer for the Trenton Times newspaper. The middle and "most rebellious" of the Goldmans struggled with two currents running through him, i.e., being the writer observer or the political activist doer.

His friends at college said Zach led a strange life. He'd spend the morning walking the Trenton State College campus in a white T-shirt and jeans, carrying a cup of coffee to his literature class. He loved discussing the symbolism, metaphors and book characters. By noon, he'd be headed back to his apartment in Trenton to put on a suit or sports coat and go down to the State Legislature and lobby members of the State Assembly or Senate. He was usually joined by other students who shared his passion for changing the world.

Each would keep a checklist of names and votes needed to pass a funding bill for state colleges.

He could care less about the wild parties his older roommate would sponsor at their cramped one-bedroom apartment. He was not into the drinking or recreational drug use that flowed at these shindigs. He was always mindful of trying not to be somewhere in case the police showed up. He was too serious and preoccupied to fully join the college scene. But he did let loose on nights going to dances on campus. He also didn't mind having a steady relationship with a girl.

Against all odds, Zach did begin to change the world in 1969. With two friends from nearby schools, they led an effort that won passage for a bill in the New Jersey State Legislature to lower the voting age to 18. New Jersey became one of the first states in the country to push changes in voting rights. Three other states followed in 1969. Within a year, 13 more states followed and this growing movement became a catalyst for Congress in 1971 to eventually approve the 26th Amendment to the U.S. Constitution.

The historical significance of these efforts wouldn't sink in until years later. This was the 1970s and student activism was everywhere. Student lobbied and protested to end the Vietnam War, to protect the environment and to stop racial discrimination. Zach joked with Alan that he learned public speaking when he had to address 1,500 students, without notes or a prepared speech in the College's Kendall Hall auditorium. These were the days when you spoke from your heart—and you hoped that would be enough to move the audience to action. This was only partly true. Zach always researched subjects well in advance and he also spent time studying public speakers, like the Kennedys, Martin Luther King—and, yes, Malcom X.

While always an activist at heart, he began to wonder if he could reach and influence more students (and those beyond the college campus) by writing and publishing his ideas. He regularly wrote columns in the college newspaper. He needed to find out if he could write something worthy of publication. He'd spend weeks researching issues and gathering facts. He'd write and edit for days, away from his college courses. He saw the publishing of his work in newspapers across New Jersey as a test of his writing skills—and, more importantly, a way to bring changes in the world around him.

At college, he met David McGrail, an English writing professor who regularly graded his papers an "A" over an "F". He was thrilled with the "A" for his ideas and frustrated by the "F" for the execution of his writing. Mr. McGrail encouraged him to work on his writing. He suggested Zach read the New York Times editorial pages to improve his vocabulary and phrasing. "Zach, you will find some of the best writing in the Times," McGrail would tell him. "You should read the editorial pages every day, circle words you don't recognize and look them up in the dictionary. If you read good writers, you will learn how they construct sentences that have impact."

The challenge McGrail gave him was perfectly aligned with his thirst to read about what was going on in the world. You could find Zach in the Student Union each morning, drinking coffee and reading the newspaper. The exercise helped him learn how newspaper columnists used facts and statistics to argue persuasively. He gained insights on how to structure a 750 to 1,000-word article, so you could open with a basic premise and bring the reader back to that premise near the end. He knew it would be years before he could ever hope to write like columnists in the New York Times, but McGrail had whetted his appetite to write with clarity and impact.

As he neared the end of college, Zach toyed with the idea of following his older brother by attending law school. He felt confident his vocabulary and writing skills might finally be an asset. Alan Goldman was not kind when his brother called to discuss his future.

"You're not fucking smart enough to be a lawyer," Alan shouted into the phone. "Where did you come up with that idea?" he asked. "Maybe you should consider getting a job at the Post Office," his brother advised. "At least, you'll have steady work and a pension."

Zach was not thrown by the conversation. His older brother could be brutally harsh. He had heard him during similar discussions with his younger brother. Alan was a "take no prisoner" type of guy. He wondered if he was just too competitive with his brothers. He knew that every Goldman could accomplish what they wanted, once they set their mind to it.

More than two months passed. Zach concluded he didn't really want to be a lawyer. He was not intimidated by the task. He was just not clear on the goal. Unlike Alan, Zach was less interested in the minutiae and fine details that consumed lawyers. He loved politics and trying to influence change. He excelled at grassroots efforts organizing students and later going into the north ward of Trenton and registering black voters. His writing had become tools of his trade. He was thrilled when he earned his first byline at the Trenton Times.

Zach couldn't be certain where the road would lead, but he feared a legal career would not be satisfying. He was not keen to give his older brother any victory, as if he talked him out of going to law school. But he decided worrying about Alan's opinion was an empty exercise. The only test worth winning was the one he set for himself.

In July, after graduation, he went to celebrate with his father. He wasn't certain what his father might say about his future. Zach had no mechanical skills. He'd go with his dad on jobs to try and learn, but a natural aptitude wasn't there. He did have Murray's strength. His father would, on occasion, take Zach out of high school to help him on a job. While he started his business over, he was on his own. But he just didn't have the strength for some plumbing jobs. He would drain and disconnect the broken hot water heater. His son would drag and carry out the 150 lb. boiler on his back. Murray accepted his sons might never be plumbers. Most importantly, he was grateful they lent their strength to help him.

Zach sat with his dad in the VA Hospital canteen. He talked about his love of politics and writing. He often keep articles Zach sent him from the college newspaper or the Trenton Times. He told his father about his conversation with Alan. Murray could see how Alan's comments caused his brother pain. No one wants to be written off so quickly.

With excitement, he explained his summer internship working for David Vonman, the New Jersey State Public Defender. He landed the summer job, while waiting to attend graduate school in the fall. Vonman encouraged Zach, "if there's an issue or project that interests you, go for it." After coming across a Federal Report on Criminal Justice, Zach started researching barriers inmates faced finding jobs when they left prison. Georgia had a program helping former inmates get jobs. The report found this cut the recidivism rate by two-thirds.

He had written a 100-page report comparing "best practices" among state laws on the subject of ex-offender employment restrictions. So, at NJ's Rahway State prison, inmates were being trained for jobs as barbers. But existing law prevented them from getting a license required to be a barber. Zach found a book on how to draft legislation in the Public Defender's law library. He drafted four proposals to change state laws. When he presented the report and the draft legislation to Vonmon, he was offered a full-time job on the spot. Zach would become his Legislative Assistant, tracking bills and preparing reports on issues before the State Legislature. He also encouraged Zach to leave work early three days a week, so he could complete his Masters degree at Rutgers University at night.

Murray waited for Zach to finish his stories before speaking.

"You have it wrong," Murray told him. Zach paused. He had no idea what his dad was telling him. Did he not approve his decision to accept the job offer?

"Look, Zach," he started. "There are times when each of you may think I favor Alan. Yes, he's the first born. We waited almost a decade to have a child, so I can see where you and Gary may think we favor him. But you have something your older brother does not have. And I've never worried you'd find your way or be successful."

Murray stopped for a minute, as if he lost his train of thought. Zach started to break the silence, when his father waived his hand. This was always the signal to stop talking.

"So, my advice," again Murray paused. This time it seemed his father wanted to put emphasis behind his comments, "Don't, don't listen to anyone.

Don't worry about Alan's opinion. Be your own compass. Let your inner voice guide you. Remember, it's always darkest just before dawn. When you face the darkness, call upon your inner voice to remind you that you're my son. Trust your gut to show you the way forward. It will serve you long after I'm gone."

That was it! After 22 years, he had waited for wisdom to guide him as he ventured out into the world. His father's words were brief. This was indeed his nature. "What did he mean, it's always darkest just before dawn?" Zach asked himself. There were never long walks together in the park or sit-down lunches with dad to discuss his future. Still, Zach was not surprised by his dad's expressions of confidence. A child often knows. The unspoken is as powerful as the spoken. But this time, his father's words did carry extra weight. He realized his dad trusted him to make his own decisions. He was indeed giving his son the wisdom so often sought by their children. No one shares your journey in life. Rely on yourself, even when you have doubts.

This is your great adventure.

Without really understanding the import of events, Zach's career began to take off. The following year, Vonman was appointed to the cabinet of the new Governor. At 23, Zach would become the youngest Special Assistant to a Commissioner in New Jersey state government. He was Vonman's point person in the State Legislature. He actively lobbied on legislation and he guided the department's lawyers with research on nearly 350 bills being considered by various legislative committees. Vonman knew Zach had the right political instincts. He trusted him to coach lawyers when testifying before committees, when to stand up or sit down. At night and on weekends, Zach would be fine tuning his skills working on local political campaigns, writing press releases, speeches, marketing and advertising copy. He was recruited to work on Congressional campaigns and eventually the Governor's re-election team.

By the time Gary graduated college, Zach had grown close to Vonman. He had written and prepared Vonman's first testimony before a Congressional Committee in Washington. He also knew Gary needed a job.

Vonman had almost one thousand employees in his department. After hearing Zach's pitch about Gary struggling to start a career and working his way through college, he decided to add another Goldman to the payroll. Vonman knew what it was like to struggle, growing up in a single parent home and working his own way through law school. He had become a highly respected lawyer in New Jersey, recognized and appointed to his jobs by both Democratic and Republican governors. He had the discipline to see past the emotions of partisanship and pragmatically figure out what could work. He'd school Zach that "after the election is over, you have a responsibility to work with folks on both sides of the aisle. If you are responsive and treat elected legislators with respect, regardless of party, they will remember you."

Gary started working as a criminal investigator in a small area of Vonman's department. He would learn from experienced investigators about how to network and the technical skills used by professionals to unearth evidence. He was excited by the work, which seemed so much more challenging and rewarding than selling shoes. The gambit on college was paying off beyond his expectation. He was able to keep up with child support payments. He would see Matthew every other weekend. Staying a dad was still a priority. It would take two years before his income would grow and give him some breathing room. But Gary, being Gary, didn't hesitate to resume his life pursuing women.

CHAPTER 61

The Prosecutor

Alan, meanwhile, had moved on from his clerkship for a State Supreme Court judge to a job prosecuting crime in the U.S. Attorney's Office. At the time, New Jersey had one of the most visible U.S. Attorneys in the country. Every bright young lawyer wanted to work in this office. To get the job, Alan competed against young lawyers from Harvard, Yale and Stanford. He was not intimidated. Graduating "first" in your law school class, regardless of the university, spoke volumes about your commitment to the law. The endorsement of a State Supreme Court Judge was also not something overlooked. He went for multiple interviews, before getting the job offer. This role as an Assistant U.S. Attorney truly brought out Alan's command of the law and was complemented by his aggressive personality.

During the first year, Alan mostly prosecuted smaller federal crimes. This pattern was consistent with how lawyers were slowly trained as prosecutors. However, cases pursued in federal court were more complicated than petty crimes in state courts. The expectations for prosecutors (conviction rates) were high as well, and lawyers who didn't succeed didn't last.

Alan gained a reputation as a trial lawyer, who always had command of facts in the cases worked on. Defense lawyers cringed, if their client were being prosecuted by Goldman. Lawyers would sooner make a deal than go to court against Alan Goldman as lead counsel.

Before long, he was working on very sensitive cases involving charges against elected officials and some organized crime figures. His cases were always kept secret from his family or friends. He initially worked as "second chair" with his boss leading the prosecution. This arrangement was bound to change over time. It moved along somewhat faster, however, following an incident in a major drug conspiracy trial. He had been asked to handle the cross-exam of a critical witness, who was vouching for the "bad guys."

Alan started out his questioning sounding pleasant and even friendly, reviewing facts the witness had given. After 30 minutes though, the questioning got tougher. He caught the witness lying twice in court. He pounced on him. He could recall and cite testimony of other witnesses. He brought up evidence linking family members of the witness to the defendants. The grilling increased in speed and intensity. Alan was in absolute control, but he feigned anger as his voice grew louder. He moved closer and closer to the witness box.

"Isn't it true?" he kept saying to the witness. "Aren't you now lying to this court?" The witness had been perspiring during the cross-exam for 10 minutes. Alan's energy was high, his voice kept repeating questions. And then it happened.

The witness stood up without warning. He looked straight ahead, as his arms rose up to clutch his chest. His eyes rolled back in his head. His neck jerked backward twice. He keeled forward and collapsed in the witness box. He was dead before he hit the floor.

Alan took three steps back, as the witness fell. Everyone in the court room froze in their seats. No one could have predicted this result. Yes, he had done an effective job discrediting the testimony. His cross exam was not out of character for a prosecutor in this type of situation, but that's not how the world would remember it.

As Sherriff's officers ran to the witness, shouts to call a doctor could be heard. The judge banged his gavel and asked jurors to be removed from court. There was chaos for several minutes, until a semblance of order could be restored. The medics who arrived put the witness on the court room floor, tore the man's shirt open and worked on him for 15 minutes before pronouncing him dead. There was no pulse and electric shocks could not get the heart to restart.

Alan wasn't certain what was happening. He was in a daze as he turned and walked to his seat at the Prosecutor's table. He remained in his seat, until the man was carried out of the court room. "I think I'll go home now," he said to his boss. This was the most shocking incident he had ever experienced. He felt terrible, when he had to explain to Grace why he was home so early from work. He sat on the porch in the backyard with a drink. His hands trembled.

But, by the next day, Alan was back at his desk preparing for the resumption of the trial and next witness. The judge postponed the trial until the following week, which gave the jury and the lawyers several days to recover. His boss heard he was back in the office. He walked down to check on his assistant prosecutor. He offered some words of condolence and encouragement, but he could see Alan was trying to bury himself in the work. Some of the staff in the

U.S. Attorney's Office spread rumors that Goldman was a heartless bastard, who showed up for work after killing a witness. This characterization was furthest from the truth.

When death comes, what will you do? It's a question everyone must face at some point in their lives. Death isn't polite. It doesn't send an invitation to join and watch. Death often punches you in the face. The Angel stands and smiles, while you bleed and mourn. Nothing is as unpredictable as the moment your life leaves your body. Your soul is pulled off the line where you were waiting to find out why you were here. Your journey of self-discovery ends. What's next is an unknown. You're not even certain you'll recognize the next phase, beyond the darkness, beyond the silence and beyond the words of goodbye you never got a chance to express.

The drug trial resumed the following week. Alan's boss moved the timing of the next cross-exam to give his protégé more time. When his turn came, he began slowly with his next witness. But his questions and his confidence in asking them gained traction as he went along. The witness was fidgeting in the witness box. His story began to crack under pressure, but was it the questions or the questioner? The folklore began about a young prosecutor who was so laser focused and aggressive that he could cause witnesses irreparable harm. The case was completed in 10 days with a conviction by the jury.

Within months, Alan moved up to first chair, prosecuting major cases on his own. Some would argue Goldman just scared people, so it was be easier to get defendants to plea bargain. His boss knew better. He had seen in Alan Goldman someone who could keep his composure in the most difficult of circumstances. He won in court not because of some false bravado or bad behavior. He won because he was more prepared than his opponent and his impressive command of the law.

His reputation grew as a "lawyer's lawyer" (someone who other lawyers sought out for advice on legal strategy) took root during those early years as a federal prosecutor. His presence in a finely tailored dark grey suit, with blonde hair and hazel blue eyes stood out in the court room.

After hours, at a bar with colleagues near court, he was often sought out by women who wanted to know and be with him. "I've concluded, you're the best-looking man in this bar tonight. Why don't you come home with me?" At times, he could just feel a woman pinch his ass as she leaned next to him to retrieve her drink. The attention he received, reminded Alan of the days working at Petak's deli delivering food and sampling the corn beef. He would be tempted many times by the liberated and aggressive women he'd meet, but at the end of the day there would only be Grace. Like his father, he would grow and mature to understand the value of having a woman who stood by him. Grace and his children were a blessing he wasn't certain he deserved. But as he had travelled a road knowing there was uncertainty in life, Alan's family was his anchor.

CHAPTER 62
Navigating

Zach liked the romantic idea of dating. He wanted his relationships and the more intimate moments he might share with someone to evolve naturally. But his schedule always worked against keeping relationships. If he wasn't working overtime or on weekends to complete a project for his job, Zach was running around New Jersey helping some political candidate.

In 1975, he was smitten with a New Jersey staffer working in the Governor's Washington office. Elena Rossmore was one of the brightest operatives he had ever met. He was always attracted to women who seemed confident, in control and knew how to navigate to influence people and events. Powerful women were an aphrodisiac to him. Perhaps there was some deep seeded desire in him to be with someone who he didn't have to take care of.

Aside from her street smarts, Elena had the most amazing hazel green eyes. Her long brown curly hair flowed down past her shoulders. She wasn't tall, but this was not important. He was impressed by her quickness and instincts about politics. Her mom was a big deal in Jersey politics for decades. Perhaps she just benefitted from the DNA. Zach would see her for drinks whenever he had an excuse to be in Washington, representing his boss, Vonman with the congressional delegation.

During an especially difficult day running from the House side of the Capitol to the Senate offices, Zach hit a low point. He had not succeeded in getting the support his boss wanted on critical legislation. It was both a professional and personal failure, as he saw it. He was always toughest on himself. He took pride that he knew how to work the system and sell ideas. The drink with Elena was planned ahead of time, but it came at the end of a stressful day. Zach poured his soul out to her, by the second drink. She had that quality about her, she could listen patiently and then offer the most insightful advice. After 30 minutes, Zach couldn't believe how he babbled on. He apologized, when Elena excused herself from the table.

Zach feared he might have bored her with work related stories. "If I thought about impressing this girl," he said to himself, "I've really ended the day in a mess." He was taken by surprise, when she returned from the ladies' room and without warning leaned down and kissed him. This was not a peck on the cheek. She kissed him slowly and with passion. Was she just trying to cheer him up, he wondered? Was it remotely possible, she felt a connection? His head started to throb with excitement. He stood up, pulled Elena close and returned the kiss. "Elena, I don't know how to tell you this, but I really did dream about this moment for so long. I adore you beyond words. I want so much for us to be more than friends."

Elena sat down and returned to her drink. She sat strangely quiet. He couldn't take the silence. "Please, Elena, say something."

"Zach, there's no easy way to tell you this," she said. The pause in their conversation seemed like it would last forever.

"Look, I adore you as well. I have for some time now. But, I'm gay."

"So," Zach responded. "So, you're gay. Do you really think I care? Do you really think that changes how I feel about you?"

Now, it was her turn to sit stunned by his response.

The two young political activists sat in the bar staring at each other. Neither of them knew what to do next. Zach's response took her by surprise. "How could this possibly work?" she asked herself. "How could he not care that I preferred being with a woman? Who says something like that?"

"Come with me," Elena stood up, breaking the silence. She grabbed his hand, as she led him from the bar to his room in the hotel upstairs. There was no explanation given. There was no explanation needed. She had made a decision she had never made before. She wanted to make love to Zach. Their intimacy started slow, as if they were two young people who had never been with a man or woman before. The passion built after that. He couldn't stop kissing her. And she could not get enough of him. What had they discovered in this moment? They were soon drenched in sweat. Elena brushed her wet hair away from her face. They stayed in bed, falling asleep in each other's arms.

After that, Zach would make a point of calling her almost every day. Most of the conversation was small talk, like kids who don't want to leave even though they have nothing left to say. Three weeks would go by before he found an excuse to be in Washington again. The couple met for dinner at the Capital Grill, where they drank wine and talked about the political landscape back in New Jersey. As the evening wound down, Elena moved to the subject she had come to discuss.

"Listen, I don't think we can keep seeing each other," were the words that seared Zach's ears with pain. "You are the first man I have ever been with—and loved, but I can't keep doing this. I think about us daily, but I have a girlfriend. We've been together for two years. What's going on between you and me, well, there's just too much conflict here. I can't handle it."

Zach sat patiently and listened. He hadn't planned this relationship, but he wanted it. "I don't care," he would interject in the conversation. "I can live with this. You set the boundaries and I'll try to live with it."

"What?" Elena asked. "You're going to share me with another person? Could you possibly love one woman and let her love another?"

"You matter to me," he responded. "I just want to have you in my life. If the compromise is to share you, I'm prepared to do so."

Elena was stunned. Her instincts about Zach were right. He was the real deal. She had never met someone like him before. He made it so tempting for her, but she knew he could not change her. She loved women.

He didn't really know if he could share Elena. In his mind, he was ready to try. He hadn't considered what his life might be like in the future. He clung to his romantic idea of being with Elena, regardless of the consequence. He was lucky Elena was more realistic. She left Zach that night without so much as a promise to remain friends. He would never know if she did that to protect him from wanting her and pursuing something he could no longer have—or if she feared she, too, might change her mind.

He never discussed this relationship with anyone. Elena would remain in his heart for many years, long after their brief time together. She agreed to keeping the friendship, though there were limits on how often they'd see each other. Zach's best friend, Mitch Moran, would joke with Zach that it was time to find someone and settle down with. He could never confess to him he had found the girl. It was just complicated.

Mitch had married his high school sweetheart, Linda. In those years, Mitch was more athlete than girl chaser. He pined for Linda for three months, until Zach drove him to the store where she worked. He told Mitch to get out. "I want you to walk into that store and ask Linda Didonato to go to the movies. If you don't come back with a yes, you're walking home." Mitch returned 20 minutes later. He had the biggest smile on his face. These two friends could talk about any subject in their lives. Mitch dealt with meeting his alcoholic father for the first time. Zach agreed to go with him to the bar in New York, where his dad kept offering the two young men drinks. Mitch was taken in by his Aunt Millie at 5 years old, after his mom was sent to a state hospital for schizophrenics. Zach would be there for Mitch, just as his friend would help him when the Goldmans faced health issues. But Elena was not a subject he wanted to share. It would remain someone he valued too much to cover in casual conversation.

It would be a year before Zach found someone again. His life revolved around work, running around New Jersey working on political campaigns and spending time with his nephew, Matthew, whenever he could get Gary to drop him off.

He knew he would fall for Gabby the first time they met at the New Jersey State House. Gabrielle 'Gabby' Bernstein had energy in her eyes and a smile to set a house on fire. She worked in the Governor's Office in Trenton doing research and drafting policy papers. Zach was introduced by a mutual friend, as he waited by the State Assembly chamber to button hole several legislators. She had a mix of humor and sarcasm that hinted at the smarts she brought to the job—and to life.

She also had a way with people that brought them into the conversation and made them feel comfortable. Partisans on both sides of the aisle were drawn to Gabby. Some because they admired how well she operated and succeeded in the male-dominated environment of influence and politics at the time. Some were just attracted to this raven haired, dark skin beauty.

In the months leading up to the Governor's reelection campaign, Zach and Gabby would regularly run into each other at political events. She, like any good operative, had done her homework on Zach, talking with a circle of friends they shared. At first, she saw him as a resource she might call upon. She wanted to leverage Zach's editing skills on major policy papers she prepared for the Governor's office. Gabby wanted polishing on these critical documents, since they would likely become public over time.

He was only too happy to give Gabby a hand. He initially saw it as a way to network and develop relationships with members of the Governor's team. The two operatives would disappear back to her apartment in West Trenton, where Zach would pour over and edit documents. Gabby would try to play host, making them lunch while he worked. She admired his skill for getting documents to be clear and impactful.

She was soon drawn to her new partner in crime, the longer they worked together. He never criticized her writing. Often times, he'd rearrange the structure of the policy papers, based on his experience working at the newspaper. He hadn't actually learned about the "inverted pyramid" style of writing. Trenton State College didn't have a journalism program. But Zach focused on the lessons of getting the most salient information in the first two paragraphs.

Gabby surprised him one day, after pouring glasses of grapefruit juice. He had finished editing his third policy paper. Zach was standing in the kitchen waiting for her to finish making lunch. She set the plates down on the table. She then turned and kissed him. He could taste the grapefruit juice on her lips, tangy and sweet at the same time. This was likely an omen of their relationship.

Zach had never been a "first move" kind of a guy. He hated chasing women. Using one-liners in a bar or party seemed so false and conjured up. Even talk, like, "you are really attractive" or "you have beautiful eyes," would seem contrived and never come across as he intended.

He was definitely attracted to Gabby, but he was leery about stepping over the line from simply being a good friend. He felt let off the hook, when the girl made the first move. She stood in the kitchen French kissing Zach for almost 20 minutes. It was Friday. She was certain no one at the State House would miss her if she didn't return before the weekend. "Do you think we could go upstairs?" she asked him. He stood motionless for a minute, as his brain registered the invitation. His feet followed her to a more private place.

She had shared stories about her German boyfriend, during small talk over their many months together. The details of lovemaking were more than he cared to know. Now that it was his turn. He struggled to recall all the do's and don'ts. But to his surprise, the time in the bedroom was effortless. That's not to suggest it wasn't strenuous. Gabby had a comfort level with herself and her body that he had not experienced. She knew where he had to be and what he had to do in the moment, to fully enjoy their time. She didn't hesitate to stage direct the action. And his physical endurance would be put to the test. He didn't mind learning from her. This had always been his priority, to satisfy his partner. She was equally tuned in to finding Zach's favorite places, which she exploited.

The moments of rest that Friday afternoon were filled with laughter. He wiped the sweat from his forehead. At the end, he could still taste grapefruit juice on her lips. He leaned on his elbow as they made small talk, each expressing how they wondered if this time would ever come. It appeared they both thought about being more than friends, almost from the first time they met. Both were thankful Gabby broke through Zach's reserve. The rest period ended when she decided to start touching him again. He met a self-confident woman, ready to take charge. "Could life get any better than this?"

Zach was several years older than Gabby. He cautioned her they each had visible jobs. They needed to be guarded about their relationship in public. She agreed. She knew the rumor mill would spread stories whether they were true or not. Besides, she knew more time was needed for them to figure out if their passion would grow into a meaningful, long-term relationship.

CHAPTER 63

Selling Insurance

Gary Goldman had made steady progress in his job as an investigator. He learned to take meticulous notes. The attorneys he supported complimented how well he organized files, before cases went to court. And his ability to track down witnesses over the phone won high praise from his immediate supervisor. The one aspect of the job he hated was going out and pounding the streets of urban cities.

Before finishing college, Gary had quit the shoe store and switched jobs to a New Jersey insurance company. He was excited with the idea that he might actually learn about financial products and the insurance business. He was certain that his selling skills had been fine-tuned by convincing women to buy shoes. He liked that insurance companies paid commissions on every life policy paid. He spent a month in classes to learn the basics. At 4 pm, he'd leave to attend courses.

He completed his insurance certificate. The company's headquarters were located on State Street in the City of Trenton. He was given a territory that covered the West and parts of the North Ward. These were primarily minority areas of the City. He discovered that instead of selling insurance policies, his job entailed being a glorified collection agent. He would visit homes to collect delinquent premium payments on car, health and home insurance policies. Instead of commissions, he was paid based on a percentage of the funds he collected.

There were many times Gary knocked on doors where homeowners lived in abject poverty. He had not seen this before. It broke his heart to ask these people to decide between paying their health insurance or buying food. Sometimes to cover his tracks, when he returned to the office, he'd mark on his "call sheet" that no one was home. It wasn't like him lie. It's not how he was raised. Yet, he could not afford to report that his collection efforts failed.

He also experienced the "gamers" or folks who pretended they couldn't pay, because they prefer to spend money on other things like alcohol or drugs. He had compassion for customers who were straight-out poor. He was friendly and, in a few instances, took money out of his own pocket because he couldn't bear to return again. However, the "gamers" were a different lot. He'd arrive at a house. The woman would come to the door with her breasts busting out of her top. Sometimes she'd be holding a child to plead she didn't have the funds to pay. It only took him a minute to figure out who was truly poor and who were the gamers. These women would sweet talk him, telling him how good looking he was. She'd put the child down and touch her breast, while asking him if there were some way for them to have an arrangement. He would resist any invitation to come into the home.

Gary was not street smart. Luckily, he was coached by a friend, Malcom Sandler. Malcom grew up and had worked in Trenton for nearly six years, before getting a promotion to the insurance office in Ewing Township, a nearby suburb. He had a good idea of what Gary would face, when he heard he was given his old neighborhoods. The gamers would trade sex to cover their health or car insurance payments. He also educated Gary about the well-known shake down with Larry Standoff. Larry was a white-guy from Bordentown, who came to work in Trenton before Malcom came on the scene. He didn't mind hooking up with a gamer, if she looked good. He had some regulars that he saw once a month, which is about all he could afford to take out of his pocket. He was sneaky with the home office, sometimes paying only a small part of the premium he had gone to collect. The insurance company added interest charges in these situations, but they weren't about to cancel a client who payed something. The gamer never knew Larry was only giving a partial payment. This allowed Larry to continue the sex he was having with 2-3 different single moms.

His world came crashing down, when he took up with a strikingly good-looking gamer who lived near Calhoun and Spring Street. Maybe Larry was doing this own scam for so long, he got careless. Cora Rodgers came to the door, much like other gamers Larry had met in his travels. She had a beautiful, wide grin and stood almost 5' 8" without shoes on. She had invited Larry into her home several times. She had signaled that she was ready for anything that could help her cover expenses. By the third visit, Larry dove in. She sent her two children into the living area to watch TV. She then took Larry into the back bedroom, where she took off her clothes and lay back on the bed.

Cora didn't look like she had two children. Her stomach was flat and tight. Her breasts were modest in size, but perky. Larry couldn't resist any longer. He stripped off his clothes at record speed. He never wanted any gamer as much as he wanted Cora. She took her time with him, though he behaved like the house was on fire. He was just at the cusp of finishing business, when he heard a man's voice. "Oh, shit," Cora said, "that must be my husband."

"Your husband?" Larry responded.   "Since when did you have a husband?"

"Well, I didn't think it was important to tell you, Cora said. He's usually at work until 10 pm. He's a security guard downtown."

He couldn't get off Cora in time, before an angry voice pushed through the bedroom door.

"What the hell is going on here," the voice grew louder?

"I think I'm going to kill someone today."

Larry had no idea that this was a setup. Cora had done this many times before. Her so-called husband would come in, find her in bed with someone and then threaten physical violence to the both of them. Once the man allowed him to dress, he was given "one opportunity" to make things right. He would agree to the blackmail. He would agree to keep giving money to pay Cora's insurance payments for the next two months. He couldn't believe how lucky he was to get out of that house alive. He would never figure out the whole thing was a scam. Cora split the money with her make-believe husband. Ironically, Cora wouldn't find out until six months later she was also scammed. Larry only paid the company enough money to cover part of her premiums, before he quit the job.

Malcom schooled Gary well. He scared the hell out of him. There were indeed times when Gary was truly tempted to sleep with a client. He wasn't looking for a single moms, but some had just fallen on hard times and were quite attractive. They weren't all gamers. He treated these women with respect. If an overture was made by a woman, it likely happened because Gary was so nice to them. He recognized most of his clients were just struggling to get by. Once he fixed a woman's front door, so she could lock it at night. But regardless of whether the women were genuinely appreciative for an insurance man who gave them advise or tried to help them, Gary knew he could not cross the line.

His experiences while working in Trenton as an insurance salesman influenced him when he became a professional investigator. He had become street smart about cities, but this only made him less enthusiastic about pursuing witnesses for the Public Defender's (PD) Office. Many of his colleagues in the PD, including his supervisor, were former law enforcement officers. Helping clients who were being defended for an alledged crime was safer than serving as a police officer in crime-ridden neighborhoods. Gary, however, had been in the streets of Trenton for 2 years. Being white did not make his job for the PD any easier. He still ran into gang members and drug dealers. No one cared if you were helping anyone. They cared if you were there asking questions about crime and their friends.

During his time at the PD, Gary had learned and excelled in investigative techniques. He had terrific instincts about where to look and find information. His boss thought he was resourceful. While never serving as a police officer, his colleagues still took to Gary. They enjoyed his irreverent sense of humor and his willingness to help others who were working on difficult cases. In return, his colleagues took him to the police firing range to learn how to use a gun. PD staff did not carry weapons, but he wanted to learn if he found himself in a difficult situation. His colleagues also taught him valuable insights on the operating procedures used by local, state and federal law enforcement agencies. After 3 years, Gary knew how to get inter-agency cooperation. He decided it was also time to move on from the PD.

Nick Navarro, who had worked with Gary at the PD, transferred to a new agency called State Gaming Enforcement. New Jersey had legalized gambling in Atlantic City by 1976. However, they wanted to keep organized crime from taking over the casinos. The State Legislature set up very strict rules, which included doing background investigations on all employees who applied to work in a casino. Nick told Gary the job had all the investigative requirements of the PD, but did not require chasing down witnesses in cities across New Jersey.

Gary was ready for any assignment that wouldn't remind him of his days selling insurance. He was also intrigued by the close working relationship Gaming Enforcement had with other law enforcement agencies in New Jersey and at the federal level. As Nick explained, "You might be checking out a front-line casino employee, but you were really investigating any direct or indirect connection he or she might have to a larger criminal enterprise."

It took Gary several months to apply and complete the lengthy job interviews. At the time, there was a lot of competition for these gaming enforcement jobs. The Gaming Enforcement Agency reported in to the State Attorney General (AG), so the staff spent considerable time coordinating with the Criminal Division's efforts to prosecute violations of the Gambling Act.

His application for the job got a boost, with a recommendation from the Public Defender, David Vonman. His reputation for integrity and excellence really counted. Gary stopped by to thank Vonman, before accepting the job.

"I could never thank you enough. You've given me an opportunity to learn and grow at the PD. I will try to make you proud of your endorsement, by the work I know is ahead of me."

"Gary, I often tell your brother, one of my favorite quotes is from a Robert Frost poem, which states that 'nothing gold can stay'. I doubt Frost was referring to "Gold—man," but you've done a good job here. I wish you well. And don't be a stranger, keep me posted on your progress at Gaming."

Gary began his third or fourth career move. He'd joke with friends he was not quite perfected yet. He was like a caterpillar that was slowly growing wings. His days as a butterfly were still ahead of him. Fortunately, in the new job he wasn't completely on his own. Nick introduced him to his fellow investigators, when he arrived. He was able to leverage this goodwill.

CHAPTER 64

The Struggle with Age

Murray Goldman's life had taken an odd turn, and he struggled to accept the infirmities he suffered. He lived at the Veteran's home for almost five years. He prided himself on his independent nature for so long, and, yet, he could no longer be independent. He took to the routine at the home, since he had no choice. His walking was slow. His balance and gait were off. His mind, for the most part, was sharp. He did experience some short-term memory loss.

On occasion, the old Murray would make an appearance. He was never one to be held down or held back. He tried to escape from the home three times. Once, he limped across the hospital grounds to reach the main road. He hitchhiked to the next large town, where he called a taxi to take him to Newark Airport. When he arrived at the airport, he asked the driver to wait so he could go inside and get his son to give him the money for the taxi fare. Except, there was no son inside. He had successfully devised a plan to get himself to the airport, but he had no money and he had no destination. When the police called Franny, she asked Gary to drive to the airport and pay the taxi driver. Murray was brought back to the hospital with a grin of defiance on his face.

Franny and the boys didn't believe Murray was undertaking these adventures to protest living at the VA home. If he was rebelling, it was at the physical condition that sidelined him in life. The VA home was filled with men who, like him, had served their country. Many suffered physical ailments or long-term mental handicaps. Some did not have family or had been estranged from loved ones for decades.

The commitment of Murray's sons to visit him every weekend never wavered. The boys were fast becoming men. Alan and Gary had children. His sons were also workaholics. The pine cones didn't fall far from the tree. Weekends included time for his sons to catch up on projects at home. But, regardless of family or work, making time for their father was a top priority. They tried to bring him home for holidays, though at times that could be difficult.

Visiting their dad was stressful. The first person they'd encounter at the VA home was Luke. He had been a fighter pilot during WWII. The boys never got the whole story, but Luke had been at a VA facility of some sort for more than 25 years. His blond hair was thin and unkempt. He always had more than 3-4 days of beard growth. But the most telling part of Luke's story was how he'd pick up cigarette butts he found on the floor or in ash trays. You'd find Luke pacing back and forth in the entrance hallway. He'd be talking out loud. The story would begin as the fighter squadron was bearing down on the enemy, somewhere over Europe. They didn't notice the German pilots coming at the squadron from the east.

"We lost men that day," Luke would say over and over again, shaking his head as he paced….and paced. "Why did we have to lose so many, many men?"

The story was always the same. Luke was always at his post by the front entrance. He'd look for a butt on the floor and then launch into the attack somewhere over Europe. If Gary or Zach tried to engage Luke, his head would look down at the floor. He'd look to walk left or right, to avoid eye contact or any direct communication. The boys, over time, learned to respect Luke's space. He was not lonely, as they thought. He was simply lost in time. It was a time warp they would never come to understand.

The men at the VA home lived in a small dormitory like setting. Each had their bed and a dresser next to them. Bathrooms were down the hall. The place was always clean. The walls were painted a light blue. This was nothing like the awful conditions the boys found at the Bronx VA hospital, when their dad had his second brain tumor surgery. The Bronx hospital was not clean, the staff tending to the young veterans coming back from Vietnam could care less about them and few of the foreign-born doctors could communicate easily with those suffering war injuries.

Luke was not the only veteran who stood out to the Goldman boys. Harold lived three beds away from Murray. He was near 70 years old and bald. His face looked like he had suffered a stroke. He never spoke. It was unlikely that his sons would ever take notice of Harold, except when Murray pointed him out. The boys would bring their dad snacks or supplies, if he needed anything. While his hair had thinned, Murray always asked for combs. The supplies would be put in his dresser.

"Dad, where's the box of tissues Gary brought you last week?" Zach asked.

"See that guy over there," he responded. "He eats them. I see him come over at night."

Zach looked over at Harold in disbelief. His father must be joking. He walked over to Harold. "Excuse me, but are you eating my dad's tissues?"

Harold's eyes rolled up toward the ceiling. "Oooh, aaah; Oooh, aaah, Oooh, aaah," was all he could get out of Harold. As he spoke, Harold shook his hand up and down. In each hand, he held tissues loosely. The white tissue would fly up and down. It only took a minute for Zach to fully understand the situation.

He backed away and returned to his father. "Ok, dad. Do the best you can to keep the box of tissues in your dresser draw so Harold can't find them. I'll ask Alan to bring another box, next visit."

Luke and Harold were among the Vets who stood out at the home. Many others were simply men who faced physical or psychological issues as they grew older. If the weather was good, the nurse's aides would take men in wheelchairs for a walk around the grounds. If the weather did not cooperate or the men wanted to stay indoors, they had several rooms where they could watch TV all day long.

The boys understood their dad resisted giving in to slow pace and the lack of freedom. He was like a furnace; whose embers have all but faded. And yet a spark still remained. Gary and Alan would bring their children to visit their grandfather. Outside the children would run on the grass, while Murray watched and smiled. He accepted Gary's decision to divorce. In matters of love, their father rarely offered comment or opinion. Gary made a point to visit his father on the weekends when he had Matthew. He was only a toddler, but he gave his grandfather special attention as he ran up and hugged his leg. Grace, Alan's wife, would sometimes come along during the visit. She could still remember Murray, before the second brain surgery. She liked him, because he reminded her of her own father. She had more sympathy for Murray, because he was always such a proud and strong person.

Zach preferred to visit by himself. On a rare occasion, he might bring a girlfriend if he was going to a political event after seeing his dad. He enjoyed taking his father for coffee at the canteen. He would give his dad an update on the campaign or his job. Murray would always ask about Franny, who still struggled with pain daily. Zach would try to coax stories from Murray about growing up in Brooklyn. His dad wasn't always in the mood. He was never a guy who talked a lot. It was an extra special Sunday, when his dad did open up.

Franny Goldman's life became more solitary over time. Her sons were off on their own, raising families and pursuing their careers. She woke each morning with aches and pains. The night was never her friend after the car accident. It seemed like forever, before she could find a comfortable position for her body to relax. When she did finally fall asleep, it was like being drugged. She often woke at 4 a.m. Her body had not moved from where she drifted off. She didn't like taking pills and tried to avoid them. She might lay in bed an hour, before giving in to swallowing pain killers. Again, she'd wake near 8:30 a.m. She got her crutches and walked to the bathroom. The first few steps in the morning hurt the most. She might let out a short scream of pain, but no one was there to hear her.

By 9:15 or 9:30 a.m., she made her way to the kitchen. She didn't have much of an appetite. However, she knew eating was important with more than 15 pills she took throughout the day. She was always mindful to sit close enough to reach the phone. Invariably, one of her boys would call every morning and evening to check on her. Often, she'd hear from more than one son. She felt special when receiving their calls. She loved to hear about her grandchildren. She didn't always understand her sons' stories about their job. She might remind Alan that he should be nice to people, without realizing this was not a trait associated with prosecutors. She might caution Gary about walking around in Newark, when his job was finding witnesses to help defend someone in court.

Franny was very strong willed when it came to her independence, but she didn't like living alone. She often talked about how much she missed having Murray at home, though she knew it was no longer possible. He could not help her and she was not healthy enough to help him. There are times in life when love just isn't able to overcome these limitations. The boys would fight with her to accept help, until she finally compromised. By late morning, an aide would come to the Goldman home. Her name was "Lou," which was short for Louise. Her family had come to the U.S. from Poland. She left her husband in Poland, something to do with his drinking habits. She worked cleaning homes, until her two children were grown. She now worked as a nurse's aide, which paid better money and was easier on her back.

Lou would come three days a week. She'd help her wash and dress. They'd make a point of planning their next great adventure together, where the aide drove them to lunch. Franny's favorite would be the Jewish deli in Fair Lawn where she could get a corn beef sandwich, "extra lean" she'd insist. "And don't forget the pickles." Sometimes, they'd go for Chinese food, when she had a hankering for shrimp with lobster sauce. Wherever they went to eat, Lou knew half the meal was coming home. Franny thought she was always being so economical, buying lunch and dinner at the same time. Lou would follow her instructions to wrap and put half a sandwich etc. in the freezer. During visits, the boys would discover the freezer held more food than anyone could eat in a year.

On occasion, Lou would also drive Franny to the local McDonald's in Paramus. Franny so loved a large order of French fries. She listened to her doctors' instructions on all things, except eating fries. "Lou, it's ok. I can eat the fries. No one has to know. Just don't tell my children. I trust you to keep our little secret."

After lunch, Franny planned some retail therapy. She had plenty of groceries and a closet full of clothes, some not worn for decades. She was not a hoarder. She just didn't have the physical strength to clear out dressers or shelves in the closet. Her children might think she was hoarding, because she had multiples of virtually every kitchen product available. What the boys didn't understand is that the shopping was a way for her to engage with the world. She didn't want to be locked up at home. If she got tired while walking with her crutches, Lou would get her a wheelchair. She'd circle aisles in a clothing store like a vulture smelling blood on the carcass below. Lou would stop often, so Franny could look at price tags on the sleeves. Her father was a tailor. She'd teach Lou that the quality of clothes could be found by rubbing your fingers against the material. "My father knew the schmata business. Here, feel this Lou."

A purchase was finally made by her, if the ticket said 40% off or she fell in love with the color. These shopping adventures created a level of excitement and unpredictability in Franny's life. After a few hours, her energy level was gone. Lou brought her home. She helped her into bed to rest for an hour, while Lou made dinner and relaxed in the kitchen. She'd feed Franny and set her up to watch TV in the bedroom. While she had a remote "gizmo", it was not uncommon for the TV to be on late into the night. Franny could watch only so much TV, but she didn't mind leaving it on. It kept her company to hear the sound. If she got up for the bathroom, the TV lit up the whole bedroom.

Her routine didn't change much. On the days when Lou was not coming to help her, she got herself up, dressed, fed and then back into bed to rest. Her most special time of the day was in the afternoon. She would take her saxophone out every day. She'd begin by playing her scales. This was a warm up for what would follow. She grew up learning and loving music. Her jaw had never fully healed from the car accident. She lost teeth and had to wear dentures. Franny figured out a way to hold the mouthpiece for the sax near one side. So much had been lost in her life, but she would not quit on playing her instrument. She was near 60 years old, but the sound was if it was being played by someone half her age.

The boys would come regularly on weekends with their wives and children. Sometimes they'd just drop by the house if they had an excuse to be in Bergen County. A highlight of a visit for the grandkids was if grandma Franny would play music on her saxophone. Her signature tune was Autumn Leaves. The boys would tell their children it was grandma's favorite song. Not true. She played it because the song was Murray's favorite. She'd get melancholy at times, but this song also reminded her of the special love they shared.

Grandma would also play, "When the Saints Came Marching In." The grandchildren would be encouraged to dance or march around the house. The Goldman boys were amused that mom still had a way of getting their kids to participate in this musical ritual. As youngsters, their mom was insistent each child learn an instrument. Alan began with the accordion, but switched to the saxophone. Zach took up the trumpet and Gary tried his best to learn the clarinet. She'd teach them this one song so they could play together, like they do in a marching band. This was long before the car accident. The boys were young. Franny made them practice walking around the house or in the front yard, while playing. By the time she was done, the boys could almost play the song in their sleep. They'd refer to it as a "lifelong lesson" in music appreciation.

Their mom told the grandchildren about her brother, Lennie, the band leader. She still idolized him and she'd describe how many instruments he could play. None of the Goldman boys argued with their mom. If it made her happy to share these stories, she deserved to enjoy these memories from her childhood. But Lennie meant little to Alan, Zach or Gary. When it mattered most, following the accident, Uncle Lennie was AWOL. From their point of view, he didn't even have the decency to call and check on the boys—or to see how Franny was coping with her recovery. Uncle Lennie only cared about Uncle Lennie. While accomplished as a musician, Gary would still describe him "as a legend in his own mind."

During the holidays, the boys brought Murray home to see Franny— and the grandchildren. If this was not possible, they'd bring their mom to the VA home to see dad. Each of the boys understood how important it was for their parents to maintain the connection, even if their individual health issues worked against them. Nothing ever diminishes love.

CHAPTER 65
Striving for Progress

———

Zach wondered how frustrating it must be for his older brother not to be allowed to discuss his legal cases. Alan couldn't even mention to his family the nature of the cases he worked on or the parties being prosecuted. It was typical to hear details only after the case was finished, from a press conference where his boss, the U.S. Attorney, announced a result or the deal struck with an offender. Even at that point, Alan would not comment or provide any details. "Off limits," he'd tersely reply, if anyone in the family asked him questions.

The two brothers were both rising in their own careers. Zach and Alan spoke, but rarely about anything other than family matters. Zach guarded talking about his career, once it was clear his older brother thought a job at the Post Office should be his life objective. The Goldman boys were independent to begin with, but Alan's strong personality alienated Zach and Gary. In his mind, Alan may have thought he was being protective. His brothers felt he tried too hard to be controlling. And this often sounded like he was discouraging them from pursuing their dreams.

However, it was only a matter of time before the two brothers found their career circles intersecting. Zach had a growing profile in State Government, working for Vonman, and in Democratic politics, from his work on campaigns. The State Chairman contacted Vonman to see if he'd talk to him about joining the Governor's re-election campaign in the late 70s. The Governor had several candidates running against him in the Primary election, which was a clear signal that he lost popularity while in office. This situation made it difficult to find campaign operatives willing to give up their jobs to go work for the Governor. When Vonman asked Zach about the campaign, he emphasized that it was completely his decision. He didn't mind being asked. He liked the Governor. He also valued the Governor's support of Vonman.

Zach volunteered to use the five weeks of vacation time he saved up and take a leave from his job. He didn't want any questions being raised about working in the Primary election from his state job in Trenton. Within 3-4 weeks, a Star Ledger newspaper editorial talked about "the blizzard of endorsements" being won by the Governor. Behind the scenes, he was generating a steady stream of press release announcements for citizen groups that were sent to daily and weekly newspapers across New Jersey. The strategy was to create the perception of a groundswell of excitement.

In the general election, Zach was asked to serve as Chairman of Citizens Committees, which essentially were all the special interest groups who supported a candidate because of a particular issue they championed. The Citizens Committees became a sizable operation in the general election campaign. If you weren't a regular Democratic party member, you could easily fit and work as a member of a special interest group.

Zach strategically targeted 65 major interest groups. These groups included Labor groups for the Governor, lawyers, doctors, teachers, police, firemen, Black Americans, Women and a broad assortment of ethnic American groups. If someone came into the headquarters to volunteer, Harry Landon, Campaign Manager, would send them over to Zach. "That guy just has a knack for knowing how to give folks something meaningful to do."

Since Zach believed volunteers needed tangible things to do to feel connected to the campaign, he'd ask everyone to write a "letter to the editor" of their local daily newspaper and to send copies to their weekly newspaper. The daily papers would only publish a small percent of the letters they received. This steady stream of letters reinforced the perception of widespread support for the Governor. These were not canned or scripted letters. Folks were asked to express in their own words why the Governor should be reelected. Weekly newspapers and special interest magazines were always looking for content to fill their pages. They welcomed publishing letters and photos from local readers.

Zach's staff in the general election included five professionals he handpicked, who had particular knowledge of or connection with a subject or group. The Labor coordinator, for example, had a decade or more experience working with various labor unions across New Jersey. The ethnic coordinator spoke several languages and had a healthy respect for diverse cultures, from South American Latins to distinct Southeast Asian and Far East Asian communities.

The campaign victory in the fall would be celebrated for weeks after. Dinner parties, breakfast celebrations and a long line of social drinking after work. The long struggle to overcome several Primary candidates and then struggle to regain support among voters surprised even the most hardened news commentators. Everyone had written off the Governor's chances of reelection, but he did win. And in the end, he won in a virtual landslide election with 56% of the vote.

Election nights are cathartic and strange. The hotel ballroom is often filled with supporters who may not have done any real work on the campaign. Nothing wrong with these folks wanting to share in celebration. Campaigns have a way of attracting people who want to be part of something. They may show up at campaign offices, just to see what's going on. They don't always volunteer to do any work.

Then there's the campaign staff. They walk around election night hugging everyone they worked with or met during the campaign. There is a kinship the actual workers feel with each other. Victory has a way of setting aside differences and hard feelings that erupt over the three-month pressure cooker of deadlines and campaign setbacks.

The candidate's family often crows with confidence, "We knew he'd do it. Never a doubt in our mind." But everyone working on the campaign knows better. Everyone doubts the campaign strategy and the people managing the campaign. Victory is the only vindication.

Campaigns bring together people who are passionate about candidates, issues—and life in general. When the campaign is over, the energy sparked between people may explain how love affairs happen. For some, these affairs set a new bar for measuring how they want to spend the future. Some may never return to their normal lives. Some may find themselves drawn to another campaign staffer in a moment of shared passion and sacrifice, but recognize these involvements are artificial. They welcome returning home to families. Lastly, there are many who just go through the campaign season wanting to do a good job; win an election and go about the rest of their lives feeling at this one time they had "made a difference."

The greatest friendships are forged in the heat of battle during a campaign. Some of the most embarrassing moments of your life may also be laid bare or open to criticism, since campaigns are always under the microscope from those who have traveled this road before you. Years will go by. Stories will be told and retold with varying shades of detail and truth, as memories fade. But everyone who works on a campaign will be changed by it, to a lesser or greater degree. These are life altering –and, hopefully, enriching times.

Almost six months after the campaign, life for Zach was returning to normal. He had returned to work with Vonman.

Gary, meanwhile, had been working on his biggest case ever. He was reviewing files for a new casino, The Beauregard, in Atlantic City, when he first started to notice some strange patterns and connections. The "Pit Boss" application for Roddy Roberts had several gaps of employment. The second tip off was his movement around the country, including New York, Vegas and Miami. Gary could not find any criminal offenses, but there was something about the guy that made him want to probe further. He kept Roddy's application in a folder on his desk, marked suspicious.

A few weeks into his review, Gary found another odd employment form for Peter Pratrici at the same casino. Patrici's application also had gaps in work. Gary decided to check among his colleagues and encouraged them to begin looking at overall hiring patterns by the casino, instead of separate employment forms. Gary and Ward Seagirt, a former State Police officer, teamed up to drill down on this casino. Seagirt had been with the State Police for nearly a decade, before an "on duty" accident chasing a guy down the

Garden State Parkway permanently messed up his left leg. He was older than Gary, but they worked well together.

Gary's experience at the PD prepared him. The two investigators found 10 questionable employment applications. This was not a large number among hundreds of people who might work at the casino. Their supervisor wasn't certain these "isolated" cases warranted more investigative time. The N.J. Gaming Enforcement had the right by law to simply deny employment to anyone, without justification or appeal. Why not just deny the 10 applications and move on?

A friend of Gary's at the FBI helped break the case open. He found Roddy Roberts was really Ralph Robertini, with a well-established record of minor crimes stretching back 15 years. Seagirt wanted to hold back sharing the information until the investigators could complete the background checks on the 10 suspicious forms. Several weeks would pass before their back and forth with the FBI could corroborate their findings. Both Gary and Seagirt were shocked to find aliases and varying degrees of criminal behavior for all 10 of the applicants to The Beauregard. "Walt, this is no longer a coincidence," Gary told him. "How could this occur without someone in management of the casino being aware? Is there more going on here below the surface?"

The goal in New Jersey was to stop organized crime from slowly infiltrating and taking over the casino industry. Granting a casino license was so strict that no legit company would dare jeopardize their investment by lax hiring of new employees. After reviewing their finding with their supervisor, it was clear someone high up at The Beauregard was trying to cover up. Gaming Enforcement put the regional FBI office on notice. The NJ Attorney General's office alerted the Justice Department in Washington. Gary and Walt Seagirt were assigned to work on the Task Force to quietly investigate, as they moved up the food chain at The Beauregard.

The work of the Task Force continued for several months into the spring of 1978. Gary and Walt traveled to Maryland and Delaware to compare findings with local law enforcement in those states, where legalized gambling was going on. They did eventually identify Louis "Lou" Lebowski, Executive Vice President at The Beauregard, as the key contact who was helping organized crime. The Board of Directors at The Beauregard were unaware of Lebowski's criminal connections, which only underscored how insidious the threat could be.

New Jersey publicly announced the shutting down of The Beauregard casino for six months, until the Board and management were forced to restructure the company. Half the executives and a third of the employees initially hired to launch the casino were gone. For some, it was tragic they were caught up in the steps taken by investors to salvage The Beauregard's casino license. Many of these folks were innocent of any connection to organized crime, but the Board of the casino was determined to show New Jersey they would take whatever drastic actions were needed.

The actions taken against The Beauregard included a substantial fine, which was intended to set the bar in the industry for what New Jersey would not tolerate. Owners were responsible for their employees, whether on the front lines or sitting in the executive suite.

While Gary and Walt Seagirt were just doing their jobs, their snooping uncovered the largest effort ever undertaken by organized crime. Their names were never mentioned in the press, since the work of Gaming Enforcement was done in secret. Each of them, however, would receive a commendation from the NJ Attorney General and a small bump in pay. But it was never about the glory. These two were motivated in their own way to simply prove they were right about their investigation. Whatever baggage Gary may have had from his years growing up a Goldman, these insecurities were replaced by a new-found confidence. He would never doubt himself again.

For weeks after the investigation was concluded, Gary was walking around on a cloud. He took Matthew with him to visit his father at the VA home. His brothers warmly congratulated Gary once he took them through the behind the scenes action. Alan, of course, started off the conversation the way he always did, "Look, I'm sorry, but I don't know what the fuck you do for a living? Ok, so you figured out where the bad guys were hiding. Did they give you a medal for that?"

Alan really did understand what Gary had accomplished, having served as a federal prosecutor. However, it was not in his nature to heap praise on his brothers.

For his part, Gary only cared about one opinion. He took his father for a walk outside on the grounds of the VA home, pushing his wheelchair as Matthew ran onto grass. His son was still very young, but Murray so enjoyed watching him. Matthew chased butterflies and picked yellow dandelion flowers. He sat with his dad explaining the work he did on the casino investigation. His father listened for nearly a half hour. He was surprised at how his dad followed the story. He actually understood what he was talking about and why it was so important. At the end, his dad simply smiled and said, "Good, Gary. You did good." While some might have expected more, it was more than enough for this proud son.

He called Matthew over and watched as his son scrambled onto Murray's lap. His father sat quietly as Matthew reached up and softly grabbed his face. Matthew was talking to himself, sitting on his grandfather. He clapped his hands. After a short period, he was ready to climb down and run off onto the grass again. Gary's day was complete. He could see how pleased his father was to have this time with Matthew. How could he know how short lived these opportunities really are?

The ride home was joyful. Gary played the radio. He tried to find songs that Matthew might recognize, but it didn't really matter. The boy was happy singing to himself, until half-way home when he fell asleep. He kept looking in the rear-view mirror. He loved watching Matthew. His son was living with his mom. He missed waking up in the morning, when Matthew called out to come get him. There is always distress for a parent in divorce. Gary, however, was not about to let this day be marred by his circumstance. He dropped Matthew at Alicia's apartment and drove home, still excited about his day.

CHAPTER 66

Knock on the Door

The week ahead went by quickly. Zach was finishing remarks that Vonman would give at a mental health conference in Miami. Vonman's department had been given responsibility for representing the rights of the mentally handicapped. The lead lawyer working for Vonman was Michael Bremberg, who successfully argued before the NJ Supreme Court that someone being committed to a psychiatric hospital had a right to be represented by a lawyer. In the decade before this case was brought, it was common to find senior citizens who were locked away and committed because their children didn't want to take care of them. The hospitals for mentally ill patients were also used as a dumping ground for juveniles, who acted out at home with parents. The hospitals had little oversight or controls. Patients were beaten by staff, food was withheld to force compliance, drugs were administered to control behavior and patients were held in solitary conditions for indefinite periods of time.

Greystone Psychiatric Hospital in the 1970s had space for 350 patients, but it housed thousands. These institutions were "out of sight, and out of the public mind." Bremberg brought several lawsuits that resulted in landmark decisions in New Jersey—and precedent setting across the U.S. The right to counsel at a psychiatric hearing was guaranteed to protect against unnecessary commitments. A second case required patients to be held and treated in the least restrictive setting possible. This litigation forced the State of New Jersey to eliminate overcrowding and horrible hospital conditions. The State had to build a series of group homes to house patients who didn't need to be locked away.

Vonman shared Bremberg's passion for protecting those who were most vulnerable in society. He worked with Bremberg on legal strategy, found resources to fund additional lawyers to help on these issues and he regularly spoke out to further these issues at public forums. The New Jersey legal cases would help establish new national standards reshaping the treatment of the mentally ill or mentally handicapped across the U.S. Zach admired Bremberg. He was one of the smartest lawyers he had ever met. He was thin and wore thick wire rim glasses. Zach guessed he was six years older than him. He would never be mistaken for the athletic guy. He was always carrying books and reading them in his office. Colleagues would joke that he was likely that way since he was a kid. But his colleagues shared Zach's view that he was one of the smartest lawyers around. He worked closely with Bremberg on bills introduced into the Legislature that would further codify the rights and treatment of patients. Bremberg came to respect Zach's ability to navigate the politics at the state house.

Vonman had been invited to give a major speech at a national mental health conference. He would outline the issues and strategy pursued in New Jersey. Vonman would advocate the urgency of changes required by Congress. Zach's speechwriting skills were never fully tested, since Vonman was such a gifted speaker. Perhaps it was his training as a trial lawyer, but Vonman could get up and speak for almost an hour without notes or a script. He was also very down to earth when he spoke. He often interjected humorous stories to reinforce points he was making. His speechwriter's best hope was that the 10-12 pages he'd written could be used as an outline. Zach always included statistics and quotes that his boss could lift from the remarks, if he chose to depart from reading the text. He was confident that Vonman would make him look good, especially when he started out by saying, "I have a speech prepared by a bright young man from my office."

Zach and Vonman traveled to Florida on Sunday afternoon to get settled before the conference began Monday evening. Vonman was scheduled to serve as the luncheon speaker on Tuesday. It was not uncommon for Zach to switch hats, from lobbyist representing Vonman in the state legislature, to speechwriter, to political lieutenant working with the NJ congressional delegation and sometimes as an advance man, coordinating Vonman's appearance at venues and working with the press who covered these events.

At dinner, he told Vonman he planned to check out the ballroom in the morning. He'd meet with the conference staff to walk through the order of speakers and the introduction material he sent the week before. Where Vonman would sit and who was next to him was all part of the briefing he planned to give his boss mid-morning. He assumed Vonman would spend a quiet morning, reading the newspapers, going over the draft remarks and checking in with the office back in New Jersey.

Vonman and Zach enjoyed an easy rapport, especially when traveling. Away from the office, it was easier to let their guard down. Vonman was an unassuming guy. If he had an ego, it was not apparent. In the years when he served as a General Counsel to the Governor, he would often arrive early at the state house. He would head down to catacombs under the capital and have coffee with the janitors, where they would talk sports or local news in Trenton. No one referred to him as Mr. Vonman during these regular visits. It was just a group of guys drinking coffee with David.

In Miami, they swapped stories about their early years. Vonman grew up with a single mom, in an urban area. He was a brilliant lawyer and a street-smart kid. He worked his way through college. He was ambitious but he didn't wear it on his sleeve. He could tell a joke and he enjoyed hearing funny stories. "You can do serious stuff with your life," Vonman was fond of saying, "but you also have to laugh at yourself occasionally." I He particularly enjoyed hearing some of the behind the scenes stories from Zach about the Governor's reelection campaign. Zach had a knack for imitating some of the major characters in the campaign. The mannerism in these impressions were on target and poked fun at their peccadillos. The two of them would laugh late into the evening.

Vonman didn't hesitate to have a few "pops" or drinks at dinner. On a trips to Washington, he'd quote Winston Churchill that "you should never trust a man who doesn't drink." The attribution of that quote has been disputed for many years, but Vonman didn't care who said it. He believed that nondrinkers were somehow afraid of letting their guard down—and having others discover their true selves. Zach, of course, had a different view. He wasn't shy pointing out to Vonman the harm drinkers can cause, if they're out of control. Vonman knew about Zach's family. He understood his reserve, when it came to drinking. He never tried to keep up with his boss' tolerance for alcohol. Rather than get sloppy, he would nurse his drink.

The night ended early. The two men did not lose focus on why they had come to Miami. There was plenty of time to laugh and celebrate afterward. Zach had a mentor who shared his passion for trying to change the world. He admired Vonman. He challenged him to learn and sharpen his skills; to work harder; and to recognize that leadership was leveraging the best from people around you.

The knock came suddenly. It was very early the next morning. Zach had showered but was not fully dressed. Vonman's room was next door. Zach heard the knock from the door adjacent to his room. He turned the lock to let Vonman enter.

His boss spoke slowly, "Zach, your mom is trying to reach you. The hotel put her through to my room. I'm sorry, but she has some bad news. I'll wait for you downstairs."

Zach couldn't fully process Vonman's message. He worried his mom might have fallen and injured herself. He sat down on the bed to wait for the call. Vonman left and closed the door behind him.

"He's gone," Franny said. Zach could hear her crying. She tried her best to calm herself. She fought through her tears, "Your father is gone. He died this morning. The hospital contacted me an hour ago."

"I don't understand," he replied.

"I just called Alan. I'll call Gary next. The only information they gave me is that they found him slumped over in his chair at breakfast. You'll have to make arrangements to get home."

As the words started to sink in, Zach refused to accept the news. His mother and father had weathered many storms. How could this happen now?

"Mom," he began, "I'm so sorry. I'm sorry you're alone. I wish I could be there right now." She could hear the emotion in Zach's voice. He began to cry. She knew this moment would be difficult for her boys. Murray was only 61 years old.

The conversation with mom was short. Zach called the airlines, but the earliest flight home would not leave until late afternoon. He would be trapped in Florida for nearly six hours. The plane would not arrive in Newark until dinner time. He arranged for a car service to pick him up and take him to Paramus. After completing his travel arrangements, he sat in his room. "Why did I have to be so far from home?" He knew his older brother would have to handle things until he got there. The custom was to bury the person by the next sundown. Zach felt angry and frustrated to be so far away from his family.

He packed his bag and threw on some clothes. Vonman was waiting in the lobby. He put his hand on Zach's shoulder. "I'm really sorry about your dad," he told him. "Do you need help with the travel back to New Jersey? Look, my talk isn't until this afternoon. Why don't we get some breakfast? We can spend time together before you have to leave for the airport."

Franny had given Vonman the bad news. He tried to assure her that he would look out for her son and get him home. He knew the family history. Unlike Zach, he did not grow up with a father. He enjoyed hearing the stories Zach shared. He admired all the Goldman boys for their dedication going to see their father so regularly at the VA home.

Vonman asked him if his dad had been ill lately. His mom told him that he died at breakfast. "I understand the nurse's aide asked my dad if he wanted more coffee. My dad said no. The aide turned around to give food to another patient. When he turned back a few minutes later, my father was gone. They believe he had a heart attack."

There are times when even the most gifted orator can find him or herself speechless, unable to express their feelings. Until this crisis, Vonman may not have consciously realized how fond he was of Zach. He could see how much pain he was in, but he didn't have wisdom or words to offer at breakfast. He waived his hand at Zach, when his valued staffer started to change the subject and talk about work or the speaking engagement. His reaction reminded

Zach how his dad would sometimes waive off one of his sons from dwelling on a subject. Vonman wanted Zach to talk about his dad and how his brothers would handle the news. He had trouble finding answers to offer him. Mostly, he listened.

Zach figured he'd need extra time to reach the airport and get his ticket. He was mindful that Vonman still had to get ready for the big dinner Monday night. He thanked his boss as they walked over to the taxi line. Vonman put his hand on his shoulder again. He would not make the funeral, since the conference ran for two more days. He asked him to give his mom and his brothers his sympathy. He apologized for not getting back in time. Zach made it into the cab and to the airport without letting go of his emotions.

He called his mom before boarding the plane. Alan contacted the VA nursing home to see if he could learn any more details about dad's death. His body would not be released until evening. Zach did not have to worry about delaying the funeral. Alan still needed a funeral home to pick their father up from the VA facility. He contacted Robert Schoen's Menorah Chapel on Route 4, which the Goldman family had used when Murray's father passed away. Zach started to cry on the phone, "Mom, please tell Alan I'm sorry I wasn't there to help him. I wish he didn't have to handle this alone."

Franny tried to calm Zach, "I don't want you to worry. You'll be home tonight. Tomorrow, you can go with your brother to make the arrangements."

Sitting on the airplane ride home, he obsessed that Alan had to handle getting their father's body from the VA facility by himself. "I should have been there," he'd tell himself over and over. "I can't believe I'm so far away. I feel so helpless." This was the first time he had ever agreed to sit by the window on an airplane, but this was the only option on short notice. It turned out to be a blessing. Zach cried half-way home, looking out the window to hide his red face from the two travelers sitting in his row of seats. So much had been lost.

Alan Goldman had been sitting at the kitchen table with his children, Sara and Blake, when the phone rang. He had just finished a cup of coffee. He knew immediately when he heard Franny's voice that something was terribly wrong. She had trouble getting the words out. Alan could tell she was crying.

"Mom, what's going on?" he asked.

"Alan, you father died this morning."

The words pierced Alan like a jagged knife. He had not known this type of pain before. He paused for a minute, asking his kids to go in the other room so he could hear grandma.

Franny did not have many details. "They think he had a heart attack. He was finishing breakfast. The aide asked him if he wanted more food or coffee. Dad said he was ok. They began feeding another patient. When he turned back, your father was keeled over in his chair. It was very quick, they told me."

Alan stood silent for several minutes. "Alan, are you there?" his mom asked. I need your help. Can you call the hospital to see how we can make arrangements? Your brother, Zachary, is in Florida. I have to call him to let him know what's going on." Murray's sudden death brought to the surface many conflicting feelings Alan had struggled with over the years. His teenage anger had given way as his dad's health failed him. As he became an adult, he was gripped by feelings of sympathy. But the overriding emotion that engulfed his father's death was guilt.

He never questioned whether he was his father's favorite. It was obvious to him—and his brothers. For much of his life this idea both inspired and challenged him to succeed. His confidence came from the special status he held in his father's life—and now it was gone.

After he hung up the phone, he sat down and buried his head in his hands. He cried until his body trembled from exhaustion. Sara went to find Grace. "Mommy, daddy is crying in the kitchen. I think he was on the phone with Grandma."

Grace knew better than to coddle him. It was not her way. It was not what he wanted. Grief is solitary. Alan needed time to come to himself. Grace went over and put her hand on his neck. She leaned down to tell him how sorry she was. She knew only the loss of his dad could unsettle him in this way. "Alan, I'm here. I'm so so sorry. I love you. Take whatever time you need. I know there are things you'll have to take care of."

Grace broke the news to Sara and Blake. She encouraged them to go in and hug their dad. There would be no school today. After 30 minutes, Alan had calmed himself. He called the office to postpone motions he had in court. He then called the VA home and Schoen's funeral home. Once he knew his father's body would not arrive until evening, he decided to wait for Zach to make the arrangements with Robert Schoen.

Sara had just turned 7 years old and Blake was 5. They understood the idea of death, but they never thought their grandpa would die. Alan spoke with them in the kitchen. "Grandpa died this morning. This is a very sad day for me, for uncle Zach, Gary and especially Grandma. Your Grandma had known Grandpa for almost their whole life. They grew up in the same neighborhood. Like your mom and me, they got married and raised a family."

Sara began to cry. She knew there was no coming back. When a person dies, you never see again. Blake sat quietly, his head looking at the floor. "Can you tell me what you remember about Grandpa?" he asked the children.

"He was very large," Blake responded. "I liked it better when he was sitting down so I could see him. He use to grab me, as I ran through the house. He could pick me up with one hand. I'd sit on his lap and he'd tickle me. Then he'd put me down and I'd run off."

"Sara, what do you remember?"

"I remember Grandpa had trouble walking. At times, he'd limp when he walked around the house. What I remember the most was the way he smiled, when we played with him. He couldn't chase us, but if he grabbed us there was no getting away. He was so strong."

"What I want you both to think about today is what you remember about your Grandpa. It may be hard for you to understand, when a person dies we don't see them again. We can look at photos, which we'll do tomorrow with the family. We can tell you stories. Each of us will have a favorite story about Grandpa. But the most special thing to keep with you is your own memories about the time you spent with him.

I know it wasn't easy for you. Visiting Grandpa at the VA nursing home couldn't have been as much fun as when we brought him to Grandma's for the holidays. As you grow up, there are many things you experience that will fade in your memories. I don't want you to think this is the day my grandpa died. I want you to save all the things you remember about him. Tell these stories to Grandma. Tell them to your uncles, and don't forget about your cousin Matthew. Tell the stories to your friends when you go back to school. If you do this, Grandpa will always be with you. His kindness and love will guide you, just as it guided your dad all these years."

The tears streamed down Alan's face, as he spoke to his children. A young child can see pain. They don't have to be told their father was hurting. He was trying his best to encourage them not to let death rob them of their memories. Sara did what she always had the wisdom and insight to do, she went over to her dad and hugged him. She hugged him so tightly that he had to take notice through his tears. Blake would follow her lead. He grabbed his father's arm and hugged it.

Grace always had an intuitive sense of what needed to get done and the planning required. She waited for Alan to finish with the children and complete several calls to his boss and colleagues at the office. She asked the children to watch TV or play in their room. Mom was headed out to get food for the larger Goldman family who would gather tomorrow, a day before the funeral. Alan never worried about the social aspects of his life. He had a partner, who thought ahead about what was needed and she always stepped up.

Franny called Gary last. He was still in bed, though he was not alone. Gary's weekends were filled with women. He could never get enough and he had little regard for standards. He was not looking to find someone and settle down again. He had been there and done that. On the alternate weekends, when he had Matthew, Gary would try to be the best dad possible. He'd take Matthew to the park. He had his son work with him so he could teach him about tools, just as his father had done. But on free weekends, he would start his regular routine on Friday at the local bar.

He was always honest with the women he dated. Dinner, dancing, drinking and shtupping were his priorities, but not in any particular order of importance. Gary never rushed the moment. If he didn't have sex with every woman, he didn't see it as a loss. Alan and Zach could never figure out why girls, later women, were so drawn to their younger brother. The secret was that his priorities did not have to include sex. Women were drawn to his low-key and fun-loving style. The women set the expectations and they made their own decisions, free from the pressure most guys put on them. Ironically, women who are free to choose for themselves can be quite aggressive.

One of Gary's favorite girlfriends was laying naked in the bed with him, when his mom called. Her name was Eva Perez. He often called her his "gypsy woman," because of her jet-black hair and dark features. Her eyes were light blue. Gary wasn't always that particular about the women he dated. Some were less than attractive, but then he often saw something in them that others overlooked. However, Eva was different. She was strikingly beautiful. She was tall, five foot eight inches, with athletic shoulders,….and a flat mid-section. At first sight, she might be taken for a dancer, a yoga instructor or a volleyball player.

Franny's voice sounded strange on the phone. He sat straight up in bed, when she began to speak. "Gary, I'm sorry to disturb you this morning, but your dad passed away two hours ago."

"Wait. What? What did you say?" Gary asked in disbelief. He stood up and walked out of the bedroom to the sliding glass door in the living room of his apartment. The sun was bright and shining through the drapes.

"Gary, he's gone. Your father is gone."

Gary held the back of the phone to his face, as the tears rolled down his cheeks. He paused to let the news sink in. "I don't understand. I just saw him last week with Matthew. He seemed fine. I can't believe this. Are they certain it was dad? That place has so many people. Maybe they made a mistake?"

Franny repeated the story she had shared with Alan and Zach, about Murray keeling over at breakfast. "They believe he had a heart attack, but it was very quick. There was nothing anyone could do."

It took Gary several minutes to fully grasp the situation. While he had lost his father, his mother had lost her soulmate. Gary began to realize that a separation did not diminish the loyalty and love his parents shared for more than 40 years.

"Mom, I don't know what to say," he said as his voice cracked with emotion. "You and dad struggled for so long together. I don't think I've ever known two people more devoted to each other. I will drive up to be with you, as soon as I can shower.

Mom, I love you. We tell you as often as we can. Please, you have to be strong now. We need you in our lives. You have to help us get through this."

As he hung up the phone, Eva came into the living room with a sheer robe covering her. She had heard most of the conversation. She could see Gary was in shock staring out the window. Her instincts were to try and comfort him, but she knew he needed space. She walked over to him and hugged him gently. "You need to shower and go see your mom. I'll try to straighten up the apartment. Take as much time as you need. It's the weekend, there's no work today. I will be here when you get back. I do not want you to be alone."

Gary put his arms around Eva and pulled her close. He valued her above many of the women he dated. She truly cared about him. He appreciated that her first thought was to be there when he returned. He went to take a shower and dress. Eva made coffee. She toasted muffins she found on the kitchen counter. Gary was gone in 45 minutes. It would take him a little over an hour to get to his mom from his apartment in East Windsor.

Alan drove from his apartment in Fair Lawn to pick Zach up early on Monday. His younger brother arrived at the family home in Paramus late the night before. He was drinking coffee with his mom in the kitchen when Alan walked in. Alan spent several minutes hugging Franny. He then went over to Zach. It was out of character for Alan, but he reached down and hugged his brother. It had been a long time since the siblings showed feelings like this.

The two brothers left for the funeral home to discuss arrangements. Gary had spent Sunday afternoon with Franny, driving back to East Windsor in the evening before Zach got home. He told his mom he would be back mid-day on Monday to go over the funeral details with his older brothers. Franny spent part of Sunday and Monday speaking with friends and family. Each of the Goldman boys would alert their office and let them know a time on Tuesday for the funeral service. They all agreed to ask Rabbi Rackowitz to conduct the service.

Robert Schoem was very kind to Alan and Zach, when they arrived. This was a large and well-known Jewish funeral home near Paramus. Mr. Schoem insisted on personally helping the boys with the arrangements. He had known their father for many years, working and living in the same community. Mr. Schoem had served on the Board of the Jewish Community Center with Murray.

Mr. Schoem could tell from the conversation how much these sons loved their father. He was so proud of these young men, since he had such respect for Murray's honesty as a businessman and for his contributions to the Jewish community. He tried to guide the boys. "As you can see, we have a room filled with different types of coffins. You can spend a fortune for some of these ornate ones, but please understand that it won't bring your dad back.

If you're asking me, Jewish customs call for modesty when dealing with a funeral. I can't always say that to a paying customer. Traditionally, a plain pine box like this one on your left is appropriate. The idea is simple, whether rich or poor, in death we are all equal. The Rabbis teach us, the only thing that matters at this point is a person's spiritual nature.

I think your dad would prefer this simple pine casket. My memories of him was a hard-working guy, a guy who worked with his hands, a guy who respected and treated people well.

He didn't wear his wealth or religion on his sleeves, like some folks at the Synagogue. Your dad was always looking to help someone who may not have money. I guess it was his way of giving back."

Alan and Zach listened intently to Mr. Schoem. They spent a half hour with him and found stories about their dad that lifted them up during this painful period. There was paperwork to fill out. The funeral would be scheduled on Tuesday at 11 a.m. The service would be held in the funeral home's Chapel, followed by the drive to Beth El Cemetery in Paramus. Mr. Schoem had called ahead to Beth El to coordinate the details. It was just like their father to have planned ahead for the entire family. The boys just shook their heads smiling, but in disbelief. They were unaware that dad had bought an entire section of 12 plots at the cemetery, enough to cover the family and future spouses of his sons.

As they finished their business, Mr. Schoem stood up, "Do you want to see him?" he asked? "Give it some thought, I'll be right back." He left the room so Alan and Zach could talk. Their father's body had been picked up late yesterday. The boys had brought a suit dad hadn't worn in years. Normally, the deceased in buried in a shroud or cloth robe-like garment, but this didn't seem appropriate for their father. "Maybe we should take one more look," Alan asked his brother.

This was not the right move. Zach knew it in his heart. "No, you are not going in there. You need to remember him as he was. If you go inside, the memory you will carry the rest of your life will be how he looked after he died. No, that is not the way you should remember him."

He had never been so emphatic with Alan. He wasn't asking his older brother, he was telling his older brother. The entire trip home from Florida, all he could think about was how his family would handle his father's death. Yes, he mourned. But there would be time for that. Zach focused on what he could do to help his siblings and his mom cope.

The two sons thanked Mr. Schoem when he returned to the office. Alan accepted his brother's decision. They wanted to remember dad as he was. Seeing him now would be very difficult. Mr. Schoem wanted them to have the option, but he agreed with their decision. The boys returned home to have a family discussion about the funeral.

Gary arrived mid-day on Monday. Franny ordered a food delivery, so the boys could eat and talk. Aside from the Jewish holidays, this was the first time the family had been together in a few years. Alan started to take charge, as he often did, defining how the service should be conducted. It wasn't that his brothers didn't have their own point of view, but since they were children Alan always felt it was his responsibility as the oldest. He outlined that the Schoem staff would bring dad's coffin into the Chapel. The boys would walk in with Franny, helping her to a seat in the front row. They would sit next to her. The Rabbi would then say prayers and make remarks. Afterward, everyone would exit. Some family would follow to the cemetery and then back to the Paramus family home where the boys agreed to sit Shiva.

"No. NO!" Zach interrupted. "That's not how it's going to happen."

Gary and Alan sat back, in shock at Zach's forceful behavior. They had never seen him act like this before. The family sat hushed waiting for him to speak.

"This is our father. I don't want strangers describing or defining his life. I agree it's great to have Rabbi Rackowitz participate. But no one knows this man the way we do. I don't want anyone saying 'he was ill a long time, maybe it's better he's not suffering.'

Alan, you're the first born. This is your responsibility. You have to step up and speak for dad—and for our family. It's time for you to deal with your feelings about dad. I'm not sitting here quietly. Our father deserves better than this."

He had planned these comments for two days. This wasn't just about eulogizing his father. Zach felt confident he was plenty capable of giving this speech himself. And part of him really wanted to give this speech. He had so much love and emotion to share in telling stories about his dad. But he thought it was more important for Alan to come clean; to deal with the years of pent up guilt and conflict he felt from his teenage years. As he matured, he grew to understand more about the nature of relationships between men and women. The world was not as black and white as he initially believed. However, as he gained insights about life and his father's actions following the car accident, this only increased the guilt he carried around. He professed hating his dad for several years. He couldn't let go of the guilt over things he said out loud and harsh feelings he harbored. As an adult, Alan tried his best to be kinder to his dad. His father likely never understood the source of his son's disrespectful behavior, but Alan knew. He would grow up, but Alan's greatest difficulty was forgiving himself.

Zach's insisting that Alan speak at the funeral was an act of love. He wanted his older brother to heal old wounds. He needed, in this moment of grief, for Alan to move on. It seemed an odd decision, considering how he suffered beatings from Alan when they fought over their dad. A certain distance would always exist between them. But Zach didn't care. He believed at this critical moment, Alan needed to finally confront and let go of his guilt.

The room stood quiet for several minutes, before Alan spoke. He tried twice to deflect Zach's insistence that he speak at the funeral. Then Gary joined in, "Maybe Zach is right. I'd rather have someone from the family talk about dad."

Alan got up from the table and paced around the kitchen. Zach had touched a nerve. They could all see it. Alan couldn't let go of his anxious energy. For a few minutes, it almost seemed as if he was talking to himself as he circled the room. Finally, he left to walk down to the end of the house by the family room. "We're not done here," Zach called after him. His younger brother was not letting him off the hook. The use of the words, "first born," were purposeful. He was certain this euphemism would remind Alan he was not only first, but also his father's favorite. He did not want him to walk away, without realizing his family had thrown down the gauntlet. He would not escape their expectations of him.

By the time he walked back to his brothers, he looked at his mom, "Ok, I'll do it. I'll talk tomorrow."

CHAPTER 67
He Never Quit

———

The Chapel at the funeral home was full by 10:30 a.m. There were two ante rooms where a steady stream of visitors flowed to express their regrets to the Goldman family. Alan, Zach and Gary would periodically introduce a colleague or friend from work to their mom. She sat off to the right side of the room, where relatives of the Sugar and Goldman families would congregate. Uncle Sammie stood with the boys for several minutes when he arrived. His eyes kept tearing up at the loss of his big brother. After, he went to hug and sit next to Franny. Murray's brother, Asher had driven from New York with two of his sons. He circled the boys asking questions about what happened.

The boys were respectful, but Asher had never visited his older brother during the years he lived at the VA home. Berta, Murray's sister, arrived just in time for the memorial service. She expressed regrets to Franny and then took her seat in the Chapel. The Goldmans were surprised that she showed up at the cemetery. She came with two of her daughters.

The sight of Bob O'Brien lifted the boys. He was one of Murray's oldest friends in Paramus. He was crying like a baby when he came up to Murray's sons. Each of the boys had their memories of meeting O'Brien, either at work or on the little league field. Further back in the funeral line, Alan could see the blonde bouffant hairdo that belonged to Dottie Gleeson. He had last seen her sitting on Murray's lap following the car accident. She seemed so old now. Her hair was like a blinking signal on a truck, but it was teased and thinning. Her lips were still painted bright ruby red. It appeared she was limping, though he couldn't figure out why. He carried hatred around for this woman over the years. Now, he could only feel sorry for her. He accepted his mom's story about dad. Maybe Alan never really understood what he saw that day. In death, none of this history mattered anymore. If there was a choice, he preferred an imperfect father than to lose his presence in life.

Gary was the first to observe how many people showed up for the funeral. He kept asking his brothers if these folks were people they knew from work? Many of the visitors went up to the sons and introduced themselves as former friends and customers of dad's business. Eventually it became clear the room was packed with people who knew and respected Murray Goldman. One elderly guy from Teaneck explained to Alan that his father did a major plumbing job in his home, even though Murray knew the man couldn't pay him. "Years later, I came to your father and brought cash to cover some of the money I owed. Your dad wouldn't have it. He'd say over and over, "what's done is done. I'm glad I was in a position to help you. Take care of your family. If you find yourself able, offer that help to someone else."

Your dad was a good man. He was a person everyone could trust. He never tried to take advantage of someone. His word was his bond. I'm so sorry for your loss."

Alan shared this story with his brothers, as they sat Shiva in the days ahead. Each of Murray's sons came away with a story from someone their dad worked with. It seemed remarkable that so many came to pay tribute. Their dad's business had been gone almost 15 years. How strange and yet impressive that people still remembered him.

The Chapel filled. Murray's casket lay near the front, a simple pine box with the Star of David on the cover. The Goldman boys walked their mom to the left side of the pews and took their seats in the front row. Rabbi Rackowitz read several prayers and spoke of the man they had come to remember.

He told the personal story of Murray Goldman's quiet behind the scenes effort to help build the first Jewish Community Center in Paramus. He also spoke of Murray's devotion to his family and to his wife, Franny, after the car accident.

Alan then stood up. He paused for a minute, as he walked to his father's coffin. His hand rested on the wood surface. He took a deep breath. Then he turned and looked at his brothers, before taking the small stage in the Chapel.

"On behalf of our family, I want to thank everyone for coming today. My dad would have been surprised to see so many friends.

My father didn't have an easy life. No one would say, he had an easy life. He faced poverty as a child during the Depression. He came from a home rocked by divorce. He struggled as a teenager, leaving home at 15 years old.

He became a boxer to find a route out of poverty. He worked odd jobs—let me correct that, he worked "any" job to earn money. He made it his priority to bring some of that money back to help his family. He went to war to service his country, in the Navy during WWII. And when he returned from war, he married the love of his life and started his own plumbing business.

If this sounds like a simple rags to riches story, it is not. His path was never easy. My father struggled to overcome anti-Semitism. He moved the family to New Jersey and struggled to grow a business in a town where he was not immediately welcomed. By sheer force of personality and long hours, my dad did achieve success.

However, each triumph would face setbacks. He would be challenged by a brain tumor that threatened his life at 40 years of age. He overcame a year of being physically debilitated from the brain surgery, to the credit of the woman he married and who was as tough and determined as him. He built a small business empire, before much of it was taken away by a drunk driver on a narrow highway near Atlantic City. In the aftermath of this accident which crippled my mom, my father cared about one thing. He could care less about the money or the business. What he could not accept is seeing his wife in a wheelchair the rest of her life.

He was ready and willing to give it all away. He would commit and sacrifice whatever was needed to change the course of our family's future. He moved us to Florida so mom could heal and learn to walk with crutches. I think many of us would consider this a crazy life's journey, but this was not the end. He faced a second brain tumor as my brothers and I reached high school and college. This tumor took a larger toll on him and he required several surgeries over the past eight years. When they called us and said your dad died suddenly of a heart attack, my brothers and I reacted in disbelief.

Now, I've heard from some family members today that maybe it's better this way. Maybe Murray suffered enough in life.

Alan's voice cracked. Tears rolled down his face. He paused, trying to gain control of his emotions. Zach sat in the front row crying uncontrollably. Gary tried to hold his feelings inside, but the tears rolled down his cheeks. Franny took turns putting her arms around each son. Alan began again,

"Yes, some of you may have believe "maybe it's better this way? But you are wrong!

Our father never quit! He never quit on any challenge he faced in life. And thankfully, he never quit on us. Even now, his courage and spirit lives on in each of his sons. His family was everything to him. Our mom was his one great love. His children became his inspiration. It was always in our father's nature to persevere, to overcome, to simply win in every life competition he faced.

Yes, we are grieving today. This loss and this pain will never leave us. But no one here should walk away believing that my father would be better off not suffering any longer.

Our father would never, never, never give up in a fight. He would never accept 'maybe it's better this way'. He loved his life, regardless of the difficulties he faced. He still had so much to teach us. My brothers and I honor his memory by remembering the high bar he set for us. My dad use to say, 'We all get knocked down. It's the gumption to pick ourselves up and show the world what we got left that makes the difference.'"

Alan stepped down from the stage. He walked several steps to the coffin. He said something to himself as he bent down and kiss the box that held his father. He returned and kissed his brothers. His last gesture was to kneel, as he hugged and kissed his mom.

The Goldman boys refused to stop until they filled the grave dug for their father. The Jewish custom was followed to allow family and friends to throw one shovel of dirt on the casket, but Alan, Zach and Gary returned to the task when everyone had finished. The workers at the cemetery looked on from a distance. This was one funeral that would not require their help. Each son stood between the mound of dirt and the grave. They cried as they tossed the dirt. The sound crashed on the coffin, until the grave was almost filled. There would be no mistaking among the children of Murray Goldman that he was gone. Accepting death may take a lifetime, but filling the grave settled any doubt of the loss.

The family returned to their home in Paramus to sit Shiva. A small crowd of about 80 family and friends cycled through the house over the next two hours. The dining room table was filled with food. Franny sat in the living room. The grandchildren, Sara, Blake and Matthew, sat with her for about 10 minutes. Soon they began squirming, until Grandma said, "Go, go play in the den. Just be careful not to break anything." That was all they needed to hear. They were gone. Sara decided it was safer to play in the finished basement, where they had the freedom to run almost the whole length of the house.

By 4 pm, the house was empty of visitors. The family would have maybe three hours before people returned to say prayers at night. The boys had long ago shed their ties and suit jackets. Franny's aide, Lou, was helping clean up the kitchen. The deli had also sent two women to help straighten up after all the company had left. Zach and Gary were still trying to grab some food to eat in the adjacent dining. Alan sat with his mom on the living room couch.

"You did a good job today," Zach told his older brother. "We are all very proud of you."

In normal circumstances, Alan rarely cared what his brothers thought. He set his own standards and kept his own counsel. It was never clear if this was a defense mechanism to cover up any doubts he might feel at times. But something had changed after Murray's death. Maybe it was a new-found closeness the brothers might find, as they rallied together to bury their father. Zach's comments suddenly did mean more than at any time growing up. "Thank you," he replied. "I wanted people to remember dad the way we knew him. He may have had his physical issues, but his mind was still sharp and his courage never wavered."

At this point, Alan couldn't sit any longer. He walked across the room to his brothers. He hugged each of them. He told them he loved them. "Mom taught us to stick together. I hope we will follow this lesson."

Whatever wrongs had gone before in life, Alan wanted a new beginning with his siblings. Zach believed forcing him to speak at the funeral had been liberating. The two brothers had shared many nights together sleeping in chairs or on a hospital floor to protect their dad. Zach could see how much his brother cared, even if the words escaped him. At the funeral, Alan had found a way to let go and openly profess his love for Murray. He was free now. No more guilt. No more conflict in his emotions. He could tell stories and celebrate his dad.

The Goldman boys grew up to be more secular than religious. However, they wanted to follow Jewish customs during the seven-day Shiva period. After the funeral, the sons would sit on low chairs that did not have any back for support. The idea is that you're supposed to feel uncomfortable: someone has passed away. There's psychology to these customs. In spite of your grief, you get tired of sitting in uncomfortable chairs and want to resume your life. Each of the sons wore a torn sports coat to symbolize that someone has been torn from their life. None of the boys shaved, which is another custom.

Each morning they drove to the Synagogue to say the Mourner's Kaddish. A minyan or group of ten people is required to say morning prayers. Volunteers came to the Synagogue each day to ensure a minyan was available. The mourner's prayer, ironically, never mentions "death". The prayer praises God for his infinite wisdom and compassion. Jews believe that they do not have the right to question God; why things happen or don't happen. Many things in life are just beyond the comprehension of human beings. "Only God, who created the universe, can fathom the intricacies and interconnections between the physical and the metaphysical."

A service was also conducted each night so the Goldmans could say the Mourner's Kaddish. The sons did not pray seeking an explanation for their father's death. Each son in his own way accepted the loss, hoping in time they could find a purpose in death that would fill the hole in their hearts.

The evenings were filled with stories about Murray Goldman. Their mom delighted in telling the boys how their dad stood on the steps of their apartment building waiting for her to come home. "Your father wouldn't let anyone past the front steps. He'd stand there with his arms crossed. Buddy this is as far as you go." Your dad did not take "no" for an answer. I'd make a protest, but he knew what he was doing. I didn't think anyone would want to date me because of him, so I guess I just decided he had to be the guy."

Gary and his brothers loved that story. It sounded so like their dad. They'd ask Franny about him going up to Harlem dance clubs?

"I thought your father was much older. He'd come down the stairs to meet Artie Schwartz in his floppy hat and dark grey zoot suit, wearing spats. My sister thought he was a gangster. He was so tall and thin in those days. The suit was buttoned at the waist. He didn't walk as much as he glided down the street.

In those days, his outfit was very popular with the dance crowd. Your dad would take the train all the way to Harlem to jitterbug the night away. He didn't really drink like Artie. Your dad was always training in the gym. He was still boxing in those days, so it was more likely he'd be found at Rosie's Bar to earn some money. That was your father."

By the fourth day, the Goldman boys focused on the children. They needed an outlet, being at home for such an extended time. Uncle Zach decided it was time to share a tradition started with his brothers, when they were kids. He took Sara, Blake and Matthew to the bedrooms at the end of the hallway. He'd look for old clothes in Grandma and Grandpa's closet. He wanted strange combinations of outfits to dress up the kids. Sara wore a wool rain hat with a yellow robe and red socks. Blake had a pair of woman's stockings on his head, which draped down across his shoulders and looked like reindeer ears. He gave Matthew his hat and coat from military school. The hat was too large and slid to the side of his head. The coat had room for two more children. Zach did not have any music, but he led the group in a parade from the bedrooms past the living room and down to the den. The family was spread out between the rooms. You knew the children were coming when you heard the applause and cheerful laughter. Franny recognized the parade, just like her crazy children did when they were young. Grandma laughed and laughed. She cheered them on, "go show your mother and father," she'd yell out.

It had been a long time since the family gathered like this. The pain of dad's passing, at times, would bring tears to the sons. But it also forced them to start thinking more about their own legacy as fathers. By the end of the Shiva period, each Goldman would return home with a beard growing, a desire to work again and a need to talk about their dad.

CHAPTER 68

Reassessing – Changing Course

___

Life events always have a way of changing our course. We may not be conscious that our decisions have been influenced by the loss of someone, but the brain processes this information at varying speeds and reboots without notice.

Alan was the first to begin reassessing his career after he returned to work. He had joined the U.S. Attorney's Office with a mission to serve the law and to prosecute those who violated it. Many are drawn to this work because they want to influence the world around them. "Justice for all," was a slogan he often responded to at law school. For him, this meant there should be accountability for white collar crime. He was offended that so much attention was focused on prosecuting people at the lower end of the economic ladder. In his view, economic crime cost society way more than petty theft. He shared a righteous indignation over the idea that if you had money you could afford better lawyers to defend you—and escape justice. He worked his butt off for several years to disprove that assumption. Alan was willing to go up against the best defense lawyers in his prosecutions—and win. Regardless of your stature in the community or your ability to use ill-gotten gains to buy your way through the system, he learned to exact justice in a court room. Trial lawyers are always about winning. Alan had earned his well-deserved reputation.

As he returned to work, Alan dove in and tried to distract himself by taking on a heavier than normal case load. His supervisor asked if he was really ready for this, but he waived his hand almost mimicking the way his father signaled he was done talking. It was strange that while he juggled motions in court and spent hours screening jurors for different trials, Alan still spent time reflecting on his father. Interaction with strangers often brought back memories. One witness response during a trial brought a flashback to an incident he had with his dad as a child. He answered the response with humor that broke up the court room with laughter. This was not the serious, stoic and deliberate prosecutor everyone associated with Alan Goldman.

He was eventually assigned a case that challenged him unlike any other. The prosecution involved a State Senator, who was alleged to have taken an illegal campaign contribution. He told his boss about the potential conflict, since the State Senator had been a friend of his father for many years. Alan didn't know the Senator personally, but he recalled the man showing up at his dad's funeral. His supervisor asked a dozen or so questions. He then asked him to proceed with the case. His boss agreed to take the lead in the case, if it went to court. He trusted Alan would do his usual thorough preparation.

In fact, it was so good that after the discovery process, the defense lawyer asked to make a plea deal. Alan was saved from having to go to trial. The plea deal recommended a fine but no jail time. The Senator was a Captain in the Marines and a war hero during WWII. He was also a very successful local Mayor. No one believed those mitigating factors would result in a Judge sending the man to jail. Over time, the Senator's good deeds would prove the federal prosecutor and the Judge made the right call. The Senator was reelected for public office another 20 years, passing historic legislation along the way. Alan did his best to win the case, but he came away feeling justice was served. He was relieved by the outcome.

He didn't realize it right away, but after his father's death Alan had found his humanity and a certain peace in his life. He was still driven to perform, but he wasn't angry. He had come to terms with his guilt and his love for his father. His perspective had matured. He was apt to be more patient and friendlier with people, even if his killer instinct in the courtroom remained. As the months came and went, he began to think about life beyond the U.S. Attorney's Office. Beyond his passion for law, it was time to focus on a career that would financially secure his family. Going through papers with his mom, Alan could see how much time and energy was given to planning for the future. He let it be known to a very small circle of friends that he was thinking about moving to a law firm.

Word spread quickly. Within six months, he had been contacted by three firms that offered him a partner track. In matters where choice was involved; choice of cars, choice of clothes; choice of buying something expensive, Alan was always his own man. He didn't lack confidence in his own judgment. However, he respected and valued his wife's opinion. Grace's input was required on all decisions that could impact the family. He didn't expect her to always understand his rationale, but his wife was his life partner. Her voice mattered.

He finally chose an offer from Rauchwerger, Wallach & Zimmerman in Essex County, New Jersey. He would make the move a year after his father passed. He wished his dad was still around to see—and bless this transition. He convinced himself that he would be proud and moved ahead with his decision. The law firm had been around almost 15 years. They were looking to recruit the next generation of talent, who could serve as the future backbone of the firm.

He would join the litigation section of the firm. He became a defense lawyer in certain criminal matters, leveraging his experience as a prosecutor. But he quickly diversified to work with corporate clients on commercial and securities matters. His trial experience was sought after by major businesses. Alan did not disappoint.

Leslie "Les" Zimmerman would hear from clients about how prepared Alan was at trial. They also admired his ability to get under the skin of his opposing counsel. To them, it was almost as if he could anticipate a motion the opposing attorney might make in court. He seemed to wait for it and then grab his notes and convince the judge the arguments being made were not consistent with the law or rulings by other judges. Winning in court was no different for Alan, except these cases often involved large sums of money.

Gary Goldman struggled after Murray's death. He felt he didn't have enough time with his father during his short lifetime. He couldn't see—or accept—that he was not alone in feeling this way. His brothers had likewise felt cheated. But for Gary, the loss seemed magnified.

As the youngest, he always felt his pain was greater. He had less and his obstacles were always bigger or more difficult than his brothers. He also felt his successes were never adequately recognized or respected by his brothers. "Sometimes I feel no one truly appreciates what I've accomplished," he often told his girlfriend, Eva Perez.

Eva came from a large Latin family. She couldn't understand why Gary felt this way. Everyone in her family, from the oldest to the youngest, felt equally loved by their parents. She had been with him many times at Goldman family functions. "Gary, I can see your brothers care about you. I can see it in their eyes. I can tell by the questions they ask. I think you believe they are always critical, but it looks to me that they are proud of the work you are doing."

A year before his dad died, the Gaming Enforcement agency created a specialized unit to handle investigations requiring coordination across state and federal law enforcement jurisdictions. Gary and Walt Seagirt were the first two investigators to be handpicked for the new unit, along with four other colleagues. The group was moved to a different floor in the building, where they could be housed in secure office space. Like the early work Gary and Walt had completed on The Beauregard casino, the cross-jurisdictional investigative unit would review work of their own agency employees to spot suspicious relationships within a casino or between two casinos. Anything that might suggest a link to organized crime would be reviewed with the FBI and other states where casinos were policed. The work of this unit would be confidential. No public announcement would be made.

The new assignment included a promotion for Gary and a raise. Matthew would soon be turning 7 years old. He lived with his mom, Alicia, but his dad still enjoyed the alternative weekends when he got to spend time with his son. Matthew did not share his cousins, Sara and Blake's interest in sports. He initially preferred puzzles to tossing a football or baseball. Later, he only wanted to work on projects with his dad. There was no question in anyone's mind that Matthew had his father's (and Grandfather's) natural mechanical ability to fix things or work with tools. His dad enjoyed that Matthew wanted to help him, whether it was working on a car or a project in the apartment. Gary also bought his son a mountain bike, which he would ride in the park as many hours as his mom would let him.

Matthew had also grown quite comfortable being with Eva. The three of them would go to dinner together. Eva often stayed over, when Matthew was around. Like his uncle Zach, she was very skilled in making pancakes, his favorite breakfast. She was also quick with hugs, which the boy welcomed.

Gary had strayed from Eva many times. Perhaps that was his nature. However, he always came back to her. Zach was certain he would eventually settle down with Eva. He could see the positive impact she had on his brother, whenever she was around. She encouraged him. She calmed his nervousness. She boosted his spirits when he doubted himself. It was perhaps his biggest mistake in life that he eventually looked to marry again, except it wasn't Eva.

Gary had so many good qualities, but at times his stubbornness led him to make bad choices. His mom would say, "he's stubborn like his father." In his case, however, he wouldn't listen.

Each of the Goldman boys had to deal with their own catharsis following their father's death. In truth, this process, after losing a parent never ends. It dissipates. It can be turned into something positive. In Gary's case, his emotions always took longer to resolve. He would achieve success at work, which gave him a place to put his energy. But he would struggle to find peace with himself. Questions would linger for years about his place in the world.

The Goldman family rallied to love and support Eva Perez. Over the next two years, Franny would attended holidays and celebrations at the Perez family home. Eva was always at the table during the Jewish holidays, sitting next to Matthew. These were happy times. Eva's personality helped light the room. She had become a fixture in the Goldman family.

Life without Murray was difficult for Franny. While he had not lived at home for several years, it didn't feel that way. She would walk around the house. Her husband's presence was everywhere. In the large den at the end of the ranch home was a white Georgian marble fireplace. She smiled thinking about how he insisted on an entire wall of white marble. The Goldmans never actually used the fireplace, but Murray loved the look. Like the deck he added on the back of the house, he had a vision for the home they built.

Franny and Murray would always be childhood friends, and later, lovers who weathered so many storms together. When times were toughest, their shared values and tenacity binded them. No one ever knows what truly goes on in a marriage between a man and a woman. We are onlookers in someone else's life. We often fill in the blanks across the space of time with our own interpretation of the relationship these two people shared.

Dad's reaction to the NY fire department phone call about his luncheon-ette burning down was a classic. Franny never lost her love for the young man she beat at handball.

During his time in the VA home, Franny tried to see him frequently. On some occasions, she'd give Lou extra money to drive her to the home. More often, the boys would take her and she'd push them to bring him home for holidays and celebrations. When Sara and Blake were graduating from Jewish Sunday school, Franny insisted their Grandfather attend. She wanted him to be a part of her life right up until the end. Bringing dad home was increasingly burdensome on the boys traveling back and forth, but mom had a way about her. She asked for these moments, so he could always be in their lives. Her sons understood. Franny would remain their moral compass.

She had spent more than a year alone crying and grieving for her husband. A lifetime of love, even cut short, stays with you. She began to thinking about what to do with herself. She asked Alan and Grace to come to the house for a family discussion.

Following the car accident, Franny stayed in touch with her friend, Diane Shulman. Diane's husband had passed away from cancer. She was living in West Palm Beach Florida, in a small condo community. Franny asked Alan to consider moving into the family home from their 2-bedroom apartment in Fair Lawn. She had long thought about moving to warmer weather, which would help her reduce the pain she suffered. She wanted Alan to buy the house, but at a fraction of the real cost.

She knew Alan could only afford a small mortgage. Franny would use the proceeds of the sale to buy a condo in Florida. The house was worth three times the amount Alan would actually pay. She told him the savings he'd get from buying the house cheaply would represent his portion of her will. Whatever was left of the investments and real estate Murray owned would be split with Zach and Gary, after she was gone. To her, this was a fair arrangement.

Alan and Grace were taken aback. They had talked frequently about getting out of their cramped apartment, which they shared with two children. Interest rates for mortgages were unusually high at the time. Alan pointed out to Grace that his mom was offering them a huge bargain. He expected his income to increase following his move to the law firm. This would also help.

"Mom, we really appreciate the offer," he told her. "Living in the home dad built is beyond anything we could hope for. I guess I want to understand, however, how you might feel if at some point down the road Grace and I wanted to sell the house."

"Alan, if you live here and then decide to move somewhere else that's your decision. Right now, you're still trying to get ahead with your career. I don't need such a big house. I may need to stay here with you for six months, until the condo is completed. I'll only ask that you help me make the move to Florida."

On the drive back to Fair Lawn, Alan and Grace were giddy talking non-stop about living in the large ranch home on Koman Drive in Paramus. The children would have their own rooms. They discussed fixing up the house, which had not been updated in a decade. They talked about the kids changing schools. Alan knew he had to crunch the numbers before giving his mom a final yes. He would speak to William 'Bill' Barton at the bank about the mortgage. Barton had been his father's banker and friend for years. He had developed a close relationship with Alan since high school. Alan sought his advice about college and law school.

Over the next month, a plan was put in motion. He flew down to Florida with his mom to put a deposit on the condo. Diane Shulman had done homework to help find Franny an aide to look after her. Alan spent more than an hour interviewing a woman from Haiti. Her name was Ayida Saint Louis. She was near 40 years old, with a family of her own. She spoke with an accent, but Alan and Franny could understand her. He didn't tell his mom, but Ayida's former client had recently died. An agreement was struck for Ayida to help Franny three days a week, until right after dinner. Over time, Alan would talk with his brothers about increasing the hours and days.

Ayida had some education, back in Haiti. Her husband drove a truck. Her two children were in middle school and pretty self-sufficient. If Franny was having a bad day, Ayida promised Alan she would stay as long as needed. She would never leave Franny alone, if she was not well.

The condo community was new, but modest. There was a large swimming pool where Franny could exercise. The community was set up for seniors, so all of the amenities made it easier for them to get around. Franny was close enough to walk to the clubhouse, but they also had small shuttle buses to give you a lift if needed.

Diane Shulman told Franny about the community band. According to her, Franny characterized it as "six partially deaf guys, who couldn't always tell if they were in tune." But Diane knew her friend well. It had been years since she even thought about picking up her saxophone. She didn't really tell her sons about the band. She decided this was something she'd look into and tackle once she got settled.

Life after Murray Goldman was quite difficult for Franny. She wouldn't let on with her children how lonely she could be. Especially on nights where she experienced pain, she would cry herself to sleep. Murray's name was always on her lips. It was not in her nature to wear her emotions on her sleeve with friends or family. She hoped the move to Florida would give her a chance to meet other women. In Paramus, she was locked away in this large beautiful home.

Her sons called her daily to check on her progress. Zach remarked to his brothers how happy mom sounded. During her first year, each son made it a point to pay their mom regular visits.

She was delighted to show off her family. She had seen so many children and grandchildren pass through the Condo Clubhouse. When it came to her turn, she beamed with pride. Sara and Blake were dragged along with Grandma to see band practice. "I swear," Sara told her father, "Grandma was the only one who could play in tune. The trumpet player was just loud. The guitar player was a very nice man, but he couldn't read the music. It's like he wasn't in the band. He just strummed along." Alan would smile listening to his children critique the group. He was thrilled his mom had taken up her instrument. It gave her a new purpose in life. She had the saxophone case in her bedroom, near the bed. She would take it out every day to practice. Nothing had changed for her. She started each practice session rehearsing the music scales learned as a child. She'd play scales for almost 15 minutes before launching into a song. When she did play a song, her neighbors would always remark about the quality of her tone and sound. It became "a thing" if you lived next door to Franny Goldman.

She rarely had a pain free day following the car accident and the hip replacement surgery. She took pain killer pills regularly to take the edge off. The hip replacement improved her ability to walk with elbow crutches, but it did not eliminate the pain. Franny often tried to push past the discomfort. There were days, however, when the muscles in her legs would cramp up. Her calves and her hamstrings would start to contract violently. She'd try to jump out of bed and move around. If she couldn't move fast enough the pain would overtake her. She'd cry out.

At night, there was no one to help her. She'd breathe slowly to try and calm her body, waiting for the pain to subside. During the day, these events often happened after walking with Ayida in a store for more than an hour. Once home in the condo, Ayida was very skilled at massaging her legs with lotion. She had strong hands and dug into the muscles to relax them. Ayida was so pleased that after these sessions, Franny would fall asleep. In these instances, it was more than just a job for Ayida. She felt sympathy for her. Her employer was such a warm and giving person. Knowing her history led her to care more about helping Franny than the normal employer employee relationship.

Ayida found a friend in Franny. She would buy clothes for her children. She encouraged her three sons to give Ayida money for the various holidays, to reward her for being so kind to their mother. The Goldman boys valued having help in the home over the years. These relationships were a lesson learned as children about different cultures, ethnic backgrounds and the human decency shared between people. Like Effie, who took care of the Franny and the boys after the accident, Alan, Zach and Gary would hug Ayida during their visits. She would become a member of their extended family. If she faced difficulties, the Goldmans were there to help her. They would gladly help read mail Ayida received from government agencies and draft letters of response for her. The Goldmans also insisted their children treat Ayida with respect. "Don't forget what Grandma taught you about the Golden Rule," Alan would remind Sara and Blake. Ayida would tell stories to the children about her home in Haiti, describing the struggles people faced with poverty and the lack of proper medical care. Alan hoped his children would grow up to understand the challenges people faced in other countries, not as rich as America.

The year following Murray's death passed quickly. The Jewish custom of unveiling the headstone at the cemetery is meant to occur within a year. Their father had bought a large plot of land at Beth El Cemetery in the late 1950s. He wanted to ensure there was room for everyone. The best option was to create a family headstone for "Goldman" and to place a smaller footstone at the top of each individual grave. The headstone would have to be quite large, since it was meant to spread across two rows of six graves. The Rabbi explained to Alan that there was nothing strictly religious or magical about the one year unveiling. His opinion was that the timeframe could be extended, if needed. The ceremony for the unveiling at the grave site was set for 15 months after his death. Franny would travel north for the ceremony. Alan invited his brothers to stay at the family home in Paramus.

During the ceremony on Friday morning, the family literally removed a cloth covering of the headstone, followed by the Goldmans reciting prayers including Mourner's Kaddish. Afterward, the family returned to their home to spend time with each other. This allows everyone to talk about the loved one who has died.

On Sunday, before heading home, Alan and Zach made one more trip to Beth El Cemetery. Gary had left earlier in the day. The boys stopped at the Cemetery administration building to get a map where Grandpa Isaac and Grandma Tonia Goldman were buried. Zach would recall many years ago, how he went with his dad and Grandpa Isaac to pay their respects to Tonia. Murray helped his father, who had difficulty walking, get in and out of the car. Zach knew Murray blamed Isaac's gambling for breaking up the family, but he still loved his father. Murray would kiss his father's cheek and hug him, openly showing his affection. This is what his dad believed. He didn't have to be told. And he didn't have to teach it to his own children.

The boys visited their grandparents' graves, before driving to the other side of the cemetery where dad was buried. They rarely saw their grandparents, but it was important to put rocks on the graves out of respect for their father. This is what he would do, if he were here.

As they reached the far side of Beth El, Alan and Zach could see the very large headstone, "Goldman." They parked the car and walked over to the single footstone marking Murray's grave, surrounded by trimmed green grass. Suddenly, Zach burst out crying. Alan was taken by surprise. He expected they would all cry at some point during the unveiling ceremony Friday. He did not, however, understand why Zach was crying on Sunday. "What's going on?" Alan asked. "Are you ok?"

"I'm sorry," he responded. "After the weekend with the family, it really hit me. Dad will never get to meet or know my children. I always considered it a blessing that Sara, Blake and even Matthew would grow up with their own memories of dad. Even if we are filling in details they may not fully remember, they will recall how he hugged them, kissed them and held them on his lap. I have lost the greatest gift in life I could ever hope for."

"Zach, I don't think you should feel that way," his brother responded. "Someday, you will have children. And while they don't have a physical connection or memory of dad, I know you will tell them stories. You're the writer in the family. You know how to make the words come to life.

The truth is, none of us were prepared to lose dad at such a young age. We can't change this. You weren't ready to settle down. When you are ready, you'll have both a wife and children to share stories with. I believe you will keep dad alive in their eyes. I believe the love you share with them will help each of them understand where it comes from. I know how important this is to you. We have all lost something, after dad died. It may take the rest of our lives to realize how deep a loss. What we do with this loss matters."

He walked over to console and hug his younger brother. At the funeral, Zach insisted that Alan speak because he thought it would help his brother heal from years of guilt. A year later, Alan's new-found perspective and compassion would now help Zach heal from loss of their father.

"What we do with the loss matters," was something that would stay with Zach. Life yields choices between dwelling on the negative or focusing on the possibilities we still have ahead of us.

Zach Goldman had not experienced changes in the year following his father's death. He was back at his job, still working for Vonman. His stature in political circles had grown, based on the work he did on the Governor's re-election. Zach had always felt confident about his organizing skills, but he was pleased he got to prove himself working on a statewide campaign.

The success of the campaign did cause Zach to start thinking about his next steps. From the prediction of the Governor being a one term office holder, the campaign won in a landslide. Zach had straddled the fence between being viewed as a campaign operative and a "professional" working in state government. If his priorities were weighted, he preferred the view of the substantive work he did representing Vonman in the State Legislature. This work resulted in getting legislation passed that impacted people's lives. Before the Governor's campaign, he worried that the life of a political operative was too nomadic for him.

Zach thought about trying his talent out on a national campaign. He watched as colleagues he met started to interview for jobs working for different Presidential candidates. He had reservations. Zach had seen firsthand the politicking and jockeying that occurs in a state campaign to gain the ear of senior staff or the candidate. In many instances what you accomplished was not as important as whose ass you were kissing.

But Zach soon faced a reckoning in his personal life that changed him forever. Unlike his brothers, he did not feel the impact until a year after his dad died. In a social setting, his natural engaging personality would shine through. Yet, there was a darkness that plagued him well into the night. He had lost something. He had lost someone, who provided the light and always pointed the way. There were nights and weekends Zach spent alone. He shed tears and he felt depressed. He withdrew more and more, hoping the silence would help him find answers.

Gabby Bernstein had always been there, encouraging Zach, whether he wanted to work in a national political campaign or move to a new job in state government. She and Zach had been together almost a year. It was remarkable that for most of that time, no one knew they were a couple. Yes, they'd attend the Governor's Inaugural dinner or other post-election fundraising events, but they'd arrive and leave separately.

Gabby had become Zach's lover. He looked forward to her laugh. Her eyes could communicate such energy without saying a word. She was funny. She had a knack for pointing out people's foibles. She had an energy that could light up a room when she walked in. She hugged and engaged each person, as if they were the only one that mattered in the world. As Zach pondered a life in politics and campaigns, he was certain she would be a perfect complement. They shared a very passionate open physical relationship. Gabby had few boundaries. There was never judgment or awkwardness. Their time together was how he suspected lovers are meant to be. She set the tone. Both were ready to learn from each other. So much of their passion and laughter were perfectly aligned.

Yet, Zach still felt doubts. Gabby was quick to offer her guidance, but maybe too quick. She had so many opinions he wondered if she had the ability to make good judgments. Today's good direction became questionable the day after. At times, she could be so carefree, "Go with the flow. If it doesn't work out, you can switch directions. This part of her nature was antithetical to Zach's deep-seeded need to control outcomes and methodically consider a strategy before taking action. Her boundless energy often seemed to take her in disparate directions, almost at the same time. Zach tried to coach her on narrowing her focus.

Gabby came from a family that had long been politically active. Her mom, Mindy Bernstein, held several paid positions. Her dad, Ted, was a quiet man, who worked very hard at his CPA job doing taxes. While not a public person, he supported his wife in every way possible. He shared her passion for social issues, but he could care less about being directly involved in the fray.

Zach had been to the Bernstein home many times. Dinner at their home was always going to devolve into a discussion or debate over politics. He enjoyed listening to Gabby's brothers argue. What surprised him, however, was how Mindy weighed in during these discussions. When she was challenged, she took no prisoners. She could almost be dogmatic in her point-of-view. Zach could see clearly where Gabby got the sarcastic side of her nature. Her mom could be tough on her sons with caustic comments. He observed that during these exchanges, Ted rarely participated. He'd sit back and let Mindy do her thing.

It was clear to him that Gabby admired her mom's opinionated nature. This was not your historically polite and passive woman of the 1950s. Mindy was a scrapper. She was ahead of her time. She loved showing men she would not play second fiddle to anyone. She didn't hesitate to cut someone off mid-sentence, to criticize them or their position on an issue.

If there were concerns lurking in the back of Zach's mind about his relationship with Gabby, he traced them back to her mom. Zach admired Mindy's strength, but in Gabby he saw transience and insecurity. Before attending the unveiling of his father's gravestone, she was being particularly critical about a new high-profile job he was offered. Zach couldn't tell if there was jealousy mixed with her sarcasm. During the argument that followed, she said, "Look, I'm not certain you're ambitious."

"What are you talking about," he responded.

"You aren't willing to give up everything else in your life to achieve your goals. You'll never be a CEO."

Zach was shocked by the outburst. The comments seemed to ignore the success he had already achieved, compared to his peers and others older than him. It also presupposed that he wanted a life of blind ambition.

After the unveiling, Zach came to the most difficult realization. Unlike Alan and Gary, his life was not moving forward. A year had gone by. He concluded he could not find in Gabby the support, the certainty and a shared vision about the future. She would always be unpredictable.

The break up took all the energy he could muster. This was one time he could not be completely honest. He didn't want to hurt her. He could not bear to tell her why he had reservations. There was so much natural chemistry between them. Ironically, it was Zach's leadership qualities on the campaign that Gabby first found attractive. But he saw a future where he could not navigate on his own. He feared Gabby would always push and pull him, when he needed someone to simply give him the space and time to make the right decision.

Zach had to free himself from the comfort of his circumstance to grow and find his purpose. He was certain that she was never going to forgive him. He was right. He could tell below the skin there would always be a wound that never healed. It was a nagging hurt Gabby felt about what could have been.

He tried his best in the years ahead to keep the bond and friendship with Gaby. He would tell himself, "You don't stop loving someone, just because you realize they are not the one to spend your life with."

CHAPTER 69
Finding Eliana

Nine months passed after Zach broke off his relationship with Gabby. He did not pursue a job on a presidential campaign. Instead, he accepted an offer from the Attorney General (AG) to become a State Ombudsman. He would investigate complaints about the worst government agency in New Jersey (or any state)—the Division of Motor Vehicles (DMV). Zach led a team that would handle individual complaints from the public. However, his real focus was to find patterns of complaints and recommend sweeping changes in DMV operations, rules or state laws.

Zach thought this was the best job he could have imagined. The AG was a friend and respected his talent. His confidence in Zach's organizing skill and hands on approach was very strong. There was no question in his mind that Zach could help rout out inefficiencies or discriminatory practices. In his first months on the job, Zach was able to stop DMV officials from detaining Hispanic looking citizens until the local U.S. immigration office could come and interrogate these folks. This type of behavior was clearly illegal.

Zach thought it was outrageous that any ethnic group was singled out. His investigative report to the AG and the Governor found this unknown cooperation between state and federal agencies was going on without their knowledge. Ironically, most of those detained (98%) were legal residents. They just spoke with an accent or broken English. The practice was ended immediately.

Other issues he tackled were highly visible in the news media. The public couldn't get through on the toll-free phone lines, when they called. Forms sent to N.J. residents were written in legalese, which most people didn't understand and ignored. Zach completed a string of successful projects, which newspapers applauded as major reforms going on at DMV. However, he took the job knowing he would not stay beyond two years. He had never thought about a career in the private sector, but like his brothers he felt it was time to take a risk. He had started talking to friends and associates about companies and jobs he might pursue, but this effort kicked into high gear when Zach found a new source of inspiration.

His friend, David Mazursky, worked as a Special Counsel to the Governor. He handled the review process for nearly 3,000 appointments to senior level jobs in State Government. Aside from his day job, David was active and well-known in the New Jersey Jewish community. Everyone loved David. He was such a smart, warm and outgoing personality.

David would frequently try to serve as a matchmaker. He regularly invited Zach to social events. Most of them were political dinners, but on several occasions he'd drag his friend to a Jewish dance. "Oy vay," he would joke with David, "I remember….This was a throwback to another era…relationships very young."

David would not let him off the hook. He seemed to take on the mission that nearing 30-years old, it was time for both he and his friend to settle down. As November came, David kept nagging him to attend a dance in Springfield, New Jersey. Zach finally gave in, but he insisted on driving his own car so he could leave early.

After 20 minutes at the dance, he met Sarah Freeman. She was very nice, Zach thought, but he soon discovered Sarah's talent for keeping a conversation going—endlessly. Sarah came from North Jersey. She worked for a Jewish community organization near Englewood. She was clearly a good-natured person and she had a good sense of humor. However, he wasn't prepared for her high-pitched laugh that took forever to settle down. It reminded him of that person who keeps laughing long after the joke has ended, except in this case her voice could likely be heard on the other side of the room.

He made several attempts to try and excuse himself. The objective at a Jewish dance was to meet people and move on, with the hope that at some point you'd find someone interesting. The key to this strategy was to "keep moving." He figured Sarah must have been to many of these functions. She was well schooled in the various explanations given for moving on. She had no intentions of letting Zach escape. When he got quiet, Sarah kept the conversation going. He could see that Sarah had lots of good qualities, but he could not imagine himself with someone who talked non-stop and might break a glass with her laughter.

After 30 minutes, Zach decided that he hated David Mazursky for the drama he introduced into his life. He was certain, at one point, that he could only save himself if he agreed on the spot to marry Sarah. His imagination kicked in. He wondered if in the Ketubah (Jewish marriage license), he could require that his wife refrain from talking between dinner and going to bed. Since he didn't see a way to escape his fate, this might be the only way to keep his sanity.

Suddenly, David appeared out of nowhere. Zach's brain was already numb. He actually hesitated, when David looked at Sarah and told his friend it was time to leave. He looked at Sarah for only a second, shrugged, said good night and then started for the door. Sarah reluctantly waved goodbye. She gave him her phone number. He was certain she blamed David for breaking the rhythm of her effort to win a husband.

Walking through the event, Zach realized the crowd had grown rather large, from when they first arrived. "You owe me big time," David said as they pushed through people congregating in areas of the large catering hall. They were getting near the front entrance when Zach suddenly stopped in his tracks. He had been looking at folks in the side anterooms, as David walked ahead of him. He spotted her in this last room on his left. She wore a soft beige collared blouse with brown slacks. Her hair was a thick strawberry blonde and short. She was tall, maybe 5' 7". Her arms and hands moved expressively like a dancer, slow and with grace.

David was almost out of sight, when he realized Zach was missing. He doubled back to find his friend standing by himself and staring at a girl in the other room. "Now that's what I call a beautiful woman," he told David.

"Oh, that's Eli," David replied. "She was born in Israel, but lives near me in Linden."

Zach looked incredulously at his friend. "You know her?" Zach asked. "If this is true, then why are we standing here? Please introduce me."

As they walked over, David gave Eli a big hug and introduced Zach. Then David stood there for what seemed like an eternity talking to her in Hebrew. Zach was guessing it was Hebrew. It wasn't a language he immediately recognized. Initially, Zach didn't mind. It gave him time to just stand and stare. He could not get enough of her. Her clothes draped so naturally across her body. Her body was lanky, with small breasts and long limbs. He guessed she must be athletic. The browns and beige colored clothing looked perfect against her light, rosy skin. This was not how he envisioned an Israeli woman. In the NY Times advertisements for Sabra liqueur, the pictures of Israelis were dark skin, dark hair and dark eyes.

From where he stood, next to David, he could also see she had the most amazing green eyes. He wouldn't repeat his first thought. Her eyes reminded him of the yellow green you see with a Weimaraner.

Zach started to lose his patience quickly. He wanted to talk. He wanted to know this amazingly beautiful woman. But he didn't speak Hebrew. He began to wonder if this might stand in his way? David could see his friend was ndgety waiting. He finally turned and told him he'd return in 15-20 minutes. As he walked away, Zach struggled to get his footing. While always outgoing, he became shy in the presence of a girl he wanted to know. Suddenly, he heard the music piped through the event hall. He asked Eli to dance. What a graceful hand she had.

He soon realized she spoke perfect English. The pressure was off. They talked casually, as they danced. Eli taught elementary school in Elizabeth, New Jersey. She lived in an apartment near Maplewood. She didn't have any siblings. Eli asked him about his work and how he knew David? The music stopped, but they stood on the side of the room and continued to talk. Eli was uncomfortable, at first, she couldn't get over noticing how he kept staring at her. She eventually concluded he wasn't weird. "Maybe he didn't know he was staring," she said to herself. She did have one reservation. She thought he looked young, maybe about 25 years old. Eli had recently turned 30. This might be too big a gap in age, for a new boyfriend.

Zach asked her what she did in the summer months, when school let out. She told him she liked to travel. She had backpacked through Europe, after college. However, for several years, to earn extra money she worked at a nursing home. "My father is the director of the home," Eli explained.

"That's interesting," he replied. "What's the name of the nursing home?"

"It's the Workman's Circle Home in Elizabeth."

"Wow, that's so funny. My grandfather was in that nursing home during his final years."

"What was his name?"

"His name was Sugar."

"Saul? Are you kidding me? Saul Sugar was your grandfather?" Eli asked.

"Wait," Zach began, "you knew my grandfather?" He stood there in shock. How could this be? How is it possible that he'd meet a woman who may have won his heart at the first sight of her—and she knew his grandfather. He could not wipe the smile from his face. If that wasn't a sign from the heavens, what was?

"Yes. Your grandfather use to sit outside the office where I worked. He was always dressed in a shirt and tie. He might have some grizzle on his face if he didn't shave that day, but he'd insisted on wearing his suit. We persuaded him to leave the jacket on the back of the door in his room. But, yes, he would sit by the office and wait for the employees to punch the clock, as they arrived for work. Saul would look at his watch. He'd call out to them, "you're late" if they did not show up on time. It's been many years now, but he was a very nice man."

Zach's head was still spinning with delight, when David Mazursky returned. "Ok, are you two done talking?" There was no way he wanted this

night to end. "Do you think we could leave the dance and go for coff
asked looking at Eli. David suggested they meet at the Springfield
Route 22. Each drove their own car.

As Eli slid into the booth at the diner, Zach blocked David fron
thinking about sitting next to her. David's relationship with Eli was pla
which became more apparent to him as they shared stories about atten
Jewish events. Both David and Eli had also traveled to Israel many time
visit relatives. Neither of them had many friends who spoke Hebrew, so so
ing each other gave them a chance to practice their language skills.

David praised Zach's talents in his government job and working or
the Governor's campaign. The guys shared war stories from their time working together. After coffee and dessert, Zach leaned over and asked Eli if he
could call her? He was careful to put the napkin with her phone number in
his pocket with his wallet. For once, he couldn't complain about attending a
Jewish dance. Waiting to call Eli would torment him for days.

They arrived at the Steak & Ale restaurant. Zach picked Eli up at her
apartment. He was so excited she accepted his invitation. He brought flowers.
A girl friend who lived down the hall was waiting to see what this new guy
looked like. He caught her out of the corner of his eye giving Eli a thumbs up.

From the start, they seemed to have so many things in common. Neither
one of them were drinkers. As they ordered dinner, he asked her if she wanted
to share an order of mushrooms. She accepted. This exchanged buoyed his
spirit. He wanted so much for the date to go well.

Zach had so many questions, he didn't know where to start. His curiosity and training as a reporter kicked into high gear. He tried not to seem too
aggressive. It was better to let Eli tell the story at her own pace. "So, how did
you get to the U.S. from Israel? Were your parents born there?"

"Well, I was born in Israel and came to the U.S. with my parents at
eight years old. My parents were Holocaust survivors. My mom was born in
Berlin. She had three siblings and they left Germany for Israel before the bor-
ders were sealed. My mom's parents wouldn't let her go, since at the time she
was only 14. My grandfather was later deported to Poland. My mom and her
mother were left in Berlin. They survived Kristallnacht in November 1938,
with help from non-Jewish neighbors who hid them in their home. After that
my mom and grandmother were sent back to Poland. Both my grandparents
perished at Auschwitz. Mom survived for nearly four years in different concentration camps. These were labor camps, not death camps. There was little
food and horrendous living conditions. Everyone understood, if you got sick
or injured and couldn't work, you would be transferred to the closest 'death
camp.'

Listen, maybe this isn't the conversation you wanted to have at dinner?" Eli asked Zach.

˙ded. Zach encouraged Eli to continue with

ın the camp near the end of the War. My dad
⹁sh army, fighting the Germans. He was wounded
man POW camp. During the transport at night, he
⹁d hid in the woods for two days. He returned home to
⹁, but was arrested by the Gestapo for not having identity
μaid a ransom to local officials in Sosnowiec, so he wasn't
⹁ans. A deal was struck, sending him instead to labor camps
then Poland."

⹁plained that her dad lost his entire family during the Holocaust.
⹁'s parents and his 12-year old brother died in Auschwitz. His younger
⹁mazingly survived the horrors of Bergen-Belsen. But tragically, she
six months after camp's liberation. Like the more well-known story of
⹁ne Frank and her sister, Margot, Eli's dad lost his sister to Typhus. She
μointed out to Zach, "more than 52,000 people died from starvation and disease at this camp, with more than 1,000 deaths per day in the spring of 1945.
Before the war, my dad had 13 uncles and aunts, and they and their extended
families all perished. Only two cousins from her father's family survived.

"At the end of the War, after liberation, my parents would marry. They
eventually contacted mom's siblings in Israel to let them know she was alive.
The oldest brother, Jonah, got her telegram at his Kibbutz and he contacted
Micah who was based in Belgium. Her middle brother, Micah, fought with
the British in the Jewish Brigade. He borrowed a jeep and a woman's British
uniform. He drove across the war-torn continent to find his sister in Poland—
and bring her home. He had not seen his sister in nearly a decade. She literally
passed out, when her brother came knocking on her door."

Zach sat speechless. He couldn't get over the story. The Holocaust
would always be part of his Jewish heritage. But he was the son of a couple
born in New York. He wasn't overlooking the pride he felt about his dad's
service in WWII. In fact, it made him prouder that his father fought to help
liberate Europe. Eli's story, however, was one of survival—beyond anything
he could ever imagine. Suddenly, the fist fights he joined to protect his brother,
Alan, on the school playground and the beatings he faced being Jewish at a
military school in the South meant more to him.

Eli spoke calmly about these events in her parents' lives. This was a
woman who seriously understood the meaning of life. Eli's story put into perspective the unpredictability and fragile nature of life itself.

After her parents reached Israel, Eli was born. She explained her mom,
Ruth, was initially afraid to have children. She was forced to work with chem-
icals at a German ammunition factory, which frequently turned her hair green.
"The first language I spoke in Israel was actually German," she shared with

Zach. "My mother spoke only German, so my parents spoke German at home. My dad speaks several languages, Polish, German, French. He speaks and reads Hebrew and he learned English before we came to the U.S. I didn't learn Hebrew until I started school."

"Can I ask, did your parents named you for someone lost in the Holocaust?" Zach knew it was a Jewish custom to name children after a deceased family member you admired. Eli smiled.

"My parents wanted me to represent the start of a new life in Israel. They gave me the name Eliana, which in Hebrew means, 'My God has answered me.' Zach could not put into words what his heart felt at that moment. He had been looking for a sign in his life, after his dad passed. Was this it? Had this person come into his life to answer his own prayers?

Eli had the most easy-going personality, but he knew almost immediately that she had a serious nature. There was nothing cavalier about this woman. She had a core set of values that no one could shake or compromise. He had never met someone in his life that came with such clarity. It was also obvious her parents' experience did not dissuade her from traveling the world. Her curiosity to learn about people and cultures was quite strong.

The conversation turned to Zach's family. He started by connecting the dots between the grandfather, Saul Sugar, who Eli met and his mom's musical family. The stories about Brooklyn and his dad came next. He tried to tell funny stories about growing up with his brothers, yet the car accident still loomed large as the event that changed everything for the Goldman family. "How is it possible that your parents' siblings didn't come to help you?" She asked. "You were only 11 years old. Did they really leave you and your brothers to be alone for two months?" Zach stared off, unable to respond.

A feeling of melancholy came over Zach as he talked about losing his father. It was in this point that Eli could see Zach was more than the outgoing personality she met at the Jewish dance. There were several times when they experienced silence. Again, Eli's patience impressed Zach. She understood that life had serious moments. She never rushed the silence or tried to minimize it.

They arrived back at Eli's apartment. Zach walked around the living room trying to figure out where the bathroom and bedroom were located. He soon discovered there was no bedroom. This was a studio apartment. The brown couch they sat on opened up into a bed. Eli made tea. She set out brownies for dessert.

The first kiss between them was effortless. Zach doubted he had ever felt lips like hers. Was it just his excitement over meeting this woman? He was certain it was the fullness of her lips, like his own, that seemed unhurried and welcoming. He held back with all his strength as their tongues shared the same space. He did not want to cross a line or act too aggressively. He paused several times, as they sat on the couch and shared this intimate time. They spent more than a half hour hugging and kissing. He kept one hand on her shoulder, where he could pull her close to him. His other hand held hers. There would be plenty of time for them to explore beyond this point. Zach could only hope this first date would mean a new beginning with Eli.

On the ride home, he played quiet music. He wanted his mind clear to think about Eli. He had asked to see her again. He was pleased she said yes.

Three weeks would go by. Zach and Eli would call each other several times a week. He would return to Maplewood each weekend. On Saturdays, they were fond of visiting the flea market on Springfield Avenue. These shopping excursions gave them time to share stories. "What was it like coming to America? How old were you?" Eli had a certain reserve about her. Zach often had to ask questions. She was at the opposite end of women who were self-centered. She had the most incredible life story, but to she didn't think it was necessary to talk about it.

"Zach, as you can imagine, I was excited and terrified. I didn't speak a word of English. From Israel, my father wanted to stop in Belgium to see the one uncle who survived the War. There are things that I remember so well. We went to a department store in Antwerp. I had never seen an escalator. I drove my father crazy. I made him go up and down the escalator for almost an hour, 'Abba, Abba, Abba.'

My parents put me in an elementary school in Linden within weeks of our arrival. Again, I didn't speak English, so I didn't have a clue on what was going on."

"How did you survive in that environment?"

"I was lucky. There was one teacher in school who spoke Yiddish, which I could understand because of the similarities to German. That teacher worked with me every day to help me learn English. She was terrific. I stayed in touch with her through college. I can't say for certain, but her kindness may have been the reason that I decided to study teaching elementary students as my career."

The couple wandered and talked until Zach became hungry. Their favorite place for a late lunch was the Greek souvlaki sandwich stand. Eli said it reminded her of the shawarma meat in pita bread that she'd eat in Israel with falafel.

"Have you ever been to Israel?" she asked Zach.

"My parents talked about going there when I was a child, but I think it's one of those places most Jews in America have on their wish list. Eli, maybe you can take me one day. I'd like having my own interpreter."

"While we're on the subject of travel. Listen, the holidays are coming up soon. Would you be willing to go with me to Florida," he asked? Yes, they had only been together a short time, but he wanted Eli to meet his mom. He felt certain this was going to be more than a casual relationship.

"Are you joking," she asked? "Do you think you can get a reservation so close to the holidays?"

"If I can get a reservation, will you come with me?" She nodded yes, in response.

"Good morning, Eastern Airlines. This is Mrs. O'Douley, how can I help today?"

The voice at the other end of the phone was deep. He spoke slowly, making certain to clearly enunciate his words:

"Mrs. O'Douley, Mrs. O'Douley, Mrs. O'Douley.....do you believe in miracles?"

Zach could hear the laughter at the end of the phone. "I need two tickets to Florida....really bad. I want to take my girlfriend to meet my mother."

Again, he heard laughter. He had given it his all. After several minutes, the long pause of silence was broken.

"Ok, Mr. Goldman, I think we can get you those tickets." Zach was giddy. He thanked Mrs. O'Douley several times and wished her a good holiday. He couldn't wait to call Eli and tell her he succeeded. She laughed out loud, as Zach shared his sales pitch. Only one step still remained. Both Eli and Zach were pushing 30 years of age, but he knew it wasn't right to take her away without meeting her parents.

The following Friday night, Zach was invited to the Berger family home in Linden New Jersey for Shabbat dinner. He could not recall attending a Shabbat dinner, though he was certain his family must have observed the holiday when he was a young boy. The word "Shabbat" literally means "rest" or "day of rest". The holiday comes from the Ten Commandments, to "set aside a day that is holy" and, to thank God for creating the universe.

He was so nervous. He wanted so much to make a good impression. The three piece suit he wore was definitely overkill for Shabbat. He was welcomed into the Berger home by Eli's father, Sam. In Israel, it was Shmuel. He was a 5'10" tall, thinly built man, who looked studious with thick glasses. His handshake was welcoming. He took Zach's coat. Ruth Berger came out briefly from the kitchen to also greet the young man Eli talked about. Ruth was maybe 5' 2" tall. Her hair was already gray. Eli had told Zach the story her mother's naturally blonde hair at 14 convinced many during the early days of the War that she was German. This protected her up until she was required to wear the yellow Jewish star on her clothes.

Zach's eyes lit up as Eli came downstairs. She motioned for him to join her in the dining room. He could see Ruth had already lit the candles signaling the start of Shabbat.

What Zach knew about the Holocaust, he learned from books and movie newsreels. He had never met survivors of the camps before. What happened to Jews during WWII seemed distant to his life in America, but Zach felt a strong emotional response each time he saw the images of suffering and death. The warmth he found in the Berger home was hard to reconcile with the thought of their suffering in concentration camps.

Soup was always first on the menu for Shabbat. Sam started with a Hebrew blessing for the wine, a Riesling, and the Challah. Ruth would disappear to the kitchen and return with the soup. Eli explained her dad was particular about one thing. He wanted the soup to be hot, very hot. Tonight, Ruth made beef barley soup. Zach could see the Bergers were very European, especially when dining. The soup spoon didn't dive into the bowl, like in America. His hosts scooped the soup with the side of their spoon. The soup plates were never lifted up to scoop up the soup. And, most importantly, there was no slurping noise.

The cooking was straightforward and simple. Ruth made a broiled chicken, broccoli and roasted potatoes. The Bergers held the fork and knife in the opposite hands, as they cut the chicken. Zach was the only one at the table that had to cut and then switch hands to pick up the food. Other than noticing the European etiquette, dinner was relaxed and the conversation flowed.

Sam asked Zach about his current job working in New Jersey government. He tried to keep his explanation simple and short. What was most important, he thought, was that he was trying to help people who may have been treated poorly. Eli mentioned Saul Sugar being in the nursing home, which took the dinner conversation in the direction of Zach's family. He talked briefly about his parents, including his father's passing.

The Bergers explained they had come to the U.S. in 1957, on the Queen Mary. The ship was so loaded with passengers that Sam Berger stayed in a dorm room with men at one end of the ship, while Ruth and Eli had a small room at the other end. Neither Ruth or Eli spoke English, which made them fearful to be on their own. Even after nearly 20 years in the U.S., Ruth still spoke with a heavy German accent.

Ruth Berger came from a very religious family. She did her best to keep the traditions passed down, though she compromised on many orthodox customs followed by her parents. The Bergers belonged to an Orthodox Synagogue in Linden. On the High Holidays, cars were not driven. The Bergers walked almost two miles to and from the Synagogue.

If it were up to him, Sam Berger would not attend Synagogue services. His point of view was not uncommon among Holocaust survivors. Some remained religious through the horrors of that period, even thankful that God had delivered them from certain death. Others could not accept how many lives had been lost. Why hadn't God saved more? Sam had learned and spoke

Hebrew fluently, which was not an easy task. He could say the prayers without looking at the Siddur or prayer book. But he mostly followed Jewish customs out of his respect and love for Ruth.

As the evening went on, Zach became more comfortable asking Eli's parents questions. A year after liberation from the concentration camp in Poland, the Bergers arrived on the last ship reaching Israel before the British diverted Jews to Cyprus. "My parents were caught by the British," Eli interjected, "and held in a detention camp called Atlit in Israel. The Jews were required to strip, be sprayed with delousing chemicals and put through showers...just like the Nazis did in concentration camps. Men and women were then separated in the camp. The British put these people through hell, just to try and dissuade Jews from returning to Israel."

Eli went on to explain that since her dad served in the Polish army, he was eventually drafted into the Israel military as a Captain during the War of Independence. Zach had read the book, Exodus, about the Jewish migration to Israel after WWII. Here he was at dinner with Ruth and Sam Berger, who lived this history.

Ruth served coffee and apple cake, which she had made special for Zach's visit. She was surprised when he got up from dinner table and insisted on helping clear the dishes. "Mrs. Berger, don't be shocked. In our home, my brothers and I grew up helping clean the table, take out the garbage or complete whatever chores our parents needed us to tackle." Eli was not surprised. All of her instincts about Zach were proving correct, during the short time they had been dating. She didn't know how strongly Zach felt about her, but she felt certain "he was the one."

Zach wanted to hear before the evening ended how the Bergers wound up in Linden New Jersey. Most folks know the name of the town, from the oil refineries they pass (and smell) driving along the New Jersey Turnpike. Those refineries are actually on the outskirts of town. Still, why would the Bergers move from Israel to Linden, of all places?

"We have family here," Eli said. Zach looked confused. He was certain the Bergers told him they lost everyone during the War except Ruth's siblings, who were still in Israel. Eli explained, "When my parents decided to come to the U.S., they wrote to friends here in Linden. There must be 25 people who are part of this circle. These were fellow survivors from the concentration camps. They risked everything in the camps to help and protect each other. My dad, for example, tried to sneak bread for the others that he was given from a 'good' German soldier. He almost died that night. A group of soldiers caught him with the food. They threw him on the ground. They stabbed him in the back and neck with bayonets trying to find out who gave him the food. He still bears the scars on his neck.

These 25 people lost everyone in their families. Helping each other has become a life-long commitment. In many ways, they are closer than family. If someone loses a husband or wife, the group still makes certain the remaining spouse is included in their lives and social get togethers. In a few instances, two survivors have married after they lost spouses. These bonds were strong, because they shared the worst of humanity. Now they found comfort celebrating with each other the new lives they created in America. You'll meet them soon enough. They spend every holiday or special occasion together."

Zach could not let go of these stories. Petty differences and different opinions didn't matter, when compared to the desperate struggle to survive the Holocaust. The Bergers represented a lifetime of experiences beyond his comprehension. He found their stories enriched him. There's was a journey quite different than his own. He was fascinated to know this family—and the daughter he was falling in love with.

CHAPTER 70

Done Waiting

He told his mom Eli was the woman he would marry. "There is some-thing here, between us, that is just different than any relationship I have ever had before. This is a person who really knows who she is—and what she wants from life. She never gets excited about issues that don't matter. Her experiences have given her a perspective I'd value having in my life."

During their first visit to Florida, Franny acknowledged she could see how calm Eli could be. She was not a primadona. She was gracious and loving. She thought it was early for Zach to reach a decision, but she would support whatever decision he made.

The courtship would grow over nine months. Both of them were nearing 30. Life was done waiting for them. They were ready for the next Chapter, which included talk about starting a family. "Eli, I guess I don't understand. We've been together almost a year. Whether at a party, wedding or social event, I've never really seen you let loose. I don't think I've ever witnessed a time when you got tipsy. Have you always had such self-control?"

"Zach, you have learned about my parents' story and you've sat at the holiday tables where their friends in the camps shared their survival experiences. The most important priority in my life is to never add to the burden they have already lived. I can never let go of the responsibility I have not to cause them hurt or more suffering. This includes even small stuff like having them worry about when I'll come home, where I might travel or who I might go out with."

Eli's conversation stayed with him for weeks. How could a person be so controlled and driven to avoid causing her parents pain? What sacrifices would this require in her life? This just seemed remarkable. She felt certain this was someone who would be more than a great love, she would be the best life partner he could ever hope for.

The couple planned a trip to Israel near the fall, so Zach could meet Eli's family. Her uncle, Micah, had two daughters who grew up with and were like sisters to Eli. Everyone had heard about her boyfriend, long before their airplane touched down. Before leaving, Zach was keenly aware that he was taking the Berger's only child on this long trip. He planned for a month to propose marriage, but he wanted to wait until they reached their visit to Masada. This mountain fortress symbolized a place of commitment. It was at Masada that Jews rebelled and held off the Roman army. When all seemed lost, 960 committed suicide rather than submit to slavery. Zach wanted this to be a gesture of his commitment to Elie. The engagement ring sat in the freezer ice tray at his apartment for three weeks.

However, as the trip got closer, Zach decided not to wait for Israel to propose. He felt certain the Bergers would feel better, if Eli was traveling with her future husband versus just a boyfriend. As his relationship grew with Eli, very few decisions would be made without respect and growing affection for Ruth and Sam Berger,

He planned dinner at "Jenny's", a small bistro near New Hope, Pennsylvania. They were sipping a glass of wine. Zach just couldn't contain himself any longer. He put a small blue box on the corner of the table. "Eli I have loved you before I ever met you. You are so much of what I ever hoped to find in this world—and more. Will you marry me? Eli sat for a minute. Surprised. Quiet. She took nothing in life for granted. Had she also been thinking about this moment and who she might commit her life to? After a few minutes, a smile broke the silence and she nodded her head in agreement. "Zach, I love you too. Yes, yes, I will marry you."

Dinner was served, but Zach and Eli were too excited to eat. They sat staring at each other, unable to get the smiles off of their faces. He told her about keeping the ring in the freezer and his plans for Masada. Eli laughed, "Zach, when we get to Masada, it will likely be 110 degrees at the top. I think we both might pass out." They picked at their food, trying to figure out next steps. He wanted Eli to call her parents. He had already planned to call his mom. However, they agreed the night was theirs….and theirs alone. The calls could wait until the morning. The trip to Israel was a week away. Neither one of them wanted to wait six months to get married. Eli didn't care if they had a big wedding. She hoped they could get married when they returned from their trip.

The phone rang early at his apartment. Eli was already awake. He could see her looking at her outstretched arm and the ring on her finger. As soon as he picked up the phone, he knew it was his younger brother Gary. He was the only one Zach confided in. He thought it was important that someone know a diamond and sapphire ring was in the freezer. He passed the phone to Eli, "So is your finger cold," Gary asked?

"Yes," she replied. "But it's getting warmer, every time I look at it."

"Well, congratulations," Gary said. "And welcome to the family."

The call to Ruth and Sam Berger did not go as Eli planned. Her parents were thrilled to hear the news. They really liked Zach. For them, he brought a warmth and commitment to family that they had wanted in a son-in-law. The Bergers realized their experiences in life had actually made it hard for Eli to find someone to settle down with. Her expectations were so high. She had dated before. Some of the men were quite nice and generous, yet there was always something missing. Ruth could see that Zach was different.

Mid-way through the conversation, Ruth began to cry on the phone. Eli told her she wanted a small wedding after returning from Israel. "Eliana, your father and I have waited our whole lives to see you married. How many weddings have we attended for children of the camp survivors, wondering if our turn would come? It is so important to all of us who made it through that dark period, to see our children under the Chuppah and hopefully, have children of their own. I cannot speak now."

Eli felt awful, as she heard her mother weep. Her father got on the phone and congratulated her. He told her that he understood her eagerness. "We want you to be happy," he told her.

Eli ended the call and began to cry. Zach could not imagine the burden his future wife carried around throughout her life. After all her parents had suffered, she couldn't bear that she now the source of their pain. She had waited so long for this moment. She simply wanted to marry and move on with her life. He understood. But now he also loved and worried about her parents. He tried to comfort Eli. He suggested they give the decision a few days and work on finding a compromise on the wedding.

After arriving in Israel, Eli and Ruth had several more emotional conversations. Zach intervened, "Eli, couldn't we agree to wait three months? That's not too long to wait, if it allows your parents to find a wedding hall. They can pick the venue based on the availability of dates, even if it limits the number of guests."

She agreed with Zach to find a compromise. Ruth sighed with relief, when Eli proposed waiting three months. Her mom embraced her daughter's request to handle all the details, while she was away in Israel. "Mom, you can choose the food, the colors for the reception and the invitations. We only want to pick the band." Ruth was satisfied with the arrangement. She and Sam set about calling and organizing the wedding.

Zach realized how right Eli was when they reached the top of Masada, with temperatures reaching 120 degrees. Proposing marriage would not have been feasible without air conditioning. Her cousins took them touring all over Israel from their home in Tel Aviv to Haifa and the Golan Heights in the north and on a memorable drive through the Negev desert to Sharm El Sheikh at the bottom of the Sinai Peninsula. Zach never imagined he travel through the desert and see wild camels roaming across the roadway.

Upon returning from Israel at the end of August, Eli and Zach were speechless to find that 220 guests were already invited to their November wedding. The Bergers secured a date at the Patrician catering hall in Livingston, New Jersey. This was a rather fancy and well-known wedding venue. Her mom wasn't kidding about waiting her whole life to see her only child married under the Chupah. As they agreed, Ruth had taken care of all the arrangements.

The day of the wedding felt like a whirlwind for the couple. First, the Rabbi was MIA (missing in action). It really unsettled Eli when she heard the Rabbi was late. She sat in her high neck white dress in a side room near the wedding hall. When Zach heard about the Rabbi's delay, he went to check on her. It looked like her father's orthodox cousins from Brooklyn might have to perform the ceremony. She peaked her head out, hearing Zach's knock on the door. "Eli, are you ok? Please don't stress. Your dad has these two big guys with Payots making certain I don't leave." She laughed nervously. She wanted this day to go perfectly. Her mom wasn't the only one who had dreamed about this moment.

The Chupah canopy filled with family. The Rabbi apologized to the audience for being a half-hour late. He redeemed himself with a beautiful wedding ceremony. He did the blessing over wine. Eli circled her husband 7 times in keeping with Jewish custom. The Rabbi explained "a marriage is a union of two halves of the same soul." He went on to share comments from his discussion with the couple weeks before the wedding. "I asked Eli and Zach to come up with one word that best describes their future spouse. Eli used the word "gallant". She said "Zach was always brave, heroic and self-sacrificing. He cares about others and will go out of his way to be thoughtful. I'm grateful for the special attention and respect he gives me."

Zach said, "The best word I can use to describe Eli is "elegant." She is a person with deep opinions and convictions but rarely will voice them, especially if they might offend others. She always is graceful and dignified. She has incredibly good taste, but never showy or opulent. Everything in this woman's nature is refined and elegant; her good heart, her empathy for people and her commitment to family and faith.

The stomping of the glass at the end of the ceremony launched a celebration of new beginnings, for the young couple and the Holocaust survivors
who joined them in the first Hora dance. Some things did not change. As the
band played Hava Nagila, the tempo picked up. Zach was joined by his friend,
David Mazursky in the center of the circle to do their Kazotsky dance. It
didn't take long before Zach started doing hand springs across the floor. Eli's
cousins from Israel would tell the story for years about her husband doing
flips at his wedding.

CHAPTER 71
Celebrating Her Influence

"Zach, it's bad. You better come right away. We can drive to the
Catskills as soon as you get here. The doctors aren't certain whether mom
will make it through the night."

Alan received the call from the small medical center near Monticello.
Franny Goldman was in the early stages of heart failure. She had seen a musical show earlier that night at Grossinger's hotel, where she spent part of the
summer. After returning to her room, she began to experience breathing problems. She called the front desk and the EMTs took her by ambulance. At the
hospital, her conditioned worsened.

Zach drove from Hamilton Township in New Jersey. He reached Alan
in under an hour, which meant he was speeding on the New Jersey Turnpike.
From Alan's house in Upper Saddle River, the boys still had an hour drive.
They would reach the hospital near midnight. Franny was sleeping when her
sons arrived. They asked to see the doctor.

Dr. Emanuel Duarte, the Cardiologist on call that night, explained
Franny was having "congestive heart failure." Essentially, her lungs were
filling with fluid because her heart wasn't pumping the blood properly. The
medical team were giving her several medicines to try and stop her body
from shutting down. He told Franny she needed heart bypass surgery, if she
expected to survive. She was adamant she didn't want surgery. She had been
through enough in her life. She wasn't giving up, but she did not want another
operation. Dr. Duarte told the boys there would be time to address this issue,
if she survived the night and the following day. The doctor kept repeating,
"she was very weak." It was clear to Zach and Alan the doctor was trying to
prepare them.

"When does it end?" Alan asked out loud as they left the doctor in the hallway near their mom's room. The Goldmans had grown into adulthood never knowing what might be next around the corner. Issues of life and death traveled with them, like a suit that fits too tight. A flood of emotions came rushing forward, as the realization set in. This might be the last night they have with their mom. How many times had they been at this breaking point? How could they begin to accept the inevitable? "We've gotten her this far," Zach responded, "we can't give up on her now. Whatever it takes. What... ever it takes."

Franny opened her eyes as her sons entered the room. They agreed after hearing from the doctor to wait until the following day to discuss his surgery recommendation. Based on the doctor's assessment, the issue would be moot if she didn't make it through the night.

She was smiling, as they approached her bed and kissed her. It was like Franny to forget her own pain and circumstance, when she saw her children—and grandchildren. She was thankful for the blessings she could see and touch. She held onto each son's hug a tad longer on this night. She understood how fragile the situation was, as the tightness in her chest came in waves.

"Mom, I'm sorry, but I couldn't reach Gary. He wasn't home. Alan and I didn't want to wait. We'll call him later."

Alan and Zach stood next to her bed. "How are you feeling?"

"I have trouble catching my breath," she responded. "The nurses have been in my room regularly giving me medicine. It has helped me, but I feel so very tired."

"Well, we're not leaving you, so you can rest." Zach motioned for Franny to lay back and sleep. The hospital had put her in a small private room. He turned to his older brother and suggested they take turns. One of them would sleep in the chair or on the floor next to mom's bed. The other would sleep across several chairs in the waiting room down the hall. Neither of the boys actually slept much that night. They would get up regularly to check on her—and on each other. There was little conversation between them. Life for each of them had seemed like a perpetual hospital waiting room. They accepted the part required of them. The woman who had given them life and nurtured them might die this night. These Goldman boys had to be resourceful. No stone or treatment option would be left unexplored. No gap in taking care of her by the nursing staff would be tolerated.

Alan, Zach and Gary had hoped, after their father died, that mom would be around to fill the void. Grandma Franny would instill the values they so desperately wanted their children to learn. These Goldman values reflected their parents' struggles growing up in Brooklyn, during a Depression and WWII.

As she got older, Franny Goldman's biggest treat was to travel north in the summer and stay a month at Grossinger's hotel in Liberty, New York.

Grossinger's was one of the largest hotels, in what was called the "Borscht Belt". At one point, the hotel had grown to 35 buildings across 1,200 acres and hosted more than 150,000 guests per year. Only kosher food was served at the Grossingers. Aside from attracting Jewish families from New York City, the hotel in its heyday was a hot spot for the rich and famous. Elizabeth Taylor was married at the hotel. Rocky Marciano would train there and Jackie Robinson vacationed with his family.

As a musician in the 1930s, Franny had played so many of the Catskill hotels. She had such fond memories of visiting these symbols of growing wealth. The staff and musicians stayed in dumpy housing on the far side of the hotel grounds. But Franny would always remember the festive and romantic atmosphere of these large hotel ballrooms, where people dressed up and danced at night.

The world had changed since that early period of her life. The Catskills declined, as soon as the airlines industry grew and started to offer vacation destinations in the Caribbean. But as long as the big hotels like Grossinger's existed, there would be an aging population of guests trying to recapture a simpler and happier time.

It was a long night at the hospital. Her two grown sons were less resilient dealing with the stress and the difficulty sleeping across a row of plastic chairs. Alan had the last shift with his mom before morning. She was still very weak, but she was alive. After an hour of talking to her, he took a break. He headed to the waiting room, where his younger brother was laying on the floor sleeping. "Zach, time to get up. The doctor has just been in to see mom. She told him she's not having any surgery. I can't get her to come around. If we can't change her mind, Dr. Duarte told me they will try to make her comfortable—but she'll be gone in a few days."

The words were shocking and Zach knew it was his brother's way of asking for his help.

"Ok, I will talk to her," he replied, as he tried to shake off the cobwebs.

Zach got a cup of coffee at the hospital canteen, as he thought consciously about his strategy with mom. When it came to medical stuff, he felt a special connection with his mom. To her, Zach would always be the more compassionate son. He was the one that never lost his patience, especially when she was in pain.

He asked Alan to take a walk, so he could talk to her privately. "Alan, I know what I want to say to her. Give me some time. Trust me, I'll do whatever it takes to change her mind."

Zach returned to his mom's room, with his cup of coffee in hand. He spent a half hour talking to his mom about her trip to Grossinger's this year. He asked her about the days playing in an all-women's band. He wanted to lighten the mood, before he began twisting her arm.

"I need you to have the operation," Zach said bluntly. The comment came at her from left field. Franny thought that conversation was over, when she talked to Alan. She sat quietly for several minutes, trying to avoid her son's stare. Zach met her silence with his own.

"You have to understand," Zach finally told her. "My children never got to meet my father. I'm the only one in this family who didn't get to share this blessing. They will never hear my father's voice or be held in his arms. If you don't have the surgery and fight to stay alive, I will have nothing to share with these children. I can't have them lose the influence of your love in their lives."

At that point, Zach broke down and began to cry. Franny was taken aback. She wanted to hug and comfort her son, but he could not be consoled. He sat on the bed and then reached out to hug his mom. The crying grew louder and his body trembled. He no longer cared. He knew this could be the end. He let his emotions flow out of him. "Please, mom, you have to do this. You have to think about all of your grandchildren. Please do this for me. Do it for them. I never saw you quit on anything. Please, mom—please."

He buried his head in her arms. He had given it his best. He stopped crying to blow his nose. As he came up for air, Franny was staring out the window. She took his hand, "Ok Zach, calm down now. I love you so much. I love your brothers. I know how hard it has been for all of you since dad passed away. I will do it. Tell Alan and Gary, I will have the surgery. I understand now how important this is. I will listen to my sons. I won't give up."

Zach stayed with his mom for another 15 minutes. He calmed down and left the room to call Gary. He wiped his eyes and found Alan at the end of the hallway. "How did you get her to come around?" Alan asked. "I just tried to impress upon her the important responsibility she still had with our kids. Dad's gone. If she doesn't teach them, who will?"

The boys took turns speaking to Gary. Bypass surgery would not be a walk in the park, but it was the only chance their mom had to survive. Dr. Duarte helped arrange Franny's transfer to Hackensack Medical Center, where they specialized in open heart surgery. She would arrive the next day, still in heart failure but her condition was stable.

The triple bypass surgery was scheduled almost immediately. Zach coordinated with his brothers to bring their respective families to see their mom, with special instructions that the grandchildren would each express their demands. "Grandma," Sara told her, "you have to get better. I expect you to be cheering for me at sports this fall." Sara was the oldest grandchild and her prowess as an athlete made Franny especially proud.

The day before surgery was filled with visits by each son's family. An effort was made to space out the timeframe to give her time to rest and avoid pushback from the nurses. By the end of a long day, Franny was just overjoyed. The doctors cautioned her sons about her weakened condition, but she was mentally ready for the unknown.

Alan, Zach and Gary met at Hackensack hospital the next morning. They stayed with her, as long as the nurses allowed. Once the staff finished prepping her, the boys each took turns giving mom a final hug. Each held on to her longer than what might seem necessary. She had reached this point in life, but no one could be certain about the next several hours. Gary went with his mom to the operating room, while Alan and Zach found the surgical waiting room.

Alan just stared out the window. Three hours had gone by without any updates from the nurses. As Zach approached Alan, he could see the tears flowing down his brother's cheek. "Are you ok?" Zach asked.

"I don't understand? Hasn't she suffered enough? When I think about what mom has been through, it tears me apart inside. How will I face my children, if she doesn't pull through this?"

Zach put his hand on Alan's neck. He pulled him close and hugged him. With all their history, this sign of affection was unusual. "Alan, she's going to come through this. We may never have the answers you're looking for. You can't really expect that. It was tough enough losing dad. I don't think it's her time yet."

The two brothers stood together for almost 10 minutes without speaking. Each had their own way of coping. They each had their doubts but tried to stay optimistic.

Gary suddenly appeared. "Hey, I spoke to the nurses. The surgery is not over yet. They said she was hanging in there."

The boys clung to the news, though they would not let down their guard until the operation was complete.

Franny Goldman was rolled out of surgery and returned to her room at 3:30 p.m.. Zach thought Alan was going to puke when he saw her. You could still see blood on her hospital gown. The incision was visible down the center of her chest. Her coloring was ashen. They had delivered a patient to Franny Goldman's room, but she was unrecognizable. Zach asked Gary to take Alan for a walk outside the hospital, to regain his composure. The nurses wouldn't let anyone in her room. He assured his brothers, he would stay close to keep an eye on her.

More than a week would go by before her coloring returned. The boys took turns at the hospital watching and hoping she'd avoid any post-surgery infections. Often, they would rotate, with Alan coming in the morning and Zach or Gary driving up mid-day for the afternoon or evening shift.

From the worst fears, Franny slowly emerged with a new level of vigor. She was ready for the rehab center, where she'd gain strength and return to normalcy. And like with their dad, the boys made the most of it. They'd take turns visiting her in Florida. Each son would call regularly, even if they had less discipline than the weekly visits to the VA hospital. Franny's grandchildren would come to know—and love her—for years to come. They would see her physical pain and struggle, but they'd be influenced more by her tough and competitive nature.

CHAPTER 72
Did We Meet His Expectations?

Nearly a decade had passed since the death of their father. Every year, the boys would spend dinner as a family during the Jewish High Holidays. Alan and Grace would sponsor the dinner at the Goldman family home. Later, they sold the Koman drive home and the yearly gathering moved to their new residence in Upper Saddle River.

Basia Jasinski and Gary Goldman were married in 1981, after a year courtship. Surprised? Every member of the Goldman family walked around in shock, when they heard the news. Gary was married to his first wife, Alicia, at 18 years old, divorced by 25, with a child, Matthew, who had to divide his time between their two homes. Everyone rallied to his girlfriend, Eva Perez, who for two years was such a warm, welcoming and would-be member of the Goldman clan. Why did Gary break off their relationship? No one could figure it out. Alan and Zach felt certain Gary, himself, didn't know why he ended it.

Their younger brother had a stubborn streak. Not all of his decisions were easy to understand. While Eva felt very comfortable with the Goldmans, Basia was not keen to be with the family. The wedding was held at the Rutgers University Chapel and conducted by her Minister. The basis for the marriage to Basia would remain a mystery to the rest of the family. She almost never invited Gary's siblings to their home. The one bright spot was the birth of Lilly Goldman, nine months after they married. She was a gentle, sweet child.

Life does not stand still for anyone. In your mind, you may try to hold back the changes going on. Sometimes we yearn for simpler times or for simpler answers. The one constant, however, is change.

During the Jewish holidays, the sons of Murray Goldman always paused to take stock of their lives. Alan, Zach and Gary had grown more confident, as they grew older. They each shared an instinct to control events, rather than let them just happen. Zach would tell his niece Sara and his nephews, "You have to choose. In your life, you can be a hammer or an anvil." The Goldman boys knew the early trauma in the lives robbed them of a childhood, but they quietly agreed this was a sacrifice they'd gladly bear if it meant their children could escape the pain and stress in their lives..

Competitiveness among siblings notwithstanding, they all celebrated each other's success. Dad was no longer there to praise them. Each brother confirmed the deeds of the other. "Dad would have been amazed at what you've achieved." Each of them felt their accomplishments could not be fully appreciated, unless celebrated with their siblings.

Alan had become a senior partner at his law firm, in record time. His success in court was recognized by would-be clients and the founders of the firm. Increasingly, he'd be asked to serve as Chair of the firm's legal strategy committee, which involved reviewing and guiding the growing litigation portfolio. His reputation as "a lawyer's lawyer" was already well established. He was singled out as someone seen as an expert in the law and sought by other lawyers for his counsel.

His career progress was coupled with financial reward he had not imagined. But his progress in the law could not outweigh his commitment to his children. There were sacrifices in the early years, when Sara and Blake watched their dad disappear in the bathroom to study.

Where does the foundation of being a father begin? When does it take hold of you? Who provides the bar of expectations to measure your progress? Each of Murray's sons would wrestle with these questions, as they sought to fill in the blanks.

Alan's daughter, Sara, was an accomplished athlete in three separate sports. She was a standout in soccer, basketball and softball.

Alan made it a point to show up at her games, to cheer her on. In her Junior year at Paramus High School, Sara had been selected as "All County" Short Stop on the softball team. The newspapers were filled with articles praising her accomplishments. However, Alan was soon beside himself, when her coach asked her to switch positions and become a Catcher in her senior year. "Who does that," Alan demanded? "Why switch positions? You are certain to get scholarship offers playing short stop."

At times, Alan could be overbearing. He acted out of love, but he didn't always accept he could not control his children's lives. In time, he learned his children had good judgment.

Alan resisted the move from shortstop to catcher, until Sara put her foot down. She was indeed "his daughter". She was strong and very tough when it came to making her own decisions. She told her coach, she would make the switch to catcher. Much to her father's surprise, by next season she would become an "All County" Catcher in her last year of high school. The scholarship offers came pouring in. However, Sara had her own ideas about the future. She would forgo a sports career at college. She wanted to pursue her interest in nursing—and helping save lives.

Sara's brother, Blake, was also gifted as an athlete. He was a hard driving point guard on the high school basketball team. As a young man, Blake's school performance seemed less important. Alan and Grace were financially able to send Blake to a private boy's school, where he would get extra tutoring and support for college entrance exams. With fewer students in each class, Blake found there was no place to hide from doing homework or participating in class discussion.

The private school turned out to be a good investment. Blake would eventually be accepted at several universities. He chose to pursue a degree in business and accounting. Afterward, he'd complete his CPA and scale the ladder at a major accounting firm.

The Goldman boys kept the promise they made to their mom to always look out for each other. At times, they didn't like each other. Each had learned to fend for themselves. Independence wasn't a virtue, but it was often seen as a critical survival tool. Each resisted "brotherly advise" whether it came from an older sibling or, even worse, if Gary or Zach tried to coach Alan. But if one them faced a work, family or health crisis, brotherly conflicts were left outside the room. They would race to be there and do whatever was necessary to support each other.

This unspoken rule in the family applied to their children as well. Each brother would create a special one-on-one relationship with their nieces and nephews. Alan get tickets for football games and take his nephews and nieces to the Meadowlands Arena. He'd make a point of calling each child to check on school progress. Zach would take Matthew on weekends. He'd attend sporting events to see Sara and Blake compete. And Gary would look to involve his brother's children as helpers, whenever he visited to fix something in the home. Gary also brought his dogs. His brothers didn't have dogs for the kids.

Matthew, Gary's son, was often a ping-pong ball between his parents, during the early part of his life. Over time, however, Gary and Alicia matured so their son benefitted. His outlet was his passion for mountain biking with his best friend, Peter. They were both very introverted kids at school, but they found a shared love of the outdoors. Each talked their parents into getting them thick wheeled bikes they could take to the park and go off-trail. Riding or fixing bikes became their escape.

"Do you think he knew how much we loved him?" Alan asked.

"He knew we loved him," Zach would reply. "None of us will truly know what he thought, but I'm pretty confident he felt his influence with his sons."

"I just wish I could be certain," Alan continued. "I don't believe there is anything more challenging in life than not knowing whether I've lived up to his expectations of me."

"I agree with you," Gary said shaking his head in agreement. Zach sat quietly. This was one of those occasions when he agreed with his brothers.

"But how does any son or daughter ever figure this out?" Zach asked. "And why does that matter?" he wondered. "Wouldn't his father love him, even if he didn't live up to expectations?" But it would always be true for the Goldman boys nothing mattered more than pleasing their parents. They saw suffering most children never see. They would have given anything to lessen the pain Franny and Murray experienced in life.

"Dad had such a terrible life," Alan said. "He suffered so much. I don't know why? Mom has also struggled for so many years. What the hell is this all about, when two good people have been put through a meat grinder? I can't accept this. I can't understand. I still struggle with the guilt of not having answers. I ask these questions every day of my life. Part of me is grateful when I look at Sara and Blake. They haven't known from this type of suffering. But for me, this is still not enough."

On this point, Zach agreed with Alan. He too felt the boys were driven to succeed by a deep need to offset the pain in their parent's lives. The smile on dad's face, when the boys spoke of the progress in their careers was worth more than any accolade or financial reward. Dad didn't dwell on his diminished physical health. He didn't care he was living alone in a VA home. Yes, the boys were inspired because it was a chance to affirm their parent's purpose in staying alive. "They had to live," the boys would say, " so they could witness what we each achieved."

The brothers spent the Rosh Hashanah holiday together reminiscing about their father. It was an exercise they had completed many times since his death. Ironically, there were so many stories they didn't know.

There were stories that even their mom didn't know. How does anyone truly have the perspective of the person who is living their life? Murray would always be the composite of the experiences he lived and the prism through which he saw the world. If Franny told the boys a story about their dad, her sons could only imagine what it must have been like. How could children fully grasp stories handed down to them from second and third hand sources?

As adults, Alan, Zach and Gary began to create their own versions of stories about dad. In their versions, each son projected onto their father the qualities they wanted him to have—and those they wanted to find in themselves. The reality of someone's life is never as interesting or as glamorous as the one we create using our imagination. Zach would sometimes ask his brothers the oddest questions.

"Is a father someone we use in life to guide us toward a destination? If we didn't have one, I'm guessing we'd invent them to fill the gap in our lives? Many families don't have fathers. What do those children do? If we lost dad when we were younger, what would we have done? Who would we have become? Like everything in life, we each bring a perspective. Why do we each remember the same stories about our dad, but with different facts and changed endings?"

Gary responded, "What matters the most is how much dad loved us. Wouldn't you give up anything you own, just to have one more day with him?

I remember him towering over us, as kids. He was such a large guy. I remember his voice, as if the heavens opened up when he spoke. I remember the strength of his hand, when it swooped down to send my bottom almost to the sky. No, he was not a push over by any measure. But I also remember our Sunday naps together, how we'd crawl up next to him."

"I guess what I remember is his work ethic," Zach said smiling. "I recall at 10-years old, when dad took me on a job in Lodi New Jersey. It was a Cape Cod house. I remember it so well. We climbed the stairs to the second-floor bathroom. I could smell it, even as we walked down the hallway. Dad walked into the bathroom and lifted the cover of the toilet. What he saw was a toilet bowl filled with paper and brown waste. He slowly turned to me, 'Zach, stick your hands in the toilet and see what's stopping it from flushing.'

The words hung in the air. I looked down at the toilet bowl and then up at dad. I felt dwarfed next to his 6'2" frame, 250 lbs., with those long arms (like Gary) that reached down past his waist and connected the largest set of hands I had ever seen.

You both know dad never gave instructions more than once. If we didn't hear him or respond, the next experience was the back of his hand. The crack was so fast and furious; it would take several minutes before the pain registered in our brain. In dad's day, there was no sparing the rod. The boundary lines and expectations were clear.

I wasn't about to challenge his instructions. Yes, I did hesitate, but dad was not smiling. He was serious. So, I took off my coat and rolled up my shirt sleeves. I reached deep into the toilet bowl, with a determination that I hoped he would be proud of. After several minutes fishing around for an answer that I did not have, I pulled my hands out. The brown goo clung to my fingers. I literally had poop all over me. Once again, I looked up to dad for direction.

Dad paused for a minute to reinforce his message. He looked down at me. He then spoke slowly, "Zach, now you know the meaning of work! If you're not afraid to get your hands dirty, you'll be ok. Now, go wash your hands."

I've never shared this story. However, the lesson from Lodi New Jersey stayed with me. In the moment, I was proud I obeyed him. It wasn't a pleasant experience. But it's a lesson I have also used to shape my own ideas about life and work. I have to believe, both of you would understand. The things dad did made a lasting impression with us ."

"Well, I'm glad it was you," Gary responded. "I have to agree with Gary on this one," Alan joined in. They all started laughing. "Maybe this is why you decided to go to college," Gary continued. Alan started laughing. For once, Gary was not the butt of the family jokes. Gary got his share of ribbing, but they all had their moments.

Their older brother then shared a story about his father, when he was in law school. "I wanted to talk with him about my fears looking ahead to my career. Dad waved his hand. He bluntly told me, "Look, don't have shit in your blood." I sat there shocked at his language. At the time, I didn't really have a clue what he was trying to say to me. Like all of us, when he spoke we listened. There would be time to try and understand his message. However, during this visit to the VA home, he did try to explain himself.

He shared a story—his story—to make a point.

He warned me, "fear prevents blood from reaching the brain." The story was from when he fought in the 1932 Golden Gloves. He was losing a fight. His breathing became labored. Each punch he took caused him to feel dizzy. It was the only time an opponent had literally knocked him down, or so he claimed. He grabbed the guy in a bear hug so he could be saved by the bell. When he got to his corner, Frank Celentano, his trainer started yelling at him, 'Hey, Moe, you got shit in your blood? Don't you know who you are? Don't you know where you came from?'

Dad said he was groggy, but Celentano's kept yelling. He thought to himself that he knew he came from Brooklyn. What he didn't know until that moment was who he wanted to be? Celentano started in on him again, "the kid I trained don't know no fear. He don't know how to quit. Give him the best shot you got, but he'll still keeps coming at you."

By this point, dad told me his head cleared. His breathing was normal again. The bell rang to start the next round. Celentano grabbed his arm, as he was leaving the corner. His last words to him were, 'Moe, it's time to show that guy what you're made of. Don't come back here, until you've done that.'"

Alan paused for a minute and smiled, as he looked at Zach and Gary. "I don't think I've ever shared that with either of you. For the longest time, it bothered me. I wondered if dad didn't feel I was on the right track or whether I somehow had disappointed him. But that was not his message. Over time, I figured out that dad wanted me to look past the fear we face in life. Dad wasn't afraid of losing a fight.

'He just didn't want to lose, because he feared not succeeding'. I think about that story, when I'm struggling. I can hear him remind me, 'don't have shit in your blood.' Now, it's a story for the two of you as well."

Something was changing in Murray Goldman's sons. His presence had always brought them together. Often this unity was driven by the need to manage a health crisis in the family. The brothers depended on each other to navigate and overcome obstacles. Alan could be very congenial as he questioned doctors and hospital staff about medical treatment, yet he gagged if he saw blood, urine, etc. Zach was more aggressive, signaling an unwillingness to accept answers he didn't believe addressed his father's medical condition.

Gary always seemed to be running around the outside of the family circle, yelling out questions from the sidelines. But this characterization wasn't fair to him. When he did ask questions, his brothers realized it was something they hadn't thought of. Gary also had a way of bringing laughter to situations, even when his jokes might seem corny. Alan and Zach never wanted to encourage Gary, but his ability to look for humor in the most dire circumstance was needed and valued.

The holidays always brought Murray's sons together, and they would use the time to share and remember their dad. But the boys were grown now, with families of their own. They wanted to talk about their father from their own experiences with him. These would be their stories about fathers and sons.

Murray Goldman was more than a guy who survived the Depression and worked hard to create a successful business. Their stories included how he survived brain tumors and restored the family after a horrible car accident. Yes, he was all of those things. But as his sons would become fathers, the most meaningful stories would focus on what they learned from him—about life—and about love.

Before the holiday dinner, the boys would drive to Beth El Cemetery. Each of them would remember to bring rocks to put on the gravestones. The boys stopped at the Cemetery administration building to get a map to guide them to the graves of their grandparents, the Sugars and the Goldmans.

The boys would recall how their father helped Grandpa Isaac walk to pay his respects to Grandma Tonia. They knew their dad blamed Isaac's gambling for breaking up the family, but he still loved his father. Murray would kiss his father's cheek and hug him, openly showing his affection. This is what their father believed. He didn't have to be told to show this affection. His example was the best teacher they had in life. And they didn't try to teach this to their own children.

The boys visited their grandparents' graves, before driving to the other side of the cemetery where Murray was buried. They rarely saw their grandparents, but it was important to put rocks on the graves out of respect for their father. This is what he would do, if he were here.

As they reached the other side of Beth El, Alan, Gary and Zach could see the very large headstone, "Goldman." They parked the car and walked over to the single footstone marking their father's grave, surrounded by beautifully trimmed green grass. The boys stood quietly for several minutes. This time, Gary began to cry. Alan and Zach were taken by surprise. Gary wasn't one to show emotions. Gary was complicated. He had difficulty expressing himself.

The rough edges of his personality were always hiding so much more. He never let go of the feeling that he had suffered the most, as the youngest of the litter. "What's going on?" Zach asked.

"I miss him so much. I have lost the greatest gift in life I could ever hope for. I should have told him—before he died, how much I loved him."

"Gary, you're not alone," Zach told him. "We all wish we had more time with him. You can't change this. We all wish we spoke more openly about how we felt. He was proud of you. He was proud of all of us. His measure of us was not in the words, it was in meeting his expectations for us to succeed."

CHAPTER 73

The Special Bond Between Fathers and Sons

———

Zach Goldman would finally become a father. It was a destination he waited for his whole life. As teenagers, Zach and Mitch Moran talked regularly about what it would be like to be a dad. These conversations may have started from their notions of training future sports competitors. But quickly, they would digress into long philosophical and serious discussions about instilling values and righting wrongs in the world.

These were not typical talks between two teenage friends. Mitch's father was an alcoholic, who left him and his mother. Mitch was a fierce athletic competitor, a long-distance runner, who was determined to do better in life than he experienced as a child. Zach and Mitch bonded because of sports—and their shared desire to take control of events in their lives.

Zach and Eli married at 31. They both wanted children. It was a subject talked about at length while dating. They realized there was no time to waste. Zach hoped to have four children, but he conceded this was not realistic. Eli had been an only child, but she wanted her child to have a sibling to go through life with.

Aaron was born December 3, 1981. His grandfather had been born December 1, 1915. No one ever forgets how they became a parent. The labor was long and difficult. Eli woke at 1 a.m. with contractions five minutes apart. The doctor previously told her this was the point, at which you should go to the hospital. Zach thought it was way too soon. He encouraged Eli to call before they got out of bed. The doctor "on call" told her it was too soon. Based on her symptoms, she likely had 4-6 hours to go yet. A first-time mom, Eli laid in bed and stared at the clock unable to sleep anymore. Zach, a first-time dad, rolled over and slept another three hours.

As the contractions grew more intense by morning, she woke her husband. But instead of getting nervous, Zach went to take a shower and pick out clothes to wear. Eli was mortified. She was so anxious to get to the hospital. He hurried his pace for Eli's peace of mind. But along the way he'd remember how his father would always be "calm in the middle of the storm."

They arrived at the hospital at 6 a.m. The labor dragged the entire day. Zach would massage her shoulders and lower back to help with discomfort. By early afternoon, when the baby's heart rate dropped, the nurses called the doctor. After checking her vital signs, the doctor said it was necessary to check on the baby. He stuck his hand deep inside of Eli, while Zach stood by nervously. The child's head was in malposition. Essentially, his head faced up and couldn't get past her pubic bone. "Are you ok with this?" the doctor asked as he looked up at Zach. "Please do what you have to," he responded. The doctor waited for a contraction to slowly turn the baby.

In the delivery room, the doctor invited Zach to stand next to him. Many dads are leery about seeing the birth. The baby's head was quite large, so there was more cutting down below than normal. There was blood everywhere, but Zach was not phased. He just watched as his son entered the world.

"If anyone ever questioned whether God exists," Zach thought to himself, "you realize in the minute before the baby's first breath what a miracle you have witnessed."

His first instinct was to have Eli hold him, but she was exhausted. She lay back on the bed, while the nurses wrapped her son in a soft white cloth blanket. He took his son in his arms for the first time. He quickly checked he had all his fingers and toes. "He's perfect," Zach told his wife. He stood there as tears filled his eyes. These were tears of joy. He brought the child over to show his wife. More than 20 hours of labor, she had done more than her part. She reached to touch the baby's hands. Her husband leaned down to allow the new mom to kiss the child. He then bent over to kiss Eli. The nurses took the new born to be cleaned up, giving mom a well-earned rest.

Zach made calls to Eli's parents and to Franny. He left the hospital an hour later to get some food. His first stop was the newsstand, where he bought the New York Times. He thought it was important that his son understand what was going on in the world the day he was born.

The day would end quickly. He called his brothers to share the good news. Later, he surprised Eli with an early dinner. The best he could do was a souvlaki sandwich and a vanilla milkshake. "No hospital food for the mother of my child," Zach told the nurses. The doctor came by to check on her. "What's that smell? Did someone sneak in food?" Both Eli and Zach thanked the doctor, but neither one of them was about to share their souvlaki.

A week later, the Berger home was filled with Holocaust survivors and the Goldman family for the Bris. Few of these survivors thought they'd live to see grandchildren. On cold winter nights in the concentration camps, there was little food and the only thought was to try and live one more day.

The celebration of a new baby (to the Third generation) brought every camp survivor to the Berger home. Franny Goldman was treated as an honored guest. Strangers came up to hug and congratulate her. Sam invited the men into the dining room, where they toasted the new child with shots of Slivovitz. It was said, this beverage made from plums "had an alcoholic punch that could knock a Cossack off his horse," between 80 to 100 proof.

The Goldmans had grown up largely as a secular Jewish family. Being secular didn't mean there wasn't a strong identity with Jewish culture and customs. But no one in the Goldman family attended Synagogue regularly. Perhaps the hardest thing for their friends to understand was the idea that every Jewish person, religious or not, feels a one-on-one relationship with God. Each Jew feels the same obligation to follow the Ten Commandments; to do good deeds (mitzvahs) and help others.

Zach—and his brothers—always welcomed the opportunity to visit the Berger home, especially with their friends who survived the war. Each one had a unique story to tell. Each story enriched Alan and Gary's understanding of Jewish history.

Eli and Zach would name their son, Aaron Maxx Goldman. The Jewish custom is to give a child a Hebrew name after a deceased family member or friend, someone who had qualities you wanted the child to emulate. Normally, the naming is done with the first name. However, Zach was firm. He wanted his son to be his own person, which meant he should have his own name. He could never be comfortable calling his son Murray.

The Rabbi explained they could use an "M" for the first or middle name. This would allow Zach's son to be given his father's Hebrew name, "Moshe". Zach was thrilled beyond words. He was the last of his family to have a child. But he would be the only Goldman son to honor his father, by giving the child his name.

The Bris was completed on the Berger's dining room table. Zach had given Alan the honor of being the Sandek, which is the person who holds the baby while they do the circumcision. He had not consciously considered how white his brother's face would turn when he saw blood, but Zach had a mischievous smile on his face.

Afterward, little Aaron was carried around the Berger home on a silver tray. Four camp survivors filled with Slivovitz danced around the baby. Zach, nervously, stayed close by, ready to catch the baby if he rolled off.

Eighteen months later, Sofia "Sophie" Rose was born. This time it would be a naming ceremony at Anche Chesed Synagogue, followed by a community celebration. For the survivors, the birth of a girl was just an important as a boy. The Slivovitz was poured and the hugging, eating and joyful words were exchanged nonstop.

Sophie's Hebrew name would be "Rivka," after Sam Berger's sister, who perished at the end of the war. Her name was Regina. She had survived the Bergen-Belsen concentration camp, where more than 50,000 died from disease and starvation. However, she died from Typhus six months after liberation. Zach wanted a strong and independent daughter. Her first name would be her own. Her Hebrew name would come from the "R" in her middle name.

As the family returned home from Sophie's naming, Zach sat in the dining room thinking about the future. Life was complete now—or was it?

"How do you know? How does anyone know if a child will become the person you dreamed of? You feel so energized by the birth of a child, but does this mean your job is done? The child will grow, regardless of your presence. If you try to control their lives, you often take away their ability to find the right course on their own. Pushing and pulling them may actually produce the opposite result from what you intended. So, if it's not the quantity or quality of time spent, is it better to just step back and give them room? Won't a child simply manufacture the father that doesn't come naturally?"

Zach could not resolve his inner turmoil. Would nature or nurture prevail with Aaron and Sophie? "How would a father know when they should bend steel to their will or allow the seedlings to grow strong on their own?"

Zach, Alan and Gary would enjoy success in their lifetime, beyond anything Franny and Murray could imagine was possible. Alan's reputation as a trial lawyer would continue to grow. Honors would follow. Famous clients would seek him out, though he would quit working for any client that might compromise or harm Alan's sense of integrity and reputation.

Imagine a lawyer unwilling to accept large retainers, if the work might raise questions about their "good name?"

Gary's career at Gaming Enforcement was both long and satisfying. The casino industry matured over the decades, so the requirements to police the hiring of employees declined. But experienced and senior folks like Gary were still needed, when there was a need to investigate the behavior of casinos.

He was perhaps less successful in his relationships, as his second marriage resulted in divorce. Over time, he came to realize he was marrying the wrong women. He wanted these relationships to work so badly that he often compromised his own happiness to keep them going. At the end, the divorces were financially costly—but liberating. Gary would find a new footing, as he got older, where marriage was not important. He found happiness in a relationship that valued his good nature, sense of humor and work discipline. Finally, he found a woman who had her own resources. She made him the priority and his life became more rewarding.

Zach poured his energy into his job at Citibank. His three VP colleagues had Harvard MBAs. Zach brought writing skills and a work ethic. He was the first one in the office and the last one to leave at night. He didn't manage his career looking over his shoulder. He had the capacity to see the big picture and an innate understanding of how to be a catalyst for change.

He joined so many others on the train each morning at Princeton Junction for the nearly four-hour commute there and back. He was determined to succeed and he wanted his children to have a backyard.

Like his brothers, Zach would achieve success, because he didn't know any other way. He would become a senior strategist, author and spokesperson in financial services. His political experience helped him see the world three dimensionally. Successful political campaigns required the three C's"… Clarity, Consistency and Constancy in messaging. The campaigning also taught him to prepare "ahead of the curve"; to anticipate the opposition and plot "if P, then Q" messaging. Eventually, he'd be chosen by several CEOs to represent them with major media in the U.S. and overseas.

But Zach was also the last Goldman to have a child. He had waited decades to be a father. He found himself asking, "Am I up to the task? I've wanted this for so long. I have a son and daughter now. I wonder if I'll measure up in their eyes?" He couldn't be certain if his brothers shared this anxiety?

Each of the Goldman boys wanted to be an influence in the lives of their children. There would be no light shining down from the sky to guide them. The books about raising kids would not provide any answers either.

A father's role in a child's life is left undefined. No doubt trial and error is a constant threat to the whole exercise. Gary and Alan followed Zach's example to tell their children stories about growing up with their father. These stories would be embellished to suit the circumstance and the values each Goldman son wanted to reinforce.

In the months and years ahead, Zach could not let go of the uncertainty. Like a generation before him, he would not spare the rod. However, he was slow to anger and even slower to use the rod, when his voice was enough to modify the children's behavior.

One night, after reading a story to Aaron, Zach finally had an epiphany. The answer to his purpose in life would come from Aaron, who was almost 6-years old. His connection to Eli's parents was a great blessing in Zach's eyes. Aaron and Sophie would grow in their understanding of the Holocaust and the lessons Sam and Ruth Berger's life instilled in them. But on this night, Aaron surprised Zach. For the first time, he asked, "Dad, what was your father like? Can I see a picture?"

The questions were difficult for Zach, even after 12 years from his death. Aaron didn't immediately understand, when he saw Zach's face. "Please don't cry laddy. I'm sorry."

Aaron began to cry, too. He could not see Zach's tears were "joyful expressions of loss." Through the eyes of his children, he realized someone would always remember. Someone wanted to know.

"It's ok Aaron. It's ok," Zach said as he hugged his son. "You didn't do anything wrong. I just miss my daddy. I loved him, just like you love me. That's a good thing."

The next day, Zach sat in his office in New York for several hours. He closed the door, which often signaled to the staff that he was writing. On this day, Zach decided it was time to write about his father. He would finish the article by the late afternoon. His eyes were rarely dry, as the emotions came pouring out of him. More than a decade had passed, but there was no resolution. Maybe there would never be a resolution.

The Goldman boys had reached their mid or late thirties. They had shaped the life they wanted—just as life had shaped them.

There was still more to do, more to accomplish and even more to celebrate, in time.

What do you put in its place, when death robs you of someone you love. Aaron's questions about Murray Goldman found their way onto the page. Zach hoped the article would give Aaron and Sophie a place to find answers. At least it was a place to start.

Zach sent the article to the Trenton Times newspaper. He hadn't written the article for public consumption, though he wondered, afterward, if others might feel as he did. This had been a cathartic journey for him. He had struggled for so long to make peace with his loss. In the end, he wanted to create something his children—Franny and his brothers could read with pride.

After the article appeared in the Trenton Times, Zach received calls at home for over a month. Each stranger had their own story about their father. The newspaper granted Zach's request to publish the article on December 1, 1987, his dad's birthday.

Zach wanted to find the answers to questions that nagged him for much of his life. What was it about his father that meant so much? What is that magic between fathers and sons? As he tried to tell his father's story, Zach realized he found his own story as well. Murray Goldman had loved his children every day of his life.

He had given them the most meaningful and lasting gift in life: unconditional love. It wasn't a starting point or a destination. Their father was the sun in a clear blue sky. Alan, Zach and Gary would know his presence, whenever they struggled. As they looked to their own growing children, each knew that what dad handed down to them was a gift he bequeathed to this future generation.

"As long as we tell the story," Zach would remind them.

*   *   *

A Special Bond Between Father & Sons
The Trenton Times

His hands remain a vivid image; years after his chiseled features became blurred in my memory. To a young boy, he seemed tall as a tree. Our treat was when he'd come home from work before we went to sleep.

Most of the time we were already in bed for the night. We'd hear the front door and abandoning any sense of parental rules, we'd charge from our rooms to greet him.

Effortlessly, he'd swoop down. His huge hands would lift us upward for a hug and a kiss. At that moment, the ascent seemed rewarding beyond any earthly satisfaction. Dad was home.

As we grew up, the pattern never really changed that much. His was a generation of sacrifice, doing whatever had to be done, providing for his family. Years later we would hear the stories about my father growing up in the 1930's. Independence and self-reliance was not a fad then, just a way of life.

At 15, he hopped freight trains to Philadelphia from New York for fun. He worked one summer in a traveling circus setting up the tents.

At 17, he would carry steel radiators weighing over two hundred pounds up six flights of stairs for $5 each (often making $20). Even then, I'm told, he seemed larger than life -- a huge man, incredibly strong, with a presence well beyond his years.

Mom grew up in the same neighborhood, and told us how he would walk down the street in his pinstriped dark grey zoot suit, floppy hat and spats. Usually he was headed with a friend up to the Savoy Ballroom in Harlem, where he'd dance the night away. No one ever suspected that beneath the confident air and bold swagger was a boy of 19.

But these images were not the father I knew. My dad was a plumber. His clothes were gray and usually soiled. He didn't go to ball games with us or play sports. He worked six days a week. Our worlds came together usually on Sundays, when he'd wake me or one of my two brothers for our weekly tradition of buying bagels and lox, and picking up the newspapers.

After a late morning breakfast, the three of us would be led into the master bedroom for our ritual nap--with dad. We would all protest against sleeping, which usually gave us fifteen minutes to wrestle with him. Always our protests would give in to the comfort of his arms holding us so we couldn't sneak out of the room. How special Sundays were.

With great pride in having three sons, he occasionally would take us with him to work. Usually we travelled in two's, some-times solo, but almost never as a tribe. He was a large plumbing contractor. We'd watch as he directed his men puffing the cigar that was his trademark. He was the only man I have ever seen inhale a cigar.

The roar of trucks on route to fix the pipelines of New Jersey, gave way to ringing phones and heated business conversations. In the back of the shop we'd scale the wooden bins containing more plumbing fixtures than I had ever thought existed.

Afternoons consisted of lunch at local eateries and visits to inspect what the workers were doing. Always he would introduce us to customers and friends, "this is my number one, number two or number three son." I was never certain if he forgot our names or watched too many Charlie Chan movies. In time, it became natural to introduce ourselves as number one or two son. Nothing could please us more than for someone to say, "He's Murray's number two son."

As I grew older, his health declined. At each turn, life-threatening illnesses stalked him. He never complained. His humor could not be dampened nor his spirit extinguished. He was sick at the time I heard the story about bootleg boxing. It was 1934, and people crowded in the back of a bar where two men fought to please the patrons and earn some money. He used the name Moe Fields as an alias. He knocked out twenty some opponents and had his nose broken twice. He told the story with a smile and a gleam in his eyes.

My father feared nothing, or so it seemed. We laughed a good deal that day--a proud son and a defiant father. But I didn't understand why he used a fictitious name. His voice grew soft, softer than I had ever known.

"My father would never have approved of boxing," he explained. "And he would have come down there after me." He did not want to choose between the independence he valued and the love of his father. Instead, he became Moe Fields.

I often wonder what that strange magic is between father and son. I'm convinced it has nothing to do with time spent or games played. And rarely are words spoken that capture it. We came to know my father more than most sons learn until well into their own middle age (if they ever know their father at all). His life became the silent values that guided us. Most of the lessons he taught us were not from instruction, they were indirect. He led by example. He was not perfect. As sons are apt to do, I tried to understand him.

The humor of his business card, "Murray's Plumbing and Heating--your sh__t, is my bread and butter." His combativeness when he felt wronged, like the time he punched and broke some guy's jaw over a series of anti-Semitic remarks. His belief in hard work, which I learned about at 10 years old in Lodi, New Jersey. The toilet on the second floor was stopped up and full. I was instructed to reach in with my hands to see why it wasn't working. When I finished, he said ever so bluntly, "now you understand the meaning of work." He was right.

I've read that as we get older, it's the images of childhood, which remain sharpest in our memories. I still remember my father's hands. His large and strong hands.

It has been years now since he passed on. And now I look at my own son and wonder what silent values he will find in me. I look deep within for the answers, hoping the irrepressible spirit of Moe Fields lives on.

*   *   *

AUTHOR'S BIO

Stuart Z. Goldstein was one of the longest serving PR Spokespersons on Wall Street. As Managing Director of Corporate Communications & Public Affairs for the Depository Trust & Clearing Corporation (DTCC) in New York, the largest trade clearing house ($5 trillion daily) and central securities depository in the world.

"Goldstein surely was the highest profile corporate communications executive in the securities services industry," according to Global Custodian magazine. "In a position where few survive more than 5 years and one CEO, Goldstein managed four times the average tenure, and served three successive CEOs."

Prior to this, he was a spokesperson for American Express and led National Public Affairs at Citicorp. Earlier he served as a State Ombudsman in New Jersey and as Legislative Affairs director for the NJ Public Advocate.

Mr. Goldstein has co-authored 2 books in plain English explaining the inner workings of U.S. Capital Markets. He has published numerous articles in PR trade magazines and was a contributing author to Public Affairs in an Era of Change. His by-lined articles on public policy issues have appeared in USA Today, the Washington Times, the Star Ledger, Trenton Times, Global Financial Markets magazine and made trade journals.

He graduated from The College of New Jersey (TCNJ) with a B.A. in English and earned his M.A. in American Government from Rutgers University. During college, he wrote for the Trenton Times and helped lead the effort in NJ to lower the voting age to 18 and ratify the 26th Amendment.

He's lectures on crisis communications and media relations. He has also served on the graduate school advisory board in Corporate Communications at Fairleigh Dickinson University and was a founding member of the Corporate Communications Institute at Baruch College.